DEADLY WORDS
Witchcraft in the Bocage

DEADLY WORDS

Witchcraft in the Bocage

JEANNE FAVRET-SAADA

Chargée de Recherche, Centre Nationale de la Recherche Scientifique, Paris

Translated by Catherine Cullen

CAMBRIDGE UNIVERSITY PRESS

Cambridge
London *New York* *New Rochelle* *Melbourne* *Sydney*

EDITIONS DE LA MAISON DES SCIENCES DE L'HOMME

Paris

Published by the Press Syndicate of the University of Cambridge
The Pitt Building, Trumpington Street, Cambridge CB2 IRP
32 East 57th Street, New York, NY 10022, USA
296 Beaconsfield Parade, Middle Park, Melbourne 3206, Australia
and Editions de la Maison des Sciences de l'Homme
54 Boulevard Raspail, 75270 Paris Cedex 06

Les mots, la mort, les sorts
© Éditions Gallimard, Paris, 1977

English translation © Maison des Sciences de l'Homme and
Cambridge University Press 1980

First published 1980

Phototypeset in V.I.P. Baskerville
by Western Printing Services Ltd, Bristol

Printed in Great Britain by
the University Press, Cambridge

British Library Cataloguing in Publication Data
Favret-Saada, Jeanne
Deadly words.
1. Witchcraft – France
I. Title
133.4'0944'1   BF1582   79-41607
ISBN 0 521 22317 2   hard covers
ISBN 0 521 29787 7   paperback

CONTENTS

Appendices

TRANSLATOR'S NOTE

This book has long quotations of peasant dialogues in the regional dialect. In agreement with the author, I have chosen to translate these into standard English and not into some rural English dialect. It seemed preferable to give up some of the local flavour rather than instil an arbitrarily-chosen one.

Catherine Cullen

This book owes much to the Laboratoire d'ethnologie et de sociologie comparative of the Centre national de la Recherche scientifique which accepted me and allowed me to follow my own line, which might have led nowhere. Let it be thanked here for its extreme patience.

Sa grande inquiétude était de savoir si réellement il avait assisté à la bataille et dans le cas du oui, s'il pouvait dire s'être battu, lui qui n'avait marché à l'attaque d'aucune batterie ni d'aucune colonne ennemie.

Stendhal
La Chartreuse de Parme

His great anxiety was to know whether he had really been part of the battle at all; and if so, whether he could say he had fought in it, since he had not marched to the attack of any battery nor of any enemy column.

Part I

THERE MUST BE A SUBJECT

'They say there are savages in Africa; but you who've read so much, do you know — anyone more savage than us?

'Here, one is immediately caught — to the death: death is the only thing we know about around here.'

An unwitcher, to the ethnographer

THE WAY THINGS ARE SAID

It seems that even the pure light of science requires, in order to shine, the darkness of ignorance.

Karl Marx (1856)

Take an enthnographer: she has chosen to investigate contemporary witch-craft in the Bocage* of Western France. She has already done some field-work; she has a basic academic training; she has published some papers on the logic of murder, violence and insurrection in an altogether different, tribal society. She is now working in France, to avoid having to learn yet another difficult language. Especially since in her view the symbolic shaping out of murder or aggression – the way things are said in the native culture – is as important as the functioning of political machinery.

I. The mirror-image of an academic

Getting ready to leave for the field, she looks through the scientific (and not so scientific) literature on contemporary witchcraft: the writings of folklor-ists and psychiatrists, of occultists and journalists. This is what she finds: that peasants, who are 'credulous', 'backward' and impervious to 'cause of effect', blame their misfortune on the jealousy of a neighbour who has cast a spell on them; they go to an unwitcher† (usually described as a 'charlatan', now and again as 'naïve') who protects them from their imaginary aggres-sor by performing 'secret' rituals which 'have no meaning', and 'come from another age'. The geographical and cultural 'isolation' of the Bocage is partly responsible for the 'survival' of these 'beliefs' in our time.

If that is all there is to be said about witchcraft (and however much you try to find out from the books of folklorists or the reports of trials in the French press over the last ten years, you will learn no more), you may

---

* *Bocage*: countryside of Western France marked by intermingling patches of woodland and heath, small fields, tall hedgerows and orchards.

† *Unwitcher*: The Bocage natives use the word *désorceleur* rather than the more usual *désensorcel-leur* [ensorceller = to bewitch]. I have translated it by *unwitcher* rather than *unbewitcher*. Similarly, *désorceller* is translated as *to unwitch* and *désorcellage* or *désorcellement* as *unwitching* or *unwitchment*.

wonder why it seems to be such an obsession. To judge by the public's immense curiosity, the fascination produced by the very word 'witchcraft', the guaranteed success of anything written about it, one wonders what journalistic scoop could ever find a greater public.

Take an ethnographer. She has spent more than thirty months in the Bocage in Mayenne, studying witchcraft. 'How exciting, how thrilling, how extraordinary . . .!' 'Tell us all about the witches', she is asked again and again when she gets back to the city. Just as one might say: tell us tales about ogres or wolves, about Little Red Riding Hood. Frighten us, but make it clear that it's only a story; or that they are just peasants: credulous, backward and marginal. Or alternatively: confirm that *out there* there are some people who can bend the laws of causality and morality, who can kill by magic and not be punished; but remember to end by saying that they do not really have that power: they only believe it because they are credulous, backward peasants . . . (see above).

No wonder that country people in the West are not in any hurry to step forward and be taken for idiots in the way that public opinion would have them be – whether in the scholarly version developed by folklorists, or in the equally hard faced popular version spread by the media.

To say that one is studying beliefs about witchcraft is automatically to deny them any truth: it is just a belief, it is not true. So folklorists never ask of country people: 'what are they trying to express by means of a witchcraft crisis?', but only 'what are they hiding from us?' They are led on by the idea of some healer's 'secret', some local trick, and describing it is enough to gratify academic curiosity. So witchcraft is no more than a body of empty recipes (boil an ox heart, prick it with a thousand pins, etc.)? Grant that sort of thing supernatural power? How gullible can you be?

Similarly, when the reporter, that hero of positivist discourse, goes along on behalf of a public assumed to be incredulous, and asks country people whether they 'still believe' in spells, the case is decided in advance: yes, people do still believe in spells, especially if you go to the Lower Berry or the Normandy Bocage. How convenient that there should be a district full of idiots, where the whole realm of the imaginary can be held in. But country people are not fools: they meet these advances with obstinate silence.

But even their silence about things to do with witchcraft; and more generally about anything to do with illness and death, is said to tell us about their status: 'their language is too simple', 'they are incapable of symbolizing', you won't get anything out of them because 'they don't talk': that is what I was told by the local scholarly élite. Why not say they are wild men of the woods, since they live in a 'bocage'; animals, even? 'Medicine is a veterinary art round here' a local psychiatrist once told me.

So all that was known about witchcraft is that it was unknowable: when I left for the field, knowledge of the subject boiled down to this. The first question I asked myself when I met the peasants, who were neither credulous nor backward, was: is witchcraft unknowable, or is it just that those who say this need to block out all knowledge about it in order to maintain their own intellectual coherence? Does the 'scholar' or the 'man of our own age' need to comfort himself with the myth of a credulous and backward peasant?[1]

The social sciences aim to account for cultural differences. But can this be achieved by postulating the existence of a peasant who is denied all reality save that he is the mirror-image of an academic?

Whenever folklorists or reporters talk of witchcraft in the country, they always do so as if one were facing two incompatible physical theories: the pre-logical or medieval attitude of peasants, who wrongly attribute their misfortunes to imaginary witches; and ours, the attitude of educated people who know how to handle causal relations correctly. It is said or implied that peasants are incapable of this either because of ignorance or of backwardness. In this respect, the description given of the peasant and the '*pays*', the canton, that determines him is governed by a peculiar set of terms which necessarily imply that he is incapable of grasping causal relations. Witchcraft is put forward as a nonsense theory which peasants can afford to adopt because it is the local theory. The folklorist's job is then to underline the difference between his own theory (which also happens to be a 'true' one) and the peasant's, which is only a belief.[2]

But who can ignore the difficulties involved in postulating the co-existence of two incompatible physical theories which correspond to two ages of humankind? Do you really have to do thirty months of fieldwork to be in a position to say that country people are just as well able to cope with causal relations as anyone else, and to make the suggestion that witchcraft cannot be reduced to a physical theory, although it does indeed imply a certain kind of causality?[3]

---

[1] I have published an earlier version of the above: Jeanne Favret, 'Racontez-nous des histoires de sorciers', in *Le Monde*, 6–7 October 1974. Appendix I. (*The explorer of darkness*, cf. p. 225) reproduces a comment I wrote on a television report about witchcraft in the Berry: 'Sorciers et paysans', in *Critique*, No. 299, April 1972.

[2] Arnold Van Gennep introduces the subject 'Magic and Witchcraft' in his well-known *Manuel du folklore français contemporain* (1938) as follows: 'When one looks more closely at the facts, almost the whole of French folklore could be substituted here, since the acts and concepts which are designated *popular* [i.e. the subject of folklore] contrast exactly with acts and concepts which are designated *scientific*, through a *mistaken application of the law of causality*. The importance of this '*logical error*' has varied with time . . .' I have italicized what goes without saying for Van Gennep. Appendix II, *Ignorance as a profession* (cf. p. 227) analyses the folklorists' attitude to witchcraft.

[3] In theory, anthropology is a more sophisticated discipline than folklore. However, its remarkable naïveté is illustrated by the fact that it was not until 1966 that a distinguished researcher, Edmund Leach, put his own reputation at stake by criticizing the dictum (which had so far been totally accepted) according to which some primitive people ignored the causal relation between copulation and birth. Cf. Edmund Leach (1967).

II. Words spoken with insistence

I began by studying the words used to express biological misfortunes, and used in ordinary conversation: about death, sterility, and illness in animals and humans. The first thing one notices is that they distinguish between ordinary misfortunes and their extraordinary repetition.

In the Bocage, as anywhere else in France, ordinary misfortunes are accepted as 'one-off'; so, a single illness, the loss of one animal, one bankruptcy, even one death, do not call for more than a single comment: '*the trouble with him is that he drinks too much*'; '*she had cancer of the kidneys*'; '*my cow was very old*'.

An onslaught by witchcraft, on the other hand, gives a pattern to misfortunes which are repeated and range over the persons and belongings of a bewitched couple: in succession, a heifer dies, the wife has a miscarriage, the child is covered in spots, the car runs into a ditch, the butter won't churn, the bread won't rise, the geese bolt, or the daughter they want to marry off goes into a decline . . . Every morning, the couple ask anxiously: '*What on earth will happen next?*' And every time some misfortune occurs: always unexpected, always inexplicable.

When misfortunes occur like this in series, the countryman approaches qualified people with a double request: on the one hand for an interpretation, and on the other for a cure.

The doctors and vets answer him by denying the existence of any series: illnesses, deaths and mechanical breakdowns do not occur for the same reasons and are not treated in the same way. These people are the curators of objective knowledge about the body, and they can claim to pick off one by one the causes of the misfortunes: go and disinfect your stables, vaccinate your cows, send your wife to the gynaecologist, give your child milk with less fat in it, drink less alcohol . . . But however effective each separate treatment may be, in the eyes of some peasants it is still incomplete, for it only affects the cause and not the origin of their troubles. The origin is always the evil nature of one or more witches who hunger after other people's misfortunes, and whose words, look and touch have supernatural power.

Faced with a bewitched, one can imagine that the priest is in a more awkward situation than the doctor, for evil, misfortune and the supernatural mean something to him. But what they mean has become singularly blurred by many centuries of theological brooding. The dividing line between the ranges of the natural and the supernatural has been fixed by Catholic orthodoxy; but the reasons given have scarcely been assimilated, especially since each late pronouncement does not categorically cancel former ones. So theological knowledge is no more unified in the mind of a country priest than it is in the body of doctrine.[4]

Hearing the various stories told in his parish, the priest can choose between three different and mutually exclusive types of interpretation:

1. He can dismiss these misfortunes as part of the natural order, and so deny them any religious significance: by doing so he sides with medical ideology, and in effect says the bewitched are raving or superstitious people.

2. He can acknowledge that these misfortunes do pertain to the supernatural order, but are an effect of divine love: so the bishop of Séez preaches 'good suffering' to a congregation of '*luckless*' peasants.[5] A universally aimed (Catholic) discourse can turn him who is '*luckless*' into the most lucky. The man whom God loves best and so chastises, is only a victim in the eyes of the world. This reversal of appearances sometimes has its effect.

3. The priest can meet the peasant on his own ground and interpret his misfortunes as the work of the devil. He is permitted to do this by at least one branch or stratum of theology. He then has two alternatives.

He may consult, as he is supposed to, the diocesan exorcist, the official expert in diabolical matters appointed by the hierarchy. But in Western France, the priest knows very well that he is not likely to convince the expert, who has held this position for thirty years precisely because he is sceptical about the devil's interest in so-called 'simple' peasants: you have to be clever to interest the devil. So the diocesan exorcist, in the elitist style of any country priest who has risen in the Church or any peasant who has risen in society, offers the positivist interpretation. He refuses to give any religious meaning to the peasant's misfortune except by mentioning 'good suffering' or saying he will pray for him. Like the doctor, he refuses the peasant's request for a meaning by advising the man to consult a psychiatrist, to live a more balanced life, and to apply better the rules of the experimental method. The village priest knows in advance that to send a bewitched to the diocesan exorcist is to ask him to take his troubles elsewhere, and in effect to direct him to a doctor by way of the ecclesiastical hierarchy.

Alternatively, the priest comes and exorcises the farm and its inhabitants without consulting the hierarchy. As a more or less willing distributor of blessings and medals, holy water and salt, he plays the role in his parish of a

---

[4] Sometimes the dogma changes, but it is always expressed in an a-historical form and guaranteed by the infallibility of the Supreme Pontiff: 'The dogmatic truth consists in effacing its historical trace from writing', writes Pierre Legendre (1974). Anyone could lose their way in it, and the country priest must have a hard time trying to find the religious code which is appropriate to the dramatic situation presented to him by the bewitched. For although the priest is concerned with dogma, he is much more concretely involved in the a-theoretical use that the ecclesiastical hierarchy makes of an institution (here, that of the diocesan exorcist) at the particular point in time when the bewitched comes to consult him.

[5] To use one of their own expressions.

small-scale unwitcher who protects people from evil spells without sending them back to the witch.

'*If it's a small spell, it works*': the series of misfortunes stops and everything returns to normal. It works, but the origin of the misfortune and its repetition are still not satisfactorily symbolized. For when the peasant talks about being bewitched to anyone who is willing to listen, what he wants acknowledged is this: *if such repetitions occur, one must assume that somewhere someone wants them to*. I shall show later that witchcraft consists in creating a misunderstanding about who it is that desires the misfortunes of the bewitched. Note here that the Church's rite merely clouds the issue by attributing the evil to some immaterial spirit included by half-hearted theology in a list of '*preternatural facts*'. For the victim, the witch is some familiar person (a neighbour, for example) whose aims he can at least hope to discover.

If '*it doesn't work*': if the priest '*isn't strong enough*' because his parishioner is '*caught tight*' in the spells, the bewitched is left with his question: why this series of events, and why in my home? What is at stake here, my sanity or my life? Am I mad, as the doctor says, or does someone have it in for me to the point of wanting me to die?

It is only at this point that the sufferer can choose to interpret his ills in the language of witchcraft. Some friend, or someone else who has noticed him moving deeper into misfortune and seen the ineffectiveness of approved learning makes the crucial diagnosis: '*Do you think there may be someone who wishes you ill?*'[6] This amounts to saying: 'you're not mad, I can see in you the signs of a similar crisis I once experienced, and which came to an end thanks to this unwitcher.'

The priest and the doctor have faded out long ago when the unwitcher is called. The unwitcher's task is first to authenticate his patient's sufferings and his feeling of being threatened in the flesh; second, it is to locate, by close examination, the patient's vulnerable spots. It is as if his own body and those of his family, his land and all his possessions make up a single surface full of holes, through which the witch's violence might break in at any moment. The unwitcher then clearly tells his client how long he still has to live if he stubbornly remains defenceless. He is a master of death; he can tell its date and how to postpone it. A professional in supernatural evil, he is prepared to return blow for blow against '*the person we suspect*', the alleged witch, whose final identity is established only after an investigation, sometimes a long one. This is the inception of what can only be called a cure. The séances later are devoted to finding the gaps which still need sealing, as they are revealed day by day in the course of life.[7]

---

[6] An essential character, whom I have called the *annunciator*.

[7] I have published an early draft of the above, although it now seems to me confused and inadequate: cf. Jeanne Favret (1971).

III. When words wage war

In the project for my research I wrote that I wanted to study witchcraft practices in the Bocage. For more than a century, folklorists had been gorging themselves on them, and the time had come to understand them. In the field, however, all I came across was language. For many months, the only empirical facts I was able to record were words.

Today I would say that an attack of witchcraft can be summed up as follows: a set of words spoken in a crisis situation by someone who will later be designated as a witch are afterwards interpreted as having taken effect on the body and belongings of the person spoken to, who will on that ground say he is bewitched. The unwitcher takes on himself these words originally spoken to his client, and turns them back on to their initial sender, the witch. Always the 'abnormal' is said to have settled in after certain words have been uttered, and the situation persists without change until the unwitcher places himself like a screen between the sender and the receiver. Unwitching rituals – the actual 'practices' – are remarkably poor and contingent: this ritual or that, it makes no difference, any one will do. For if the ritual is upheld it is only through words and through the person who says them.

So perhaps, I was not entirely mistaken when I said I wanted to study practices: the act, in witchcraft, is the word.

That may seem an elementary statement, but it is full of implications. The first is this: until now, the work of ethnographers has relied on a convention (one too obvious to be stated) about the use of spoken words. For ethnography to be possible, it was necessary that the investigator and the 'native' should at least agree that speech has the function of conveying information. To be an ethnographer is first to record the utterances of appropriately chosen native informants. How to establish this information-situation, the main source of the investigator's knowledge, how to choose one's informants, how to involve them in a regular working relationship ... the handbooks always insist on this truly fundamental point in fieldwork.[8]

Now, witchcraft is spoken words; but these spoken words are power, and not knowledge or information.

To talk, in witchcraft, is never to inform. Or if information is given, it is so that the person who is to kill (the unwitcher) will know where to aim his blows. 'Informing' an ethnographer, that is, someone who claims to have no intention of using the information, but naïvely wants to know for the sake of knowing, is literally unthinkable. For a single word (and only a word) can tie or untie a fate, and whoever puts himself in a position to utter it is

---

[8] The anthropologist's task is like learning an unknown symbolic code which must be taught him by the most competent speaker he can find. Cf. for example: Royal Anthropological Institute (1971), S. F. Nadel (1951), John Beattie (1964).

formidable. Knowing about spells brings money, brings more power and triggers terror: realities much more fascinating to an interlocutor than the innocent accumulation of scientific knowledge, writing a well-documented book, or getting an academic degree.

Similarly, it is unthinkable that people can talk for the sake of talking. Exchanging words just to show that one is with other people, to show one's wish to communicate, or what Malinowski called 'phatic communication' exists in the Bocage as it does anywhere else.[9] But here it implies strictly political intentions: phatic communication is the expression of zero-aggressiveness; it conveys to one's interlocutor that one might launch a magic rocket at him, but that one chooses not to do so for the time being. It is conveying to him that this is not the time for a fight, but for a cease-fire. When interlocutors for whom witchcraft is involved talk about nothing (that is about anything except what really matters) it is to emphasize the violence of what is not being talked about. More fundamentally, it is to check that the circuit is functioning, and that a state of war does indeed hold between the opponents.[10]

In short, there is no neutral position with spoken words: in witchcraft, words wage war. Anyone talking about it is a belligerent, the ethnographer like everyone else. There is no room for uninvolved observers.

When Evans-Pritchard, founder of the ethnography of witchcraft, studied the Zande, he made it his practice to interpret the events of his life by means of schemes about persecution, consulting oracles and submitting to their decisions: 'I was aided in my understanding of the feelings of the bewitched Azande', he says, 'by sharing their hopes and joys, apathy and sorrows [...]. In no department of their life was I more successful in "thinking black" or as it should more correctly be said "feeling black" than in the sphere of witchcraft. I, too, used to react to misfortunes in the idiom of witchcraft, and it was often an effort to check this lapse into unreason' (1937). But we learn from his book that actually the Zande had given him the position of 'Prince without portfolio', which is no slight consolation if one remembers that in Zande society, a prince can only be bewitched by another prince (a rather reassuring thought for an ethnographer established many miles from the court) and that by not giving him of portfolio, the Zande were exempting Evans-Pritchard from having to play the role, so important for the effectiveness of the cure, of symbolic guarantee of the return to order.

[9] Under the term 'phatic communion', as part of 'ordinary conversation', Malinowski identified a particular type of discourse which is not aimed at giving information, but at a communion through words: 'inquiries about health, comment on the weather, affirmations of some supremely obvious state of things' ... (B. Malinowski, 1923). These remarks are exchanged in order to establish and maintain communication between the speakers. On this problem, see also T. Todorov (1970), E. Benveniste (1970), R. Jakobson (1960).

[10] R. Jakobson (op. cit.) remarks that the prototype of this kind of utterance is '*Hallo, can you hear me?*'.

In other words, the ethnographer could not himself possibly be involved in a case of witchcraft.[11] In the Bocage, the situation happens to be less comfortable: nobody ever talks about witchcraft to gain knowledge, but to gain power. The same is true about asking questions. Before the ethnographer has uttered a single word, he is involved in the same power relationship as anyone else talking about it. Let him open his mouth, and his interlocutor immediately tries to identify his strategy, estimate his force, guess if he is a friend or foe, or if he is to be bought or destroyed. As with any other interlocutor, speaking to the ethnographer one is addressing either a *subject supposed to be able* (a witch, an unwitcher) *or unable* (a victim, a bewitched person).

It follows that wanting to know could only be – for me as for anyone else – in the name of a force which I claim to have or which my interlocutor credits me with. If I were not equipped to confront it, no one would believe I could survive unharmed, or even survive it at all.

'*Are you strong enough?*' I was often asked when I tried to establish an information-relationship, that is to get people who had experience of witch stories to tell me about them. A mere desire for information is the sign of a naïve or hypocritical person who must at once be frightened off. The effect that the person telling the story is trying to achieve is either to fascinate or to frighten: nobody would talk about it who did not hope to fascinate. If my interlocutor is successful, he says I have '*weak blood*' and advises me to change my course of research towards folk song or the ancient papegai festival. If he fears that he has not brought it off, he anxiously asks me how I can bear to hear such stories every day, and offers various assumptions: '*You've got strong blood*', or else '*you've got something*' (to protect yourself with). He then tries to identify my fetishes, to find out whether or not they are '*stronger*' than his own. Otherwise, he may identify me with a certain unwitcher who has just died, a double-edged compliment which I am bound to appreciate: to say that my '*hands tremble like Madame Marie's*' means that, like her, I'm '*quite strong*' – but also that in the end she met her master in witchcraft, and he did away with her quite recently.

As you can see, this is not exactly a standard situation, in which information is exchanged and where the ethnographer may hope to have neutral knowledge about the beliefs and practices of witchcraft conveyed to him. For he who succeeds in acquiring such knowledge gains power and must accept the effects of this power; the more one knows, the more one is a threat and the more one is magically threatened. So long as I claimed the usual status of an ethnographer, saying I wanted to know for the sake of knowing, my interlocutors were less eager to communicate their own knowledge than to test mine, to try to guess the necessarily magic use I intended to put it to, and to develop their force to the detriment of my own. I had to accept the

[11] He only recounts one incident (p. 460) in which the Zande were able to say he was bewitched.

logic of this totally combative situation and admit that it was absurd to continue to posit a neutral position which was neither admissible or even credible to anyone else. When total war is being waged with words, one must make up one's mind to engage in another kind of ethnography.[12]

[12] It is not surprising that Clausewitz (1968) was an important point of reference at the beginning of my work: war as a supremely serious game, trying to dictate its laws to the enemy; as an extension of a duel on a wider scale and over a longer span; as a continuation of politics through other means, and so on. It was not always easy to decide which one was speaking: the discourse of war or the discourse of witchcraft, at least until I realized that it was meaningless to think of witchcraft in terms of the categories of game theory.

2

BETWEEN 'CAUGHT' AND CATCHING

There is one precept of British anthropology – perhaps the only one in the name of which I can call myself an ethnographer – by which the native is always right, if he leads the investigator in unexpected directions.[1] If the ethnographer is led astray, if nothing he finds in the field corresponds to his expectations, if his hypotheses collapse one after the other in contact with native reality even though he set up his investigation with great care, these are signs that we are dealing with an empirical science and not a science-fiction.

I was soon forced to change my plan to study the beliefs and practices of witchcraft – problematical concepts which haunt ethnographic literature – into that of acknowledging the truth of a discourse: in what way are the bewitched right when they say they are suffering? and the unwitchers, when they say they '*take it all*' on themselves? (And what of the alleged witches, who remain obstinately silent, or claim they do not believe in spells?) What, then, is at stake when such a discourse is being used?

These questions led to other, more fundamental ones, about the effect of spoken words and the very rationale of this discourse: why is talking in this way so like the most effective kind of act? How do words kill as surely as a bullet? Why do people talk rather than fight or die, why do they use precisely these terms? And why this kind of language rather than another? If one talks in terms of witchcraft, it must be that the same things cannot be said any other way. I therefore established, as a methodological principle, that the discourse of witchcraft and, for example, the scholarly terminology considered above cannot be interchangeable: since peasants know both and can use both, we must assume that referring to one or to the other does not involve the same relationship of meaning.

[1] As an example, this passage in Evans-Pritchard: 'The anthropologist must follow what he finds in the society he has selected for study: the social organization of its people, their values and sentiments and so forth. I illustrate this fact from what happened in my own case. I had no interest in witchcraft when I went to Zandeland, but the Azande had; so I had to let myself be guided by them. I had no particular interest in cows when I went to Nuerland, but the Nuer had, so willy-nilly I had to become cattle-minded too, eventually acquiring a herd of my own as the price of my acceptance, or at any rate tolerance' (1973).

What I have said about the political or aggressive function of speech suggests that this first step is bound to produce others. My route through this 'field' can be summed up as a progressive understanding of one proposition and its implications: *nothing is said about witchcraft which is not closely governed by the situation of utterance.* What is important, then, is less to decode what is said than to understand who is speaking and to whom. In the field, the ethnographer is himself involved in this speech process and is just one speaker among others. If he then chooses to write a scientific report on spells, it can only be done by always going back over this situation of utterance and the way he was 'caught' in it; this interchange between having been 'caught' and 'catching' things (from a theoretical viewpoint) is precisely what must be pondered.

I wish to suggest that what is needed is a second 'catching' and not a 'getting uncaught' – leaving it to the rest of this book to establish this necessity. I suggest that this marks unequivocally the distance that separates me from both classical anthropology and post-structuralist thinking in France in their shared ideal of 'a totally a-topical theorizing subject'.[2]

I. Those who haven't been caught can't talk about it

Witchcraft, remember, is not the only language available to account for misfortune, and the Bocage cannot be seen as some cultural island which has never been reached by the categories of experimental thought. The most superficial observation shows that everyone here can reinvent them for himself in explaining everyday events, or what I have called ordinary misfortune. In short, unlike a Zande who in all circumstances only has the choice between '*witchcraft*' and '*sorcery*' – two concepts which in the Bocage are totally indistinguishable – the countryman knows perfectly well that there are explanations of another kind.[3] He can say that he does not believe in them at all, or that they account for everything but his own circum-

---

[2] In a review of a book called *Politiques de la Philosophie: Chatelet, Derrida, Foucault, Lyotard, Serres* (1976), Bertrand Poirot-Delpech quite rightly says of its authors: 'They are all trying to stop being taken in by words [. . .] their "politics" – in the full sense of the term – are defined by words from the family of prefixes "*de*" – *dé-voiler* [to reveal], *dé-caper* [to scour], *dé-crypter* [to decipher], *dé-pister* [to detect], *dé-construire* [to deconstruct], in short, *dé-penser* [to unthink]. *Dé-river* [to drift] too: not to *dé-pendre* [depend] either on God, on Being, on Man, on any centre or even on any locatable place. The spatial comparisons used by them all refer to the same, total a-topia, an absolute nomadism: to talk from nowhere, to become ungraspable, unapproachable, irrecuperable in every way' ('Maîtres à dépenser', in *Le Monde*, 30 April 1976).

[3] The Zande of South Sudan, fortunately visited by Evans-Pritchard (1937) in the thirties, enabled a distinction to be made (since then held to be essential in spite of its ambiguities) between *sorcery*, or instrumental magic, and *witchcraft*, or magic operating without the help of a material prop: 'Azande believe that some people are witches and can injure them in virtue of an inherent quality. A witch performs no rite, utters no spell, and possesses no medicines. An act of witchcraft is a psychic act. They believe also that sorcerers may do them ill by performing magic rites with bad medicines . . .' (p. 21).

stances: he cannot prevent their being the official theories of misfortune. The priest assures him that God alone, or occasionally a hypothetical 'evil spirit', can will the series of events in which he is struggling; the doctor claims this series is only an illusion, or a set of pure coincidences. These official theories are backed by powerful social agencies: the School, the Church, the Medical Association. They constitute both the social order, and since this order prevails, social 'reality'.

Note here that when a Zande says he is bewitched, he is acting as a social being, who accepts his group's symbolic code and knows how to use it. But a peasant of the Bocage who says he is bewitched shows he has seceded from the official theories of misfortune, or that he lacks the capacity to use the positivist or religious set of terms which express *this* particular story. From then on, he deliberately shuts himself off and enters the state of secrecy.

The others shut him off by their criticism or scorn: he is superstitious, backward, raving, say the priests, the other villagers and the doctors. But the bewitched himself only reinforces his own isolation by justifying their attitude with such statements as '*you have to be caught to believe*'. For he thinks that only a raving, backward or superstitious person could believe theoretically in spells, and talk about them without having specifically experienced them himself. He also says: '*For those who haven't been caught, they [spells] don't exist*'; so unbelievable seems the reality of his misfortunes to anyone who has not been caught in such a series. Finally, he asserts: '*Those who haven't been caught can't even talk about it.*' By the same token, one cannot talk to them even if they have enough good will to accept the truth of this discourse: for it cannot even be uttered in front of anyone who is exempted in advance from having to withstand its effects.

Of course such assertions were being made long before any ethnographer arrived in the Bocage. All the same, they prompted me to ask myself: what ultimate authority could I invoke, in talking about spells to a bewitched person or an unwitcher?

For when a bewitched person talks to an ethnographer, who is supposed to hold only to the official theories on misfortune, he starts to talk about himself in just the same way as he would to the doctor, the teacher and the ethnographer. He says that he only has a distant, indirect knowledge of spells, as well as of the '*superstitions of backward people*' or the '*beliefs of the old folk*' whom he also calls the '*back*' people: from '*back*' to backward is but a short step.*

At first, when witchcraft is put forward as the belief of other people, any information is bound to be loaded or unrecognizable. What is important to the native is that the listener – for instance, the ethnographer, who is presumed to partake of objective language – must not recognize him in

---

* The expression 'the back people', 'les arrières' is essentially a term of 'generation reference', i.e. of reference to the second generation from 'ego' – in the present context the generation of the 'arrières-grands-parents', the great-grandparents.

what he says. He will only talk about witchcraft provided he can set himself apart from it, and describe it as a particularly childish, preposterous and ridiculous set of beliefs.

Because the peasant is talking to the 'other', the scholar, he objectifies himself, and says nothing. The ethnographer, for her part, does not listen – either she is looking for empirical facts and in these fantastic stories there are none which could satisfy any criteria of plausibility; or she adheres to this language and understands that it simply expresses a refusal on the part of the peasant to speak in his own person. Hence the arrogance of a folklorist's attitude in this particular matter: as long as she adopts an external position, the ethnographer hears nothing but wanderings meant to convince her that the speaker is quite as adept as herself in keeping his distance from an 'object' called witchcraft.

II. A name added to a position

In pursuing the ethnography of spells, the first point to grasp is being clear about whom each 'informant' thinks he is speaking to, since he utters such radically different discourses depending on the position he thinks his interlocutor holds. To someone who *'isn't caught'*, he will say: *'spells don't exist'*; *'they no longer exist'*; *'that was in the old days'*; *'they were true for our back people'*; *'they exist, but not here: go and look in Saint-Mars* (or Montjean, or Lassay: somewhere else ...) *'over there, they're really backward'*; *'oh, spells! I don't hold with all that rot!'*[4]. To someone who is *'caught'*, one speaks in a different way, depending on whether the person is given the position of bewitched or unwitcher. (No one talks to the alleged witch, but this very silence is in itself a whole discourse, the silent assertion of a fight to the death, which always has some effect.)

When an ethnographer works in an exotic field, he too has to take up some sort of stance. But common sense and the handbooks point out the virtues of distance and the advantages to be derived from the status of rich cannibal.[5] To claim, on the other hand, that one wants to hear about peasant witchcraft yet remain alien to it is to condemn oneself to hearing only objectivist statements and to collecting fantastic anecdotes and for unwitching recipes – i.e. to accumulate statements which the stating subject formally disavows. So for the last hundred and fifty years, the native and the folklorist have been looking at themselves in a mirror each has held up to the other, without the folklorist apparently ever noticing the ironic complicity that this implies on the part of the native.[6]

---

[4] All the names cited in this book belong to the stock of local names. However, to preserve the confidentiality to my former interlocutors, I have systematically changed them: no name corresponds to the person who actually talked to me, or to the place where the event described occurred.   [5] To adopt an expression of Jean Monod's (1972).

[6] One can also say, and this is another aspect of the same problem, that the peasant is thus signifying his eminent right to participate in the same symbolic system as the scholar.

When I left for the Bocage, I was certainly in no better position than any of my predecessors, except that I thought their findings trivial compared with the reality at stake in a witchcraft attack. Within a few months I had myself done much the same collecting as they; it left me unsatisfied, and gave me no guidance about how to pursue my investigation. It would have been just as futile for me to try and win over the peasants with large-minded statements of good intention, since anyway, in matters of witchcraft, it is always the other person who decides how to interpret what you say. Just as a peasant must hear the words of the annunciator, if he is to confess that he is indeed bewitched, so it was my interlocutors who decided what my position was ('caught' or not, bewitched or unwitcher) by interpreting unguarded clues in my speech.[7]

I must point out that I knew nothing about this system of positions, and that the main part of my work has been to make it out little by little by going back over puzzling episodes. For several months my notes describe a number of situations in which my interlocutors placed me in this stance or that ('not caught', 'caught'–bewitched, 'caught'–unwitcher) although at the time I did not see anything but a classic situation of ethnographic investigation, even if a somewhat difficult one because I was after something particularly secret.

I was probably not yet ready to maintain this speech process in the only way conceivable to my interlocutors: by accepting that being given such a stance committed me to utter my part in this discourse in the same way as they did. Of course this position existed before me and was acceptably occupied and maintained by others. But now I was the one being placed there, and my name was being attached to this position as well as to my particular personal existence.

Although I went through the whole experience in a state of some confusion, I can say today that it is actually patterned around a small number of characteristic situations in which my interlocutors required me to occupy a position that they indicated. They were conveying that they had no need of my ability to listen, for what mattered to them was not merely to be understood, or, in the language of communication-theory – they had no need for a decoder. In witchcraft, to receive messages obliges one to send out other, signed messages: it was time for me to speak.

For example, here are some instances of the manner in which I was put to the test: (1) the first time that the bewitched told me their own story (and not that of some hypothetical 'backward people'), it was because they had identified me as the unwitcher who could get them out of their troubles. (2) A few months later, a peasant interpreted my 'weakness', took on the role of annunciator of my state as a bewitched, and took me to his unwitcher to

---

[7] Anyone who called himself bewitched on his own authority would simply be thought mad: a warning to apprentice sorcerers who try to make peasants talk by simply declaring themselves 'caught'.

get me 'uncaught'. ③ For more than two years, I subjected the events of my personal life to the interpretations of this unwitcher. ④ Several bewitched asked me to 'uncatch' them. Although at this point I had become quite competent at handling magical discourse, I felt quite incapable of taking the speech-position upholding it, and I sent them on to my therapist. ⑤ Lastly, this unwitcher, with whom I had a complicated relationship (I was her client, agent, and guarantor of the truth of her words during the cures in which I was invited to participate) instructed me to bring her a healer who would relieve her of her bodily pains and to assist him in his task.[8]

You could say, given the ideal assumption that I might have made my choice in full consciousness of the situation, that every time these were the alternatives: either I refused this assignment of my identity to a position and withdrew from the speech process pointing out that I was being mistaken for someone I was not (*I am not who you think I am*) or I agreed to occupy the position assigned to me, unless I could propose some other which I felt more able to occupy (*I am not where you think I am*). In the first case, I would have had to leave the Bocage, where I no longer had any place; in the second, the speech process would go on but I had to place myself in the position of subject of the enunciation.

It emerges from the asides of investigators that I was not the first person to be offered this alternative. Some folklorists, for example, tell of their amusement at having been invited, at one point or another, to act as unwitchers. This type of occurrence is worth looking into. Note in the first place, that it is out of the question for the investigator to be assigned the position of bewitched. He would have had to give some sign that he knows he is mortal, vulnerable or at least subject to desires – all things one can freely admit, but only to close relations and in confidence – certainly not to uneducated farmers and while practising one's profession. In the field, the investigator therefore routinely presents himself to his interlocutor as someone who does not lack anything: or to take up the expression I used above,[9] he displays a continuous surface without holes in it. Everything in his behaviour suggests he is '*strong enough*'. This especially since he does not omit arguments likely to loosen their tongues: he may say he belongs to a local line of magic healers (he might claim, for example, that his maternal grandmother, who is still remembered in the area, '*passed the secret*' on to him); and in his conversations with 'informers', he shows he knows many unwitchment recipes, magic formulae and fantastic anecdotes. Without being conscious of it, the investigator has done everything necessary for his interlocutors to assign him the position of unwitcher. But if he is actually told this, and asked to perform, he is amused. He recounts this episode as if it were just an entertaining anecdote, and a particularly conclusive evidence of peasant gullibility, to a listener who is confidently assumed to feel

[8] These situations are discussed in the third part of this book and in a forthcoming volume, which will be almost entirely concerned with analysing unwitching séances.   [9] Cf. p. 8.

equally superior. Indeed, there is cause to smile: there has been an error, a mistaken identity, the investigator was not the person he was thought to be.

But one may wonder who is more naïve, the peasant or the folklorist. The former cannot understand that one might collect formulae without putting them to any use, just for the sake of information; the latter judges that he has satisfied the demands of science by collecting information, without realizing he cannot do anything with it, neither science nor magic.

Not science: the folklorists failed to recognize the existence and role of the power of therapists in unwitching cures. They strained to find out what these therapists knew, and this in the particular form of secrets to be collected. In other words, whatever in their discourse most resembles an utterance, a statement which can stand on its own independent of the stating subject.

The content of the secret (the utterance) is for the most part neither here nor there: it does not matter whether one is told to pierce an ox heart, twist steel nails, or recite misappropriated Church prayers.[10] Magicians know this, when they quietly say: *'to each one his secret'*, and show themselves in no hurry to increase their knowledge. For what makes an unwitcher is his *'force'* and its links with a world of language (the very one which produced the content of the secret). The power of the magician, thus referred to a symbolic set, places him in the position of recognized avenger (and not, for example, of a criminal settling private scores), but on condition that he openly declares his readiness to assume this position.

Not magic: unwitching does not consist in uttering formulae or practising magic rituals. If they are to have any chance of being effective, a set of positions must first be established, by which someone who is not the magician places him in the position of subject supposed to be able; and the magician himself must acknowledge he is in it, and accept what this implies in terms of personal commitment to a discourse, and of assuming the effects of magic speech on his own body and so on.[11]

So when the folklorist reacts to a request for unwitchment by laughing as if this were an inappropriate proposal, and excuses himself by saying he cannot do anything, or by sending the patient to his doctor, the peasant gathers that this academic does not want to commit his *'force'*, if he has any; or more likely, that he has no idea what *'force'* is or just how much is involved in speaking. The folklorist's mirth simply shows that he does not think he can cure anyone with magic formulae, and that for him such knowledge is pointless. And so it is, unless a subject agrees to become the support of these magic utterances and to proffer them in the name of his

---

[10] But the writings of the folklorists nonetheless rely on these small differences.

[11] It would be a great mistake to imagine that it is enough to propose the position of diviner or unwitcher to have it enthusiastically accepted. Everyone in the Bocage is sufficiently aware of the dangers and servitude attached to magic power to know that it is a poisoned gift which one must not touch unless one's desire to do so is sufficiently strong.

own *'force'* taken as part of a symbolic universe – i.e. to convert this knowledge into a power.

III. Taking one's distances from whom (or what)?

So one cannot study witchcraft without agreeing to take part in the situations where it manifests itself, and in the discourse expressing it. This entails certain limitations which will seem most unwelcome to those who favour an objectivizing ethnography.

(1) You cannot verify any assertion: first because there is no position of impartial witness in this discourse. Second, because it is pointless to question outsiders: to be bewitched is to have stopped communicating with one's presumed witch as well as with anyone not involved in the crisis; so other villagers know almost nothing of the matter. Finally, it is inconceivable that an ethnographer to whom someone had spoken as to the legitimate occupier of one of the positions in the discourse might step outside it to investigate, and ask what is the truth behind this or that story.

(2) You cannot hear both parties – the bewitched and their alleged witches – since they no longer communicate. Not only do they not talk to each other, they do not speak the same kind of language. If, exceptionally, it were ever possible to obtain both versions of the same story, they could not be set face to face, since witches always claim that they do not believe in spells, object to the discourse of witchcraft, and appeal to the language of positivism.[12] In any case, the bewitched prevent any such confrontation by warning the ethnographer to avoid meeting their aggressor, for fear of becoming his victim. To take no notice of this advice would be a sign either of disturbing masochism, or of a rash faith in the powers protecting you, or indeed of an intention to work some betrayal. Note that such daring would be just as disturbing to the 'witch', however imaginary he may be: knowing that the ethnographer sees people who call themselves his victims, he would, on receiving a visit from this stranger, see him as an unwitcher come to fight him. In time of war, nothing so resembles the characteristic weapons of the magician (words, look and touch) as an innocent 'how are you?' followed by a handshake.

(3) One cannot investigate in one's own *'quartier'* [neighbourhood] so dreaded is the magic effectiveness of speech. The peasant thinks it wise to maintain a certain distance between the speaker and the listener, to prevent the latter from taking advantage of the situation. A serious crisis will never be taken to the local unwitcher. People prefer to choose their therapist beyond some boundary (in a neighbouring diocese or *département*), in any case outside the network of acquaintanceship. For this reason, I never worked less than ten kilometres from where I was living. So in general, I

---

[12] A dodge which an Azande would never have imagined, since he can only choose between *witchcraft* and *sorcery*.

remained unaware of the sociological context of witchcraft matters and especially of the particular positions of the opponents in the local struggles for prestige and power – and these usually constitute the subject-matter of ethnographic investigations into witchcraft.[13]

(4.) One cannot set up any strategy of observation (even a 'participating' one) which keeps the agreed amount of distance that this implies. More generally, to claim an external position for oneself is to abandon hope of ever learning this discourse: first (remember) because those concerned react with silence or duplicity to anyone who claims to be outside. But more profoundly because any attempt at making things explicit comes up against a much more formidable barrier: that of the native's amnesia and his incapacity to formulate what must remain unsaid. These are the limits of what one can ask a willing informer (in so far as such persons exist in the Bocage), and they are soon reached.

To take one example: if you want to know the substance of a diviner's consultation, you can simply ask him what usually takes place in a séance, or what his clients consult him about. But you should not be surprised at trivial answers: *'They come because of illness, love affairs, animals, to recover money they have lost . . .'* – 'And what about spells?' – *'That might be the case, but I don't deal with that'* will be the diviner's systematic reply. A barrier, then, of silence and duplicity: the diviner can only admit *'dealing with that'* in front of someone who puts forward a personal request for divination. About the séances, on the other hand, he claims he honestly has nothing more to impart than a few matters of technique: *'I begin with the game of piquet and go on to tarot cards.'* – 'But how do you guess their story?' – *'Well, I have the gift.'* Even when the ethnographer's questions are more subtle, they soon come up against the bounds of the unstatable, represented here by the reference to a *'gift'*. Pressed to make himself more clear, the diviner can do no more than illustrate his statements by recounting the enigmatic circumstances in which, one day, a long time ago, when becoming a seer had not yet entered his head, a patient seeking for revelations sensed the *'gift'* in him, and announced it to the professional diviner who then initiated him.

---

[13] In the forthcoming volume, I shall show the relative autonomy of the discourse of witchcraft in relation to the sociological determinants usually proposed to account for its use. Here it is enough to point out that this discourse as it was spoken to me in the Bocage would make me tend more to question the basis of ethnography's most obvious assertions. Thus one often reads in scholarly publications that the 'witch' is always a 'jealous neighbour' (followed by descriptions of neighbourship relations as opposed to kinship relations; or on the topographical distribution of cliques, etc.). In the Bocage too, it is said that the witch is a jealous neighbour. But 'empirical reality' is not so much in question here as a system of naming: it is because X was first classified as being my *'witch'* that he is said to be my *'neighbour'*, *'jealous of me'*, etc. References to topography are therefore suprisingly elastic, and motives of envy too obvious to need detailing. In the forthcoming volume, I shall return to this point, and the mechanism of imputation, i.e. the way in which one constructs an answer to the question 'Now, who is my witch?'.

If the ethnographer resorts to the patients, he obtains uniformly improbable statements: the diviner, he is told, 'reads me like an open book', or again, 'he's extraordinary, I never tell him anything and he knows everything'. But if he has ever accompanied peasants to the diviner's and sat in the waiting room during the consultations, the ethnographer knows that they never stopped talking: it's just that, as after a hypnotic trance, they do not remember.

So the diviner and his client have a common 'misknowledge' which is not the same as the simple complicity of sharing a secret: no winning of trust will ever make the persons concerned capable of explaining what the terms 'gift' and 'seeing everything' really mean, because the whole institution of divination depends on the fact that they do not want to know anything about it.

For anyone who wants to understand the meaning of this discourse, there is no other solution but to practise it oneself, to become one's own informant, to penetrate one's own amnesia, and to try and make explicit what one finds unstatable in oneself. For it is difficult to see how the native could have any interest in the project of unveiling what can go on existing only if it remains veiled; or for what purpose he would give up the symbolic benefits of such important resources.

(I am well aware that there is a fundamental gulf between my present aims and those of my Bocage interlocutors. Until now, I have been content to state that the discourse of witchcraft is such that to gain access to it one must be in a position to sustain it oneself. And yet, it is one thing to have access to it – it was a memorable adventure which has marked me for my whole subsequent life – it is another thing to want to go on to develop its theory.)

If you want to listen to and understand a diviner, there is therefore no other solution but to become his client, i.e. to tell him your desire and ask him to interpret it.[14] Like any native – or any desiring subject – the investigator is bound on this occasion to be afflicted by misknowledge: so for several months, however carefully I tried to take notes after each divination séance, a certain part of the consultation, always the same, was censored by amnesia; similarly, when a seer, who I was hoping would teach me the everyday tricks of divination saw the 'gift' in me and gave me her life-story for interpretation, claiming she had nothing to teach me that I did not already know, I could not help being amazed.

Persistent amnesia, dumbfoundedness, the inability to reflect when faced by the seemingly unstatable – i.e. a vague perception that something in this cannot be coped with – this was my ordinary lot during the adventure.[15] It may

[14] To consult without asking the seer to 'see' is futile, since the latter sees nothing and there is nothing for the ethnographer to understand.

[15] I might just as well express it as 'can't be thought' or 'can't be said'; in talking of what 'can't be coped with', I am trying to point to an element of reality, that at some point escapes the grasp of language or symbolization.

be wondered how, at a certain point, I managed to surmount this inability, that is, try to get it out in words, to convert an adventure into a theoretical project. But this question cannot be answered simply by invoking one's duty towards the demands of the scientific approach, or one's debt to the scholarly institution which acts as patron: if that respect applies, it is somewhere else and in another manner. To have been engaged in the discourse of witchcraft beyond what can be required of an ethnographer in the ordinary practice of her profession poses first the problem of motive; what could have been my own desire to know; why was I personally involved in the ambition to give a solid basis to the 'social sciences', and why, in the case of divination for example, was I not content to resolve the issue by invoking the concept of *'gift'*, or, even sooner, by accepting the findings of the folklorists.

So the distance necessary if one is to be able to theorize does not have to be established between the ethnographer and his 'object', i.e. the native. But of all the snares which might imperil our work, there are two we had learnt to avoid like the plague: that of agreeing to 'participate' in the native discourse, and that of succumbing to the temptations of subjectivism. Not only could I not possibly avoid them; it is by means of them that I was able to work out most of my ethnographic work. Whatever you may think of it, it must be granted that the masters' predictions do not always turn out to be true, which state that in such cases it becomes impossible to put any distance between oneself and the native or between oneself and oneself.

Anyway, I was never able to choose between subjectivism and the objective method as it was taught me, so long, that is, as I still wished to find an answer to my initial question – what are the people involved trying to shape out through a witchcraft crisis one? Working in this way has at least preserved me from one limitation regularly met by the objectivizing ethnographer and which is never emphasized, since it is taken for granted: I mean the ethnographer's dependence on a finite *corpus* of empirical observations and native texts collected in the field. This kind of ethnography meets any new question with the answer that it is included, or not, in the *corpus*; it can be verified, or not, in the empirical data – and of anything not referred to in the *corpus*, nothing can be asserted. In my case, the fact that Bocage peasants forced me to come up with a number of statements in the same way as they did (i.e. to be an encoder) enabled me to break away from the limits of the *corpus*; or, and this comes to the same thing, to include my own discourse in it. For the sort of question posed by comparative grammarians, I was able to substitute that posed by transformationalists: can this utterance be produced or not? Hazarding my own words in the presence of native decoders, I became able to discriminate accepted from unacceptable meaning whatever the utterance and whether or not it was produced during my stay in the field. The limits of ordinary ethnography are those of its *corpus*. In the case of the ethnography I was practising, the problem was, each time, to evaluate correctly the limits of my position in speech. But my having occupied at one time or another all the positions in this discourse, knowingly or not, or willingly or not, at least enables me to have a view on everything that is statable.

It is now time to give a little information about the position of the witch. No one, in the Bocage, calls himself a witch; it is not a position from which one can speak. A witch never admits his crimes, not even when he is delirious in a psychiatric hospital (this is considerably different from exotic witchcrafts). The witch is the person referred to by those who utter the discourse on witchcraft (bewitched and unwitchers), and he only figures in it as the subject of the statement. His victims claim that it is unnecessary for him to admit he is a witch, since his death speaks for him: everyone laughs at his funeral because he died in a significant way, carried off in only a few hours as a result of the diviner's curse, or neighing like the mare he had cast an evil spell on, and so on. This makes it highly unlikely that there are witches who actually cast evil spells, but this is surely not in the least necessary for the system to function.[16]

[16] The only position I did not occupy was that of witch. And yet the magazine *L'Express* published a report on my investigations and decided to call it 'The witch of the C.N.R.S.', thus succumbing to the cult of the dark hero I alluded to above (Gérard Bonnot, 'La sorcière du C.N.R.S.', in *L'Express*, No. 1206, 19–24 August 1974).

3

WHEN THE TEXT IS ITS OWN FOREWORD

On re-reading my field-notes, I find that nothing directly concerning witchcraft lends itself to ethnographic description. Remember that any information on the subject is not informative, but only moments in a strategy: either a peasant, not himself behind what he says, insists how unlikely it is that there should be bewitched and how he could never be one himself. Or else the speaker is involved in what he says, but is talking in order to engage me in his own fight to the death against a witch and not just to give me information. The facts of the case are then simply a speech process, and my notes take on a narrative form.

If I am to describe witchcraft in the Bocage, it can only be done by going over the situations in which I was myself given a position. The only empirical evidence I have of the existence of such positions, and of the manner in which they relate to each other consists of fragments of narrative. My mistakes, and sometimes my refusals or evasions are part of the text; each answer I gave my interlocutors was, like their question, part of the fact under investigation. It should be remembered that these positions only gradually became clear to me through the later repetition of the same request: this time, I was able to perceive (or admit) that I was meant to occupy them. The ethnography of spells consists in the description of this system of positions. It was by comparing several similar episodes that I was able to abstract such a description.

It may – quite justifiably – be deplored that ethnography can depend so much on the ethnographer's moods. Readers of my narrative may wonder how, on this occasion or that, I could have been so stupid. Of course I have regretted this myself. Others, more bold or more resourceful, would have behaved more dashingly. And yet I claim that the ethnographer's stupidity, for instance her refusal to realize where the native is wanting to lead her, is inevitable in such circumstances. *That there must be a subject to uphold the verbal exchange* is a necessary condition for the ethnography of spells. It does not really matter what sort of person the investigator is (and another would react differently to the same situation); the bewitched person addresses himself to the person in front of him and to him only; and that is why the person cannot be eliminated from ethnographic description (or at least from the narrative on which the description is based) any more than you can eliminate the words and deeds of the native.

Ethnography as I learnt it – and even taught it – is considered a science so long as one covers up the traces of what fieldwork was like. This is both an apprenticeship, during which an outsider is taught to decode a symbolic system he did not know before, and a long dialogue between the outsider and his host: that is to say a process of verbal exchange. It is understood (it is even a rule in this kind of literature) that these two elements can only be mentioned outside the text: either in another book of a different genre (a diary or a philosophical journey) which does not claim to be scientific precisely because it chooses to admit these traces;[1] or in a scientific report, but only in the form of a 'foreword'. The scientific *text* as such is for the results of the ethnographer's decoding work.

Thus scientific status or objectivity is usually made visible in the split between the stating subject of ethnography, and the set of statements on the native culture: in other words, in the difference between foreword and text. A noteworthy feature of the ethnographic text is that the stating subject (or rather, the author) is regularly hidden. He withdraws in favour of what he states about his object. It may well be asked – and my colleagues never tire of questioning me about this whenever I talk to them about my research – whether the material I have produced on witchcraft in Western France can be called 'science', since the stating subject of ethnographic work cannot at any moment disappear as a person behind what he states about his object. Just as the native, throughout the fieldwork, continually appealed to the particular personality of the investigator, similarly readers of the opening remarks of this chapter may fail to see how the ethnographer could abstract himself from the narrative on which his description of witchcraft is based. Can you still talk of science when the text is its own foreword?

The reader will understand that, faced with this question, I have a number of arguments (or excuses) based on the peculiarity of the situation in which I found myself. But I think it is more interesting to develop here a completely different argument which questions this conventional withdrawal of the stating subject behind the usual topic of statements in ethnographic writings. Yet there cannot be any statement which is not upheld by its relationship to the stating subject that is what recent linguis-

[1] This difference is seen in a particularly striking way in the work of Michel Leiris. Compare *L'Afrique fantôme* (1934), the diary of his expedition through Africa, and the scientific reports written on his return, for example: *La Langue secrète des Dogons de Sanga* (1948). But one could also take C. Lévi-Strauss as an example, and note the unbridgeable distance he established between *Tristes Tropiques* (1955), (the phrase 'philosophical journey' is from Madeleine Chapsal) and the rest of his works. Similarly, Balandier expresses his desire to admit the original workings, but 'in parallel' with his scientific work proper (*Afrique Ambiguë*, 1957, p. 19).

tic studies, or for that matter everyday experience, have taught us.[2] I was forced to face this by the borderline situation of witchcraft, where I could hardly avoid understanding that it was a matter of one subject calling forth a response from another subject.

I could develop my arguments along the following line:[3] ethnography, as the science of cultural difference, has legitimately constituted its research procedures and criteria of validity around the notion of objectivity. It is by talking of the native as an object, as someone 'other' and by referring to him as a 'stating subject' ('he' has this practice or says this or that) that we reach the possibility of a discourse on a different culture, on an object which is not me. Yet if one wants this discourse to be plausible or even intelligible the 'I' must announce himself and say to whom he is addressing this discourse about the other: for *only a human being who names himself 'I' can refer to another human as 'he'; and he can only do so by addressing a 'you'*. Now, in ethnographic writings, neither the speaker nor his partner – in other words, neither the stating subject, author of the scientific report, nor his reader – are defined. It is implied that the 'I' need not introduce himself because he is taken for granted, just like the 'you' who is talked to. It is so much a matter of course that the 'I' and the 'you' converse about 'him', that the stating subject can withdraw behind an indefinite subject, and call himself 'one'.

Etymologically, the French *on* [English 'one'] is *homo*, anyone, everyone, people – any subject as long as it is indefinite. The fact that it is a subject gives it the right to predicate something of 'him'; the fact that it is indefinite means that, like any personal pronoun subject, it replaces a proper name without ever having to identify itself. 'One' is 'we': I who am talking and you who are listening. It is everyone and anyone except 'he' the only definite term in ethnographic discourse. Thus the stating of scientific discourse is spent in the act of designating, leaving open the question of who designates and to whom.[4] As a result, what is designated – the other, the native, the third person – is bound to become unreal in the eyes of the reader, as for instance De Martino[5] notes: 'Once the book was finished', he

[2] Cf. Emile Benveniste, *Problèmes de linguistique générale*, vol. i (1966): 'Structure des relations de personne dans le verbe'; 'Les relations de temps dans le verbe français'; 'La nature des pronoms'; 'De la subjectivité dans le langage' And vol. ii (op. cit.): 'Le langage et l'expérience humaine'; 'Structure de la langue et structure de la société; 'L'appareil formel de l'énonciation'; 'L'antonyme et le pronom dans le français moderne'.

[3] This argument claims less in relation to the one I defended above on subjectivity (cf. pp. 20–4): I prefer to come back to it only after I have provided some means of dealing with it other than basic principle. The present argument acknowledges the importance given by the ethnographic approach to objectivity, but points out that to reach this aim one will have to go about it differently.

[4] This is how I would today define the statements I have defended before on this same point (cf. Jeanne Favret, 1969).

[5] De Martino, an Italian historian who thought he ought to read some ethnography in preparation for a study of contemporary rituals of exorcism in Taranto. The following quotations come from *La Terre du remords* (1966), pp. 13 and 14.

says, 'the Aranda [described in the monumental study of Spencer and Gillen] appeared to the reader like some dubious form of humanity, a monstrous joke in human history, the futility of which could not be compensated for by its very conventional weirdness'. Unable to perceive that they have anything in common with the natives talked about, the author who talks and the reader who is talked to are lost in 'a world of visiting and visited shadows, insignificant and trivial for all their meticulous prattle'.

Another peculiarity of ethnographic writing is that the native, the 'he' who is so freely predicated, never seems to have been engaged in his own person in any speaking process. Scientific works do not refer to the original speech situation except to illustrate a point and to explain a native statement by referring it back to the speaker's social position: 'he talks in this way', we are warned, 'because he is a warrior', an 'aristocrat' or a 'shaman'. The remarks he once made to the ethnographer had no aim other than to represent the interests of his faction. In other words, an implicit convention of ethnographic discourse holds that a 'he' can never be an 'I', and that the position of the stating subject in the original speech situation must thus always be left vacant: at best, a social group sometimes offers its identity. The situation would be no more plausible if the author presented the social group as a person (which no social group can ever be) or even as a fiction of a person. For this subject in the third person, as he speaks in the text, does not seem to speak to anyone, in any case not to the subject the ethnographer may very well have been at the time when the words were exchanged. In ethnographic writing, a native faction talks to a universal science, a non-person to an undefined subject.[6]

So ethnography seems to be carried forward between a native confined for all time to the position of subject in the statement, and a scholar who assigns himself the role of stating subject, though an indefinite one. The native then turns out to be a conceptual freak: no doubt he is a speaker, since ethnography is based on his words; but he is a *non-human speaker*, since he can never occupy the position of 'I' in any discourse. As for the ethnographer, he presents himself as a *speaking being*, but without a *proper name* since he refers to himself under an indefinite pronoun. A strange dialogue, between these two fantastical beings...

---

[6] In his *Problèmes de linguistique générale*, vol. I (op. cit.), Benveniste remarks that the pronoun 'il' [he] is improperly labelled 'third person' since it is 'the non-person, whose mark is the absence of what specifically qualifies the *je* [I] and *tu* [you]. Because it implies no person, it can take any subject or contain none, and this subject whether it is expressed or not is never stated as a *person*' (p. 231).

Part II

THE REALM OF SECRECY

'Of course, you aren't taught about that [spells] *at school. No fear of you being taught that. It's never mentioned in your books. No fear of anyone talking about it.*

'And yet, for all your sciences, you believe in it.'

The unwitcher, to a schoolgirl

4

SOMEONE MUST BE CREDULOUS

When I went to live in the Bocage in July 1969, I took it for granted that no one would talk to me about spells for quite some time. So, for several months – until about December – I was content to get acquainted with some of the people in my area, to let my intention to study witchcraft be known, and to make notes after any conversation which had to do with witchcraft.[1]

These notes from the early stages are more revealing in what they do not say than in what they say. Until I was myself *'caught'* in spells, i.e. until I stopped being just an inquirer, the people I spoke to very efficiently concealed the existence of one essential person: the professional spell-breaker or *'unwitcher'*. To be more precise, they acted as if there were only two or three unwitchers in the region, who had hit the headlines through scandals or court-cases. In other words, they mentioned the people whom I could hardly miss hearing about by simply looking at the back numbers of the local press. No one bothered to tell me that these notorious characters were complete outsiders so far as the system was concerned, and that they were being shown off like carnival masks so as to allow the numerous clandestine unwitchers to carry on in the background and go about their business without attracting unnecessary attention.

So my work on spells was being confined to an inquiry into the *'Blonde Lady'*, an unwitcher who originally came from the North of the Mayenne and lived in Le Mans.[2] If I was told about her and her only in relation to witchcraft this was first because she no longer operated in the area: she had been threatened here and there by disgruntled villagers; second, and principally, because her methods were so grotesque that no one could possibly

---

[1] I lived in a village of the Bocage from July 1969 to September 1971; in the following year I spent eight months there, and from then on two or three months a year, until 1975.

[2] As I mentioned earlier (cf. p. 16, fn. 4) all the names of places and people in this book have been altered. Except, of course, those printed in the newspapers: in this chapter, for example, the *'Blonde Lady'* and the *'Magus of Aron'* are the names given by the press; on the other hand, M. Derouet, Mlle Jalus, Mme Paillard – or, in the following chapter, the Fourmands, Lenain, Chailland, Quelaines, etc., are fictitious names for people or places.

believe in them: '*You had to put a hundred-franc note, folded in four, in a keyhole, or well-cleaned chunks of pork out in the yard, and you were forbidden to go out at night. If the money or the pork were no longer there the next day, it meant it had worked*': one was unwitched. Or else the farmer's wife, stark naked, had to bring the cows into the stable, riding them backwards. Or else, naked and standing backwards astraddle on two cows, she would have to go over a fire into which a handful of salt had been thrown while her family formed a circle around her. Or else ... there was a long list of her eccentricities, but why bother to give it in detail:'*The Blonde Lady? You can find out about her in a book.*' This refers to an issue of *Constellation* containing an article appropriately entitled: '*Incredible: a bewitched country district!*'[3]

'*Read this, I can never remember stories about spells*', apologizes my 'informant' as she hands me the precious copy of *Constellation*. Against all likelihood, she insists that she had never heard anything about spells before the scandal of the '*Blonde Lady*' – whereas usually disclaimers consist in admitting that one has heard a lot about spells, but only as a child and always about the '*old people*'.

This issue of *Constellation* belongs to M. Derouet; he lent it to old Miss Jalus who lent it to Mme Paillard, who lent it to me. What a Godsend this '*book*' is for local slander; thanks to it, gossip is transformed into text – perhaps even into objective truth, since it has been sent back from somewhere else. Everyone can pass on this piece of scandalous information because it is given in the doubly irresponsible form of a text printed elsewhere and written by a stranger.

The important thing is to respect the custom: if the '*book*' is to be handed around, its circulation must be explicitly forbidden. For it is not forbidden to reveal the misfortunes of the bewitched family, as the article by the journalist does; but only the name of M. Derouet who started the rumour in his neighbourhood. So one can peddle scandals but not mention names, or else one must disavow them in every possible way. So I was told about witchcraft, but only through disclaimers; which was a way of transmitting the following message, in the words of Mme Paillard:

(*a*) Some bewitched people go to this '*Blonde Lady*'; this is not what I say myself, but what that other person, the journalist, says. As for me, I have nothing to say about it. I am just repeating a reported speech ('Incredible: a bewitched country district!'): I can only talk to you about witchcraft by switching you on to official discourse, on to the '*enlightened*' version of these events as they were reported in the '*book*'.

(*b*) In any case, don't take that '*book*' too seriously. '*A lot of things in it are false*', the ethnographer is warned without comment. In other words: this (official, enlightened) reported discourse is unreliable; it is inadequately informed; but to correct it I would have to break away from it and speak in my own person.

Only one reservation is explicitly formulated: the journalist made the

[3] Cf. Marc-Ambroise Rendu (1965).

mistake of classifying as 'superstitions' both the vagaries of the *'Blonde Lady'* and the pilgrimage to the local saint, protector of animals: 'We carry out a pilgrimage in good faith.' This qualification is easily expressed, because it involves an eminently authoritative institution, the Church.

(c) Because the *'Blonde Lady'* is so eccentric and her clients so willing to be deceived, I cannot risk being identified with them. The only explicit discourse I can offer on spells is one which will emphasize the unbridgeable distance separating me from them: I am not bewitched, the *other* is; the person who is credulous enough, stupid enough, to place a hundred-franc note in the keyhole, and who will not stay to find out who arrives to pick it up; or the one who, wanting to cure his wife's sterility, sends her off to spend the night in the *'Magus of Aron's'* bedroom.

The *'Magus of Aron'* is another scandalous unwitcher, nick-named by his enemies *'the billy-goat of Aron'*. They often talk about him under the general heading: *'unwitching to go to bed'*. For example, the sterile wife's husband has to remain downstairs in the dining room, in front of a fireplace, a candle in each hand, while the *'billy-goat'* treats his patient upstairs, in the matrimonial bedroom.[4]

The *'Blonde Lady'* on the other hand, is talked about under the following two general headings:

1. *'Unwitching for money':* '*the number of hundred-franc notes that woman has accumulated, through a keyhole!'*

2. *'Unwitching to go to bed.* '*One week she goes to bed with the farmer, next week with his wife; that way no one is jealous'*: so they joke.

You also sometimes come across an intermediate theory according to which she spends the night in the farmer's bed with the couple while an accomplice picks up the notes in the keyhole.

The advantage of this attitude of disavowal is that it presents the people who believe in spells as being in a situation which is unacceptable or beyond understanding: only a fool or someone out of his mind could believe in the *'Blonde Lady'* or in the *'Magus of Aron'*, for we can instantly grasp the human, all too human, origins of their so-called magic powers.

This is probably why, in speaking of these two magicians, the case of a few admitted madmen who went to them for help is always mentioned: who would go, if he was not a fool or mad?

That these scandalous unwitchers agreed to treat madmen by magic (as I was able to ascertain) is a clear indication of how totally anomalous they are in relation to the system: later, we shall see that their clandestine colleagues take very strict precautions to avoid any meeting between the two spheres of madness and witchcraft.[5]

[4] The local press, Catholic and conservative, declared war on the 'Magus' when he decided to invent a religion. Until that moment, Brault had been content with the role of an eccentric but discreet unwitcher. More details about him can be found in Appendix 3: *'Robert Brault, "Prophet" of Aron'* (cf. p. 234).

[5] This topic will be further discussed in the forthcoming volume.

Of course, the fact that an eccentric unwitcher manages to attract clients in this way poses a problem. But after all, no one is totally protected from a pervert in the Bocage any more than in Paris. In so far as a nosographic category is an explanation of anything at all, and in so far as one may use it without having met the persons concerned, these two characters do evoke perversion, especially the *'Blonde Lady'*, who emerges from the narratives of her familiars as a heroine of Sade, though she would be more likely to haunt the Basilica of Lourdes than a castle.

All the same, the basic difference between eccentric unwitchers and their colleagues seems to reside in this: the former perform rituals which they have invented from beginning to end, which were not transmitted to them by anyone else, and which are not supported by any form of tradition. This is perhaps why the country people are so eager to disavow them; for they cannot really imagine that such practices bring about a symbolic end to the personal crisis which led them to the unwitcher in the first place.

The irony of fate (or the requirements of the ideology of enlightenment) have it that national newspapers see the true nature of the peasantry revealed in these eccentric characters and their clients, and seize upon a few anecdotes to turn them into emblems of peasant credulity and anachronism. Spells! – and in this ridiculous form! – you have to be a peasant to believe in them.[6]

So the journalist of *Constellation* introduces his report on the Saint-Fraimbault scandal with the following remarks: 'I've discovered the existence of witchcraft at a distance of no more than three hours from Paris. In the Bocage of Normandy, people still believe in spells, and they perform magic rituals. Electric pylons stand over the grass-land, tractors are driven along the tarred sunken lanes ... but medieval superstitions still prevail. Some farmers throw salt in the corners of their fields to protect their crops. They drive their cattle into the stables backwards to unbewitch them. In the farm fireplaces, ox hearts are kept boiling to reveal the identity of evil spell casters.' Note the use of the present, a tense which has no implied ending, to describe a timeless peasant; and rather than the restrictive 'some' (of farmers) the use of 'they', which always refers to the general category *homo*, understood here as *paganus*. 'All this takes place today, in 1965, at the confines of Normandy, Maine and Brittany. And yet the Bocage is a pleasant region ...'[7] It is indeed a pleasant region, but it is also a territory where one is likely to find the rejects of Western rationalism.

---

[6] Now is the moment to question the press's claim to have informed the public about witchcraft: for, according to a survey I made of three Western *départements* (Manche, Orne, Mayenne), about one unwitcher out of sixty, and one witchcraft story out of ten thousand are made known to the public. This does not mean that the others make no stir or are entirely discreet. But if one were to do no more than glance at these cases, the futility of the dogma according to which witchcraft is a matter for charlatans and dupes only would become immediately clear. So the press does not talk about witchcraft unless it can present a clear case of an eccentric unwitcher.   [7] Op. cit. p. 32, fn. 3.

Roger-Pol Droit of the newspaper *Le Monde* is very willing to develop this ideo-logic to its conclusion. In a review of a book on witchcraft in the Berry, he says that its authors 'make us penetrate a world, three hundred kilometers from Paris [this seems to represent the exact distance from Enlightenment to Darkness], in which magic thought still plays a leading social role [...] through their account, we are shown a portrait of a closed society [...]. To put it plainly: a primitive society, in spite of the car parked by the gate and the television in the living room.'[8] By all means let us put it plainly: but from which vantage-point and at the outposts of what progress?

This primitive, supernatural, anachronistic district where peasants of the Bocage park alongside urban ideologists is also – and mainly – the 'district of credulity'. The inhabitants of this region, haunted by 'marauding werewolves', are seen as simpletons or naïve children whose 'credulity can be quite risklessly exploited'. And the newspaper *France-Soir* amuses its public by describing the 'spectacular theatricals' of the '*Blonde Lady*', that inventive charlatan, that cunning city-dweller who knows how to fool peasants. For example, when he describes the trick with the hundred-franc note in the keyhole (childish!), the journalist ironically concludes: 'No need to be a great scholar to see the hoax'.[9] The urban reader is thus reassured that, even if he is not a great scholar, the gap between an ordinary man and a peasant, is infinite.

Held up in this way to public scorn and derision, the 'credulous' peasantry of the Bocage is bound to refuse to recognize itself in the distorting mirror presented to it, and to deflect the image in some other direction. For

[8] Roger-Pol Droit: 'Bewitched France' in *Le Monde*, 12 August 1973. On the anachronism of peasants, cf., for instance, Maurice Denuzière, 'The Witches of Perche Answer the Telephone', in *Le Monde*, 15 October 1969: 'At a time when man calmly walks on the moon, and the fairy tales of village evenings have been replaced by television programmes, one is bound to be surprised at the small but thriving trades of mystery.' Charles Blanchard, 'The accused, a pyromaniac who hoped to ward off spells, seems to have got his centuries mixed up', in *France-Soir*, 30 April 1974. The writer does not propose prison or even the asylum, but 'reinsertion into the twentieth century' for people like Blanchard (the accused); in other words, these are anti-mutants who have come straight out of the Middle Ages. Annette Kahn, 'Witchcraft at the Assizes' in *L'Aurore*, 29 April 1974, gives her impressions of the same trial: 'It's like a dream. But while some men walk on the moon [again], others see flying saucers. '[... Blanchard] looks modern enough, as if he lived in his own time. He worked in a factory, went into town, and had a lot of friends at work, all of which should have given him a sense of reality.'
   The peasant's anachronism is equivalent to an a-chronism, a point discussed in more detail later. A good example of this is in the *Journal du Dimanche*, 7 March 1976: 'A timeless crime' (the murder of a witch by two of the victims, young farmers from the Mayenne): 'But after all, we are in 1976' concludes the author rubbing his eyes, so implying that while 'we' are there, one wonders where 'they' are.
[9] 'To ward off evil spirits, the "*Blonde Lady*" would spend the night with bewitched husbands', in *France-Soir*, 5 December 1964: cf. also: 'I found the "Blonde Lady", accused by a Normandy village of witchcraft', in *Le Parisien Libéré*, 6 December 1964.

example, by pointing to the *few* mad or stupid people who are really credulous: it is not the peasant who is credulous, but the fool or the madman, in other words those outside social categories.

It is worth mentioning here the role of the local newspapers: they continually protest against the quiet cynicism with which the national newspapers manipulate the significance of local events in order to support their prejudices and provoke the laughter of Parisians, at the expense of 'naïve' peasants. The local newspapers more or less take the same attitude as anyone who says he is not *'caught'* – that is, the same attitude as most of their readers. (Those who are engaged in a witchcraft crisis cannot expect any public kind of discourse ever to support them.) For if the local news-papers talk of witchcraft, it is only resoundingly or scornfully to denounce a few scandalous unwitchers and their clients, who are then separated from the local community by a barrier of shame and derision. (Ordinary unwitchers and their clients are, of course, never mentioned.) In each case, a few individuals are sacrificed and branded as idiots or madmen so as to preserve the reputation of everyone else, and to establish the widest possible gap between them.[10]

This is why the *'Blonde Lady'*, for example, that 'evil witch', 'whore', 'pathetic character [...] of whom it is better to see the back view than the front' serves a useful purpose: she gives us an opportunity to laugh at her among ourselves, 'hearty folk of the Mayenne' and at her 'naïve victims' who after all are only individuals.[11] *Le Publicateur Libre*, a 'Christian and Gaullist' weekly from Domfort, says, for example, in its inimitable style: 'We believe that the *Négriesse*[12] got her ideas from the story of the notorious Rasputin who preached impurity to the Tzarina so that she would have sins to be forgiven. We have been informed that in a neighbouring family [just an isolated case, then], she managed to convince the father that in order to be unbewitched, he must stand naked with his arms crossed while those around him sprinkled salt and holy water.' [Note: (1) the rituals invented

---

[10] Cf. the role of the diocesan exorcist mentioned above (pp. 6–8) for whom the idea of a *sociological* survey into spells was incomprehensible: spells only concern *individuals*.

[11] These quotations are taken from a file I made of articles from the local press concerning the *'Blonde Lady'*: 'Incredible but True! An Evil Witch' in *Le Publicateur Libre*, 8 August 1963; 'Look Out! The Witch has turned up again!' id., 6 December 1964; 'In the Gorron region, there are no witches or bewitched, but only a swindler and a few dupes', in *Ouest-France*, Mayenne ed., 10 December 1964; 'Witchcraft in Saint-Fraimbault', in *Le Réveil Normand*, 12 December 1964; 'The Witch of Saint-Fraimbault', in *Le Publicateur Libre*, 13 December 1964; 'Magic, spells and charms, in the Mayenne region', in *Le Courrier de la Mayenne*, 19 December 1964; lastly, an un-identified article in *Ouest-France* cut out for me by an informant: 'A Le Mans inhabitant who "operates" in the districts of Ernée and Gorron is accused of illegal veterinary practice, para-medical and veterinary activities and of being a "troublemaker"'.

[12] A combination of *négresse* (negress) and Négrier – the real name, ironically, of the *'Blonde Lady'*. Her enemies nicknamed her 'Négrièsse' or 'Négrière'. This continual oscillation between black and white is part of the myth about this elusive woman who is always turning up somewhere else, and in a new disguise.

by these eccentric unwitchers are made fun of, but not those which belong to local traditions; and (2) the unwitcher's client is ridiculed more for letting himself be caught up in a perverse relationship rather than because he thought himself bewitched.] 'In another commune, it is a couple [another isolated case] who, also naked, had to dance on the kitchen floor just like the most backward peoples of Africa.' [Once again, an invented ritual, which produces the same feeling of bizarreness and the same defensive laughter as the sight of savages, who, as we know, are just thoughtless children easily put back on the right road.] 'What a fantastic kick in the whatsit is needed to bring peace back into these minds and hearts!' the writer concludes paternally.[13]

It is a firm principle in Bocage society that at least one credulous person other than oneself must be pointed out, for the simple reason that since the 'classical age' it has joined the national culture.[14] To call oneself a French citizen today, descended from the tradition of the Enlightenment, is to show that one is capable of repelling the irrational. When they are required to do so – as for example when the national newspapers make a fuss about the practices of an eccentric unwitcher – the inhabitants of the Bocage loudly sacrifice those who have provoked the scandal in the sacred cause of national unity. (We are far from the stereotype of the *chouans*,* dissident peasants, who are supposed to have accepted only the authority of local tradition, and who rebelled persistently against the power and values of the nation.) By deflecting the discourse which criticizes them – though without changing a comma – the peasants point to the unwitchers as charlatans, and their patients as credulous brutes.

I shall never know whether the clients of those scandalous magicians were anything but fools or madmen: for no one in the Bocage would have tolerated my upsetting this dogma about credulity, or stirring up these half-forgotten scandals and asking questions about what must never be questioned. Even the persons concerned, those who were obliged to accept the position of idiots, knew that they stood no chance of escaping once they

---

[13] Despite this calm self-assurance, the mystery of magic force does provoke some disquiet. For instance, in the confusion over the '*Blonde Lady*' (*Ouest-France*, 10 December 1964): 'To say that people fear the "witch" is an exaggeration, but some people seem to dread the so-called power she claims to possess.' If one ignores the quotation marks and qualifications ('seem', 'so-called', 'claims'), the first part of the sentence looks like a simple denial (and for all that, the witch *is* feared); the second part acknowledges what the first part denies (some people dread the power she possesses); a general confusion arises from the fact that since the undefined subjects ('people', 'some people') do not properly fill their role of referring to someone else (the peasant), the person who is speaking (the journalist) is obliged to cram his text with quotation marks, qualifications and denials. Other examples of the same type can be found in *Le Publicateur Libre*, 6 December 1964, and *Le Courrier de la Mayenne*, 19 December 1964.   [14] Cf. Foucault, 1961.

* *chouans*: band of peasants who rose in revolt in the West of France in 1793 and joined the Vendéen royalists.

had been talked about. As for myself, I have learned from experience that whatever I do or wish to convey, the newspapers will always distort my statements on this topic in such a way that they end up sounding like an approved version of the official discourse on spells. Unless, of course, I too am written off as a fool.[15]

[15] It would be boring to set out to correct the fanciful statements made by journalists about me. Starting from an initial mythical idea (Gérard Bonnot, 'The Witch of the C.N.R.S.', in *L'Express*, no. 1206, 19–25 August 1974) they found their logical conclusion in the local press, which little by little turned me into an idiot, or an academic with weak nerves who one day toppled into a nightmare (*Ouest-France*, Mayenne ed., 4, 5 and 6 September 1964; 4 March 1976).

5

TEMPTED BY THE IMPOSSIBLE

My earlier statements will seem less dogmatic if I illustrate them with a concrete example, which will bring out the play of forces involved in forcing an individual into the position of credulous person and keeping him in it whatever he may say. We shall also see how these same forces block any ethnographic investigation as soon as it shows any sign of disturbing the *status quo*.

Before beginning this account, however, I should like to make two points which will be valid for all the subsequent examples analysed in this book.

1. In the description of this first case, the reader may be surprised to find that it provides much more information than my purpose actually required. But I have made up my mind never to be afraid of exploring the full complexity of any real situation I may come across; this complexity must in any case go beyond the simple requirement of my specific concern.

2. On the other hand, it must be remembered that I myself and my story are always part of the peculiar group of individuals and events constituting a 'case': indeed if I use this term, it is more because I wish to be able to maintain a ground for my right to abstract than to suggest there is some difference in nature between the 'theorizing subject' and the 'theorized subject'.

Here, then, is the first account.

Shortly after I have settled in the Bocage, M. Fourmond, mayor of Chailland (a commune of the Manche), a practising Catholic and enlightened farmer falls seriously ill. Cancer of the skin is diagnosed, too late. The word goes around that his wife, although a responsible diocesan of the local Catholic Action, attributes his illness to a spell and has called in the '*man from Quelaines*', a farmer by day and unwitcher by night.[1] A scandal follows: some of the town's most distinguished members, calling for news of the sick man, met the '*man from Quelaines*' at the dying man's bedside. Officially,

---

[1] Any clandestine professional (unwitcher, healer) threatened with prosecution is referred to in terms intended to deflect the curious: 'the man from X', 'the woman', the 'mère' or the 'petite mère from Y', 'the priest from Z'. (X, Y and Z are placenames.)

witchcraft is barely good enough for small, backward peasants eaten up by poverty. That a modernist mayor could be involved in such things caused some indignation among his peers and the region's *'bourgeois'* élite.[2] After M. Fourmond's death, which occurs within a few weeks, public opinion turns against his widow.

'Facts' about her past and present credulity spread by word of mouth: *'mère Fourmond* believed in them before, in spells, and so did her mother'*.

Already, at the time of the scandal of the *'Blonde Lady'* in which a few Chailland families were involved, Mme Fourmond was supposed to have *'been so convinced'* that the mayor avoided the subject with her and asked everyone to say nothing on the matter: *'he didn't want anyone to mention it in front of her'*.[3]

But the mayor's wife was watching for her chance: *'Père Fourmond didn't believe in spells. His wife waited until he was on his deathbed and unable to move before bringing an unwitcher.†* *She told the whole village it was a spell.'* (Note that a bewitched person would never do anything so stupid: spells, by definition, are strictly private matters.) *'A spell, a spell! It was cancer, that's what it was!'* conclude the positivist minds.

Now that her husband is dead, Mme Fourmond is said to hold mysterious meetings with the *'man from Quelaines'* and her children: *'Yet the Fourmond girl is a nurse and married to a doctor'* [she is in fact married to a physiotherapist; but the point is to stress as much as possible how *true* positivist science is flouted in this story]. *'The Fourmond girl believes in it even more than her mother. They hold meetings all night, with their relatives: they say prayers, perhaps even masses. And the man from Quelaines is always there. He wanted Père Fourmond to be locked up in a room with no light. That surely wouldn't cure his cancer!'*

Although in principle Mme Fourmond's virtue is under no suspicion, people wonder what a widow can be up to, locked in all night with a

---

[2] 'Bourgeois' (once called the 'bourgadins' or 'bourgadiers') are the inhabitants of 'bourgs' (villages); as opposed to 'villageois' who live in hamlets and farms; if one wished to define precisely the difference in wealth or power, it is a matter of the word 'big' as set against 'small'. Among the 'bourgeois' who felt superior to Mme Fourmond on the grounds of their up-to-dateness, we can cite Julienne Angot, who hated local healers, but praised her daughter-in-law for taking an asthmatic child to Mességué: Mme Angot heard about this 'scientific' healer on the television. [Mességué: a French doctor who has written several popular books on the use of plants in medicine. The products he recommends are marketed under his name. Tr.]

* *mère Fourmond*: *'la mère'* X, *'le père'* Y are used throughout by the peasants to name the people around them. Since this form can be considered as part of the name, I have kept *mère* X and *père* Y in the translation.

[3] My interlocutors have a more or less traditional dialect, according to their level of education (and whether or not they were boarders in a religious school, where dialect is banned). I have reproduced it as such in the French edition; sometimes the topic (spells, for example) imposes traditional forms of speech – when the speaker considers himself as the subject of the discourse.

† here *désorcelaou* in the original text, a local variation of *désorcelleur*.

widower (the *unwitcher*). Of course one of the neighbours is ready to declare that they are having an affair and even that they are going to be married. Anyway, it is a case of '*unwitching to go to bed*': since there is a scandal, sex is bound to be involved.

By the time this scandal reaches my ethnographer's ears, more than a month after it has begun to furnish local gossip I have already decided not to ask questions about witchcraft scandals while they are still raging, so as to avoid seeming to play the part – a locally well-identified one – of Parisian journalist. But any possible curiosity on my part is discouraged in advance: the bewitched mayoress is described as bigoted – Mme Fourmond is supposed to have closed the door on her daughter, the nurse, who was no longer sufficiently convinced. She is now out of reach and is said to refuse visitors, including the parish priest who '*cannot get those ideas out of her head*' – in fact, she altogether refuses to talk – except with the '*man from Quelaines*'. As for the unwitcher, there is nothing more to learn about him that I do not already know, since '*he works in the style of the Blonde Lady*', '*it's the same gang*'; unless it's the gang of the '*Magus of Aron*', of whom the '*man from Quelaines*' is said to be a disciple. (In point of fact, it matters little which: in both cases, the speaker puts him in the category of eccentric unwitchers.) Lastly, I am told that the local police are looking into the matter, that the unwitcher will soon be charged with illegal medical practice, and that a *conseiller général** is after him because he wants to make an example of his case and clear the district's reputation. As for myself, I feel little inclined to go and force the confidence of a hard-pressed man, and I restrain myself from going to see him.

Fifteen months later, I have a visit from a young girl of twenty, Marie Fourmond. A geography student at the neighbouring university, she has so far been left out of all the gossip about the family's credulity because she is not significantly linked with anything which could enrich the gossip: medicine, theology, or any *real* science. She comes to ask me a question which has been tormenting her for a long time and which the teachers and priests have avoided answering: '*Can the evil be transmitted?*'

If Marie Fourmond comes to me with her question, it is because she feels she had at last found someone who will give her support. She has read an article I had just published on Michelet's *La Sorcière* and she says that it made her think: '*There's someone with whom one can talk about these things.*' Her statement causes me some embarrassment since I know perfectly well that the article was only a well-timed pretext to escape, on the spot, from the demands of my own investigation:[4] a few months before, instead of accepting a diagnosis of bewitchment made by a rather disquieting unwitcher, and seeing its obvious consequences (that is, beginning a magic cure), I had

---

* *conseiller général*: more or less equivalent to 'county councillor' in Britain.
[4] Jeanne Favret: 'Sorcières et Lumières', in *Critique*, No. 287, April 1971.

retired to the warmth of my village, avoiding all allusions to spells and delaying my decision by re-reading Michelet's text instead of facing the reality of the 'witch'. By which we see that a question left open always ends by conjuring up the person to whom it is addressed, even though by a misunderstanding.

Marie Fourmond and I thus set out to answer her question: *'Can the evil be transmitted?'* by going over the circumstances which led to it, to her father's death.

'What I cannot understand' says Marie, *'is that one can pass the evil on to someone, that one can transform bad feelings into illness.'*

'What do you mean, are you talking of your father's death?'

'Yes, some people wanted him to die. They succeeded.'

'How did you find out they wished him to die?'

'The man from Quelaines said so. We talked about it one evening at the farm, him, my mother and I.'

So, they believe in it, concludes the ethnographer, hastily. But then, why on earth does Marie come and tell me about it, so confirming the gossip of the people of Chailland and running the risk of starting up the scandal again, now that emotions have died down? Who does she think she is talking to, and what does she want me to hear, in giving me the very version of her father's death which caused its rejection by the town, on the pretext that it made them all the prey of witches? For it cannot be denied that Marie's account, in the beginning, is exactly identical to that of a bewitched. Apart from the statement that *'some people'* wanted her father's death, there are other elements in her account of an initiate's usual prologue: (1) the inaugural denial, (2) a statement of the failure of positivist knowledge, (3) the solemn annunciation to the bewitched of her state.

1. *'It's odd'*, begins Marie: *'My father and mother had never known any witches; really, that sort of people had never entered our lives.'* She adds: *'We had never heard about them.'*

The first of these two statements is probably true; the Fourmonds had never before needed to have anything explained to them by spells. The second statement *'we had never heard about them'* – needs to be amplified to be quite true: Marie Fourmond had certainly heard of spells before her father's death, but never as something which could account for her own story. Witches and evil spells had belonged to the improbable world of fiction – they had no identifiable existence except in old peoples' stories – or in that distant world of the poor, the backward or the insane: in other words, they belonged to a long list of things she was not a part of.

We can see therefore that what is presented as a denial – the statement that one had never heard about spells – is primarily an attempt to hang on to the possibility of communicating with those who are not *'caught'*. This is why any account by a bewitched begins with an obligatory reference to an inaugural phase in which the speaker, wishing to convey how he was '*caught*', places himself in the same external position in relation to witchcraft as his sceptical hearer. In order to prevent his discourse from being discounted on the assumption that it is virtually a delirium, he begins by taking his distance from belief; by declaring that he himself would never have thought of a spell; by emphasizing that this diagnosis was given by someone else, and that it took him totally by surprise, he who had so far been incredulous, innocent, non-initiated – just like you and me.

'*Of course*' Marie conceded '*there were those people from the village, the Garniers* [a bewitched couple: the husband had several times been admitted to the psychiatric hospital with religious mania]. *Daddy told us something about it: a blonde lady would go to their house . . . that's all. But we* [the children, then at boarding school in the neighbouring town] *and especially me, we hadn't taken much notice. I said: 'So, these people aren't quite right in the head. That's all.'* In other words: those people are mad; so their witchcraft is no concern of mine.

This was at the time of the scandal of the '*Blonde Lady*'. The '*bourgeois*' of Chailland had gone about ostracizing her clients, three or four families. Only Mme Fourmond tried to break their isolation, on humanitarian grounds, by going to see them and even greeting them at the church door. Now –five years later – village opinion retrospectively interprets Mme Fourmond's charitable gesture of that time as evidence of her earlier credulity: she had approached the ostracized because '*she already believed in spells*'.

2. The whole of Marie's account, during our conversations, is concerned with what I earlier called the moment of annunciation:[5] certain bewitched, cured of their own ills, come and announce to other unfortunate people, who are supposed never to have thought or heard of spells – that they, in their turn, are caught in spells.

If this moment is to occur, the failure of positivist knowledge must first be quite unambiguously established. In the present case, for instance, the doctor had cut out a mole from the patient without realizing that he was dealing with cancerous cells. It was Madeleine, the nurse daughter, who interpreted the symptoms and corrected his mistake. Upon which the patient underwent an operation which was given a favourable prognosis: '*the doctors all thought they would cure him: for them it was a successful case*', says Marie. But two days after he came out of the hospital, père Fourmond was seized by violent pains '*it was horrible to see him suffering like that. Horrible, horrible!*' A mistaken diagnosis, plus a mistaken prognosis.

3. At this point in the story, uncle and aunt Lenain, from Quelaines, on a visit to their relative, made the following annunciation, which Marie reports to me: '*They saw how ill my father was . . . so then they said to mummy: but it's not natural! Look here, Suzanne, we can't leave poor Roger in that state. We've got to do something: it's not natural!*' Even for someone who says she had never

[5] Cf. p. 8, fn. 6.

heard about it, the statement '*it's not natural*' unquestionably means that witchcraft is involved.

If this were a typical story of witchcraft (as the people of Chailland claim it is), this prologue would lead to the sequences usually constituting this kind of account, namely:

1. The search for the witch's identity.

2. Instructions on how to do him or her harm and protect oneself from his or her evil spells.

3. The beginning of a magic ritual and the adoption of characteristic ways of behaviour.

4. The interpretation of the effects produced, i.e. for the witch, his or her downfall (by death, illness, or failure) and for the bewitched, a progressive return to normality.

5. Finally, the continuation of an indefinite transference situation between the unwitcher and his or her client.

Now, while the first phase – a search for the witch's identity – is present in Marie Fourmond's account, all the other phases are absent. And even that phase is difficult to understand, since it had no sequel.

At the beginning of my investigation, I heard a lot of witch stories which suddenly broke off. But they were not, as in this case, told by an informant, anxious to confide her personal experience to me.

Whenever I was told stories about witches, it was (1) in a tone of denial: '*I don't believe in all that rot*' and (2) by someone who was not personally involved: the stories were always about someone else's misfortunes. And they always ended abruptly with the episode of naming the witch: '*And it was père So and So who was doing it!*' (who was bewitching). If I tried to find out what happened later, all I got were disobliging comments on the irrelevancy of my questions. For a long time I had this illusion that the peasants of the Bocage were extremely sophisticated beings and, like the heroes of Agatha Christie, they underwent mortal peril simply in order to enjoy the purely intellectual satisfaction of having guessed the guilty person's identity.

Marie Fourmond's account thus raises the following problem, though it is not the only one: why does it stop short as soon as the witches are named, like the account of an informant who wishes to discredit spells, since Marie seems to be personally engaged in this search for the truth about her father's death?

For the time being, we must just note these questions. After my first talk with Marie, I wondered whether one could find out how the nurse daughter fits into the story: for after all she represents in her own way the positivist knowledge which, thanks to her, avoids total defeat. If it is true that (1) on the one hand, the people of Chailland had never stopped mentioning the nurse daughter when criticizing Mme Fourmond (either to prove to what an extent her credulity is contagious, since it even infects a nurse; or to show that superstition can lead an exemplary Christian to inhuman acts, since apparently mère Fourmond preferred to drive her daughter out of the house rather than moderate her own convictions) and (2) on the other hand, uncle and aunt Lenain were essentially afraid of the nurse's reaction when it came to the annunciation: '*Aunt didn't dare talk to her about it*', says Marie, *because she thought: Madeleine is going to think I've gone mad.*' For any nurse worthy of the calling must think one is crazy to believe in it.[6]

Madeleine, who has given up hope of a cure for her father, says that '*cancer is cancer*', that no one can survive from it and that her only aim is to relieve the dying man's pain. Uncle Lenain, the annunciator, who does not seem to have communicated his diagnosis of witchcraft to the nurse, changes his tone and says to Mme Fourmond: '*You should have him touched.*'

'*To touch*' or '*to encircle the ill*' is a traditional method of magic healing which theoretically bears no relation to witchcraft.

One '*touches*' mainly skin or stomach affections: scurf, warts, burns, shingles – called the '*ceinture de feu*' [fire-belt] – children's impetigo or '*rifle*', the swelling of the belly or '*carreau*' – either to get rid of the symptom (for scurf and warts, for example) or to remove the pain (to '*put out the fire*' of burns).

To do this a ritual is carried out which generally includes an incantation. Thus, to '*encircle the fire*' (remove the pain of burns), Louis Marchand practises the following ritual: three times with the tip of his forefinger, he outlines the burn which he then signs with a cross; at the same time he mentally says, or he mumbles inaudibly, the following formula: '*Fire, I take you from this heat, just as Judas took himself away from the Olive Garden after betraying Jesus Christ.*'

The ritual and the formula both constitute a '*secret*' transmitted through traditional channels: either from one relative to another (sometimes the sex alternates with each generation), or to a passing stranger in gratitude for some service rendered (most often to a *trimard* [tramp], a quasimythological being who wanders about the roadways, poor in cash but rich in secrets).

To possess a '*secret*' is a common advantage which does not give its owner the right to set himself up as a professional healer (one must also possess a '*gift*'). Usually the '*toucheur*' is a simple peasant who inherited one and only one '*secret*' (for example he can cure scurf, but not warts or '*fire*') and who uses it to help others, but not as any particular source of prestige or profit.

Considered as more or less independent of the particular '*gift*' of this or that '*toucheur*', the magic effect of these cures is supposed to be due exclusively to the hermetic nature of their transmission: the man who tells the

---

[6] Similarly, in 1964–5 at Saint-Fraimbault (cf. bibliography on the 'Blonde Lady') local scandal thrived on the story of a schoolmistress who considered herself bewitched: she was betraying the cause; she should have supported one of the two official versions on spells, that of the School or the Church.

'*secret*' (because, for example, he feels he is going to die and the time has come to pass it on) loses his '*force*': however hard he tries to perform the ritual gestures and say the incantation, '*it no longer works*'.[7]

'*To touch*' is thus simply to use a healing secret to alleviate the other's ill; this secondary, disinterested and sometimes beneficial occupation is so free of suspicion that priests often give it the dignity of a charisma.[8] From this description, however, it will be clear that '*to touch*' and '*to unwitch*' imply a related set of terms, amounting to magic '*force*'. So it will hardly seem surprising that uncle Lenain, fearing an outright rejection of his diagnosis of witchcraft, immediately turned to a more harmless version of magic healing, leaving it to the '*toucheur*' to announce to the Fourmonds that he was also an unwitcher.

Constant Lenain in fact goes on to suggest to the patient himself that he get a '*toucheur*', but this time without making any mention of spells. Fourmond, in great pain, approves with a nod. If this enlightened Christian agrees to take such a step, it is because his relative has helped him to it and has kept the situation ambiguous by being careful not to tell him that the '*toucheur*', as can be seen in the diagram below, is none other than Jean Lenain, the annunciator's own brother – and by implying that he is a priest: '*So, you see, Mummy, a believer, thought: Ah well! If it's a priest!*' explains Marie.

This is why when the '*toucheur*' was brought to the patient's bedside, Fourmond was astounded when he recognized his relative: '*So it's you!*' said père Fourmond – '*But he isn't a priest!*' Protested his wife – '*No, but the power he possesses comes from a priest*' explains the uncle. (Jean Lenain was initiated into magic by a priest, an enthusiast for 'magnetism'.) '*If you like, I can try and cure you*', said the '*toucheur*' to the sick man.

Père Fourmond knew that his relative had been acting as unwitcher for the previous three years : someone in Chailland had told him that Jean Lenain '*was a member of the Magus' gang*'; he had questioned his brother-in-law from Quelaines, who had told him that Jean did unwitch people but that he had nothing to do with the '*billy-goat of Aron*'. On the other hand, Mme Fourmond and her daughters seem to have been totally ignorant of the activities of the '*man from Quelaines*' until he came to look after the '*père*'. For them he was a decent man, '*a good, old-fashioned peasant*', a distant relative whom they sometimes meet on family occasions.

---

[7] '*The secret must be passed on before dying. Once you've passed it on, you can't any longer* [touch].'

[8] For example, the priest of Mézangers, among many others: 'Many people, even in Mézangers, have the gift of touching. Perhaps this in a way resembles the charisma of the primitive Church: some have the gift of tongues, others the gift of touching. It's possible, after all.' The idea of being gifted seems to be so acceptable that even a priest can allow himself to cite his parish as an example, a thing he would certainly not do in the case of the gift of unwitching. In what he says, the priest is trying to keep as close as possible to Catholic orthodoxy; but note that the last statement ('*it's possible, after all*') is an attempt to settle matters in terms of the ideology of the Enlightenment.

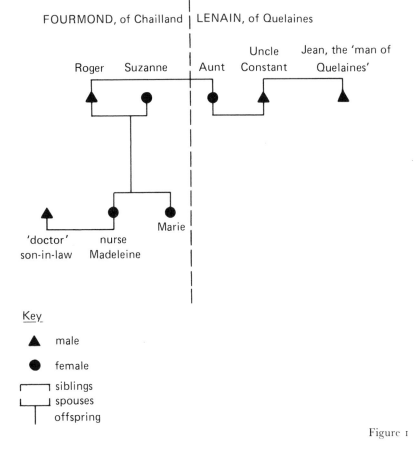

FOURMOND, of Chailland | LENAIN, of Quelaines

Figure I

Anyway, the '*man from Quelaines*' comes and works as a '*toucheur*' without the least ambiguity: he places his hands over the patient, says a few prayers and '*it works*', the pain recedes, Fourmond feels better. Note that for the second time in this story, official medicine had reached its limits, since the sedative prescribed by the doctor had no effect. Mme Fourmond, however, continues to call in the doctor, although she knows he has no chance of curing the patient, and she follows his prescriptions.

But to reduce the pain she also calls on the '*man from Quelaines*' whom she describes as a '*supplement*' to the doctor – a supplement, which, as one can imagine, becomes more and more indispensable each day as the sickness gets worse, and which she is determined to keep for her husband's sake

despite the village's disapproval. *'We were doing all we possibly could'*, says Marie. *'It's the pain we wanted to stop, by any means. And it went on like that: each time my father was unwell, we called the man from Quelaines. Towards the end, whenever he was late in coming my father would ask: "but when is he going to arrive?".*
Then the man from Quelaines would come and my father would feel better. Honestly, we could feel him reviving; yes, he would revive each time.'

Note that during those few weeks, on the one hand the *'toucheur'* never asked or received payment, and on the other, he often came without being asked. For it seems that he did not consider himself as just an anaesthetist but at the very least as a healer. In any case, magic healing and unwitching had always been closely related in his own personal experience.

As is often the case, Jean Lenain became a magic healer after personally undergoing a series of biological misfortunes: he was twice a widower of wives who had the same first name – a striking repetition – and he claimed he had then had cancer.

On the death of his second wife (in a car accident), he met a magnetizer-priest who had played the role of annunciator: *'Listen'* the priest said to Jean Lenain, *'that accident is due to a spell'* and he solemnly warned him: *'Now, it's you who are going to be attacked'.* *'So'*, said Marie, *'he gave him the power'*: the priest entrusted the initiate with a book and taught him to heal himself. So, once he had pulled himself through, Jean Lenain became a therapist of others, under the prudent and traditionally acceptable name of the *'man from Quelaines'.*

The memory of this initial cancer – which could be described as initiatory – doubtless has a part in the present story. For if père Fourmond's illness had not involved a certain repetition of what Lenain bases his capacity to heal on, one could scarcely understand why he should work for nothing (for a *'toucheur'* usually receives a symbolic payment as a sign of acknowledgement of indebtedness), or why he should be so desperate to heal his relative.

To sum up: from the women's side of the Fourmond family, the story is so far without any ambiguity: the father is sick with an extremely painful illness: uncle Lenain, pointing to the fatal aspect of the illness and its rapid development makes a diagnosis of witchcraft which, it must be remembered, no one bothers to take up. The uncle then introduces his brother who *'touches'* – i.e. soothes – M. Fourmond's pain. As for the latter, he apparently does not make the least intellectual objection to being relieved in this manner. *'The man from Quelaines' theory'*, says Marie, *'was . . . what's . . . magnetism. For my father, that was something . . . after all, why not, scientific?'* The healer will attribute a good portion of his success to the patient's faith: *'He helps me a lot'*, he will say, *'he helps me a lot because he believes in me.'* Hence we understand that Fourmond believes in Jean's power to alleviate his pain by placing his hands over him.

It is in this rather banal context of belief in an innocent practice of magic anaesthesia that the great scene of accusation of witchcraft that I mentioned above takes place.[9]

So far in the story, the discourse of witchcraft and that of magic *'touching'* have co-existed without meeting. But one evening, Marie Fourmond provokes their collision by asking the *'man from Quelaines'* for some explanations.

'All right, Daddy is ill, you act and it works. So there must be something, a relationship between you and my father, or with other people. [This can be understood in the following manner: What then is transferred, and from whom, to my father? Where do both the ill from which he is suffering and the good you do him come from?]

'Look,' begins Lenain, *'some people are very bad ...'* Marie, annoyed, interrupts him:

'But that's nothing new!' [i.e. we know there are ordinary bad people everywhere].

'Those I am talking about possess a power to do evil, they make people suffer. They've been at your father since June and they are acting, acting all the time on him.'

'But how do they act?'

'That's something we don't understand too well' the magician modestly acknowledges.

'So', says Marie to me as she relates the accusation scene, *'that's when I began ...* [she implies: that's when she began to ask more precise questions: for she is the one who started to inquire into the origin of her father's illness].

'Is it anyone we know or whom my father knows very well?' she suggests.

'Yes, people who can even be great friends of yours.'

'I didn't really believe it, I didn't believe it yet', she says to me [it's not that one can say she believes more in it now. But her account, like any account of witchcraft, inevitably poses the problem of knowing how one can both not believe in it at all and totally believe in it]. *'... I didn't believe it yet, but I said to the man from Quelaines: do you know who it is?'*

'Yes, I know who it is. It's someone from Chailland.'

'If we ask you questions, will you tell us who it is?' asked Marie, who says to me: *'I was wrong to ask that question, I wish I had never known.'*

'Why is that?'

'Because I think it's stupid to know, I think it's utter rot. I'll let it pass, but I assure you ...' (in other words: I'm not going to give you these witches' names, because spells are stupidities; but I can't help thinking about it when I meet those whose names were mentioned that evening).

The ethnographer suggests a name, just in case: that of Pottier, a distant cousin of Suzanne Fourmond, originally from Villepail like her, and now living in a farm at Chailland; Pottier is the main instigator of the intrigue

[9] Cf. p. 42.

against the Fourmonds and also its most obvious beneficiary, since he became the mayor of Chailland on the death of his relative.

'*Yes*', says Marie, '*of course Pottier was on it,*' that is, the list of witches. '*But there were several others. I can assure you that they were more than can be counted on the fingers of one hand: there was the mayor* [i.e. Pottier], *our own neighbours, and other people from the village.*'

Marie's curiosity is greatly aroused by the puzzle of this demonstration of divinatory skill: how can a human being possibly know what he has no knowledge of? '*The man from Quelaines didn't even know them* [the people on the list of witches], *he had never seen them before: how did he know it was them* [the witches]? *That's what surprised me.*' For in the case of Pottier, the main suspect, she had reason to know that the magician had never met him before this accusation scene, since Mme Fourmond introduced them to each other shortly afterwards.

A few comments on the way in which this list of witches was established will better enable us to see the peculiarities of the Fourmond case:

1. Usually, when the imputation scene takes place, on the one hand the patient is already convinced he is bewitched (he has accepted the revelation made by the annunciator); and on the other hand, quite sure of the identity of his witch or witches, for he has prepared a list of names in answer to the unwitcher who will inevitably ask him whether '*he suspects anyone*'. Later we shall see[10] that this list is never the right one. Indeed, the patient always expresses his resentment against someone with whom he is so violently in conflict that the unwitcher cannot accomplish any real cure without operating some kind of displacement – such direct naming could only lead to a fight or some other kind of clash between the parties.

The Fourmond ladies, however, have so far not accepted the first annunciation made by Constant Lenain; the '*man from Quelaines*' then makes a second annunciation, thinking himself authorized to do so by Marie's questions. But neither she nor her mother explicitly admit that they accept it; they are simply impressed by the self-confidence with which Jean Lenain claims he knows who their witches are without knowing them; and with his help, they try to guess their identity. It is quite characteristic that the Fourmond ladies are unable to give any names themselves, since they have no open conflict with anyone, and are quite unprepared to superimpose the mythical information they have about witches (taken from old stories, for example) on the features of actual people in Chailland. And so the unwitcher is obliged to put them on the right track by giving them topographical indications which will gradually enable them to bring out names which he himself does not know and which they are otherwise unable to name. He tells them, for instance: '*The person who is doing it to you lives on the road to Glières*', that is, on the way to their farm. So we can see that the real

[10] In the forthcoming volume.

purpose of a divination scene is not that the magician should guess who the witch is, but that the patient should take on the task of guessing himself, and name him.[11]

2. When they tell their story later, the bewitched are usually incapable of describing this process of imputation, which is usually forgotten. At least in this respect Marie Fourmond behaves like an ordinary bewitched: not only is she unable to tell me which divinatory method was used, but, when the question arises, her statements become typically vague:

'*I tried to remember, but then . . . No, I don't exactly remember how we got to know that so and so was doing it to us . . .*

'*I think the man from Quelaines used the road thing: the place, the village's situation, the road to Glières. . . At that point we said: Ah! It's not far away?'.*

'*As for the neighbours, the amount of time we took to identify them! Unbelievable! Lenain even said: But this is not possible! You women are so thick . . . It took us a long time. Then suddenly, it struck Mummy, she said: Ah! But that's . . . that's where the Hautbois live!'*

Note that Marie implicity admits she '*knows*' someone '*is doing it to them*', bewitching them: by helping them give the name of possible culprits, Lenain is also forcing them to admit that his diagnosis of bewitchment is relevant. The process of imputation has been forgotten, but its result – the list of names remains indelibly engraved in their memories, and with it the momentary conviction of being bewitched.

Remember that this story interests us because although it breaks off after the naming of the witches, it provokes the '*bourgeois*' scandal of Chailland which literally fixes Suzanne Fourmond in the role of bewitched, although she gives every sign of not wanting to occupy it.

What she and her daughter told me of the circumstances of père Fourmond's death throws some light on their change of attitude:

1. The most solid ground for their faith in the healer has so far been based on the effectiveness of his magic '*touch*': thanks to him, the dying man feels better. (They seemed to have listened to the naming of their witches passively, at least without integrating it into their plans for looking after the father.)

2. The dying man feels so much better that for a moment they seem to have been tempted by the impossible: they hoped or believed that Jean Lenain – who claims he cured himself of cancer a few years earlier – would, in spite of everything, succeed in saving père Fourmond.

Octave Mannoni has shown us how to perceive a typical statement of the type: 'I know . . . but still . . .', said by someone who cannot renounce an impossible desire; the 'but still . . .' cancels the acknowledgement

---

[11] The method which depends on giving topographical clues to the patient is inevitably quoted in the newspapers as the absolute proof of peasant credulity; but in my experience it is never used by itself, unless as a last resort, when the patient is quite unable to provide any name.

of the impossible, immediately after this has been admitted by the 'I know . . .'[12]

I know that *'cancer is cancer'*, is the gist of what Marie Fourmond told herself – in other words one inevitably dies of it – but still, suppose the *'toucheur'* could save my father. . .

'We thought he was going to be saved', she says: *'That's what we thought. At one point, I was so caught that . . . Yes, I know we were caught.'* A *'bourgeois'* of Chailland would inevitably see in these words the confirmation that the Fourmonds considered themselves bewitched; and yet, knowing the context, we will simply suggest that Marie and her mother were indeed *'caught'*, but only by the temptation of the impossible or by the conviction that the patient would survive.

3. What probably helped convince them – over and above the soothing power of the healer's *'touch'* – was his extraordinary personal involvement in this cure:

'While my father was in the hospital', says Marie, *'the man from Quelaines was already working on it. He was already working on my father'* [with magic means and at a distance].

'Had your uncle asked him to?'

'No, he worked just like that, because he knew my father. He said to my uncle and aunt: listen, you absolutely must tell Roger to call for me. He must call for me because what's happening to him just isn't normal' [a fatal illness, and one that appeared so suddenly].

That an initiative by the unwitcher should thus provoke his patient's call for him is a totally unusual situation; but perhaps because père Fourmond's illness reminded him of his initiatory cancer, Lenain seems to have been possessed, over those few weeks, with a tremendous zeal and frenzy to succeed; he communicated his own faith and worked ceaselessly to unwitch his patient, although officially he was there only to *'touch'*: *'And on the last night'*, Marie remembers, *'we called the doctor; and without calling Lenain, you see . . .'* [unlike the doctor, the unwitcher is always on the spot when he is needed: his acumen leads him to the right place at the right time]. *'He was at the end of the road without our having to call for him. He worked, without us calling for him, with . . . Mummy had given him a photo, I think, of both of them.'* (One can *'touch'* someone at a distance with the help of a photograph; but one can also unwitch him.)

4. In spite of all this, père Fourmond dies. The women are immensely disappointed, and they dismiss the healer: *'We talked to the man from Quelaines once more, after* [the father's death]; *but it was finished. Something had snapped. My mother told him she had had enough. I would not have allowed Monsieur Lenain to set foot inside the house again, for getting us to believe it. . .'* [that he could cure my father]. He never returned to the Fourmond house.

Lenain justifies his failure by claiming they called him in too late – two

[12] Octave Mannoni (1969), Ch. 1: 'Je sais bien. . . mais quand même.'

months after he had said it was necessary – and that in the end, the Fourmonds did not believe in spells: *'He said it was difficult* [for him to work] *at home, because basically we didn't believe in it. We didn't believe in it enough. He would say to us: of course, you aren't taught about that at school. No fear of you being taught about that. It's never mentioned in your books. No fear of them talking about it. And yet for all your sciences, you believe in it.'* Not sufficiently, however, to enable him to maintain his position as unwitcher.

This is their attitude, then – all in all, a rather sceptical one – when the scandal in Chailland takes them by surprise. To start with, the Pottiers, who have so far simply been avoiding the Fourmonds, end their relationship with them after a violent argument with the mother: *'You should have seen it, what a fight!'*, says Marie, who was told the story of the encounter by her mother. Mme Pottier accuses her relative of betraying the cause of Enlightenment, and emphasizes her astonishment at seeing Mme Fourmond opt for the side of irrationality. *'What you Suzanne, you who have such faith! and Roger who was always so opposed to it all!* [to magic healing and spells]. *You dared call in a man like that!'* [a healer-unwitcher]. *'Of course'*, says Marie *'from that moment on, the word went round all over the village'*: it was whispered that Suzanne Fourmond thought herself bewitched, that she refused to see anyone except the *'man from Quelaines'*, and so on.[13]

Yet, in the course of this discussion with her cousins, Suzanne Fourmond certainly did not present herself as bewitched. For two obvious reasons: (1) She had already been quite unable to sustain this role in front of the unwitcher, except for a brief instant, when he had asked her to give a list of her witches. (2) Since Pottier was included in the list, Suzanne Fourmond should – as a person suffering under spells who also knows how to protect herself – have avoided any form of contact with him, and she should especially have refused to meet him in her own home. After her husband's funeral, she had taken up a hint dropped by Pottier that he meant to visit her soon, and had suggested straightaway that he should come to Glières, as she was very keen to make clear to him how she felt about his cool behaviour towards her throughout her husband's illness.

So, one can see that the very fact of calling a healer to a gentleman's bedside is enough in itself to cause a scandal – and local gossip immediately confused issues and gave the name 'witchcraft' to what it knew was actually only magic healing. There is a characteristic incident: it occurred at the time when Marie was telling me her story. A woman of Chailland saw me with her and whispered: *'But do you know she's the previous mayor's daughter?'* (She obviously thought me absent minded or naïve enough to think of Marie simply as a student who, like other students in the district, had come to talk to me about her work.) I said yes in a distant way, and she made no more of it. Later, she found out that I had lunched at Suzanne Fourmond's house (in the Bocage, it is a normal part of daily life that everyone perpetu-

[13] Cf. above, pp. 39–41.

ally has an eye on everyone else). She had then taken an opportunity to invite me in for a drink in order to question me. As soon as her husband had left for work, her child had gone to sleep, and a bottle was opened, she asked me, with feigned awkwardness:

'*I don't want to be tactless, but did Mme Fourmond talk to you about witchcraft?*'

'Oh, she doesn't talk about it.' [The truth is that Suzanne Fourmond thought there was nothing to say about witchcraft, since she did not really consider herself bewitched.] 'And you know, I only met her once.'

'*But did Marie tell you she still talked about it?.*'

I chose to answer in the same terms as the question, and said: 'She never talks about witchcraft any more.'

'*That all belongs to the past, she's completely recovered now*', added a relative of hers, present at our conversation. [Note that in the eyes of these enlightened ladies, Suzanne Fourmond's supposed belief in spells is described as a passing mental aberration.]

I then put forward the suggestion that in any case, witchcraft had never been involved in Mme Fourmond's mind. My hearer loudly agreed:

'*Of course, there was never any question of witchcraft!*' [she had nonetheless just called 'witchcraft' what the mayor's wife had been involved in two years before.] '*It was all a matter about healers. She wanted to cure her husband of cancer. Of cancer, can you imagine! She thought it could be done till the very end, and so did he* [the healer]. *They could see that père Fourmond was going from bad to worse, but they still hoped to save him. Up till the last day, whenever we asked Mme Fourmond for news, she would say:* "He's better, much better".'

What upset the town is thus primarily the Fourmonds' unacceptable attempt to avoid the death of a loved one condemned by science, in other words, reality. The faith of the patient and his family in the healer's powers shocked the people of Chailland in much the same way as someone might who would *still* hope to achieve a wish for immortality. It is true that the sight of this conjuration against death was in itself scandalous; for everyone wishes to escape, and why should Fourmond succeed? It was probably feared that the patient's faith might finally save him, in the same way as his healer insisted he had recently saved himself,[14] and so the fatality of death would be publicly questioned.

Supposing that the miracle had in spite of everything *still* taken place, then the village risked toppling into the dangerous universe of a desire-which-is-fulfilled. Which is perhaps why the Fourmonds were being accused beforehand, in the name of the principle of reality, as if none of their accusers had ever nursed the desire to overcome death. When reality brought things to a definite end – through the death of Roger Fourmond – the reaction was all the more violent: Who do these people think they are, that they can bring us so close to dangerous abysses? The local context provided a quick answer: they are traitors to the cause of reason, bewitched,

[14] I never heard anyone doubt that Lenain had cured himself of his cancer.

superstitious beings. But for this statement to be relevant, the Fourmonds should have agreed to act out the position assigned to them: for instance, they should, like all the bewitched, have shunned the village's opinion instead of provoking it; they should have broken off with their witches, instead of letting the witches take the initiative, and so on. Still, the silence to which they were nonetheless condemned gave rise to all kinds of unfavourable interpretations.

As nothing is ever simple where witchcraft is concerned, I have to mention a few additional knots in the already complicated skein of the story:

1. The position of the bewitched, which Suzanne Fourmond refused to occupy, was taken over by her sister-in-law, so giving the village the objective basis it needed to keep up the slander. Here is Marie again: apart from her aunt Lenain from Quelaines, she says, *'my father has another sister in Chailland. She found out that the man from Quelaines was coming to our house: she was so caught in all that* [the conviction that her brother was ill because of a spell?], *she believed in it so much, that she went to see him for herself. It was a vicious circle.'* Whatever the Fourmonds say or do, they cannot avoid the taint of witchcraft in their family and public opinion turning this against them.

'*And then my aunt is so stormy!* says Marie.

'You mean she went to see people?, [those she accused of being her witches].

'*No, not quite that. But she glowered at them: she no longer spoke to them, no longer...*'

'But that is part of what any unwitcher teaches,' puts in the ethnographer.

'*Well, he didn't tell us.*'

'What, didn't he teach you how to defend yourselves?'

'*Well you see, we didn't believe in it. So he didn't try to teach us any dodges. He told a lot more to my aunt. To us he would just say: pay no attention to other people. That's all. Since we paid no attention before, we just carried on.*'

2. Suzanne Fourmond no longer believes in Lenain, but still . . . '*Last year Mummy had headaches. My aunt Chailland said to her: You should go back* [and see Lenain]. *Mummy said: All right, we'll see what happens. Let's try.*' She didn't come back cured, and '*ever since then, she's been saying: that's enough of that, I've had all that. My aunt from Quelaines said to her: Look Suzanne, he* [Lenain] *can't do anything for you because you don't believe in it. You don't believe in it enough; he can't act on you, you take it all too lightly*'.

3. So, the Fourmonds no longer believe in Lenain. But the aunt from Chailland, who believes and who accepts his teachings, gives them some information about the evil power of Pottier, which does have a certain effect: '*Monsieur Lenain says that those people* [the witches] *do evil through the bad books they have.*' [Note that in these circumstances, Marie no longer says the 'man from Quelaines' but 'Monsieur Lenain'.] '*Something once happened in Pottier's family. We heard about it from someone, but who from? I wouldn't be surprised if it*

wasn't my aunt, from Chailland, she would say things like that.' In fact, Mme Fourmond forbade this aunt to speak of witchcraft; and then the Fourmonds do not like her much, because she tends to be indiscreet, wants to control the girls' private lives and to have her say about the meaning of the father's death. And yet she passed on a piece of information which the Fourmonds could not use for any general interpretation but which nevertheless seems to have left its mark: '*Apparently mère Pottier, on her deathbed, wanted to burn a book. Pottier himself took it out of the fire. Well, I don't know* [denial]. *So, he would be in possession of a bad book* [affirmation].'

I try to get her to be more precise in her terms, but I am unsuccessful: 'Have you ever heard it said that mère Pottier bewitched anyone?'

'*No, not at all, at least, I don't think so. She was rather a saintly person, I think. Rather.*'

'Perhaps it was only a devotional book?'

'*I don't know. How does one get such books?*'

'You inherit them; and you can buy them in specialized bookshops.'

'*Did you ever think of buying one?*' she asks.

'Yes, I certainly did. Was there anything between Pottier and your mother, before all this, some fight over an inheritance?'

'*No, nothing at all. The families probably didn't see each other at Villepail. My mother made his acquaintance again because she got married in Chailland and lived there. That's all.*'

But just before, Marie had expressed her astonishment at Pottier's relentless efforts to ruin their reputation after her father's death: '*The way he spoke to everyone against the family, it's unbelievable. It all came from him* [the intrigue against the Fourmonds], *we know that now. He tried to turn our best friends in Chailland against us, he went to their homes and invited them to dinner; people he had never seen much before. But our friends replied: Look here, Pottier, out you get*' [leave, we don't go in for that kind of thing].

4. I've often wondered what on earth got into Pottier. One thinks of course of ambition, as well as indignation at the idea that a man like Fourmond, who represented progress, should call in a healer. But that alone is not enough. One day, Marie told me something which, if it is true, throws an entirely different light on the whole matter. Of course it was out of the question that I should ever be able to check any of it: so I shall just give my hypothesis, and no more.

Lenain had been treating a neighbour of Pottier's, Duboust, for a long time. It is plausible that the unwitcher transformed the illness into a spell and the neighbour – Pottier – into a witch. Two points favour this hypothesis:

(*a*) Pottier speaks of Lenain as a '*witch*', which is exactly what someone who is accused by an unwitcher of being a witch normally does. (Note that *at the same time* the person always insists he does not believe in spells *and* that unwitchers are witches.) So, when Pottier came to talk with Suzanne

Fourmond, he said: '*If you call for a witch, that's enough for us*', you are guilty on the sole ground that Lenain crosses your doorstep. My hypothesis then, is this: in the first place, Pottier is accused of witchcraft by Lenain via his neighbour, Duboust. Later on he gets his own back on the unwitcher by pointing to him as a witch at the death of père Fourmond.

(*b*) Lenain is particularly attached to his patient, Duboust. It is even said that his daughter is '*going out*' with his nephew, the son of uncle Constant, the annunciator. When one knows Jean Lenain's energy, where there is a spell to be driven out of the family, there can be little doubt that he talked to Duboust about spells, and he may even have convinced him. But remember, these are just assumptions. (The following diagram shows the real or hypothetical ties between the protagonists of this story.)

5. A few details about the magico-religious past of the parish and the attitude of the local priests towards a Christian activitst gone astray, which is how they judge the case of Suzanne Fourmond, will give us a better idea of the atmosphere surrounding the scandal:

(*a*) About ten years previously, Chailland had a famous unwitcher, who was none other than the parish priest, Tranchant. Of course, he had not been acknowledged as such by the ecclesiastical hierarchy, only by his patients. As always, he was not taken very seriously in the village where he lived; but it was known that every night he was consulted by the bewitched, who sometimes came from far away, and that he would go off with them and lift the spells hanging over their farms. The people in his parish remembered him as a rather boring eccentric, who had a passion for music and who died composing a hymn to the Virgin. The true scope of his activities was only seen on the day of his funeral, when all his patients came from far and wide to pay their last respects: '*We guessed they were people he had helped out*' (i.e. unwitched), I am told; and '*it was only then we realized we had lost someone of worth*'. All the same, the diocese was not too keen on the whole thing: it is not done for a priest to go about dealing with the supernatural without consulting the hierarchy.

(*b*) It will come as no surprise, therefore, that his successor, the priest Pilorge, was particularly strict on the matter of spells. He had been acquainted with the Fourmonds and still was when he left the parish. But when he heard of the circumstances of the mayor's death, he suddenly stopped his visits, and did not reply to the widow's good wishes or greet her when they met in his new parish.[15]

(*c*) The priest Faucheux, whom I met when I arrived in the Bocage, declared he had nothing to say about spells, that they were only superstitions, and so on. He seemed to me a very dry sort of engineer of the faith; but, curiously, Suzanne Fourmond said of him: '*he does believe a bit*' (later I will come back to these expressions '*he believes a bit*', '*he doesn't much believe*'),

---

[15] Similarly, the priest from the neighbouring parish refused to shake hands with her, while others took their part in criticizing the mayor's wife, in the good cause of an '*enlightened faith*'.

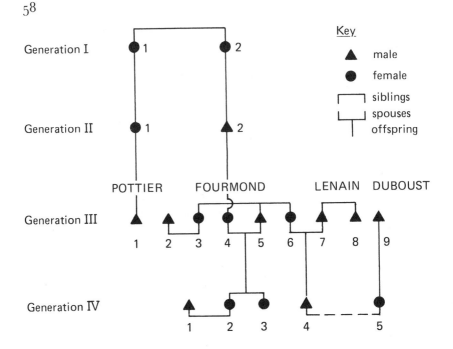

Generation I and II indicate the kinship relation between Suzanne Fourmond (generation III, 4) and her presumed witch, Pottier (generation III, 1): their grandmothers (generation I, 1 and 2) are sisters.

In generation III, I have indicated the following people:

III, 1: Pottier, the new mayor of Chailland, born in Villepail, second cousin of Suzanne Fourmond (III, 4).

III, 2 and 3: The uncle and aunt of Chailland.

III, 4: Suzanne Fourmond, born in Villepail, second cousin of Pottier (III, 1) and wife of Roger Fourmond (III, 5).

III, 5: Roger Fourmond, previous mayor of Chailland.

III, 6 and 7: The aunt and uncle Lenain, of Quelaines.

III, 8: Jean Lenain, the *'man from Quelaines'*, brother of uncle Constant (III, 7) And in generation IV, the following people:

IV, 1: The *'doctor'* son-in-law.

IV, 2: Madeleine, the nurse daughter.

IV, 3: Marie Fourmond.

IV, 4: The son of uncle Lenain (III, 7) of Quelaines, who *'is going out'* with the daughter (IV, 5) of Duboust (III, 9).

IV, 5: The daughter of Duboust (III, 9), neighbour of Pottier (III, 1).

Figure 2

in spells. '*Those who believe in it*' she says '*have to pretend they don't*' in order to avoid getting into trouble with the hierarchy. While I was talking about these things with Suzanne Fourmond, I used the epistle read in church that morning as a means of illustrating the difficulties of orthodoxy. For if it is said that the Apostles were told: 'When you enter a village, enter the houses and cure the sick', it seems difficult also to say (as in the positivist explanation, so often taken up by priests) that no one can be cured by supernatural means or that people must be mad to believe it. According to Mme Fourmond, the priest Faucheux thought hard about this kind of issue, that is, how to consider these gospel injunctions seriously and at the same time claim that magic can only be effective through the ecclesiastical hierarchy. '*Whenever he talks about it*', she says, '*he gets into a complete muddle.*' I'm not surprised.

(*d*) As for the present priest, the good Sauvage, who reads his breviary while walking through the village streets dressed in a well-patched cassock, he has decided to adopt a charitable attitude: he visits Mme Fourmond regularly and never speaks of the past (although he arrived in Chailland just after the mayor's death). Here we see how pointless is the '*bourgeois*' slander, which says that '*the priest cannot get those ideas out of her head*': Suzanne Fourmond's head, that is, of whom it is also said that she banged her door on him.

To end this chapter, I would like to mention some of the impossibilities I came up against when trying to press my investigations on the matter. Some have to do with the stubbornness with which village opinion was determined, come what may, to confine Suzanne Fourmond to the position they had chosen for her: that of a credulous person; others have to do with the necessarily ambiguous relationship any investigation entertains with witchcraft; others again, and they are important, concern the way in which my own subjectivity was '*caught*' in this story.

I. As soon as the people of Chailland saw me with Marie and heard I had seen her mother, I was literally bombarded with questions. It was generally known that I studied spells, that I had gone quite far in getting acquainted with unwitchers and that some of the bewitched gave me presents of poultry, meat and vegetables. If I was seeing the Fourmonds, it must mean that they considered themselves bewitched. Of course, I answered evasively, lied, or looked stupid, but the rumour spread quickly, and the scandal was about to break out once more on this rather flimsy basis: the ethnographer is interested in the Fourmonds. Marie's mother told her she was afraid '*everything would start up again*' because of our conversations, so I chose to put an end to them. But I have little doubt that had she been able to go on with her discourse – for what I have reported here is only a specific moment of it – there would have been several transformations. Five years later – seven years after père Fourmond's death – I was able to note that the passions had not in the least subsided: *Ouest-France* had quite inappropriately recalled my being around at the time of a witchcraft murder, and I decided to give my previous interlocutors some indication of the way I worked. But everybody in Chailland and its surrounds rushed to ask me: '*And mère Fourmond? What did she have to say?*'.

It is understandable, then, that I was unable to get to the bottom of several problems, either in 1971 or later, which would certainly have been worth investigating, especially those related to the mechanism of the scandal: What exactly had acted as detonator? Was Pottier set against the Fourmonds merely out of personal rivalry or because of a witchcraft matter between him and Lenain?

2. For Jean Lenain, the unwitcher, whom I met in 1972, the death of Roger Fourmond was unquestionably caused by a spell; '*but the Fourmonds wouldn't believe it*', he says. – 'Could you have cured him?' – '*Cerainly, up to the last day. But I have to be believed in. They didn't. I told Roger who was doing it to him. They know, and so does his wife. It was an old story* [the origin of the drama occurred long before]. *He died because he wouldn't believe in it.*'

Marie and her mother certainly do not believe in it. Or more precisely, they do not propose to draw any conclusions from the unwitcher's diagnosis. But at the same time ('*but still*', as Mannoni would say) they do believe in it. I can show this by means of a few examples of the repeated ambiguity of their remarks:

(*a*) After her father's death, Marie went to ask Lenain about the real causes of the drama, but she was disappointed by his reply. He believes in a spell, and this does not suit the young girl who nevertheless feels disconcerted by the man's goodness, profound piety and sincerity: '*he's sincere when he's passing on good*' (i.e. when he '*touches*'), she says curiously. But what about when he unwitches? On this point, Marie's reasoning is completely divided. On the one hand, she admires his strength of spirit: '*That's what surprised me in him – his indifference to criticism. Mummy would say to him: they would willingly throw stones at us in Chailland. But he would reply: please, don't bother about that. I mean, he's a strong man. Strong, really, and I admire him for that. He's not afraid to show what he's doing.*' On the other hand, it is only one step from strength of spirit to magic strength, and when it is no longer a question of her family but only of Lenain and his ordinary practice, Marie allows herself to acknowledge his gifts: '*The man from Quelaines can see whether it's a spell or just natural.*' That, in general, there are spells and unwitchers who can '*see*' them, including Jean Lenain, is something which can be admitted. But that there should be a spell in the family. . .

(*b*) Similarly, Suzanne Fourmond claims that when Lenain spoke to her of a spell, she didn't believe it: '*Cancer is cancer, and my husband was condemned even before he knew it.*' And yet, in the same conversation, she tells me this story: In Chailland she had met some clients of the '*Blonde Lady*' who didn't know how to free themselves from her hold. In the end, they got free by taking a third party's advice (in witchcraft, you always need a mediator for the subject's speech) who suggested they stop paying her: the '*Blonde Lady*' never came back. But shortly after, they felt they had been bewitched by her; they then went to consult Jean Lenain, who pulled them through. '*He's really good at lifting spells*' she concludes impassively.

(*c*) A few weeks after our meeting she tells her daughter she is afraid that if Marie goes on seeing me she too will get '*caught*'; she says she thinks I am a very agreeable person but '*completely caught, it fascinates her too much, one shouldn't try to understand these things*': note that this is an excellent way of *still* preserving a belief one is not able to accept. She had also asked me, now that I knew so much about spells, if I could lift them.

One can understand how much she needs this ambiguity to preserve both parts of the utterance: 'I know . . .' she says in effect, 'that my husband was not victim of a spell since religion, science and village opinion say so with such force and probability, but still. . . spells do exist in general.' This ambiguity has the advantage of leaving open the question of the real reason for Fourmond's death. Only one condition is required for it to remain indefinitely open: one must not talk about it, even to the ethnographer, regardless of whether she is '*caught*' or not in spells. In either case, the ambiguity would tend to resolve itself, since the interlocutor's position only leaves room for one of the discourse's two possibilities.

3. One can therefore say that objectively the investigation into the death of père Fourmond (is it a story of witchcraft, yes or no?) was extremely difficult, even impossible to carry through. An ethnographer working in the usual way, that is in the position of an outsider, would unquestionably have gone further in collecting local slander about the Fourmonds: everybody in Chailland would have been only too eager to inform a representative of science, thus using him to strengthen the cause of Enlightenment. But by this means, the ethnographer would have excluded any possibility of communicating with the Fourmonds. Things would have been no different if he had begun by visiting them: they would have refused to talk and the rumour would then have spread far enough to stop any further possibility of talking with them. I heard a lot about the Fourmonds when I was not yet interested in their story, and my indifference then provoked plenty of gossip. Once they themselves began to talk, I was no longer indifferent but everyone wanted *me* to talk. Or else attempts were made to cancel anything they could possibly say to me. Any ethnographer would have found himself faced with the choice of lending an ear either to the persons concerned or their accusers: when scandal erects a wall of secrecy between two sides, one can do no more than acknowledge the existence of this wall. Furthermore, any investigator who chooses an outsider's position would never have been able to find out whether there was a case of witchcraft between Lenain and Pottier. (Later, we shall see that I could undoubtedly have obtained Lenain's version of it, had I been able to continue our relationship, as he

suggested. But this meant I would be definitely cutting myself off from Pottier's version. Again, the wall of secrecy.) Lastly, supposing he had managed to get himself properly introduced – which any ordinary ethnographer knows how to do – another investigator could have met Lenain; but he would then have been faced by a mass of contradictory statements: the village accusing the Fourmonds of believing in it; Lenain, accusing them of not believing; and those concerned – silent. The ethnographer would probably have classified the whole affair as among those cases 'not to be used because too tricky' (for one cannot tell whether or not it is a case of witchcraft) and insufficiently documented.

It cannot of course be said that my documentation is adequate or that the case, as I have described it, is particularly straightforward. But one of the aims of this book is precisely to describe the necessary ambiguity of any belief in spells: without this ambiguity, no one could ever be 'caught'.

4. Most of what I could say about my involvement in the Fourmond story would only bring out the quite ordinary unconscious functioning, which it so happens is mine. I shall just say that when Marie came to talk to me, I had been wondering for some time about the kind of drama her mother was going through: for there was an obvious contradiction between the village's allegations, in which she was portrayed as superstitious, bewitched, bigoted and so on – and the intelligent and sensitive face whose gaze would sometimes meet mine in Chailland. It then seemed quite impossible that we should ever talk to each other, for I could not imagine how to get around the wall erected by the village between her and the rest of the world. Meeting her at last provoked a sudden worsening of the pain in my spine that I had recently been suffering from, to the point where I had to stop in the middle of the conversation so that her daughter could take me to the bone-setter who was treating me. (Let the ethnographer who has never had psychosomatic troubles cast the first stone.) I came back temporarily cured, and the conversation took on a peculiar turn: I was caught, caught fast, they would say in the Bocage.

I was not able to meet the '*man from Quelaines*' at the time: for one thing, he was busy harvesting during the day and unwitching at night; for another, the '*prophet*' of Aron had just died, and Lenain's relatives were afraid he would refuse to talk to me because I had no way of proving I was not a Parisian reporter in search of a sensational article. I waited, then, for several months, and brought him my symptom to cure – the famous backache.

By then I had been the client of an unwitcher for quite some time – the very unwitcher I had hesitated to consult for a cure while I was writing 'Sorcières et Lumières'. Lenain's therapy, apart from prayers and magnetic passes, required my breaking off with this Madame Flora, whom he soon identified as my witch (i.e. someone who desired my death, of which these pains were a premonitory sign), and in his protecting me from her, in other words, by provoking her death.

Jean Lenain gave me the impression of masterly freedom: tall, completely at ease with his body and his convictions, calmly defiant of witches, priests, and policemen: a man in full possession of his '*force*'. The way in which he worked, what he said about spells (and, of course, about the Fourmonds, the Pottiers and the people of Chailland) was of enormous interest to me. But one is not quite the master of a bond which has been tied elsewhere: I never went back to see him; I continued the cure I had started with the other unwitcher and sought to reduce my symptoms by non-magical means, by taking my ordinary unconscious functioning a little more seriously.[16]

---

[16] I shall return to this episode in Chapter 8, fn. 10, where it will be seen in a slightly different light.

6

THE LESS ONE TALKS, THE LESS ONE IS CAUGHT

Every time I spoke to the Fourmonds, they wondered why I was so eager to hear their story: *'Nothing happened, there's nothing to say, there's no story to tell'*, they would regularly protest. Since it was obvious that I did not share the village's opinion and was not trying to get them to admit what everyone else was accusing them of, they could not understand why I was interested in their story, which was not a witch story. True, they had met an unwitcher; but, after all, he had more or less invited himself; they had also named their witches, but had not followed the matter up. The fear of rekindling scandal soon put an end to these conversations, but one may well wonder whether Suzanne Fourmond was not afraid of something else when she told me it was dangerous to talk of spells and even more dangerous to try to understand them.

You can see how difficult it was to carry out this ethnographic investigation by considering together two characteristic utterances of the discourse on witchcraft. On the one hand, the bewitched declare that *'those who haven't been caught have nothing to say'*: for they cannot see how anyone would bear witness to spells without having lived through that singular experience. On the other hand, many of the bewitched also say that those who have been caught *must not* talk about it, to avoid getting caught again. For the less one talks, the less one is caught. So, if one eliminates those who cannot talk about it and those who *must* not, it leaves us with nobody. This is probably why my interlocutors usually justified their decision to keep silent by comparing themselves to some recently dead person, who would have loved to answer my questions, who knew so much about spells and who had so many stories to tell. Little did they realize that they were placing this person in the role of an ideal interlocutor precisely because he was silenced for good and all: the witches could not reach him any more, and no evil word could be turned back on him, for the simple and unfortunate reason that he was dead.[1]

---

[1] Folklorists might ask themselves what their informants mean when they talk in the past: *'in the old days'* people believed in spells and said that . . . etc. Is this not because the unwitcher – and not the folklorist, for example – is the only person to whom the bewitched can talk in the

I would like to give two examples here of the dilemma I refer to as '*the less one talks, the less one is caught*'.

I

The following episode occurred in the Mayenne at the beginning of my fieldwork. I had met Léon Turpin – a man of about sixty, vigorous, talkative and jolly – through one of his clients. He earned a comfortable living, gardening for shopkeepers and artisans in the villages of his canton. So far, every time I had tried to talk about witches I had stumbled against repeated refusals: '*One doesn't talk about that*' I was always answered sharply. This could have meant: (1) One does not ever talk about it to someone who is not caught. (2) Even among those who are involved, one only talks about it in moments of crisis. (3) On ordinary occasions, if witches are to be mentioned at all, it is only by allusion and through ambiguous sentences. For instance, the speaker declares he is '*badly neighboured*'; he enigmatically alludes to the '*other bastard*' or to that '*filth*' without ever daring to add a proper name. One does not talk about witches but only about bastards [*salauds*], a modest imaginative manipulation intended to deflect the attention of any evil beings who might still be listening around in the houses of their former victims.

This is perhaps why six months after I had begun to study witches I had still not heard the local word for them uttered – '*encrouilleurs*'[2] – except by enthusiasts of local folklore, doctors or teachers. So I was not a little surprised when Léon Turpin translated the question put by my go-between: '*Encrouilleurs?*' he said, '*I can tell you about them, because they've never attacked me.*' (In local terms, it could be said of this man that he was putting himself forward as having '*strong blood*'.) He invited me to visit him at his home where, in the presence of his daughter-in-law and his wife – who remained silent and disapproving – he mocked both witches and bewitched: '*Most people who think they are spellbound are usually under the influence*' [of alcohol], he said, repeating the cliché usually handed out to me by doctors about 'alcoholic impregnation', the main cause of peasant supersti-

present? The folklorist takes this use of the past as the basis for firm statements about the forthcoming disappearance of witchcraft (and this has been going on for more than a century) without thinking that a *discourse* on the past is perhaps not quite the same as a past *event*.

2 '*Crouiller*' is to lock up. '*Encrouiller*', '*désencrouiller*' is therefore to lock or unlock [clench, unclench] what I called above p. 8 the 'single surface' constituted by the bewitched, his family and his belongings. These terms would not need explaining and would cause no problem were it not that the unwitcher describes the two situations in contrasting terms: when he diagnoses an *encrouillage* [clenching], he adds that the surface is open to all the winds, the bewitched talks to anyone, leaves doors open, etc.; so if he attracts witches it is hardly surprising. He teaches the bewitched ways to *se désencrouiller* [unclench himself] by completely closing himself in: he must load himself with protective devices, not talk any more, put up enclosures around all his possessions, lock doors and so on.

tions. '*In the Mayenne, they believe in it because it's an under-developed region*'; '*spells come from poverty, that's where they come from*', he also declared, a century after Michelet.

But to careful listeners, Turpin seemed to have a kind of respect for unwitchers. He never failed to laugh at them and at anything to do with superstition – saying for example: '*Grippon is good at curing, especially if you pay him a calva*'* – but he granted them that 'force' which he loved to boast about in himself. The man he was speaking about, Grippon, had a considerable reputation in the canton. Always accompanied by his crow, whom he would consult when solving the riddles presented to him, Grippon treated animals by day and unwitched people by night, defying both the police and the curiosity of reporters with a violent sense of humour, which Turpin loved to quote.[3] Thus he is said to have calmly answered an exasperated reporter who had threatened to spit in his face: '*If I wipe off your spittle, nothing will be left of it. But if I do it to you* [if I spit in your face], *it'll stay there for some time.*' In other words: my spittle, as opposed to yours, is magical and you won't be able to get rid of it in the usual way, it'll stick to your face for as long as I want it to.[4] '*I don't believe in Grippon,*' says Turpin, '*but he can either cure you, or bewitch you.*' [I know that spells are a joke, but still. . .] '*The encrouilleur casts spells. Fellows like Grippon can either cast spells or cure them.*' [Describing an unwitcher's actions is very much a matter of the speaker's position: if he is one of Grippon's patients, he believes he was unwitched; but if he is the patient's enemy, he believes he was bewitched.] '*It's up to the lifter to lift the spell, it's up to him to be stronger than the other one, the encrouilleur.*' Turpin then went on to describe a locally widespread unwitching ritual, whose effectiveness depends essentially on the officiators' capacity to keep quiet about it: '*An ox heart is cooked in a pot; you stick pins into it; they claim* [*they* are the superstitious people, of whom in theory Turpin is not one] *that the bewitcher is forced to come because the pins hurt him*' [through the ox heart, the pins reach the witch, who cannot bear the pain, and who comes to beg to be relieved, thereby revealing himself to be a witch]. *When he comes, he's like a madman, but you mustn't talk to him: if you talk to him* [to the *encrouilleur*, stricken by this

---

* *calva*: a glass of calvados.

[3] Grippon, Lenain, Brault: three dissident characters, suggesting that dissidence in the Bocage is more to be found in the field of witchcraft. Other marginal figures, like the healers, are seen more as seekers of justice than defiers of the law: they claim, for example, to be '*the friends of the poor*' (or '*doctors of the poor*'). If the Medical Association left them alone, they would probably not feel so compelled to demand rights, as the late père Champ said: '*A diploma for whom? For the one who cures.*'

[4] Turpin's ambivalence towards Grippon can be seen in the advice he gave me to go and question his worst enemy: '*I know someone who doesn't like Grippon. Yes, you should go and see him, he's my conscript. Tell him you've been sent by Léon* [Turpin]. *He was a neighbour of his, he got fed up with his nonsense, he grabbed him by the throat . . .*' Turpin of course knew that by so advising me, he was leading me to a dead end: if I met Grippon's enemy, the unwitcher would never agree to talk to me.

return of the spell upon his own body], *he is cured* [he immediately recovers his magic force and begins to cast spells again: the ritual has had no effect].

I listened to Turpin carefully, wondering what he was getting at through this show of *'force'*, and was concentrating so much on how I would question him about this that I forgot to laugh with him. At which point his daughter-in-law, who had never stopped staring at me, decided to speak. The frail young woman's narrative of an event which had obsessed her in her childhood partially answered my questions about her father-in-law: she knew that his laughter was just a pretence and that she could take the risk of talking about her fear and fascination in his presence. Turpin stopped showing off his *'force'* and listened with the greatest intensity, which is a sign that the listener is *'caught'* in the witch story. She spoke to me: possibly because I had not taken up a superior attitude (I had hardly uttered a word) but more probably because she had long been looking for someone to whom she could tell her story.

So far in my experience, stories about witches had had the following characteristics: (1) The bewitched was a ridiculously naïve person who went around blaming some innocent individual for misfortunes which had an obvious, rational explanation. (2) An unwitcher was a shrewd individual who used rituals to throw dust in his patients' eyes and take advantage of them. (3) The unwitcher's predictions, once one had seen through his magic paraphernalia, were only rationally foreseeable consequences of premises which could have been inferred from the merest glance at the situation by anyone other than, of course, the stupid victim. The moral to be drawn from all these tales – always offered as the truth – was the same: in cases of witchcraft, there is no latent meaning and no mortal consequence, there are only fools and dupes.[5]

The effect of these stories on me was that I lost interest in the characters concerned, because they seemed so unreal – like dummies set up to reassure the narrator. Or, if I happened to come across one of them, as was the case with Suzanne Fourmond, there was such a tremendous gap between what I actually saw and what the legend said about them that they seemed completely out of my reach.

For the first time, Renée Turpin made me want to meet some of these people, probably because she was not afraid of admitting she was *'caught'* in her narrative.

She was about ten years old when Manceau, a neighbour of her parents, was involved in a witchcraft crisis. As is often the case, the trouble started when he got married and moved to Vautorte where he had rented some pasture-land: a short time after, all his cows died of an unknown disease. His only comment at the time was: *'No luck.'* *'He didn't consider spells in those days'*, said Renée Turpin. This raises two comments: (1) a single inexplic-

[5] I have a few examples of these stories in Ch. 4: 'Someone must be credulous'.

able misfortune is not sufficient for anyone to diagnose witchcraft. (2) It would have been strange, even crazy, to think of a spell in the absence of an annunciator.

Throughout the years, the series of misfortunes formed a pattern: first the pigs, then the calves died. When animals are affected like this, species by species, it is a sign of bewitchment. Lastly – and this brings us to the moment of crisis – Manceau himself was taken seriously ill: '*At night, he would feel compelled to bang his head against the bedpost, we could hear him scream . . . He was so ill that all he could do was lie and stare: he didn't even realize he was ill. They called Doctor Cordon from Mayenne: nothing doing, he didn't know what to say. They called the priest, nothing doing.*' [The priest was probably called as a modest unwitcher '*for good*', who protects the bewitched without attacking the witch, praying for the victim, blessing him and giving him ritual objects: medals of St Benedict, holy water, blessed salt and so on.] '*At that point the neighbours said to Manceau's wife: since the doctor refuses to come back* [for the doctor considers that his patient is lost] *we'll go and fetch Grippon*': a sentence all at once expressing the failure of positivist knowledge, the neighbour's annunciation, a diagnosis of the most dangerous kind of bewitchment – that Manceau is '*caught to the death*' – and lastly, the decision to turn to the unwitcher. Given the emergency, Grippon, who usually only works at night, comes that very afternoon. '*Along comes Grippon with his crow on his shoulder. He talks to the crow, then asks Manceau's wife to boil an ox heart and pierce it with as many pins as possible.*' He also orders all the entrances into the house to be blocked up, foreseeing that the witch will feel the pins so badly 'that he'll even try to creep through the attic window'.

Once the ox heart has been pierced with pins, the deadly fight begins between the unwitcher and the witch, who is solemnly challenged by Grippon: '*Body for body* [or '*heart for heart*', Renée Turpin is not quite sure]* *either he dies or I do.*' The outcome of the fight is by no means obvious, for Grippon, sweating heavily and shaken by spasms, had to admit the power of his supernatural enemy: '*He's really strong, this one. I don't know if I'll be able to overpower him*', he keeps repeating. He then goes home leaving his patient, helped by the annunciator, to interpret the effects of his magic duel.

Neighbours (both the annunciator's family and Renée Turpin's) stand around the house to watch for the arrival of the suspect, who is also a neighbour of the victim: '*Along comes Tripier, maddened by the pain from the pins.*' He screams, tries to break down the door, begs them to open it: '*but no one was to talk to him or touch him*': any verbal or physical contact would have immediately undone the effect of the ritual. Next morning, the witch rushes to the hospital in Mayenne, where a surgeon cuts twenty-five centimetres of intestine out of him. He is ill for a long time, but eventually comes back to

---

* In French, *corps pour corps* and *coeur pour coeur* (hence Renée Turpin's hesitation).

the village. Meanwile his victim is cured.[6] Tripier then begins to pester the legal authorities (accusing Manceau of bewitching him? It seems the most likely explanation, although Renée Turpin gave no details about this); the exasperated mayor finally has him thrown out of the village. Tripier settles on a farm in another canton, where *'apparently he's been playing tricks again* [witchcraft] *but only on animals'*: Grippon seems to have well and truly cut out his power over humans.[7]

Why did the neighbours think of accusing Tripier? Renée Turpin seems to be saying that the accusation was in their minds even before the unwitcher's appearance. During Manceau's illness, Tripier went to visit him, which in itself was suspicious since *'they hadn't been on speaking terms for a long time'* (so, there had long been bad feeling). Tripier approaches the sick man's bedside and keeps banging the bed with the toe of his boot: this contact between the witch and his victim is bound to strengthen the severity of the spell. But why should it be a spell? *'Tripier was all electrified, he was frightening'*, especially since he starts to make gloomy predictions to the patient: *'Ah! This time he's had it!*' [he's going to die] *He won't get out of it!' 'This time Manceau, you won't get out of it!'* Hearing this, the patient *'felt so weak that all he could do was roll his eyes'*, says Renée Turpin. A neighbour present at the scene then decides to act as annunciator, and goes to fetch Grippon. If he hadn't realized that Manceau had almost *'had it'*, he would never have mentioned a spell.

When Renée Turpin had finished, I realized that in fact her scoffer of a father-in-law had only been half joking when he had mentioned Grippon, his crow and his ox heart pierced with pins: which is probably why his daughter-in-law had felt free to recall this childhood event in which the same properties were involved. Compared to the stories I had been told so far, I was above all struck by the fact that witchcraft was not described as a mug's game, but as an extremely violent clash between the witch and his victim on the one hand, and the unwitcher and the witch on the other. For each protagonist, defeat meant death, or at least serious bodily harm, and for those who claimed to have strong blood – witch and unwitcher – the brutal loss of their power. Their clash, which had never been mentioned before in the narratives I had heard, could simply not be reduced to a conjuring trick or a party game. Grippon did not seem to be sure of his victory when he said: *'He's really strong, this one! I don't know if I'll be able to overpower him.'* That an unwitcher could thus enter into a battle whose outcome was uncertain and the stake was of the highest importance – life or death, force or collapse – was utterly new to me.

[6] *'We hushed up the story with the doctor,'* says Renée Turpin ironically: *'When he saw that Manceau was cured, he asked us what we had done, and we said it had happened just like that.'*

[7] *'To play tricks'* is to bewitch; but it can also simply mean to 'play a trick' without involving any notion of witchcraft. We have here an example of the ambiguity of the discourse on witchcraft: it's always the context which decides, and it is for the initiated to interpret and understand.

The whole story seems to be centred on the notion of *'force'*: who has it; who doesn't; will the unwitcher have enough; doesn't the witch have too much; will the bewitched be able to recover the force he has lost? Note that the people of the Bocage only use a single term – *'force'* – to describe both what is at stake in a crisis and what enables you to win this stake. And they are probably right; we shall see how later on.[8] But I think it would be useful to make a temporary distinction between the two categories of *'force'* involved in any witchcraft matter.

The witch has a certain amount of magic *'force'*, i.e. a force thought to produce its effects without the using of normal intermediaries: in the present case, it could be a hand-to-hand fight or poisoning. The witch's aim is to attract, by means of magic, the *'power'* or *vital* energy of a being totally lacking in *magic* means of defending himself. The bewitched, on the other hand, tries to avoid death or total loss of his *vital* force by calling on someone with magic power. Lastly, the unwitcher hopes he will be able to mobilize enough *magic* force against the witch to oblige him to return the *vital* force he stole from the bewitched. The witch's defeat consists in the loss of a certain amount of *vital* force; one can say that in a witchcraft crisis, *what actually circulates is vital force*; but *what causes it to circulate is magic force*.

In the first act of this drama, the bewitched, Manceau, is in a state of mortal weakness; in the last act, his aggressor has been relieved of a fair length of intestine – this is perhaps not unrelated to the fact that he is called Tripier* – and he is forced to go and apply his magic powers elsewhere; in the meantime, an avenger has arrived on the scene: Grippon, who dared wage a perilous fight in the name of the victim whose defeat was admitted from the start.

A witchcraft crisis, as it is presented in this narrative from the point of view of the bewitched, has three different moments:

1. *The moment of loss*

A being lacking in *magic* force, and who can *from this viewpoint* be qualified as weak (–) is struggling with a strong being (+): Manceau is suffering from a continuous loss of his *vital* force (its path is represented by an arrow) because of a superpowerful witch (+), Tripier.

Bewitched (1) ⟶ Witch (1)
(–)   (+)
Manceau   Tripier

2. *The moment of appeal*

To avoid death or a total loss of *vital* force the weak individual (–) calls on a

---

[8] Cf. Ch. 12.

* *Tripier*: in French, it means 'tripe-seller' (see p. 75).

magic avenger (+), Grippon, who is going to replace him in his unequal struggle and attempt to stop this outflow of force.

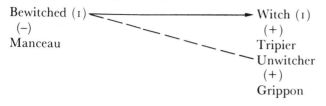

3. *The moment of reversal*

The fight then takes place between the two powerful beings, and the unwitcher gains the upper hand.[9] He now occupies the favourable position (+, witch) while his enemy is thrown back on the side of the weak (−, bewitched). When the reversal is achieved, the initially weak individual, Manceau, regains his force.

```
Bewitched (2) ─────────────────────▸ Witch (2)
(−)                                   (+)
Tripier                               Grippon
```

The logic of the crisis seems to be ruled by two principles:

(*a*) If a strong and a weak individual come into magic contact, the death of the weak one is at stake.

(*b*) The strong position cannot be occupied by two people at the same time: if they meet, it is to fight to the death.

Surely this is not very much like the petty peasant gullibility to which Léon Turpin and so many others seem to reduce witchcraft. It is not naïvety or ignorance that seems to be involved, but the mortal risk involved in conquering any unique position. For there is no room for two: it's one or the other; it's his head or mine. Jean Lenain, the Fourmond's unwitcher, had this in mind when after asking me about exotic witchcrafts, he ended the comparison with this remark: '*Here, you are immediately caught to the death; round here death is the only thing we know anything about.*'

I think it is essential to note here that the fascination of witchcraft stories lies first and foremost in the fact that they have their roots in the real, if subjective, experience – which anyone may have had on various occasions – of finding oneself in a situation in which *there is no room for two*. In witchcraft stories, these situations take on the extreme form of a duel to the death. The conviction and fascination exerted by these stories prove that this range of subjective experience, whatever form it may take, truly exists and that no one is immune to it. Otherwise it would be impossible to understand why those who went through it (the Manceaus, for example) should feel the need

---

[9] This does not inevitably occur, as we shall see later.

to recount it to others; and why their natural audience (the Turpins) should want so much to pass it on to whoever can listen; or why I myself went about collecting these stories without being deterred by the difficulty of the enterprise; and why I am now passing them on to readers who, one may assume, are not following me in this adventure entirely casually.

The last narrative pertains to this range, although it ignores its subjective character: it has to do with the mortal risk involved in the conquest of a unique position, but places it in an external reality in which only the objectivized 'force', first of the witch, and then of the unwitcher, can be operational. Everyone has good reason to be fascinated by it, although this should not prevent one from noticing that if the narrative is to have its full effect, it needs some blind spots.

For example, the reader may have noticed that the diagrams above, meant to represent the logic of the crisis – i.e. what is implied by the notion of 'force' and nothing more – depart somewhat from the way the people involved interpret this 'force'. Neither Manceau nor Grippon, for instance, would ever admit that the initial witch, Tripier, could be called bewitched, or that the unwitcher could be called a witch. In their view, the narrative simply shows that a magic aggressor is punished by a magic avenger. They do not take account of the fact that this avenger uses methods which they presume to be typical of the aggressor (working on an object to establish a metaphorical or metonymic link with the person it represents); or the fact that the defeated person uses exactly the same behaviour as one bewitched. And yet they are not unaware of this, since the story told on their behalf by Renée Turpin provides the data on which the diagrams are based. But ignoring this double reversal – from witch to bewitched and from unwitcher to witch – is fundamental to their discourse, or to their claim to maintain their position: whatever they do, they consider they are on the side of right or good; but whatever Tripier does, he is on the side of excess or evil because they accord him the first move in the magic aggression. From then on, whatever he suffers only serves him right.

If, however, Tripier, or anyone talking from his point of view, had been the narrator of this story, the chances are that the narrative would have begun with what – taking Manceau's point of view – I called the moment of reversal: Tripier feels bewitched by Manceau, he begs him to stop his magic tricks, he is suffering a thousand deaths, he has to go to hospital, and so on. The series of his misfortunes probably continues long after what for Manceau is the moment of crisis: we are told that after his return from the hospital, he tried to get Manceau thrown out of the village, which means that in his case, for some reason or other, calling on an unwitcher was ineffectual or impossible. All he could do was to turn to the law or come to a direct clash with Manceau. The fact that in the end he was asked to leave the village adds a final touch to Manceau's victory. So one can imagine the same story told by a Tripier-bewitched-by-Manceau, which would begin with the episode of his intestinal attack and continue – but perhaps not end – with the episode of his expulsion, the sale of his land and his removal far from Vautorte.[10]

Manceau's sense of being in the right is based on the conviction that Tripier is responsible for the initial magic aggression. This is a central issue, though the narrative gives no indication of it: when the initial aggression was performed, what magic techniques were used, who saw the witch at work, and so on. All that is known is that over the years, Manceau progressively developed a set of symptoms characteristic of the bewitched. Therefore he is the victim of a witch who is supposed to have touched first his animals (or something in contact with them), then his body (or something in contact with it), and confirmed his act with ritual curses.

This is not stated in the narrative, but is necessarily presupposed, or else it would not be a story of witchcraft. The evidence for this is to be found in the most startling scene of all: Tripier, *'all electrified'*, i.e. hypercharged, superpowerful, knocks the bedpost where the dying man lies, and utters curses,[11] while his victim, literally paralysed by this excess contact with evil, can only roll his eyes. The fascination that this episode evokes comes from the fact that the gap between the witch and his magic seems to be removed. For instance, Tripier is not said to own some magic instrument which he uses in some way; not at all – the whole person of the witch embodies magic violence, to the point where one cannot tell who is possessed by what or vice versa: the witch or his magic.[12] The self-evidence, the total visibility of his supernatural evil, is enough: there is no need to discover whether anyone ever saw Tripier lay spells on Manceau's stables or house: he must have done this at some moment when his magic was for him an external agent. At this present moment, in order to *'give it'* to his enemy and have done with him once and for all, he delivers all he has, and his entire being goes into action. Anyway, that is how the annunciator appears to justify his own intervention. But this intervention is probably also a desperate attempt to reduce the horror of a confrontation with omnipotence: for beyond Tripier's familiar face looms an unknown and anonymous force which possesses him. Since it is apparently boundless, it might be feared that it can no longer be held in by the system of names, which is then in danger of collapsing altogether. Was it Tripier who was seen, *'all electrified'* and terrifying, or was it something nameless, or, what

---

[10] In Appendix 4, 'The yardstick of truth', I mention the case of failed cures which lead people to resort to legal action or to physical aggression.

[11] The very bedpost against which Manceau had banged his head.

[12] All unwitchers and healers also say they are worked on by their own force: *'I've got too much, it works on me'*, *it* makes me dream, *it* prevents me from enjoying life like everyone else, and so on. Because witches never acknowledge that they are witches, they obviously have nothing to say about their force.

amounts to the same thing, something incomparable, something that no one has ever been able to measure?

So one can make the assumption that naming the witch is primarily an attempt to enclose within a figure something which in itself escapes figuration: as long as the power fatally drawing on the vital energy of the bewitched (in what I called the moment of loss) remains unnamable, it can only be absolute. It is only by naming that the symbolic manipulation of the situation has some chance of working: because one can then set the witch's name against that of an unwitcher, and try to find out whether the power of the first can be measured against that of the second. The fact that this is not automatically so (remember Grippon's words: '*He's really strong, this one, I don't know whether I'll be able to overpower him*') shows that naming, though a necessary step, does not determine the final outcome.

The following phase, which I have called the moment of appeal, could just as well be called the moment of measuring. I think it is important to examine carefully the manner in which the unwitcher chooses to measure his force against that of the witch.

Those on the side of the bewitched assume that he is 'caught to the death' because of some magic ritual which is supposed to have consisted in touching him directly or indirectly: the animals are dead, therefore they were touched; Manceau is dying, therefore he was touched. The unwitcher responds to the witch's *alleged* ritual to establish some *physical* contact with his victim with an *actually performed* (and witnessed) ritual, which consists in establishing some metaphorical contact with the witch, i.e. a *non-physical* or distant contact achieved through the use of symbolic equivalences. From that moment on, the narrative's dramatic quality is based on the idea that a real death (or serious bodily harm) can be provoked by a metaphorical contact:

1. The unwitcher pierces an ox heart and undergoes the same symptoms as if he were fighting against a real being, present there and then. Grippon responds to the witch's initial act by another act (Tripier touched Manceau; I pierce him) and to his words ('*this time, Manceau, you won't get out of it*') by a challenge: '*body for body, either he goes or I do*'. The narrator's hesitation between '*heart for heart*' or '*body for body*' shows how pregnant the metaphor is.

2. The unwitcher has pierced the ox heart and the witch suddenly appears '*maddened by the pain from the pins*': that he is maddened by this particular pain and not by something else is what those on the side of the bewitched say. Why must one avoid any contact with the witch just at that moment (not touch him, not talk to him, not let him enter the house)? In order to let the metaphorical contact established by the ritual have its full effect. For any material contact would mean communicating, therefore opening up what the metaphorical contact took great pains to clench ('*encrouillé*').

3. The witch, now bewitched or clenched to the death does not think he can get clear unless he goes to a surgeon to have his belly opened and a good length of that part of his body naming him cut out.[13]

Thus one can see that unwitching consists in responding to an *hypothetical physical aggression* (but taken for granted) with an *actual metaphorical aggression* which sets out to affect the victim's body in his *absence*. It is in this sense – and in this sense only – that those on the side of the bewitched are right to be surprised that one could subsume unwitcher and witch in a single word.

After Renée Turpin's narrative, I very much wanted Manceau himself to tell me his version of the story, and to clarify some crucial points: (1) How did the hostility between Tripier and Manceau and his 'good' neighbours begin? What had nourished it throughout the years? What elements of their common history might throw some light on the intriguing episode of Tripier's uttering curses at the dying man's bedside? (2) Was it possible to reconstitute the process leading to the imputation of witchcraft and to know how Tripier came to be accused, what other names had been suggested, and what inferences had finally weighed against him? (3) What signs, what words and what gestures had been exchanged between the side of the bewitched and the witch, from the moment when the latter was under accusation until his sudden appearance in front of Manceau's house, '*maddened by the pain from the pins*'? Of course the story raises many other questions. Those I have mentioned here were simply meant to throw light on a dark area in the narrative: I was trying to find out what exchanges had actually taken place between the two sides and how this had produced such ravaging effects on the bodies of the participants. For this exchange was presupposed in the narrative, though completely suppressed: Tripier's hatred for Manceau, for example, seems quite motivated, or motivated by the simple fact that a witch is by definition a hateful being; similarly, Tripier's appearance a short while after Grippon had operated is attributed to the '*pain from the pins*', but one wonders what signs had been addressed to the alleged witch to suggest that an unwitcher would come and fight him in the name of the dying man.

Renée Turpin willingly agreed to ask Manceau whether he would see me: at the end of the conversation, she and her mother-in-law had visibly taken a liking to me: I answered their questions on the nature of my work in a straightforward manner, and it seemed to satisfy them. Eight days later, I came back to find out what the Manceaus had answered. They were even friendlier, but very sorry: '*I'm afraid they don't want to. They said: after all we went through, we don't want to hear any more about it. It's not that they don't trust you,*

---

[13] This name, like all those used in the book, is fictitious. The real name of the person concerned is even closer to his symptom than 'Tripier', but it was the best I could think of.

but they don't want to talk about it any more.' That is, they didn't want to talk to *me* about it: after all, they had talked about it for hours to Renée Turpin. Full of good will, she reported their conversation, which confirmed her version of their story, with the additional detail of Grippon's formula at the moment of the ritual: '*Body for body, either he goes or I do.*'

It was a failure but it did teach me something:

1. The Manceaus could tell their story to Renée Turpin, since she had been '*caught*' in the event and the narrative to such an extent that there was no danger of the suppressed elements coming into the foreground – which would impugn the whole story. On the other hand, the bewitched could well imagine that although I had not mentioned my questions to my ambassadress, I was bound to do so to them. Since I was not '*caught*' in the narrative in the same way as its authors, in what cause did I wish to question them today? They had lived through a deadly crisis and had managed to survive, even if at the price of ignoring certain things. Why then should they take the risk of bringing them back, ten or fifteen years later?

2. I do not know how Renée Turpin interpreted my silence when she finished her story. The fact that I had not sneered or even smiled as the academic élite usually do seems to have been enough for her to trust me. Perhaps she even thought that I was caught in the story in the same way as she was: for I was indeed fascinated by the violence of this fight to the death and by the rigour with which a metaphorical link had three times clenched a body about itself. The Manceaus could have interpreted the account of my fascination in three different ways, each of which was risky for them: (*a*) I was new to witchcraft, and was trying to get myself initiated for reasons unknown to them, in which case they could be afraid I would use their words irresponsibly. For instance, not understanding the need for secrecy, I would go and question their witch and quote their words. (*b*) I was bewitched and in search of the truth for myself, struggling to resolve the crisis in which I was caught. But the Manceaus, who were neither my unwitchers nor even my annunciators had not the slightest reason to exchange words with me, so creating a contact between the two crises. (*c*) I was an unwitcher, and talking to me would be equivalent to asking for a magic cure. On the one hand, Grippon had done his work in a perfectly satisfactory manner; on the other, the crisis had been resolved long ago, and the participants had not the slightest intention of getting caught in it again.

It is clear, then, that the main difficulty in the ethnography of spells lies in the fact that it has to be done with words, which are at the same time a means of conveying information and an essential support to the metaphorical link established by the unwitcher. Throughout my fieldwork in the Bocage, I was continually met by this difficulty: except in those situations in which my 'informers' asked me to establish this metaphorical link myself or to assist the unwitcher in charge of doing so, I always ended up with failures. But the ethnography of spells consists precisely in recording what one has learnt from these failures.[14]

II

The story I have just analysed refers to a real episode in the lives of those concerned, but one that only exists within the terms of a certain discourse which gives it its final meaning. They had shaped the episode into a narrative, and I was trying to identify the generative rules. Like any narrative, it must be told and repeated, but only to someone who would not want to identify these rules or, and this comes to the same thing, who would be ready to share the protagonists' 'blind spots'. The narrative must not give rise to any questions; the listener is simply meant to be fascinated. If he then speaks, it must only be to evoke other narratives of the same kind, aimed at producing exactly the same type of fascination. Thus when the Manceaus said they were afraid of getting caught again if they talked to me, one can assume that meant they feared from the way in which I listened (either as an ethnographer, a position not foreseen by tradition, or as an unwitcher, a position which can always yield surprises), that I would disturb the carefully constructed sequence of their narrative and question its meaning, hitherto taken for granted.

This does not imply, however, that any witchcraft crisis ending in a successful unwitchment will automatically be transformed into a narrative. Sometimes, even though the bewitched has accepted the annunciator's diagnosis and the recourse to an unwitcher, he suddenly finds himself terrified by the consequences of his choice. He then blames the annunciator or the unwitcher and presents himself as a person who has nothing what-

[14] I met Grippon several months later, in curious circumstances: a bewitched couple I knew, who did not dare to go and see Grippon for fear that he would use eccentric methods like those of the '*Blonde Lady*' asked me to see him and bring him to them if I thought he was trustworthy. He found it incredible that anyone should confuse him with that charlatan, thought for a moment that I was some Parisian journalist disguised as an unwitching-broker and while I drove him to the farm of his future patients, he alternated between threats of magic aggression and sexual aggression. On arrival, he examined the animals with great care and declared he would come back and operate alone the following night. Although the bewitched wanted to go on telling me about subsequent events – they were afraid of Grippon and wanted me to comment on his work – I decided to stop interfering: it was better for them to decide which they were more afraid of: their witch and impending bankruptcy, or their unwitcher. I had given them other names of unwitchers, including Lenain's: it was for them to say what they wanted. Grippon's wife was uneasy about the rather pressing compliments her husband had made me in her presence: had I been a decent woman, I should have answered back sharply instead of keeping quiet. She began to make inquiries about me, to find out whether I was an adventuress in search of a rich lover: the result of her inquiry in fact proved to be in my favour, so that this woman and her friends were full of good feeling towards me. However, I decided I was incapable of sustaining such a violent relationship, and stopped seeing Grippon.

ever to say to anyone about the crisis; for as long as the interpretation can be fended off, the bewitched can hang on to the illusion that he is innocent of its outcome. In doing so, on the other hand, he forgoes the symbolic advantages of the operation: that of sharing, with all those who have been caught, the privileged use of a language legitimized by numerous generations, and he shuts himself up in a world of the unutterable.

The following story will illustrate this possibility. I was told it by Babin, the annunciator, who, wishing to oblige me (for his younger brother had identified me as the unwitcher who could at last free him from his spells), recounted the events and advised me to go and see the bewitched couple. He himself felt at ease with the traditional language of spells and had patterned his narrative on the very model of the one which has just been told. He introduced it, as is fitting, by the statement that '*we don't talk about spells to anyone; they would laugh; you have to be caught to believe in them*', a statement intended to specify the listener's position (if I am talking to you, it's because I know you are caught) and to arouse curiosity (listen carefully, I'm about to tell you an incredible story).

The Regniers had moved down from the North of the département five years before and settled on the farm of La Roche, next to his. They were honest, hard-working, churchgoing people, good neighbours of his. But Babin soon saw them being overtaken by misfortune: '*They suffered a lot of losses* [animals], *the wife was always ill. Whenever she went to Carelles* [her native village] *she got better; as soon as she came back to La Roë* [where this story took place], *she fell ill. Her husband couldn't stand her any more.*' Babin waited for a few months, then decided to act as their annunciator: '*Don't you think that some people might wish you ill?*' he asked them one day. As you might expect, they were astounded by this statement: '*Until you've been attacked*' explains Babin, '*you say: they're just stories. That man from La Roche, he was a complete novice* [in spells] *when we told him.*' The annunciator then informed them about their condition, reconstructed their misfortunes into a significant series of events, and the novices fell in with his interpretation.

To help them out, Babin first took them to the '*petite mère from Torcé*', an old woman from his native village who healed by the laying-on of hands. She came to La Roche, blessed the buildings and the people, and pronounced ritual prayers. '*Things got a bit better*', said Babin, '*but it wasn't enough: that woman can't completely stop spells. She can only do good* [she protects the victim without sending the spell back to the aggressor]. *The spell was stronger than her.*' Prayers and laying-on of hands are considered to be effective only when the spell in question is '*weak*', and has been cast by an amateur, a beginner, or a witch only mildly interested in that particular case.

Babin then said to them: '*We have the address of a woman who can turn spells away.*' This is a euphemism, since a spell which is thus '*turned away*' does not get lost in the wilderness but goes straight back to whoever cast it. For my benefit, Babin cleared himself of the charge of provoking misfortune in this way: *'the couple didn't get on well . . . François couldn't stand his wife any more, she was always ill.'* At first Régnier refused, because he hated the idea of having to deal with such a *'strong'* healer. But when his wife's symptoms became worse, he gave in: *'Where's that woman of yours who's supposed to be stronger?'* he asked Babin one day. The unwitcher was called to La Roche. She was not able to lift the spell, but she gave a diagnosis which was later used to justify the ensuing events. As soon as she had set her foot on the first step, she seemed to be shaken by an invisible force and declared; *'There's a spell here and you're caught really tight.'* She operated for several nights, unsuccessfully. I was not told of her methods, but her very failure was a sign of the witches' wickedness: *'The spell was cast on her* [the unwitcher] *by someone around here'*, whose *'force'* was superior to her own.

Babin then decided to call an unwitcher *'for evil'* known as the *'woman from Izé'*, or *'Madame Marie'*. In the past she had unwitched his wife's parents and was at the moment dealing with her brother's household.[15]

At that time (she is now dead) she occupied a position comparable to Grippon's in the hierarchy of *'force'*. Like him, Madame Marie would come as a last resort, because she was known to be capable of pushing the escalation of violence to the very end. As she entered a farm at the request of the bewitched, she would always say: *'If you don't want me to* [provoke evil], *I'll leave, but I must return evil for evil, if not, it hits me too hard, I'm not capable'* [of bearing such violence as *'hits'* me without sending it back to its original transmitter]. Babin described her in the following manner: *'she was a small, skinny woman* [in the Bocage, skinniness is usually a sign of weakness], *but was she tough, that little woman; she never slept at night, she fought, her furniture strained, it was the others attacking her* [her patients' witches]. *Her face looked tired, worn out; she didn't look very clean, but she said that if you're too clean, the witch can get a grip on you.'* In other words, a woman who knew how to defend herself as well as to attack. Her fighting ritual consisted in tossing coarse salt in a red-hot frying-pan, then saying, *'can he* [the witch] *feel it!'* He was in agony and jumped up and down on the spot like the salt in the frying-pan. Like Grippon's ritual, the aim was to drive the aggressor into declaring himself at the hour fixed by the unwitcher.

Madame Marie came several times to La Roche, operated, and said one evening: *'Whoever did it to you, won't ever do it again.'* Babin abruptly concluded: *'The woman I suspected* [the witch] *died in hospital.'* Then, after a heavy silence: *'When the woman from Izé came to La Roche for the last time, mère Chicot was at home, doing the housework. Next day,'* he said, raising his voice, *'next day, a neighbour says to me: mère Chicot is completely gone.'* He adds: *'She fell on the very day the woman from Izé said she would.'* She had such a violent fit of anxiety that her doctor had her admitted to the psychiatric hospital, where she died a

[15] This brother will play an important role in Part III.

few months later of a mysterious illness.[16] On the day of her entering hospital, the witch's husband, who knew nothing at all about the situation, said firmly to Babin: '*the mère is no more ill than you or me*'. But after her inexplicable death, he questioned the nurses, '*who said: she was suddenly beset by bad spirits. They worked on her*', said Babin triumphantly, and he repeated several times: '*the nurses said: they're bad spirits*'. The evil nature of the witch and her inevitable punishment are recognized even by positivist science, which very rarely provides the bewitched with any such satisfactions.

It is important to note that the unwitcher did not interpret the effects of her ritual, and above all that she did not name the witch. Babin says she refused to name her because once she had told a man that his witch was his brother; it had led to the witch's murder, which resulted in Madame Marie being questioned by the law.[17] From then on, she let her patients take on the responsibility of interpreting, saying, for example: '*You'll find out for yourselves*'; or else, she helped them with hints: '*he who is doing it to you passes by the end of the path*'; or else, when they were on the wrong track, she guided them in a different direction: '*you're thinking of someone, but it's not him*'. Then how is one to know? '*One suspects*', answered Babin. '*We know it's mère Chicot because she's dead.*'[18]

At this point the Régniers are extremely grateful for their annunciator's perceptiveness: '*If we hadn't met you*', they say to the Babins, '*we'd be lost.*' But everything is still not quite settled for them: '*the mère from Izé said there wasn't just one*' [witch], says Babin. I ask: 'Who else?' – '*A cousin*' – 'How do you know it's him?' Babin and his wife then throw an astonished glance at me, because my question could only come from a novice, which is not very encouraging since they hope I will operate on their brother: '*But it's quite clear!*' exclaims Babin, summarizing in one characteristic phrase the whole process discussed above, by which the code of the bewitched can visibly reveal these nocturnal witches, who only operate when they are sure they

---

[16] Later on, I shall return to the puzzle that mère Chicot posed to medical knowledge.

[17] Having found no trace of this murder, or of the action brought against Madame Marie, I am inclined to think that it is a mythical event used to justify the doctrine that the bewitched must assume personal responsibility for the interpretation. For, if a failed unwitching leads to murder (cf. p. 135, fn. 18, and p. 259) it is only rarely that the unwitcher accuses a close relative of the victim, since the object of the cure is precisely to divert the violence of the bewitched onto non-relatives. Moreover, if a bewitched murderer is arrested, he rarely agrees to give the unwitcher's name to the law.

[18] The witch is defined as a '*neighbour*' of the Régniers. This term, as I was able to check in the field and on the map of the commune bears only a vague relation to topographical reality: the Régniers and the Chicots' farms are situated in the same *quartier* [area], i.e. in the same group of properties bounded by communal roads or paths, but they are not particularly close to each other, since they are at opposite ends of the '*quartier*'. Several other farms are much closer (topographically) to La Roche than the Chicots'. Contrary to what is generally said as an explanation of the origin of conflicts between people who accuse one another of witchcraft, the Régniers and the Chicots do not share a common yard, nor do they have any lands that adjoin one another, nor any paths in common.

cannot be seen. He adds : '*it's always people who are closer to us than we think, it's not people who come from a distance*', for it is said that one cannot bewitch without touching the body or belongings of one's victim.[19] But the Régniers think it unnecessary to attack this witch who was much less dangerous than the late mère Chicot: after all, the farm is going along normally, and they have slowly recovered their health. '*Whenever they see they're getting a bit bogged down, they go to Torcé*' says Babin, to consult the '*petite mère*' who heals by laying on her hands, and everything falls temporarily back in place.

When I went to see the bewitched people, they knew that Babin had already told me his version of their story. I had a long conversation with Louise Régnier (her husband was away that day) in which we talked only about the witchcraft attack in which the couple had been the victims, but she talked to me about it from a peculiar angle: that it was impossible to talk about it. That is to say, she could only tell me she had experienced something that left her without any position from which she could safely speak.

She greeted me with a chilly bearing, which indicated her unwillingness to speak. When I told her Babin had sent me, she shuddered, and only just managed to control her anger: '*He told François, who didn't answer*', she declared. '*He even came back to the house, once, and we didn't say anything: we would have told him if we'd been interested*' [in talking to you]. My go-between had apparently been unwilling to hear their silent refusal, or had not wanted to convey it to me. So I then started a five-point negotiation with Louise Régnier on the possibility of talking about it another day:

1. How much time, she asked, would the conversation take? I proposed to go over their story from the time they settled in La Roë. '*Ah, but François is never here, either during the day or in the evenings.*' 'What about Sundays?' – '*When he's here on Sundays, he sleeps.*'

2. 'Well, could she and I talk about it? – '*No, it's better if the two of us are here, it happened to both of us. I know that when François went to fetch Madame Marie, she looked at his hand and said: you're a little caught, but it's your wife who's caught tight.*'

3. Having thus refuted her own argument, she then quickly adds a more serious one: '*If only we were sure of being free of it all, we could talk about it.*' For they are not sure of being free; at least she is not, though François says she was imagining things. '*Sometimes*', she says, '*we can feel they're around*' [the still unpunished witches].

4. A further argument: she is not sure of being '*free of it*' because she does

---

[19] The Babins asked me about town witchcraft, which they think of as rather doubtful: they cannot understand on what pretext city-dwellers would mutually bewitch each other, since there is no real contact (in town, people don't speak to each other) or acquaintanceship (in town people are strangers in the same building, tenants only stay for short periods, and so on).

not know the witches' names. *'If only we knew who it was, we could talk about it. Madame Marie said there were two of them'*, but she left them the responsibility of naming the witches and simply stated, when they first suggested a name (someone from Carelles? my interlocutor is careful not to mention it), *'it's not who you think . . . [the witch] goes past the farm'*. Not knowing who to accuse, Louise Régnier feels threatened: *'Perhaps it's someone who comes in here, who shakes hands, and then we get caught; someone we invite for a drink, we're too good to everyone.'*[20] That her cousin is the witch is obviously not as *'clear'* to her as it is to her annunciator. Unlike Babin, she seems to have the utmost difficulty in focusing her suspicions on one name.[21] As long as she can say: *'I don't know who my witches are'*, she can avoid attributing mère Chicot's death to the ritual she herself asked for; or she can pretend it was not directed at anyone in particular.

5. Finally, the reason why they are not sure of being free of spells is that they do not carry out all the instructions on how to protect themselves which were given to them by Madame Marie. She only admits this after much beating about the bush. She first talks of their disappointment: *'That's what got François, Madame Marie wouldn't tell us the names.'* I object that perhaps the woman from Izé was afraid her husband would go and *'see'* them, to which Louise Régnier replies, in a suddenly shrill voice, which shows that she had understood my euphemism (*'see'* for *'attack'*): *'No, he wouldn't have gone, he wouldn't have done anything! I know Madame Marie got into trouble over somebody* [who killed his witch after the latter had been named by the unwitcher], *but François wouldn't have done anything!'* In fact, she concluded, falling back on the wording of my remark, when one knows the name of a witch *'you avoid him, you don't try to see him'*. Now that Madame Marie was dead, perhaps they would go and ask Madame Auguste, her successor, for the names, that is, ask if she knows them. I suggested that perhaps Madame Marie thought she was protecting them enough with *'what she did'* [her rituals]. At which point she confessed: *'But we don't do everything she told us to do and we don't carry around everything she said we should!'* – 'You mean to say you no longer carry the little bag with the nail?'[22] Madame Régnier angrily exploded: *'You have to be absolutely backward to play tricks on us like that* [bewitch us] *and for us to have to defend ourselves with that sort of thing!'* [the fetish]. She had stopped carrying the little bag because she felt

---

[20] One of the aims of the cure, as will be seen in the second volume, is precisely to cure the patient of being *'too good'*, i.e. too open and defenceless against the evil person's arrows.

[21] At the start of an unwitching cure, the magician usually has to check the over-eagerness of his patients, who are in too great a hurry to suggest names.

[22] A magic protection consisting of a carefully sewn, small red cloth bag which must be worn next to the skin. Apart from blessed salt and herbs (no one was able to say which herbs), the bag contains a sort of magic lightning-conductor in the form of a bent steel nail. As far as I could understand, the steel represents the witch's force and the bending represents the diversion one hopes the force will be subjected to. But sometimes a bewitched also carries an un-deformed steel nail so as to have a reinforcement of force.

humiliated; as for François, his little bag was pinned to a vest she has sent to the laundry, and she wonders whether it will be sent back.

She then remembers the annunciation: '*To think that if it hadn't been for the Babins, we would never have understood what was going on! In Carelles* [her native village] *we don't believe in all that, we're more advanced than the people here. Just walk around the village and you'll see the difference! They're so backward round here, doing that sort of thing!* [casting spells]. *In Carelles, we're more civilized, we wouldn't dream of playing such tricks.*' This is why Babin had had to put them in the picture: the civilized Régniers '*couldn't imagine such tricks existed*'.

Note that Louise Régnier establishes a total contrast between La Roë, where she is now living, and Carelles, her native village, as if between savagery and civilization, backwardness and modernity, double-dealing and honesty. In Carelles, the cradle of civilization, no one believed in spells, no one thinks about them and of course no one casts any; which is why no one needs these ridiculous protective bags. The trouble is that one has to live in La Roë among primitives who waste their substance in dance-halls and cafés, hardly ever go to church, and play such filthy witchcraft tricks that one has to defend oneself by taking humiliating, and scarcely Christian measures. Living in La Roë means it is impossible to turn the other cheek, means that one has to live like a savage because Christianity gives no guidance about how to survive supernatural evil.[23] '*They say there are savages in Africa; but you who've read so much, do you know anyone more savage than we are?*', a question Jean Lenain once asked me. But being initiated into spells by a priest who had decided to fill in the gaps of the Christian message with his own words, Lenain was much better armed than Louise Régnier to confront the savagery of witches: for example, he did not need to state, against all probability, that at least his native village was innocent, both of all magical practice (which might be the case), and of any belief in spells. Madame Régnier, as we have seen, attempted to reproduce, without changing one iota, the characteristic utterance of those who are not willing to take any personal part in the discourse of witchcraft, so implying that they are not caught in it: spells are believed in, but somewhere else.[24] Her position is extremely vulnerable: unfortunately, that 'somewhere else' is where she stands, and where she has to try to survive: because she is, precisely, 'caught in spells'.

Babin, the annunciator, plays a particularly important role here because he is the person who has to assume responsibility for the accusation instead of the bewitched. Louise Régnier remembers, for example, that in the very year of their arrival at La Roë, Babin had already tried to warn them. One

---

[23] Shortly after the annunciation, Madame Régnier began to question the priest of La Roë: not about spells, but about the problem of the degree to which one may turn the other cheek. Asked out of context, her question was answered in vague terms which the couple thought about for a long time, wondering how to interpret them and what to do.
[24] Cf. pp. 15–16 and Ch. 4.

day, as he was making hay with Régnier, he suddenly said, between two long silences: '*Some people around here are dangerous to see.*' Régnier waited in vain for a further comment which would clarify the meaning of Babin's enigmatic statement, which he said he was only able to interpret several years later, at the time of the annunciation.[25] It must be understood that at first Babin merely reminded them that spells exist; but the Régniers did not want to listen to him, on the pretext that in Carelles spells were not supposed to exist. Perhaps Babin would have preferred not to get further involved, but his neighbours were not taking advantage of his early warning; they were incapable of relating it to their own affairs because their ears were blocked by evangelistic optimism: apparently in Carelles people think they can survive by turning the other cheek.

Louise Régnier, to whom I explain my aims and methods of work, and who says she approves – '*What you're doing is really for good*' – then begins to complain bitterly, in an effort to justify herself (this I only understood later) for having taken the decision to return the witches' evil. For more than an hour, she goes into the details of the sequence of their misfortunes, using the characteristic language of the bewitched, except that she does not once mention her aggressors: not only does she not name them, she never establishes the slightest link between the occurrence of a misfortune and the proximity of a witch. Although we both know that in the end she not only did not turn the other cheek but mortally wounded the person whom she believed had dealt her so many blows, she describes herself as the victim of a misfortune for which only '*fate*' could be blamed, using that part of the discourse of a bewitched which closely reproduces the complaints of Job.

'*The woman from Izé said it caught us just after we arrived here*' she begins. For – even though she only talks about the '*it*' which caught them, she is perfectly capable of linking the two events – two weeks after they arrived, their car ran into a ditch and turned over. '*Of course François was driving fast but that's when it started, we said so to Madame Marie.*' (I know ... but still ...). Passers-by take her to the village's old-fashioned woman doctor who only treats her abrasions, though she also suffers from concussion and has two displaced vertebrae. Louise Régnier endures vertigo and backaches for three months before making up her mind to go and consult a reputable doctor in the main town of the canton: an old man, who addresses his patients as '*tu*' and who does nothing but rebuke her to hide his own incompetence: '*You shouldn't have waited so long, now how am I supposed to see what's wrong with your back!*' Humiliated, she leaves and goes to consult a chiropractor in the neighbouring town, but it does no good. She then goes to see a healer in Laval who does '*some good*' by manipulating her backbone:

[25] Like the dialogue which took place between Louise Régnier and her priest, there is speech, but it is restrained, because something vital is at stake. One must talk about it, but the less one says ...

'but it was so unbearable', she says, *'that I fainted.'*[26] After that, the series of misfortunes begins: a cow ceases to give milk, an eight-day-old calf has to be slaughtered: *'The vet couldn't understand what was wrong. The calf was eating well, but kept losing weight.'* Other animals die for no reason; and finally, she becomes completely listless: *'I wasn't really ill, not dying, but I hadn't the strength to do anything. I had headaches, I couldn't do any work. I couldn't even give the children their bath.'* Her husband also feels vaguely unwell, but it is less pronounced.

At that point, Babin comes on the scene with his annunciation, leading to their first consultation with Madame Marie.[27] When she forthrightly declares that she returns evil for evil, the Régniers take fright and refuse her help. But the symptoms get worse, and prove her right: a few months later, Louise Régnier has a miscarriage. Before going into the clinic, she calls on Madame Marie, who agrees to visit her after the curettage.

When she talks about the woman from Izé, Louise Régnier behaves like a penitent: she lowers her head, looks down into her apron at her joined hands, and talks in a hollow voice: *'I must explain, about unwitchers: some of them take it on themselves and others send it back. They hurt those who have hurt in the first place, I mean. They can't keep it all to themselves, they say it's too tough.'* Apparently the woman from Izé forced the decision to attack the witches out of the Régniers: *'She stood there in front of the gas cooker, she was angry. She said: then why did you ask me to come?'* After so many months of useless negotiations, she is eager to toss her salt in the frying-pan. In the end, the bewitched gives in: *'She said to me: look at your children, you're not even bringing them up* [because of her ill health, Louise Régnier had been totally neglecting them]. *We did it for the children'*, she repeats several times to excuse herself. She then changes her mind and says once again that she won't talk to me about it: *'if only we could be sure we're free, then we could talk about it'*. I point out that since mère Chicot is dead, at least one source of danger has been eliminated. She immediately freezes: *'Ah, because you think it's her?'* and adds, after an interminable silence, that Babin and a neighbour are the people who interpreted in that way the results of the ritual performed by the woman from Izé. I wonder what she thought about it, but do not dare ask: *'As for us!'* she continues, *'we're more on the side of religion: to endure, endure everything to the end. Whenever I meet père Chicot, I'm so ashamed I hardly dare look at him.'* So she really does believe she killed his wife, but she cannot say anything about it because she is caught between two incompatible desires: on the one hand that it is a spell, and on the other that it should be lifted without harming anyone. Because they had suffered

---

[26] Note that the hierarchy of her medical advisers – doctors or healers – replicates that of the political-administrative authorities: it begins in the village and finishes in the provincial capital.

[27] Note that she does not mention several elements found in Babin's version of the event to me, and especially: (a) that her husband supposedly *'couldn't stand her any more'*; (b) the consultation of the first two unwitchers.

so much, the Régniers agree to hold mère Chicot responsible. But because she died, they realize, a little too late, that they would have preferred to cure an impersonal evil by means of a harmless ritual.

My conversation with Louise Régnier can therefore be summarized in the following manner: mère Chicot must and must not be a witch; she must and must not have died because of a ritual requested by the Régniers; therefore, they can and cannot talk to me about spells. My suggestion that we make an appointment to talk about it another time was thus quite out of place: it is difficult to conceive of a formalized situation in which I could have come to hear them tell me that they murdered mère Chicot. But, not yet having understood this I suggest leaving my address so she can contact me if ever she feels like talking about it. But every time I try to write it down, she stops me: 'No, look, since I'm not sure I'll talk, don't write it down. That way you too will be anonymous. It's better for you. You'll be anonymous and so will we.' Yet she knows my name and where I live; I told her when I arrived. And I know her name and address since I'm here. But she is so traumatized by the consequences of the only act of naming she ever dared to do that she prefers to cloak herself in anonymity and give me friendly advice about doing the same. In any case, she says, I could come back some time and have coffee with them, 'we're not savages, we're not like the people around here; on the contrary it'll make a change to see you'.

I could have taken advantage of her offer and come back to La Roche with the flimsy excuse of dropping in to see them: perhaps they would have told me their story, because they really did want to meet someone who could listen to them without obliging them to go any further along the path of violence or condemning them for having been driven to it. Like some other people, who ended up by talking to me, they would have asked me questions about my job and got me to tell witch stories I had heard. I could have told them some episodes concerning other bewitched who had been confronted by similar contradictions to their own, but I knew of none which had a reassuring outcome.

At that time, the Régniers had completely broken off with their annunciator: François, who sometimes worked for Babin on a casual basis, paid by the hour, decided he had received humiliating treatment, like the farm hands of old who were attached to their masters on an annual basis.[28] They also felt affronted because Babin had me go and see them, regardless of

---

[28] She repeated this incident to me several times. It seems to have really mattered to her: after a meal at the Babins', François was drinking coffee, and chatting with the boss's wife. Babin abruptly entered, sharply ordered his wife to go and do some work and handed a pitchfork to François without saying a word. Louise Régnier thinks that only his determination to keep his distance – and not, for example, jealousy – explains Babin's behaviour. Régnier, who thought he was his friend, suddenly discovered that he was only a farm hand in Babin's eyes. Louise was indignant: 'No one in the village would have done that to us! Never again! To be a farm hand today . . . that's over!' If the people of La Roë are somewhat old-fashioned in their ideas, her annunciator is extremely so.

their tacit refusal. But one can imagine that they primarily resented the fact that Babin had succeeded only too well as an annunciator, and had been too open in showing his pleasure at the death of the witch.

The Régniers had then refused to talk about the past to Babin, reserving this for the woman from Izé, on the unlikely chance that they would sometime have the courage to question her. But now she too was dead, and they were left on their own with the intolerable burden of mère Chicot's murder. When I saw the Régniers, I knew that Babin considered me an even stronger unwitcher than Madame Marie and that he wanted me to make up for Madame Marie's failure with his brother's marriage, since she had not been able to cure him of his main symptom. It is understandable, then, that the Régniers, who already thought her quite strong enough, should not have been over-enthusiastic about submitting their case to me. For what would happen if I decided to treat their remaining symptoms by punishing the other witch?[29] It was enough that they had one death on their conscience, and they obviously felt that Babin had already played too large a part in their fate. In any case, if this is what they had wanted (and I do not think it was the case), they would certainly have preferred to consult Madame Auguste, since they could at least hope her initiator had told her what she knew about them.[30]

It seems to me that by complaining of small persisting symptoms, the Régniers were trying to say that they did not completely reject an explanation by spells, but only the violent method by which they were supposed to have been cured of them. The fact that they still suffered from small misfortunes after the death of their witch enabled them to authenticate their state as bewitched, to cast doubts on the identity of the culprit, and to wash their hands of a possible miscarriage of justice. Mère Chicot was the witch because she is dead, but Babin is the one who says so; she was not the witch since I'm still suffering. Lastly, seeing how witches are dealt with in La Roë, I prefer to withdraw in a spirit of Christian charity. A disinterested but comfortable position, since after all it was because of the death that the main symptoms disappeared.

---

[29] At present time she complains of three symptoms: (a) she has begun to dream again every night. (b) She did not feel like working: '*I know I should be doing this or that, but I can't do it.*' (c) She has several warts, an especially big one on her neck. Madame Marie had spoken to her of a wart '*toucheur*', the hairdresser from Izé; but now that she is dead, how is she to find him? Would Madame Auguste tell her, would she even know? Anyway, Louise would prefer to see a doctor, for she fears she might have cancer. '*We buried someone yesterday, at Carelles, he was our age.*' These words are bound to emphasize the inconsistencies of her statements: her uneasiness shows that she feels threatened, but she cannot say by whom or what or decide on the behaviour to adopt.

[30] Although Louise Régnier considers me to be on the side of civilization and good, she cannot help being somewhat afraid of my possible '*force*'. Towards the end of our conversation, she asked me, after silently looking at me for a long while: '*You write books; but don't they* [the witches] *learn their tricks in books?*' I got out of it somehow, answering that witches' books are '*kept in the family*': they have no author and are inherited from dead relatives.

It is quite clear that the Régniers do not want to discuss spells with anyone else because their views on this point are scarcely tenable and cancel themselves out as soon as they are expressed. It can be feared, however, that by thus shutting themselves up within that which is unspeakable, they might one day find themselves in a highly vulnerable situation. Should a new series of misfortunes occur (possibly based on their remaining symptoms), it is difficult to imagine where they could turn. For they have broken off with their annunciator; their unwitcher is dead; her successor, Madame Auguste, is apparently just as *'primitive'* as her predecessor; and lastly, unwitchers *'for good'* are not strong enough to reduce the Régniers' misfortunes. But what is even less clear is how these bewitched, who have disavowed the results of a first unwitching, could ever be in a position to try a second one. Only a priest–unwitcher who knows how to manipulate both planes, the religious and the magical, could, in my opinion, give them what they are asking for: to be both cured of their ills and absolved of their past crime.

An orthodox priest would certainly refuse to absolve them of a murder he himself would consider imaginary, unless the Régniers agreed to reduce their confession to homicidal *thoughts*. But they would gain nothing by this, because it would oblige them to renounce as illusions and supersitions the explanation by spells (which still has the advantage of linking each misfortune to the doings of a single, real being) and to exchange it for the general theory of *'good suffering'* understood as a grace from God granted to a chosen few.[31] Confronted by these two statements: (1) I'm suffering, therefore So-and-So hates me, and (2) I'm suffering, therefore God loves me, whatever the Régniers may say (*'We're more on the side of religion'*), they would have liked to be able to opt for the first, since it would at least enable them to take an initiative. Because the death of the witch went beyond their expectations (or because it unquestionably revealed their desire, who knows?) they are bereft of any kind of statement, and therefore of any kind of symbolic reference.

One would still like to know why the Régniers and their annunciator were so convinced that they had provoked the death of mère Chicot. Thanks to Babin's hints, I went to consult her file in the psychiatric hospital, and questioned those who had looked after her during the seven months of her decline. No one had understood what she suffered from or what caused her death, apart from a state of intense fear which never left her. The psychiatrist treating her had left the hospital, but the doctor who had replaced him remembered Mme Chicot. Looking at the file, he assured me that there was no medical explanation of her troubles, although it was entered that she died of senile cachexia; a diagnosis which refers to a general disorganization of the vital functions that everyone was able to observe in the patient, although no one had understood the reasons for it.

[31] Cf. p. 7.

The diagnosis had nevertheless been entered in the file, to conform to the administrative rules which require doctors to give one.

Reading this document, which I now reproduce almost in its entirety, is more instructive than any analysis can be, about the catastrophic dimension of what I have previously called being shut up within the unspeakable. Medical verbalization, unable to circumvent the issue, provides a sort of loud counterpoint to it, which does not seem quite suitable even to its author.

1. *The file* has the following entries: Mme Chicot, maiden name Rebou, Marie-Thérèse. Admitted 2 February 1968. 62 years old. Born in Placé, 22 August 1906. Address: La Roë, La Basse-Bêche. Farmer, married. Deceased: 18 September 1968, of senile cachexia. [The *Larousse* dictionary defines cachexia as a 'general physical wasting and malnutrition brought about by a profound impairment of all the functions'.] Voluntary admission [probably requested by her husband].

2. *Medical hospitalization certificate* established by Dr Lécrivain at La Roë, 31 January 1968: 'patient delirious and anxious' [so one can imagine that at the time fixed by the unwitcher, the witch was seized by a paroxysm of anxiety; her words must have seemed totally incoherent to the doctor, who had her hospitalized for delirium and anxiety in a psychiatric ward].

3. *Immediate certificate of Doctor Sureau*: 'State of acute anxiety, half dumb, stereotyped sentences about her fear, without delirious motivation or explicit objective [the patient, in an acute state of anxiety, repeats over and over again to the doctor that she is afraid, but this in itself does not constitute a delirium]. Probably a case of oligophrenia [i.e. a mental defective] and perhaps a state of reactional anxiety. She is covered with ecchymoses of different phases. Under observation.'

The psychiatrist's first hypothesis is therefore that Mme Chicot reacted out of catastrophic fright to a traumatizing event. He sees the traces of physical harm on her body, and suspects she was involved in some dramatic situation.

Not knowing what exchanges took place between the witch and the bewitched after the woman from Izé operated, I cannot of course be sure that Régnier did not assault her. The fact that the bruises were of 'different phases' might imply that they were caused by something else: for if Régnier had been beating her for several months, he would hardly have needed to invoke a ritual. When a bewitched person reaches the point of fighting physically with his witch, it is because he has given up hope of the effectiveness of any ritual. If this had been the case, I believe that the discourse of the people linked with the bewitched would have been quite different.

4. *Fortnightly observations*: 'Mme Chicot arrived in the ward at 16.30 accompanied by her husband. The patient is agitated, aggressive, she tries to bite [behaviour compatible with the diagnosis of a cerebral incident, which was made later on]. When asked a question she answers by repeating

the last word several times [a symptom, in psychiatric terminology, of 'echolalia' and part of the clinical table of 'idiocy, imbecility, and of some seriously mentally deficient people'.[32] But note, also, that unwitchers often advise their clients, if they cannot avoid talking to their witch, to repeat the witch's last words to avoid letting him get a hold on his victim through the latter's words.] She has a burn on her left wrist and bruises all over her body (especially on her arm). The patient is very dirty. [As the woman from Izé would say: *'If you're too clean, he can get his grip on you'*.]

3 February, seismo. [The psychiatrist was trying to reduce the symptoms, by treating her anxiety with seismotherapy, in other words by electric shock treatment.] 'She begins to scream again towards 1.30 p.m. and goes back to sleep after the injections [. . .].'

On the following days, mère Chicot seemed to be adapting herself to asylum life, the sedatives having taken effect. But she looked terrified, refused any kind of contact and spoke only to say: *'I'm afraid.'* One day the hospital chaplain came to her bedside, and she shuddered and shouted: *'Ah, the black man, I'm afraid.'*[33]

---

[32] Cf. Antoine Porot (1969).

[33] The reader will have some idea of the atmosphere of violence, at least at the imaginary level, in which my research took place, from the story of the chaplain who was murdered by a patient in the following year. The murderer, trying to justify himself, accused the chaplain among other grievances of stealing a book on witchcraft the patient was supposed to have inherited from his mother. The ease with which the murder was committed astonished everyone: the patient entered the chaplain's house and stabbed him six times with a knife (only the last stab was lethal); no one could understand why the victim did not defend himself.

When I heard this story, I could not help remembering that a few months before, the same chaplain had lent me a book on witchcraft (*Les merveilleux secrets de l'Abbé Julio*), without giving me any indication where it had come from.

I was unable to return it to him because my unwitcher, to whom I had shown the book, had quite simply confiscated it: when I took it to her to look at, without even glancing at it, she placed it in a small suitcase containing her small library on magic, saying sharply that she would look at it in her own time. She never spoke about the book to me again, although of course I asked her about it several times. Shortly before the chaplain's death, I decided to buy another copy of it – modern and bound – and give it to him with my apologies as soon as he asked for it. I was never able to give it to him.

One cannot draw any firm conclusions from the story: after all, the patient was raving, the chaplain could have come across the book in another way, and so on. All the same, I felt very disconcerted by the whole matter, for I could not be absolutely sure that I had no part in this mad story. So as not to give it more importance, and to prevent anyone from coming to question my unwitcher, about whom I had to be totally discreet, I mentioned none of this to the doctors in the hospital. But it can be seen that I was caught in an unresolvable contradiction: I was *both* convinced that the murderer had quite rightly complained of this book's theft (how was I then to persuade my unwitcher to give it back to me in order to give substance to my allegation?), *and* that the whole story was quite unreal (here I did not lack rational arguments). My silence in this matter is closely comparable to Mme Régnier's on the death of mère Chicot: Silence alone allows for some uncertainties about the 'real' cause of a violent death to remain uncertain. Which is probably why I had completely forgotten this episode until I found it again in my field notes.

5. *Fortnightly certificate*: 'state of anxiety accompanied by stereotyped talk expressing fear. Still almost impossible to establish any contact. In the last fortnight, she went into a vigilant coma, accompanied with a left hemiplegic motor deficiency; Babinski's sign: neurological recovery is in progress. Probably a state of anxiety symptomatic of arteriopathic weakening. To be retained.'

The psychiatrist now believes she is victim of a cerebral incident, since Mme Chicot had manifest neurological symptoms. And he therefore attributes her anxiety to this. All the same, one does wonder whether the incident itself was not provoked by the terror of knowing she was the target of a ritual calculated to cause her death, as the last document in the file would suggest.

6. *Letter from the psychiatrist to the patient's doctor* who had taken the decision to hospitalize Mme Chicot, dated 20 February 1968 – i.e. shortly after the previous entry into the file.

'Dear colleague,
A recent phone call from an unknown origin (the person gave no name) urges me to give you news of Madame Chicot. First, I would like to say that I have never had any information concerning this patient, although it would have greatly helped, since I found myself faced with a silent, anxious, pantophobic patient. On examining her, we discovered a slight left hemiplegic motor deficiency as well as a Babinski.

From a purely neurological point of view, the patient has improved and has noticeably recovered her motricity, but her mental state has practically not changed at all; the patient continues to express herself with the same stereotyped phrase, i.e. *'I'm afraid'* which she repeats all day long. [Stereotypy is a well-known clinical sign, but the striking content of this one – *'I'm afraid'* – should nonetheless have puzzled the psychiatrist, were it not that he is himself a prisoner of the stereotypical character of medical discourse.] Questioning her is useless and only increases her anxiety. We are probably confronted here with an arteriopathic state, and a possible underlying intellectual weakness.

'You see then, that some information would have helped us.' [The doctor is curious about the origin of her anxiety, which seems so completely to override the coming and the going of a somatic symptom, in itself anxiety-producing].
'I remain at your disposal etc. ....'

The doctor does not seem to have answered this request for information. The patient lived on in this way for seven months, speaking only to express her fear, and refusing to eat until she died of exhaustion.

Part III

TELLING IT ALL

'*You must tell* [the unwitcher] *everything that's abnormal, you mustn't hide anything, otherwise he says he's not capable.*

Louis Babin

The narratives related in the previous chapter have presented for the first time the different protagonists in a crisis of witchcraft. Reading them will have provided a first impression of the violence which is bound to emerge, a violence characteristic of a fight to the death.

In both cases, remember, the investigation had stopped short because there was no position for me in these conflicts, whatever approach I adopted: at most, those involved or their spokesman could tell me the story, but in passing, and without my being able to ask questions.

By way of contrast, the long account in the third part of this book is remarkable in that my interlocutors spoke to me in order to win me over to their side in one capacity or another and whether I knew or wanted it or not. They interpreted my looks, my words or my behaviour as a sign that I was *'caught'* in spells. As soon as they identified me as an unwitcher, they urgently had to *tell it all* to me.

So I enter the account as playing a part in it, often a futile and stupid one, only realizing afterwards what people were trying to get across to me. This time-lag is intrinsic to my undertaking; sizing it up is what this book is about. For if I had been able to know beforehand where the bewitched were wanting to take me, I should perhaps have avoided taking such a risk. Or, if I had really found what I was looking for and if I had been able to understand it sufficiently, I might have followed the example of the ethnographer who, having spent a few years in the field, decides to settle there permanently, and finds it unnecessary to tell anyone of his findings because scientific research appears pointless compared with the fulfilment of his everyday life. For me, who lived through those years in fear and fascination (with what, I had no idea), writing this book seemed to be a suitable way (no more) of coming to understand something.

7

IF YOU COULD DO SOMETHING

When I first arrived in the Bocage, I imagined that priests and above all the diocesan exorcists would give me valuable information on witchcraft. But in contrast to the Parisian exorcist whom I had met before leaving, exorcists in the Bocage make a sharp distinction between spells and demonic possession: only the latter is of interest to the clergy. 'The devil exists', one of them said to me seriously, 'demonic possession exists, but the devil is too cunning to manifest himself in that way [in the bodies of the bewitched]. He would never enter poor peasants: the devil is not interested in peasants. He possesses some people, but not like that.' Witchcraft in the Bocage, he thought, 'is not a matter of religion but a matter of illness', of mental illness. He followed this with a down-to-earth theory of how madness seizes peasants: 'the people here are conditioned: they are poor, they don't eat their fill, they don't eat at regular hours, so in the end they go round the bend'. He proceeded to develop this theory of insanity provoked by the insufficiency and irregularity of meals, and advised me to go and consult the psychiatrists to whom he regularly sent the bewitched.[1] In the neighbouring diocese, the exorcist had recently died; no one had been officially appointed to replace him, but the priest who had temporarily taken on the role of exorcist also sent those who were not relieved by his words alone to the psychiatrist.

So I was directed to the psychiatric hospitals of the region, where I was very well received by the medical staff. They allowed me to examine administrative documents and consult as many patients as I liked.

But for all their good intentions, the psychiatrists could not give me access to what they themselves were barred from: the patients' words. And they wondered how I would manage to extract any kind of talk about witchcraft from peasants who 'have nothing to say but a few confused words', who 'know no more than about two hundred and fifty words', who 'don't talk, but somatize', and who for all that are 'incapable of symbolizing'. One of them assured me that since psychiatry in the Bocage was more of a veterinary art, he always despatched a consultation in ten minutes, and

---

[1] I already mentioned this exorcist on pp. 16–18 and 36, fn. 10.

looked only for clinical signs which would enable him to write a prescription. The patients did not speak to him, but apparently it had never occurred to him that there was a relationship between their silence and the basic principles of his treatment: 'I avoid transference-situations like the plague.'[2] His colleague, the young Dr Davoine, would take the time to talk to each patient, but his section was so overcrowded that these conversations were fairly rare.

Even at the hospital in Alençon, where a few years before a medical student had written a thesis on *Witchcraft and its psychiatric repercussions in the Orne département*, the doctors told me that the phenomenon was rapidly disappearing, as could be seen by such ridiculous vestiges as the exploits of the '*Blonde Lady*' or the sect of unwitchers set up by the 'prophet' of Aron,[3] all of which had been widely covered in the press. They themselves hardly ever heard anything about spells and generally thought that you had to be mad to believe in them. So, when I asked one of them what evidence he had relied on when writing in a patient's file (a schoolteacher about whom I had heard in the field) that she suffered from 'delusions of witchcraft', he gave me this reply: 'when she talks about spells, for us [doctors] it's just one more element in a diagnosis; it's exactly as if she told me about the voices she heard from the planet Mars'. Another doctor listened carefully to the arguments I gave for distinguishing between belief and delusions, and reached the following conclusion: 'All the same, if a person ascribes his misfortunes to witchcraft there must be some ingrained mental illness in him: it doesn't happen to other people [those who have an 'ingrained' sanity].' Doctor Davoine, who was interested in my work and who expressed less dogmatic opinions about the nature of witchcraft 'delusions', thought for a while of collecting clinical data and comparing it with the ethnographical data I was beginning to have access to. In order to secure the nurses' collaboration, he organized a meeting at the hospital, in which he explained our aims. This project, like so many others, was cut short, but for a few weeks the staff became more aware of witchcraft, understood as a symbolic system which could have its own rationale. Everyone was surprised when, suddenly, several bewitched entered the hospital with various disorders. I did not think there were more than there had been before, but that the staff's deafness had previously prevented them from recognizing any references to spells in the ambiguous words of the bewitched: remember that they talk of '*that filth*' or of '*the one who did it*' when speaking of

---

[2] We know that when Freud arrived in New York with Jung in 1909, surprised by the enthusiastic welcome he was given, he said to his travelling companion: '*They don't know we're bringing them the plague!*'

[3] On the subject of this prophet, cf. Appendix 3, 'Robert Brault, "prophet" of Aron', pp. 234–49; on the idea that contemporary witchcraft rituals have died out to the extent that they are now a mixture of tradition and personal extravagance which no longer impresses anybody, cf. Jean Morel, *La sorcellerie et ses incidences psychiatriques dans le département de l'Orne*, thesis for a *doctorat* in medicine, Paris, Faculty of Medicine, 1964, pp. 25 and 99.

their witch; they talk of a '*trick*'* or a '*trick played on me*' when speaking of
spells; or of a '*petit père*' when speaking of an unwitcher; of '*what he had to do*'
when mentioning the unwitching ritual, and so on... One must be willing
to hear these 'few confused words', to realize that they always refer to the
same experience, and accept that they cannot be reduced just to the vestige
of a primitive mentality in the Bocage.

I. A bewitched in hospital

My short collaboration with the psychiatric hospital was a turning point in
my research, because there I met the first bewitched to tell me his own
story. Jean Babin had been admitted to the hospital to undergo treatment
for alcoholism. He himself seldom spoke of the spells he suffered under, but
his wife and his elder brother – Louis Babin, the Régniers' annunciator –
willingly answered the medical staff's questions. During the month that
Jean Babin spent in the hospital, I was busy elsewhere inquiring about the
Saints' cult, but I was given his file, and I met the 'patient' on the day of his
departure.

This document, compared with others in the book, shows traces of my
short-lived collaboration with the hospital staff.[4] I have nonetheless tran-
scribed it here, because apart from the hotch potch which this kind of
document usually contains, it shows a few basic elements of the Babins'
drama which I shall emphasize whenever they appear. The file is divided
into five parts:

1. The usual administrative information: Babin, Jean, entered 18
December 1969; born in Torcé, 17 November 1931; son of the late Babin,
François and of Coquemont, Léontine; married to Letort, Josephine;
domiciled at La Croix in Torcé; has the *certificat d'études primaires*; farmer;
treated by Dr Davoine; sent by Dr Péan of Gastines; admitted voluntarily
[actually his doctor had told him to choose between a treatment for alcoholism and legal proceedings for provoking a fight in a café]; admitted for
alcoholism treatment.

2. Information given to the nursing staff by the patient's brother and
wife: he has been '*ill for ten years*' [i.e. since 1959; this way of dating the origin
of his troubles will be explained later; note, here, that it does not come from
the patient, but from his family]. Babin is 'irritable and quarrelsome,
violent out of doors; he has contemplated suicide, no action. Is depressed. A
big eater, though less so recently. He has nightmares. The cause of his
illness: unhappiness, too much drink, bewitcher. Drinks beer, pernod, and

* In the original text, a *tour de force*: a conjuror's trick, though of course '*force*' is ambiguous
here.
[4] Cf. Ch. 6, pp. 88–91 and Appendix 4, 'The yardstick of truth', pp. 250–66.

goutte.* Has a *certificat d'études primaires*. A good learner [in his schooldays].
Did his military service as a hospital attendant. Cries easily, is euphoric,
then depressed. Antecedents: cousins, treated at the [private psychiatric]
clinic of Dr Naveau in Placé. His mother, depressive. Further information:
has had no sexual intercourse with his wife since their marriage. Has had
trouble with his kidneys ever since. Thinks he is bewitched by a cousin who
wishes him ill and acts on him. The parish priest supposedly came to
witness certain things, for example the growth of a kind of '*cheese*' in the
garden or in the fields, the day after the man [his witch] came by. Is willing
to admit it's a coincidence, but does not seem convinced. [Was the patient
also questioned about his belief, or only the people close to him?] Is under the
influence of his elder brother [this is of course what the nurse thinks, not the
patient's brother or his wife, who, we shall see, always agrees with her
brother-in-law], who firmly believes in spells cast by people who read bad
books. The fact that within the last six years he has lost a significant number
of cattle can only be due to bewitchment. His wife asks us to put salt in his
pocket if he has an '*attack*'; '*it's over in five minutes*'.[5]

3. Fortnightly observations, written by the nurses: 18 December 1969:
'according to his wife, Jean Babin's impotence dates from the time of his
accident [paradoxically, these observations, which are meant to concern
the patient, actually report his wife's words. But, throughout this story, we
shall see that this is a central symptom in the couple's life: Jean Babin's wife
always speaks in his stead.] It seems that the Babin family is easily impressed by witchcraft. The patient as much as his wife and his brother.
There seems to be one particular person, the neighbour [is the witch a
cousin, a neighbour, both at once, or is there more than one witch?] who,
according to them, seems to be acting against them. This would explain the
loss of about forty calves in the last six years as well as the patient's
impotence. M. Babin was quite depressed when he was admitted; he says
he thought several times of committing suicide by self-strangulation.
    19 December: '[. . .] Makes no allusion to his troubles and sees no point
in a treatment. . .'
    20 December: '[. . .] Reluctant to talk about his sexual problems'.
    21 December: '[. . .] Is aware of an improvement since he arrived, says he
is less nervous. Still half-believes in witchcraft [we shall see that Babin's
major difficulty concerning the spells he suffers under is that he '*doesn't much
believe*'] because his cows were struck by epizootic abortions almost immediately followed by their drying up. But he says the scourge has diminished
since he no longer sees a member of his family'. A note in the margin:

---

* *goutte*: 'drop' of Calvados.
[5] According to the nurses, Josephine Babin dare not prevent their cousin from visiting them,
    but when he leaves '*we salt his arse*' she says, i.e. they throw salt in his footsteps to cancel the
    power of any charms he might have laid.

'negative brucellosis tests a few years ago' [an epidemic cattle disease, extremely widespread in that area, which causes the cows to abort and is due to a bacterium, the *brucella*].

22 December: '[...] rational conversation ... does not seem upset by his sexual impotence'.

23 December: '[...] complained of cenesthetic pains of nervous origin, like those he often has at home'.

24 and 25 December: '[...] likes the hospital but is anxious to get back home'.

26 December: 'Is adapting to the ward and looking for some diversions. Does not talk about his anxiety over the 'spells' cast on him by a malevolent neighbour. Easy to talk to, does not allude to his drinking bouts and says he has come here mostly *"for his nerves"*'.

27 to 30 December: 'Good behaviour. Apparently, he has already been treated *"for his nerves"* at Dr Naveau's clinic in Placé. Does not spontaneously acknowledge his alcoholic bouts. Is regularly visited by his family [...].'

1 January 1970: '[...] Readily admits to alcoholic excesses, but claims they have no effect on his nervous state. On the contrary, says he slept better when he drank. Says he comes from a nervous family, and that only professional worries (e.g. harvesting) disturb his appetite or his sleep. Is apparently not concerned about his sexuality or his ideas about witchcraft for the time being, makes no attempt to talk about them [...].'

So one can see that the staff tried to get him to talk about spells, but Jean Babin had decided to stick to suffering from his *'nerves'* or professional worries. When people tried hard to corner him, he admitted that his cows' abortions were abnormal, but was never willing to talk about his impotence. Apart from that, he was a model patient: peaceful, submissive and adapted to hospital life.

4. Note by Dr Davoine: Jean Babin, 38, farmer, 29 hectares [a good-sized farm, slightly bigger than the average in that southern part of the *département*]. Military service in Alençon. Irritable: *'his nerves'*. Insomnia. Fight with a farmer (facial wound). No charge lodged. *'I was half drunk.'* Voluble. Does not drink at home.

Witchcraft: epizootic abortion *'should normally end after three years, and it's been going on for six!'* [Note that Jean Babin dates his bewitchment from six years ago and not ten, i.e. 1964, not 1959.]

'Saw the parish priest of Torcé, who gave him salt which had been blessed. Puts some in his pocket: *'My wife believes in it more than I do.'*

Remember this statement: Jean Babin can afford to say he does not believe very strongly, because his wife believes for them both. Who is the witch? *'Somebody'*; does not specify. Bad books perhaps. He has been told that's the way it's done.

'Bases his conviction on the evidence that repeated mishaps stop when the malevolent person goes away.'

'Not manifestly psychotic, no hallucinations. Family conviction: wife and brother of patient.'

Note, here, that Babin does not seem in the least insane to Dr Davoine, that he admits he believes in spells, but takes refuge behind his wife's belief, which is stronger than his.

5. Note by the psychologist, which she said she wrote for my benefit. 'Saw Louis Babin, who had come especially to talk about his brother with the doctor (absent at the time). He came for the following reason: he fears his brother may not have talked about his impotence and wishes to tell the doctor about it. He would like us to take advantage of his stay here to *'do something'*: he is thinking of a surgical intervention (because of his kidney trouble, perhaps he has a *'jammed nerve'*). If the doctor thinks something can be done, then it must be done *'before he goes back home, if not, once he's back, he'll refuse to come here again'*.

Notice Louis Babin's increasing efforts to cure his younger brother, even without his knowledge, so as to make him capable of consummating his marriage. A few days after this interview with the psychologist, he phoned Dr Davoine and tried to persuade him to undertake a surgical operation without telling the patient: *'we wanted to do it underhand'* he was to explain to me a few weeks later. *'We had to take advantage of the fact that Jean was over there* [in the hospital] *to do it* [to operate on him]. *If not, once he is back on the farm, he gets used to it'*, to his impotence, this irresponsible younger brother. Louis Babin then complains bitterly about the doctor: *'I had a lot of trouble in getting the doctor's number. Then when I did finally get him on the phone, he answered: mind your own business! I asked for an appointment, and he refused to give me one. Was I furious when I came out of the post office! I'm nervous, too, although I don't drink.* [This characteristic *'nervousness'* of the Babins is interpreted as a sign of virility in the elder brother, and as the very symptom of the younger brother's impotence: he drinks, *'he is not master of himself'* etc.]. *If the doctor had been in front of me, I would have given him a piece of my mind: what can those people* [the doctors] *do that we can't do?'*

For, according to Louis Babin, the only thing to be done is to carry out a purely mechanical operation on his brother's body, which would consist in *'connecting up the cord'* which *'broke'* during the accident his brother met with before his wedding. Since Jean is by chance temporarily not in charge of his body because he is in hospital, it is urgently necessary to 'reconnect' his copulating machine: urgent for the elder brother, at least, since unfortunately, Jean, the person most directly concerned in the matter has manifestly got *'used'* to his sexual impotence over the last six years.[6]

[6] Talking to Louis Babin, I was wondering why his younger brother's sexual impotence was so intolerable to him – even more so, it seemed, than to the person concerned – when he

To come back to the psychologist's note:

'Louis Babin is the eldest by three years: he married at the age of 27 (14 years ago) and left home. His brother was already high-spirited and irascible, and although they got on well, they occasionally quarrelled because Jean Babin could not stand being crossed in any way. At that time, he was sexually normal and it was even said he had a mistress in the neighbourhood. Then he married *"late"*, at 33, the twin sister of Louis Babin's wife, three years his senior. [So, the two brothers married two twin sisters, and Jean is the youngest of the foursome.] The wedding took place three weeks after an accident caused by a falling beam apparently followed by a coma. Since then, he has not been able to have sexual intercourse with his wife. The latter informed her brother-in-law and her mother-in-law – who lived in their house at the time – one month after their wedding. He was given psychiatric treatment by Dr Naveau.

'Once you start him off on evil spells, Louis Babin talks interminably, he talks of the persistence of brucellosis on his brother's farm, of cows with no milk etc. He cites examples of evil spell-casters who were punished by spell-lifters. His examples often concern women. [Women unwitchers indeed predominate in Babin's story, although he also consulted three men, who will be mentioned only in passing.]

'To bewitch, people have to be in the vicinity, since one has to *"touch"*. So it is always people living close by who are suspect, neighbours or friends. You learn all this in *"bad books"*. They must not be read. Or else one must be highly educated so as to understand all the words.[7] Otherwise, one is caught and compelled to read on. On some pages, it is written; *"turn the page if you dare, or if you understand"*.

'*"They act through blood"*, those who have strong blood. Or through the eyes: if you can force a spell-caster to lower his eyes, your blood is stronger, you have nothing to fear. *"When my brother sees them"* [for one knows who the evil people are, or at least one suspects] *"he trembles – and then shakes hands with them – that's my brother! I always say to him: when you see them, don't talk to them, and above all, don't shake hands. You mustn't touch them"*. [Louis Babin, a giver of good advice, thus implicitly presents himself as having strong blood, as opposed to his younger brother, whom he presents as both a cowardly and an imprudent man.]

'They take the milk from animals and, through witchcraft, they transfer it to theirs [this is called *"churning the cows"*]. He gives examples of very thin cows, *"real coat-hangers"* who yield incredible quantities of milk, *"it's not*

---

suddenly made a revealing slip of the tongue, saying *'my wife'* instead of *'my sister-in-law'*. He laughed, explaining that Marthe and Josephine are twin sisters. Even so …

[7] This is true also in the imaginings of the heroes of Lovecraft's stories. But having understood everything or having exhausted the system of names, they encounter only the excessive, the incredible, or death. Cf. for example, the short stories in the book entitled *The Shadow out of Time* (London, 1968), notably the title-story.

normal"; and this happened during the war, to people who were known to be evil.

'And they know each other, they meet each other, *"they join forces"*. To fight this, one must call on monks like the trappists because they too are together and *"they join forces"*. [There is a trappist monastery at Entrammes near Laval.]

'To lift the evil spell, one must call on those who know. [Louis Babin is probably talking not so much about the magicians' knowledge as their power. They must *"go everywhere, touch everything"*, it's a long business, *"it takes years"*; but they warn you: *"I must return evil for evil."* Unless one accepts this, they can do nothing. Hence their antagonism to religion. Yet they [the Babins] have a parish priest *"who can do it"*.'

This short report tells us more about witchcraft in the Bocage than many of the folklorists' writings simply because its writer was willing to listen – she was then preparing for a meeting with the nurses – and her interlocutor was determined to convince her of the urgent need to operate on his brother's *'kidneys'*.

From the file as a whole, one can gather the following: Jean Babin has been ill for six or ten years (since 1959 or 1964). The doctor says he is alcoholic, his wife and brother say he is bewitched, but he himself only complains of his *'nerves'* or of insomnia. His family circle is mainly worried about his sexual impotence which has so far prevented him from consummating his marriage and which has two different causes: a recent one, a beam falling on his back – and a long-standing one, i.e. a spell cast on him by a neighbour and/or cousin. His bewitchment also shows itself in a significant loss of cattle, the abortion of his cows, and the appearance of *'cheeses'* on his crops. Nothing is said about how he tried to lift the spell, except that he used, with a certain degree of success, magic protections given to him by his parish priest.

II. She a magician?

On the day that Jean Babin left hospital, Dr Davoine suggested that he introduce us to each other. Before I had time to think how I would present myself, I was installed in the psychologist's office and two nurses entered, on each side of a couple of farm-folk dressed in their Sunday clothes: Jean Babin, stout, red-faced, deferential, his eyes protected behind dark glasses; and his wife, a small dark-haired woman with square shoulders, bright eyes, and a self-conscious look.

The conversation only lasted a few minutes, for a neighbour was waiting in his car to drive them home. Taking the initiative, Josephine asked me in a stiff voice: *'What's it all about?'* I said I would like to talk to them about what I cautiously referred to as their *'troubles'* – when they had begun, if their parents had been *'caught'* before them, if they still had *'losses'* among their live-stock, and so on. . . . '*Ah, about that*', said Jean, '*you'd have to come home: it takes time.*' We arranged to meet the following week, and they left.

I found out later that Jean Babin, on his return from hospital, talked about me to his brother in these terms: '*There's a woman, she's coming to see us, she a magician?*' Several months later, Josephine told me that after this first contact, she said to her husband: '*That woman, I'm sure she deals with them*' [spells]. When I asked her to explain why she was so convinced, she was only able to give me the following enigmatic answer: ''*Twas in your eyes, I mean you had blurry eyes.*' (Throughout this story, eyes – whether they are '*blurry*', '*glassy*', protruding or bulging – play an essential role in identifying the positions of magic '*force*'.)

Later it will be clear that at that point in their lives, the Babins were in urgent need of meeting a magician outside the familiar network. I was so far from suspecting this that I imagined that I would first have to explain the mystery of my presence at the hospital, since I was manifestly backed by the establishment's medical directors. But without my knowing it either, the Babins had from the start placed me in another category, for the simple reason that unlike the doctors and nurses I had not laughed when mentioning spells. Louis Babin, for example, who had not been afraid to talk of his belief, remembered the humiliation he had felt: '*the nurses*' he said '*laughed at me. They talked and talked about them* [about spells, remarkable and unusual in members of the medical profession], *but they laughed at me*'. Similarly, when he met the psychologist: '*I talked about them* [spells] *to this woman, and she laughed. But I went on talking to her and said: you can laugh; for those who haven't been caught it doesn't exist!*'[8]

So I had told the Babins I wanted to talk about spells, I had not laughed, and I had agreed to go and listen to them at their home: signs that I did not belong to the hospital staff who never dared to leave the walls of the asylum, or abandon their protective laugh. For them, the situation was quite clear, anyone who does not laugh about spells is necessarily caught; and anyone who shows he or she occupies a position of power – I was, remember, in a hospital office – has strong blood. Perhaps I was the magician they so much hoped to happen upon.

It was only later on that I realized all this. If I had to summarize my state of mind at the time I would use the term in which an annunciator defines the position of a novice in witchcraft: '*In those days, she didn't think about spells*': in other words, she didn't think she would one day be personally involved.

[8] On the other hand, when Louis and Josephine Babin took Jean to the psychiatric hospital, '*the nurses*', they said, '*wrote down everything we said on a piece of paper, like you. They asked us if it wasn't because of spells.* [As a result of the meeting organized for me by Dr Davoine the nurses had begun to investigate. Unfortunately, as we shall see, it was more like a police investigation than an ethnographer's.] *And when we said yes, they took Jean on one side, Fine and I on the other, and asked us questions, writing everything down.*' The Babins were worried at being separated to be questioned on the same subject; it reminded them of policemen; but Louis and Fine were determined to answer all the same.

Especially as, unlike novices in the Bocage, I had not grown up in that area or even in that country; no grandmother's tale, family table-talk, or witch-craft scandal had started me off in this kind of discourse. Indeed in the preceding six months I had been able to measure my cultural difference more clearly than at any time since my return to France. To give a few brief examples, silence and secrecy were fundamental values in the Bocage, whereas I grew up in a civilization of speech; the inordinate taste of Bocage people for enclosures – in the literal and figurative sense – and their obstinate refusal to owe anything to anyone astonished me: I had been taught that to be sociable is to incur obligations to all and sundry – cancelling them being equivalent to a declaration of war – and never to shut oneself off. Although such stories as the one narrated by Renée Turpin touched me or caused me to dream, I felt protected by the certainty that I was a foreigner whose maiden name, for instance, the village clerk had never been able to write down correctly.

As for my relationship with the Babins, the situation seemed to me to be as clear as it did to them, but in another way: after several months of effort, I had finally gained access to some informants who were going to tell me their own story and talk about witchcraft as from themselves. My status as an ethnographer seemed so obvious to me that for the first time I took notes throughout the conversation, since it had not begun with the usual prelude: *'People don't talk about that.'*

III. The misunderstanding

Three days before, I had written to the Babins to postpone our meeting for a few hours. When I arrived at La Croix, the first thing they talked about was the puzzle that the letter had been for them. They could not understand where I had sent it from, the postmark was unreadable. However much we look, they said, *'we can't see it'*. Indeed one could not see it, and what for me was simply carelessness on the part of the postal service, was for them another sign of my magic *'force'*, although I could not understand exactly in which way: making myself invisible, sending undetectable messages, and so on. I paid no attention to this at the time, but throughout our relationship, they came back to this incident every time they went over the evidence showing I was the magician whom they had obscurely been waiting for.

I introduced myself as I always did: as a researcher from the Laboratory of Anthropology of the University of Nanterre. I was writing a book on spells and I wanted to meet people who had been caught. The only word they retained of this short speech was *'laboratory'* which confirmed the opinion they already had of my *'magic force'*. *'Ah'*, said Josephine, much impressed, *'what we say to you is worked on in a laboratory! This'll help my husband, it'll help him'*, for *'you're for us, you're for good'*. I did not take the meaning of these words at all, for, although I had heard of *'unwitchers for good'*, I was a million miles from thinking that anyone could attribute this role to a person collaborating with the hospital who introduced herself as an academic; it can also be said that I would never have imagined that the expression '*for good*' was being used with precise reference to unwitching, for the simple reason that it had been said about *me*: *you* are for good.

The entire conversation was one long misunderstanding. The Babins told me their story, as they had progressively worked it out with the help of several unwitchers. But I did not then know that it is only to one's unwitcher that one must tell all or at any rate '*all that's abnormal*', and that the Babins were only telling me this long story because they thought I was a magician and they counted on my magic force to remove the symptom which none of my predecessors had succeeded in doing, that is, Jean's sexual impotence. As for me, I was listening to them as an ethnographer, hurriedly noting down their words without asking myself anything, even when their words conveyed a perfectly explicit request to be unwitched. For instance, when Josephine said to me '*If you could do something, return evil for evil*' (we had finished discussing the mawkishness of healers '*for good*'). Having spent six months wandering about in the realm of secrecy, it will perhaps be understood that I was so starved of ethnographical information that I began by stuffing myself, rather than stopping to think about the circumstances which had enabled me to gain access to it. I had just begun to glimpse the depth of the misunderstanding, when, at the end of our conversation, Josephine asked me: '*And how much do we owe you?*' To an anthropologist, this is an astounding question, since she is more used to paying her informants than receiving a fee from them. I should immediately have answered this question by naming a sum of money. But I could not do this, for at least three reasons: (*a*) at the time, I did not have the least idea of an unwitcher's actual fee. Each time I asked someone, I always got the same stereotyped answer: *You gives whatever you like*. I suspected that this convention existed to prevent the unwitcher from getting charged, if the case arose, with illegal medical practice or fraud: since the unwitcher did not ask for anything directly, the sum he received was not a fee but a present, and the annunciator was probably responsible for telling his initiant the magician's requirement, or what the bewitched was supposed to give freely to his saviour. (*b*) But in this particular case, there was no annunciator since the Babins had from the start identified me as an unwitcher. (One could say that the meeting as a whole was a sort of an annunciation of my state as an unwitcher, but neither I nor the Babins had any way of seeing this.) (*c*) Even if I had immediately understood the situation and named a sum of money, its small size was bound to disappoint them, since I was certainly incapable of valuing my capacities as an unwitcher as highly as they did; for example, I would never have dreamed of thinking myself the equal or superior of père Grippon or the formidable Madame Auguste. Making the best of my manifest stupidity, and in a hurry to end the conversation, I mumbled an anthropologist's reply: '*But no, honestly, it's for me to thank you and I am in your debt.*' (My bellyful of information, for example.) It was their turn to be astounded: '*What?*' they said in one voice '*but that's impossible!*' I went on to say that they were helping me to get further with my work and I was grateful to them. But they could not share that opinion: '*Fine, bring a fowl*', Jean ordered his wife. I hurriedly refused, and we parted in total confusion.

IV. Impotent against impotence

To go back to the beginning of the conversation: From the very start, the Babins told me about Jean's sexual impotence, since that was what they wanted me to cure. This symptom had indeed figured in his medical file, but was swamped by a mass of clinical data. Dr Davoine did not seem to be particularly interested in it, since he did not embark on psychotherapy, and was content to prescribe Jean a tonic for after he had left hospital – obviously an illusory kind of medicine so far as getting rid of his impotence was concerned.

According to the Babins, the situation was as follows: in 1964, three weeks before the wedding, a beam fell on Jean's head, after which he was unable to consummate his marriage. In the last six years the doctors had not been able to cure him, had even totally refused to correlate the two events, and the unwitchers had declared themselves impotent in dealing with impotence.[9]

(*a*) A short while after his marriage, Jean spent some time in Dr Naveau's private psychiatric clinic in Placé; he was admitted '*because of his nerves*', because his sexual impotence made him nervous. The doctor examined his genital organs and concluded, according to Jean, that he was normal. '*He said it would come back*', he says bitterly. '*It'll come back, it'll come back, but we've been married for six years now, and we've never had intercourse.*'

(*b*) His mother then consulted a healer. '*The mother gave Jean's photo to someone in Laval*', says Fine '*and the healer said: he's had a trick played on him.*' Note that Jean himself did not go to the consultation but was content to be represented by his picture. It seems they only used this healer for the time it took to make the diagnosis: they never mentioned him again, except to authenticate their position as bewitched by quoting his words.

(*c*) The new parish priest of Torcé said '*he was not strong enough*' to lift the symptom. He suggested they consult one of his friends, a Jesuit from Mortain, but the latter sent a reply from Paris, where he had just been posted, that he could not come.

It is characteristic of the Babins' attitude towards me that at that point in our conversation they did not allude to any other unwitchers they might have consulted: not knowing in advance which category of magicians I belonged to, they were trying not to alarm me, saying that I was '*for good*',

[9] A chronology of the events referring to the Babins is to be found in Appendix 5, pp. 267–71.

and that an eminently moral magician, the village parish priest, had already tried to treat them. It was puzzling, however, that this priest had only intervened the preceding year, in 1969: what had happened between 1964, the year in which the symptoms began, and 1969?

What is certain is that for six years they had accepted the diagnosis of the unwitcher of Laval: since, as the doctors themselves had said, Jean's genital organs were normal, his impotence was caused by a spell.

Who? The neighbour, whom they only named later, but whose identity they had long been certain of, since he had good reasons to punish Jean for marrying Josephine: the neighbour having seduced '*La Rolande*', his young servant, had unsuccessfully attempted to marry her off to Babin so as to have a mistress at hand. '*The neighbour*' said Jean '*took care of his maidservant*' [he slept with her] and, he added, obviously fascinated by the old man's amorous successes: '*He took care of them all*' [his maidservants]. Not that he was particularly attractive, but '*he had a power over them*', a magic power of course, thanks to which he commanded their desire. How did his wife react? '*Oh, his wife is as evil as he is. We know about her life! During the war, did she get it* [pleasure] *with her farm hands! While the neighbour was away* [at war] *she sometimes had five* [farm hands] *at once! Even her father-in-law took care of her*, that woman, avid for sexual experience. To be a witch is to be superpotent, but it also means one is abnormally avid for everything, and one subjects anyone who can be taken advantage of to one's desires, beginning with one's inferiors.

In 1961, the neighbour took advantage of the death of Babin's father to visit Jean several times and to try and persuade him to marry his young mistress, pointing out the advantage of being married in running the farm when he took over, as well as the fact that she had some property of her own and was thus a most advantageous match for him. At first Jean refused to answer, but when the old man insisted, he was obliged explicitly to refuse his offer. The neighbour expressed his disappointment through a pessimistic prediction he made to Babin's mother: '*in four or five years' time, things will be sad*' (on your farm). Three years later, Jean was hit on the head by the beam and became impotent just as he was about to marry his sister-in-law's twin sister.

Since they were talking to an unwitcher, the Babins never thought of clarifying how this prediction (which was supposed to take effect four or five years later) and the two events which had ensued three years later (the fall of the beam and Jean's impotence) could be understood as the effects of the same cause. Neither did they feel the least need to describe the method by which, according to them, the initial spell had been cast; nor how the neighbour had acquired his magic power: I was supposed to know all these things. No doubt a previous unwitcher had singled out this neighbour with them from the list of possible witches; six years of suspicion and then of certainty concerning his supernatural evil dispensed them from having anything more to state than a total contrast between Jean's extreme impotence and his neighbour's extreme potency.

8

THE OMNIPOTENT WITCH

In the narratives in Chapter 6, I emphasized the importance of naming the witch, an indispensable prelude to any unwitching.[1] At the dying man's bedside, Tripier *'all electrified'*, in a way declared himself when he pronounced the decisive words: *'this time he's had it! He won't get over it! This time, Manceau, you won't get over it.'* The first two exclamations seemed to be directed to someone present in the patient's room, but invisible, to whom the witch was summing up the situation; the third formally notified the patient that his last hour had come ... a thing no relation, friend or even doctor would ever do. Grippon, the unwitcher, had then magically attacked the witch: he had not been mistaken about his identity, since Tripier came and begged them to speak to him, was met with silence, and had run to the hospital to have a good length of his intestines cut out. So, naming had been the prelude to a struggle which had brought out both the relevance of the charges and the limits of the witch's magic force, since an even greater force had successfully been opposed to it.[2]

When I met the Babins, they had for a long time been quite certain of their principal witch's identity, but simply naming him had had no effect. Since no unwitcher had managed to check their attacker's *'force'*, they saw it as unbounded.[3] The manner in which they described this person confirmed at least the relative failure of all the avengers whom they had tried to set up against the witch: all Babin's symptoms had been reduced, except for the main one, Jean's sexual impotence which carried with it the annulment not

---

[1] Cf. pp. 74 and 77ff.

[2] In spite of Louise Régnier's constant uncertainties, there is little doubt that in her case things happened in the same way; she simply did not expect the ritual to be so effective as to cause the witch's death.

[3] By which one can estimate the futility of the folklorists' attempts to describe the 'portrait of a witch' without taking into account either the speaker's position (bewitched, unwitcher, alleged witch), or the moment at which he speaks: before or after the nomination, the magic combat, the interpretations of the ritual's effect, etc. . . . Compare, for example, the way in which the Babins describe their neighbour, a fearful witch because he has not been vanquished, and their cousin, who is made to look like a minor witch simply because he has been overcome.

only of his marriage but also of his plans to '*take over*' the tenant farm he had inherited on the death of his father. At the same time, since I was now the person to whom they were talking about their witch, their description implicitly appealed to the magic '*force*' they credited me with.

I. The imperishable bastard

What most fascinated the Babins about this man was that his unnatural '*force*' seemed to protect him against destruction and death.[4] Even the worst illnesses did not kill the neighbour, because he was so immensely wicked that even the supernatural entities were put off, thus ensuring him an indefinite stay among the living: '*The good Lord doesn't want him, and neither does the Devil.*' His worst symptoms were negligible: '*he's ill for half a day, then it's finished*', says Josephine. Her husband adds: '*He often falls off his tractor and stays on the ground, as stiff as anything. His sons come round to shout at him* [they hate him] *and up he gets again*', as if nothing had happened. '*And last year*', says Josephine, '*on Passion Sunday, when your black cow aborted, the neighbours thought he was going to die: two days later he was cured.*' If by chance this omnipotence were to meet the weakness of the bewitched through the mediation of speech, touch, or sight, the clash would produce catastrophic effects on the weak party.

II. Speaking

The neighbour only speaks to the Babins when he is sure of his force, i.e. of the magic effectiveness of his wickedness: '*When things are bad, he doesn't see us*', says Josephine; '*but when things are going well, he talks to us. That is to say* [he talks] *to Jean, because I won't talk to him.*' She knows the dangers of communicating with the wicked and avoids taking any risks. But Jean is forever falling into traps: '*On the eve of Ascension day*', she tells me, '*Jean went to Craon to sell a thirteen-week calf.*' The neighbour had already seized the opportunity to establish an evil contact with his victim: '*Won't you put it by for me?*' [set it on one side, I wish to buy it], he asked Jean, who ignored his offer. But had Babin been a responsible bewitched, he should have made sure he was out of reach of any demands from his witch. To allow the witch to ask a question and on top of that to neglect answering him was to be doubly foolhardy: exposing oneself to contact and provoking the '*evil one's*' resentment. As a punishment, the witch caused the calf's mother to dry up. '*The calf was sold, but the cow dried up*', concludes Josephine wearily. '*She gave two and a half litres of milk after the first meal, then two litres* [instead of twelve to fifteen litres]. '*When the cow dried up, I said: that's it, he's drawn off our milk.*' She does not seem

---

[4] Remember that the theme of immortality or survival was already present in the Fourmond story, although it was treated quite differently: cf. Part II, Ch. 5.

to think it necessary to give any details about how he did it, since she is talking to me, and I'm supposed to know.

The same attacks by the same witch happened repeatedly, but with variations. Take this one, for example: in May 1969, Jean says to me, '*a calf is born, a beautiful one. I want to sell it. The neighbour, who's heard about it, comes to see it but doesn't want it. Two or three days later, we get a "buttering"**[another local name for "*cheeses*"], *and suddenly the calf's mother dries up.*' Having failed to buy the calf, the neighbour is said to '*have travelled by night*', i.e. to have come secretly to Babin's field at night and caused the '*buttering*', a trap to '*draw off the cow's milk*'.

'*Butterings*' grow on crops during the night; they look like mildew or whitish fungus. Under the plant's transparent skin, one can see the tangled network of canals filled with a brilliant white sap. The bewitched assert it is the milk or fatty matter of the dried-up cow: the cow's produce has passed into the plant and the cow is either dried-up or produces milk of quality too poor to be sold to a dairy. To annul the effect of the transfer of animal riches to plants, one must first set the '*butterings*' on fire with petrol or methylated spirit: '*it's difficult to burn all the milk's cream*' said Jean, '*it's difficult to burn, it crackles*'. He thus seems to think that the plant is gorged with the fatty matter produced by the cow and not with its own sap, which would only be figuratively related to the cream. Once the '*buttering*' has disappeared, one must then throw holy water and salt over where it once stood. Some people, though not the Babins, add to these protective measures a magic act of aggression against the witch: when one sets fire to the '*buttering*', '*one must also throw in glass and needles to hurt whoever put it* [the buttering] *there, so as to be stronger*', stronger than the witch.[5]

Whether the drying up of cows takes place directly or through a '*buttering*', no explanation of its mechanism is given to me. When, a few months later, I had become initiated, I realized that in fact no one in the Bocage, not even the unwitcher, has any precise idea about this sort of process. It is simply thought that any kind of contact between the strong and the weak (the '*wicked*' and the good) whether it operates through speech, sight, or touch *provokes a loss of force or of wealth* – figured here by milk – *in the bewitched*. In the case of the sale of the calf, Jean exposed himself to the speech of his resentful witch: which is why the latter struck him metonymically by

---

* *buttering*: my translation for a *beurrée* [*cheese* = trans. of *fromage*]

[5] When asked how to get rid of a '*buttering*', Louis Babin answered like this: '*You have to cut it, but you mustn't touch it with your hands* [to avoid any direct contact], *pick it up with a piece of wood and put it in a tin. I burn it to ashes with nails, with anything that pricks. After that, you must bury it in a corner which mustn't be immediately ploughed.*' While it's burning, one throws coarse salt on it, '*it crackles*'. The witch is then supposed to jump up and down on the spot, like the coarse salt which crackles; he feels assailed by the nails which pierce him and he comes running, screaming that he's in pain. But Louis Babin does not say what his witch actually felt on that occasion.

'*drawing*' riches from the calf's mother. Note, in passing, a series of equivalences which will be useful to us later on:

(*a*) In the case of the witch, there is first an equivalence between force and wickedness (what, then, of the unwitcher, and what is the meaning of the opposition between '*for good*' and '*for evil*' magicians?); second, between '*force*' and sexual potency; and last, between '*force*' and enrichment.

(*b*) In the case of the bewitched, there is an equivalence between weakness and goodness or innocence (what does it mean, then, that the main aim of the treatment is to cure the bewitched of being '*too good*'?), sexual impotence, at least in the present case (in a witchcraft crisis where the bewitched is not impotent, stress is still laid on the abnormal sexual potency of the witch, who possesses all the women he wants); and lastly, impoverishment. We shall be asking what is the significance of this constantly recurring overlap of biological, moral and economic planes, although for the time being all we can do is take note of it.[6]

The Babins also told me that their neighbour sometimes made predictions which, like the one which had clinched the fate of Jean's sexual potency, inevitably came true. For example, he said: '*When the mother* [Babin's] *is gone, the farm'll be sad*'. A little later, Jean '*who's so calm*' quarrelled with her and turned her out of the farm: according to Josephine, her husband '*is no longer master*' (master of himself) from the moment he is affected by the neighbour's overpowering speech, especially when it is spoken in the future tense.

It seems to me that to explain what is involved in these kinds of situations simply by talking of the effect of suggestion is not sufficient, for this is to do no more than give a name to the very thing which is doubtful. According to the victim's version, Jean hears his witch announce an event – formulate a wish? – and he eagerly accomplishes it, all the time being acutely aware of his own strange behaviour: he does not recognize himself in this act, he is possessed by the other, he is no longer '*master*'. Note, however, that there is a glaring discrepancy between the witch's prediction – about some indefinite future in which the event is supposed to take place, in ways which are also not defined – and the haste with which the bewitched brings this event about. After all, Babin's mother could, at some time or other, have wanted to make her home somewhere else, once her son was married; or she could have died of old age. The people on the farm would have been unhappy, and

---

[6] To take the opportunity to reduce witchcraft to a matter of economic determinism, is seriously to mistake what witchcraft is all about. Not that it is not there, or that the Bocage peasants are metaphysical beings floating airily above historical or economic determinants. But it is important to remember here that *one only bewitches one's equals* or one's partners included in a relatively unequal relationship: there must be an *interaction, real or physical* – between the witch and the bewitched, for the discourse to have its effect. If a '*big man*', a rich man, is bewitched, it can only be by another '*big man*' who belongs to the same social set, sees the same people, and so on . . . I shall be dealing with this problem of historical-economic determinations in a forthcoming volume.

the prediction would have come true, but it would have been of no interest to anyone, and no one would have thought of interpreting her departure as the effect of an evil spell. So the touchstone of witchcraft is not so much the simple realization of a prediction or a malediction, as the fact that it is taken up by the bewitched, who becomes the unwilling agent of fate.

III. Touching

On this level – the most direct form of physical contact – the Babins are particularly afraid of shaking hands, such an ordinary gesture of recognition that one usually forgets what is involved: '*At père Paumard's burial*' says Jean, '*the neighbour runs to greet me: how do you explain that? He greets me hardly once a year!*' This unusual handshake clenches a cow's fate: it aborts three days later. Since the neighbour does not usually greet Jean and so refuses to consider him a friend, the fact that he exceptionally greets him can only be because he means to touch him magically: and the first misfortune to occur afterwards is interpreted as a consequence (a predictable one) of his touching. ['*And at the Smithy's*', adds his wife, '*the neighbour, with eyes popping out of his head* [i.e. endowed with attributes of omnipotent magic, bulging eyes] *comes up to say hello*' [a second anomaly, since the neighbour does not usually greet him in public or does not bother to come and greet someone he considers his junior and inferior]. '*Jean shakes his hand and says to himself: "that's it, there's going to be another misfortune."*' [As usual, Jean realizes too late that a handshake can only be a magic touch.] '*If only he'd touched his salt*', she says despairingly, [blessed salt, which Josephine puts in his pocket every day so that he has a chance to annul the consequences of his imprudent behaviour]. '*The next day, he lost the wheel of the distributor* [of fertilizers], *and he quarrelled with a man from Torcé*' [she is implying that he got drunk because he was nervous, having once again been trapped by the handshake]. Jean, who does not like to be publicly treated like an irresponsible boy, minimizes the incident, tells me that he might have lost that wheel in any case, and that '*one mustn't believe in it all, one mustn't get to the point of being credulous*' [I know . . .], but he can't understand why the handshake made him nervous to the point of provoking him to fight: he is usually so calm.

A few days later, Louis Babin told me the following anecdote to explain the drinking bout which resulted in his brother being admitted to the psychiatric hospital: '*Just before going to Mayenne*' [on a drying-out cure], he said, '*Jean meets the neighbour who goes straight up to him and shakes his hand* [once again, the same abnormal behaviour. The neighbour] *looks wild, superior* [he is showing his omnipotence]. *My brother is afraid* [since he was too fascinated to trust in his own prudence or his magic protection]. *I say to him: Don't shake his hand. Run off in the other direction.*' But Jean is not '*capable*' of following sage advice. '*My brother*', comments Louis Babin, '*is afraid*' [of the neighbour], *and the other takes advantage* [of the fact that Jean never dares to refuse his

handshake through which he is given a good dose of magic electric shock].'
After the fatal handshake, Jean began to drink systematically, abandoning
the farm during the day and spending his time in cafés in the district with
drinking companions. *'Before* [the handshake],' said Louis, ' *he only drank by
"novenas"'*, i.e. in occasional bouts. [The expression *'a drinking novena'*, often
used in the Bocage, is derived from *'a novena of prayers'* in which the faithful
pray to God with a special intention, perhaps implying that one seeks in
drinking what one has given up asking of God]. Completely demoralized by
his inability to resist the witch's fascination – and no doubt overwhelmed by
the reasonable reproaches of his wife and brother – Jean preferred to take
refuge in desperate drunkenness, which soon led him to the psychiatric
hospital, of which he has nothing but good memories: there, at least, he was
safe.

IV. Looking

Even more than speech or touch, the witch's look has devastating effects: *'If
I don't have some salt in my pocket'*, says Jean, *'I'm pushed into the ditch every time I
take the car'* after catching the neighbour's terrible look. *'The other day, I just
had time to put my hand in my pocket'* [to touch the salt, for he does think of it
sometimes], *'I was heading for the ditch.'* *'And on the 25th November'*, says
Josephine who keeps a strict account of her husband's mishaps, *'when you
came back to fetch your tools'* [he was already nervous because of this oversight],
'the neighbour was there, on the road, looking at him', she explains to me. *'Jean
lowered his eyes* [which one should never do: it leads to total rout], *and when he
got back to the farm, he had a nervous fit.'* Luckily Josephine was around and she
knew how to calm him: *'With a bit of salt, he got over it.'* The nervous fit can
only be explained by Jean's rout, caused by the staring contest: of course *'he
had been drinking, but he was calm'*, that had not been enough to make him
nervous. And as for Jean's violence and alcoholism, constantly dinned into
them in the psychiatric hospital, well: *'If Jean goes without his salt, he gets
nervous'* and *'nervousness leads to drinking'*. Her husband is suffering not from
alcoholism but from not being *'master of himself, because of that man'* [the
neighbour; note the false precision in naming him, which refers neither to a
name nor to a magic status – that of witch – but to a previous sequence in
the narrative, the object of which is also undefined]. *'We often saw the
neighbour on his tractor, looking to see what was going on in our fields'*, says Jean.
'Each time he looked, I would say to myself: another misfortune is on the way.' And
misfortunes never failed to materialize: the geese were taken seriously ill –
*'one musn't believe in it all, perhaps I would have lost them anyhow, but every time he
looked, something happened'* – the abortion of a cow, a car accident, and so on.
Josephine then summarizes for my benefit the protective measures she uses:

(*a*) *'Never accept handshakes'*, she says firmly. Later on, her brother-in-law
gives me more details: *'I never shake hands because he* [the witch] *tries to touch us'*

magically, whenever an apparently insignificant contact takes place. In any case, *'one should avoid associating with them'*.

(*b*) In the domain of speech, the best way to protect oneself is to never let the witch have the last word: *'If he says hello the best thing is to answer as quickly as possible.'* If he talks to you and you have no answer, at least repeat his last words – even though a passing psychiatrist would interpret this as a sign of 'echolalia'.

(*c*) Again, in the domain of looking: *'If he looks at you, keep looking back at him.'* Josephine, an expert in protective measures announces this precept proudly, adding for the fourth time that she is *'never ill'* or nervous because she always keeps these little things present in her mind.

Thus *direct* physical contact (through touching) must be avoided at all costs, whereas *indirect* contact through speaking or looking, if it cannot be avoided, must be withstood.

At this point, a heated discussion takes place between husband and wife: Josephine maintains that these misfortunes occur because Jean – in spite of the force of his protective devices – is afraid to meet the witch's eye and *'lowers his eyes.'* In a suddenly sharp tone of voice, she orders Jean: *'Never lower your eyes!'* and turning towards me, she explains *'When you don't lower them, you are stronger than they are'* [the witches]; *'my husband lowers his eyes whenever he is in front of the neighbour. I keep telling him: don't lower your eyes! But he lowers them every time.'* Jean mumbles a few embarrassed protests, like a guilty child.

And yet Josephine knows that the witch's force is so much greater that his victim – however he tries to protect himself – is often helpless. Fine remembers one of her parents' neighbours who, having failed to stop his witch with the force of an unwitcher – the witch was always more powerful – finally took this decision: *'If he* [the witch] *comes, I'll kill him.'* When the witch entered the farmyard, the victim's wife and children looked on in silent horror as the witch came forward while the bewitched ran to get his gun. But by the time he had the gun at his shoulder, he could no longer see his persecutor. *'That filth'* says Josephine *'he'd become invisible.'* His force was such that at the decisive moment, he had managed to conceal himself from the enemy's sight.

Jean has a similar mishap, not with his neighbour, but with another witch, related by marriage to the famous neighbour. One day, as he was chatting with friends in the café with his back to the door, Jean heard père Coquin come in. Coquin, *'who hardly greets him once a year'*, adds Josephine, silently came up to him and put his hand on Babin's shoulder. Babin could not see him, but he knew who it was. Summing up all his courage, he told himself that *this time* he would dare to withstand his look Jean suddenly turned around, but the other had disappeared. He remembered his terror most vividly and the moment of utter bewilderment during which he thought he was losing his mind. It was after mass one Sunday; there were many people present; and everyone saw Coquin enter and touch him on the shoulder. Only Jean had not been *'capable'* of seeing him, so overwhelmed was he by his witch's force. *'Coquin, that filth'* Josephine went on, *'has played a few tricks* [of witchcraft] *on my brother-in-law, Monnier'*. Germaine Monnier, one of Josephine's sisters, lives in the village of La Gravelle, where her husband is a shopkeeper: since Josephine is in charge of the family story – we shall see later that her past authorizes her to be so – it will not come as a surprise that this discourse links in a single story her family by birth (and not, for example, Jean's and her present family).

So, Coquin, *'that filthy bastard'*, who had made himself invisible on the day when Jean finally made up his mind to face him out, also plays tricks on her brother-in-law. 'What tricks?' *'His wife always has a backache.'* [Note that the husband is considered bewitched although only his wife is ill: for witchcraft always aims at the head of the family, since the goods and people who bear his name are one with him.][7] *'And then she has diarrhoea, enteritis, so the doctor said.'* [In matters of witchcraft, the fact that the medical world gives a name to an illness does not mean that it is explained: the origin of the illness continues to be a concern.] *'As Monnier doesn't own any animals, Coquin can't do much. So it* [the spell] *gets a hold of his wife'*.

Indeed, it is difficult to see how a peasant could bewitch a shopkeeper, i.e. *'draw'* his means of production, which are abstract entities – except by attacking his body or those of his dependants. Although this is not said in the story, Germaine Monnier probably suffers these onsets of witchcraft because her blood is less *'strong'* than her husband's. The pains she feels are due to the effect of those famous looks from behind: looks which are Coquin's secret: *'On a Sunday morning'*, says Josephine, *'he waits for my sister in the square, and as they enter the church he follows her closely. Next morning, she had a backache.'* Why does Coquin pursue Monnier with supernatural hatred? To get his own back on a more fortunate rival: both sit on the municipal council, but Monnier recently deprived the witch of the position of deputy mayor.[8]

V. A death at the crossroads

It will be remembered that the Babins introduced Coquin while talking about the abnormal power of their neighbour, Ribault. (They tell me his name incidentally, in the middle of a sentence, suddenly mentioning it as if I had always known it.) Apart from the battle of stares which I described above, the Babins did not seem to have any other complaints about Coquin,

---

[7] I shall return to this important notion pp. 196ff.

[8] Like all good initiants, Monnier did not believe in spells before he was caught in them. Josephine tells me she pointed out to him that he could no longer play the sceptic: *'Everything's fine when it's all going well, but when you're caught. . .'*

118

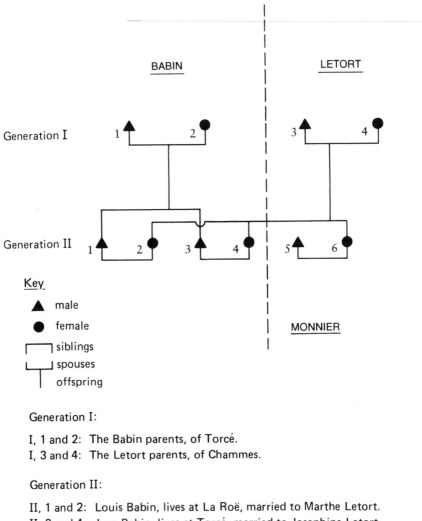

Key

▲ male
● female
⌐ siblings
∟ spouses
| offspring

Generation I:

I, 1 and 2: The Babin parents, of Torcé.
I, 3 and 4: The Letort parents, of Chammes.

Generation II:

II, 1 and 2: Louis Babin, lives at La Roë, married to Marthe Letort.
II, 3 and 4: Jean Babin, lives at Torcé, married to Josephine Letort.
Marthe and Josephine are twin sisters.
II, 5 and 6: Monnier, lives at La Gravelle, married to Germaine Letort.

Figure 3   The bewitched

perhaps because he lives outside Torcé, and so 'is only vaguely interested in its inhabitants, and has quite enough victims, in his own village, La Gravelle, beginning with the Monniers'.

They talk about him at such length in order to prove to me that witches who form an alliance are even stronger: Ribault marries his daughter to the Coquin's son and the marriage creates a natural link between the fathers' respective 'powers': 'there is a family tie, so now they communicate' explains Jean. He is implying that the fathers have pooled their evil knowledge, each one had read the other's 'books' so increasing his power: the wall of secrecy between them is completely down. This communication of each one's knowledge to the other brings out the jealous possessiveness they show toward everyone else: 'Mère Coquin [a witch like her husband] takes her book with her wherever she goes. At night she sleeps with it', says Josephine.

Only one member of the family tried to renounce this evil inheritance: Pierre, the younger son, whose marriage sealed the alliance between the two families of witches: 'Ribault's son-in-law', says Jean 'didn't have that kind of personality [a witch's].' One day, apparently, he wanted to burn his mother's book to suppress his parents' source of magic power, but his endeavour was doomed to fail, since the book is well guarded against such contingencies. From that day on, the brief life of the defenceless rebel was destined to illustrate the invincible power of his kin.

The following diagram indicates the kinship and alliance relationship between the two families of witches designated by the Babins.

To punish his son for this crime, Père Coquin bewitched his cows: 'He drew the cream from his milk', and lowered the quantity to the point where 'the people of Besnier [a local dairy which collects the nearby farmers' milk] told him that if this went on, they would no longer take his milk', i.e. if his milk continued to be so low in fats. Louis Babin was to describe to me precisely how Coquin 'drew the milk' from a cow which belonged to his son: 'Off Coquin goes to see his boy. He enters the stable, and leaning heavily on the animal's behind says: What a good cow!' So the spell consists in words that hint at the father's 'jealousy' accompanied by magic touching. Louis mimes the scene for me, leaning heavily on his elder daughter's shoulders who, in this scene, is given the role of the bewitched cow. 'Once the father had gone', concludes Babin, 'the cow was left with poor milk.' (One might ask oneself what will happen when my interlocutor's daughter breastfeeds.)

Following this episode, the Coquin son goes from one misfortune to another, pursued by his father's hatred: 'he's a handsome boy', says Josephine, 'but he's had a lot of misfortunes: he went to prison, then he was in hospital [also for drying-out], he's married to someone he doesn't get on with, and she had a negro child. Then he began to lose money.' Every time I met the Babins, they talk excitedly about the mishaps of this witch's son.

However, although they know he is innocent and that his very unhappiness is evidence of his rebellion, the Babins are afraid of him as they are of

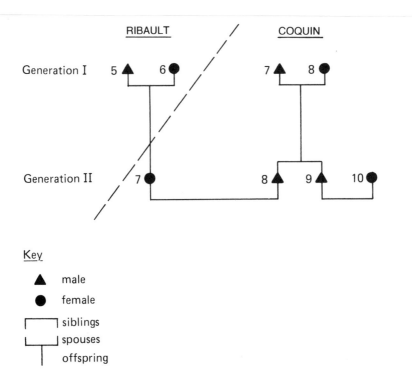

Key

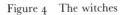

male
female
siblings
spouses
offspring

Generation I:

I,5 and 6: Jean Babin's neighbour, Ribault, and his wife; they live in Torcé.
I,7 and 8: Monnier's rival (II, 5), Coquin and his wife; they live at La Gravelle.

Generation II:

II, 7: Ribault's daughter, born in Torcé, wife of . . .
II, 8: Coquin son, lives at La Gravelle.
II, 9 and 10: The other Coquin son and his wife.

Figure 4   The witches

his father: he belongs to a *'bad'* line so he is an unwitting conductor of his parents' witchcraft, who can use his look, touch and speech to reach their victims.

The following episode will illustrate this. Interested as I was in the possibility of meeting a witch at last, even a rebellious one, who would have reasons to complain of his state and would talk to me of his parents' *'books'* and *'tricks'*, I asked Louis Babin, who seemed well disposed towards me, to arrange a meeting with him: a strange request, which would never enter a local unwitcher's mind. Louis Babin seemed astounded, he interrogated his wife with a look, saw that she was just as amazed, gazed back at me attentively and ended by asking me in a tone of deferential complicity: *'So you've got something with you?'* (a fetish to protect myself, but an incomparably more powerful one than those known to him, otherwise my question would have been simply idiotically rash). Surprised in turn, I moved my head, which he interpreted as assent. His glance rested on my left hand which I had in my confusion stuffed in my jacket pocket. *'You're not afraid of being touched?'* he asked, respectfully obviously impressed by the power I seemed to attribute to this unknown fetish. I could not answer him, and a long silence ensued, during which each person was trying to think faster than the other. The Babins were probably wondering who I could be, to be exposing myself so lightly to the magic bolts of their witches; I, on the other hand, was trying to understand who I was supposed to be in my interlocutors' eyes, and I kept quiet to avoid both disappointing them and lying to them. I had no fetishes, and indeed I had only recently realized how important they were. Although I had no magic protective devices, of course I was not afraid of meeting Coquin's son; but I was quite nonplussed at the thought of the power that my apparent self-confidence gave me in the eyes of the Babins: Josephine, remember, had asked me to *'return evil for evil'* to her witches. Louis, clearing his throat, set out to prove how dangerous père Coquin was, since he had not been overcome even by Madame Marie, who was now dead, having finally *'met her master'*, etc. He then changed the subject, no doubt to give me time to think over my strange request. When I repeated my request the next time I saw him, he had already estimated me at my true level: he asked me how one broke spells *'in towns'*, and I cautiously replied that one *'worked with words'*. This seemed laughable to him: *'That's not what'll lift our spells, ever!'* he concluded. So he refused to arrange a meeting between Pierre Coquin and the suicidal beginner that I seemed to be, with the excuse that at least he was protecting his younger brother.

Eighteen months later, in July 1971, when I asked Josephine Babin once more about the misfortunes of the Coquin son, she did not reply immediately. We had just come back from consulting our common unwitcher, and she waited to see how I would turn at a particularly dangerous crossroads in La Gravelle: *'You're right to be careful'* she approved, *'this is where he killed himself last month.'* His marriage had been going steadily downhill;

Pierre would come home drunk, and beat his children, who had finally been taken away by the Assistance Publique.* After that, he had not stopped drinking until his fatal accident. His wife had immediately consoled herself with another man and had taken her children, including the *'negro child'* of whom one could now say that he was not as black as all that.

Fine told me all this quite calmly, as if it were completely normal for a child doomed to catastrophe to meet it eventually. Her story was counter-balanced by an account of Coquin's other son, who was as much of a witch as his father and whose life prospered. As for me, I was already sufficiently shaken by the unwitching séance we had just come out of: in the warmth of a country dining room, Madame Flora, Josephine and I had been pronouncing for three hours what I could not fail to understand were death wishes. The calm statement which Josephine was now making about this young man's brutal death, the fact that these wishes actually reached their targets, petrified me. I realized that however fascinating witchcraft might be, I would never get used to it, which was where I differed completely from the Bocage peasants. For the moral of the story is that no one escapes violence: he who does not attack automatically becomes the victim; he who does not kill, dies. This had indeed been the central theme of Madame Flora's consultation: (1) As I hesitated to wish for my witch's death, she pointed out that my pains, caused by a recent car accident, were sufficient sign that I was in danger. (2) Josephine, for her part, had taken the formal decision – three weeks previously – to point to the only woman she had ever liked as her witch, and was now wishing her a painful death. Lastly, Madame Flora had told me with sinister joy, that the *'petite mère'* – the old friend who had been doing her housework since she had become an invalid, was dying in hospital, her head shattered by a car accident. I had known the *'petite mère'* for more than a year. Madame Flora would talk to me about her in a friendly manner, and now she had suddenly and brutally turned against her . . . *'the petite mère was jealous of me. And now she's punished. She's had it, now, had it!'*[9]

That one can wish the death of a loved one is a psychological common-place; however, the swiftness with which Josephine and Madame Flora had changed from love to deadly hatred was absolutely astounding. I also had good reason to fear a similar change in my unwitcher toward myself, since she questioned me sharply about a conversation I had had about her with the *'petite mère'* a few days before. I had only asked her some very ordinary questions (how long has Madame Flora been working, and so on . . .) but she took advantage of this occasion to let me know that she knew every-thing, and that she intended to remain the master in our relationship. As a

---

* A. P. National Assistance: here, the section which takes care of homeless children.

[9] The unwitcher is not saying that the accident which befell the *'petite mère'* is in any way related to witchcraft; note, however, that Madame Flora talks of her in the very terms a bewitched would use – the serious accident is a just punishment for her *'jealousy'* – and she does so during an unwitching séance.

punishment, she made me do some menial work during Josephine's consultation, sending me to the garden to look out for any late clients, adding to the little that I could overhear all sorts of disturbing anecdotes about unwitchers who are in fact witches, disguised to deceive their victims. Then, having probably decided that she had frightened me sufficiently, Madame Flora assured me of her protection, wished me luck with my book and invited me to share a copious tea.

This, note, was just an ordinary séance: the bewitched had invoked the death of the witch, and the unwitcher – even if, like Madame Flora, she was *'for good'* – had quietly pronounced death wishes and had not missed an opportunity to reinforce her dominion over a patient. And yet when on the way back Josephine told me about the inevitable death of the Coquin boy I went home in a state of utter confusion, remembering those stories by Lovecraft in which a strikingly similar situation to mine is described: out of curiosity, a person equipped with solid scientific knowledge, usually the narrator, brutally enters another world which his system of references cannot describe or name. Throughout this confrontation with the unnamable, the inconceivable, the immeasurable, and so on, he goes on wishing that this other world – which he now *knows* – could remain nothing but illusion or madness. But his wish cannot come true, and the hero has to accept the idea that he can no longer deny the reality of this other, archaic world, perpetually threatening to invade our civilization. What I had tried to take as stories – those of the bewitched as much as those of Lovecraft – had brutally been brought to bear on reality, and a young man, said by everyone to be doomed, had just died.

VI. Ex post facto

The fact that I was affected by the death of young Coquin – as I had been a few months earlier by that of mère Chicot, by Renée Turpin's story or Marie Fourmond's questions, is in a sense only relevant to my own attitude to the theme of the fight and the kill. I do not think it would be pertinent or interesting to dwell on this longer here – but I shall return to it later – once three points have been made:

1. When one wonders how, in the twentieth century, a normal individual, one brought up in the culture of the Enlightenment, can let himself get involved in the discourse of witchcraft (a question I, like anyone else, asked myself), it is impossible to give an answer by only taking into account the irrationality of this discourse. More precisely, one and only one answer is possible: it entails writing off those who are taken in by it as in the class of backward people, fools or madmen. If, on the other hand, one realizes that witchcraft generates situations in which there is no room for two: in other words situations in which one must either kill or die – and the question of the rationality of the system is considered less important – one begins to understand that anyone can be involved in it.

2. If in my case there was a feeling of adventure and moments of bewilderment in which I was overcome by fear or by what Freud calls the Uncanny, it was certainly not as an encounter with the irrational. It seems obvious to me that if one is trying to match oneself against irrationality one need not travel three hundred kilometers to do so: political commitments and even the most ordinary love relationships give plenty of occasion for it. For me, the surprise and fascination came from finding, in the society of the Bocage, a *symbolic working out* – or an accepted discourse – of what everyone is usually silently struggling with (as well as the situations I mentioned above): the repetition of biological misfortunes experienced as the path to one's own death.

3. I hope would-be refuters will not use the facile argument that I went to the Bocage to encounter my own fantasies. (1) If one can have them at home, why seek them elsewhere? (2) these fantasies are not just mine, which is why they are interesting; (3) I have plenty of others, but I will spare my readers an account of them, so ensuring, by the way, the prolongation of my own pleasure. If one looks more closely, it was the opposite that happened – I did not meet old fantasies, but only the dissolution of a fantasy. From the moment I agreed to talk about witchcraft in my own person, I was, like everyone else, exposing myself to the danger that a conflict between the discourse of witchcraft and the structure of my own fantasies would produce devastating effects. Hence, for me, the vital necessity – and the word 'vital' is not too strong – of having to recognize, sometimes, that a fantasy was operating in a certain situation. But at the same time I had to forfeit the main advantage of fantasies: indeed the only condition under which they can give pleasure is that they must never be recognized as such by the person who is to enjoy them.

These remarks will suggest, I hope, that having powerful sensations, experiencing this sense of the uncanny or finding my subjective landmarks dissolve never at any moment seemed an end in itself: this book is not meant to sum up a 'voyage into the land of the unknown', but to examine *ex post facto*, incidents which I experienced in a confused state, and to clarify what is involved in a witchcraft crisis, i.e. to use the reiterations of the same situation in order to get a better idea of its first occurrence.

On the matter of Pierre Coquin's death, my attitude was always contradictory: (1) the more I saw of the bewitched, the more his fate seemed obvious, since the position of rebellious conductor was literally untenable; (2) the more I asked myself about the reality of witches, the more it seemed to me that the secret of his death would always entirely escape me.

1. Basing myself on my experience as a whole, I now propose to show how the bewitched – together with the unwitchers – imagine the possible destinies of witches' children.

But first I would like to remind the reader that the discourse of the bewitched on witchcraft is the only one that exists – apart from the sceptics described in Chapter 4 – since witches, who never recognize themselves as such, have no position from which to speak. I dwell on this because I myself forgot it when listening to Josephine's account of Pierre Coquin's death; and that is precisely why I panicked. During that consultation, and in the hours following it, I did not doubt for a single instant that the events referred to by the speakers, including myself, which all had to do with car accidents, were realizations of the death wishes which, unlike myself, Josephine and Madame Flora uttered so freely. (This is a striking example of why I was able to consider myself *'caught'* in spells, or, what comes to the same thing, in the discourse of witchcraft.)

Despite the clumsiness of the procedure, I think my points will seem clearer if I distribute the different elements evoked during that July afternoon of 1971 along two planes: on the one hand, the death wish (whether it is or is not acknowledged by the speaker) and on the other, its presumed realization.

THE DEATH WISH	ITS PRESUMED REALIZATION
1.	I recently had another car accident, which left me with neck pains, a topic of discussion in today's consultation.
Madame Flora assures me that my witch wishes my death in a car accident. (This is what she says.)	
For my part, I *know* that naming the person whom she says is my witch, or talking about him, cannot kill him, but *still*, I cannot make up my mind to ask for him to be punished. (Therefore, I do think that naming or talking can be killing, otherwise I would play the game without the least reluctance.)	
2. Today, Josephine admitted that her best friend is her witch, brutally switching from love to hatred and asking Madame Flora for an exemplary revenge.	
3. Today, Madame Flora, without any warning, switched from love to hatred of her old friend, the *'petite*	The *'petite mère'* is dying in hospital, her head shattered in a car accident.

THE DEATH WISH	ITS PRESUMED REALIZATION
mère'. (*I know* that this has nothing to do with witchcraft, but *still*, Madame Flora talks about it precisely in this séance in which Josephine, etc. . .)	
4. Is Madame Flora, furious that I asked the '*petite mère*' some questions about her, also going to change her attitude towards me? Do the stories she told us during the séance mean that some unwitchers are really witches? (*I know* she simply meant to warn me that she alone is master, in our relationship but *still*. . .) Does Madame Flora think I am '*jealous*' of her, like the '*petite mère?*. . .'. . . . or, which comes to the same thing, '*jealous*' of her, as Josephine's witch is of Josephine. In other words: is she putting me on the list of possible witches? Is she signifying to me that she could be my witch? *Who is who for the other*, at the moment between Madame Flora and me?[10]	. . . whose head was shattered etc . . .
5. In the last few months, I have been hearing from the bewitched that there is no place for Pierre Coquin but in his grave.	Pierre Coquin died in a car accident.
6. *I know* that the person who is said to be my witch has never in the least practised any witchcraft against me; *I know* that as such, Madame Flora's rituals cannot produce the smallest effect against either Josephine's witch, mine or myself; but *still*. . ., with all these death wishes floating around. . .	. . . Am I also going to die in a car accident?

Beyond what I experienced in the form of terror and confusion, it seems that the following chain of thought was at play: a man has died, and for months I have been told that death was his only future; he died driving as though he were already in his grave and according to my unwitcher and simple common sense, I am threatened by a similar end. In other words, because I myself was *'caught'* in a series of car accidents – which started with my involvement in witchcraft – the matter-of-fact tone in which Josephine told this story was enough instantly to disperse whatever evidence I had, at the time, to reassure myself that I should not meet a similar fate and that I would be protected by my unwitcher's force or my own vital resources. But I would not have panicked had I remembered that this story was not told, for example, by the Coquin family, but by a bewitched, that is by someone for whom the death of a rebellious conductor is the inescapable end.

Now I can describe the way in which the bewitched imagines the possible futures of witches' children: we shall see how the position of rebellious conductor is untenable. But once again I have to make a preliminary détour, for this idea can only be understood within the framework of a general theory of what I will temporarily call the magic space, for want of a better name.

It is striking that the inhabitants of the Bocage use two different conceptions of a subject's relation to his social space, according to whether or not witchcraft is involved in a given situation. In the first case, they consider that the people and wealth of an individual *are one* with him to the point of declaring him bewitched even though he is not suffering from anything, for example, if his wife is ill: for the spell is pursuing the head of a family, i.e. he who gives it his name. Whatever the target of a spell – a member of his family or some material belonging – it is basically directed at what I earlier called the 'single surface' delimited by the name of the head of the family: all its points hold together, since each owes its location on the surface to this name.[11] If, for example, Josephine's sister-in-law has a backache or diarrhoea, it is only because she is Julien Monnier's wife. We will call this single surface with its solidary points the *set* defined by the name of the head of the

---

[10] Although on principle I chose not to express my moods in my daily notes, I did write on that day how bitter I felt at suddenly being excluded by Madame Flora (I was afraid she would not wish to see me any more). I also wrote that if that happened, I would go and *'denounce'* her to Jean Lenain, whom I had not yet met, but whom Marie Fourmond had told me about. When I met him, it is odd, to say the least, that he immediately thought of accusing Madame Flora of bewitching me, although I talked of her in highly favourable terms. But then I could not have had an ordinary witch (a neighbour, etc.) and Madame Flora had been unable to cure my neck pains. When Lenain proposed to attack my witch, I had of course *'forgotten'* the consultation of July 1971, and at that time my relationship with Madame Flora was idyllic. In the context I have just described, however, my refusal to start a cure with Jean Lenain can be seen in a quite different light.

[11] Cf. pp. 5–7 and 65, fn. 2.

family, and the points its *elements*. Each time there is any witchcraft, and whoever is concerned (bewitched, unwitcher or witch), it is this representation of a solidary space which holds. On the other hand, in any ordinary situation – or to speak like the Bocage people, when there is nothing *'abnormal'* – the persons and material goods marked by the name of the head of family are considered separately. Julien Monnier, for example, would then simply say that *his wife* is ill and not that *he* is bewitched; or, if he himself has diarrhoea, that he is *ill* and not *bewitched*.

Let us now turn to a witch's family: his children are included as elements of the set delimited by their father's name. Since père Coquin is said to be a witch, his children are included in a witch set. (Similarly, Germaine Monnier or Josephine Babin are, as wives, included in a bewitched set.)

According to what the bewitched say – and one must remember that only they and their unwitchers talk about witches – three possibilities are open to witches' children. These possibilities are to be understood in terms of the relation between an element and the set it belongs to.

(*a*) The child reads his parents' books, is fascinated by them, and in turn becomes a witch: since witches are never enemies of each other but necessarily accomplices – and this is an absolute rule – the child-witch thus increases the magic force-potential of the set to which he belongs. This is the case, for example, with the Coquins' eldest son, who, I was told, *'is as big a witch as his father'*. (Curiously, books of witchcraft are apparently accessible to the child, who thus freely submits himself to the family destiny.) Similarly, Jean's cousin, Gaston Chicot became a witch after his parents had been initiated.

'The Chicots knew a woman, an old mère who had books.' They read them, but Louis Babin, who reports the anecdote, wonders how they managed to do so, since *'père Chicot didn't know how to read'*: apparently, books on magic are such that they can be read by someone who is illiterate.[12] *'Chicot saw one when he was fourteen; it said: turn the page, if you dare . . . but me, I don't want to see any of those books'*, concluded my interlocutor, as was to be expected. He is telling me that he intends to stay on the side of the bewitched. Ever since his cousin *'saw'* these books, *'every time he comes back* [to La Croix], *something happens the next day'*, says Jean: a cow dries up, a tool is lost, and so on.

This situation, which I will call *'like father, like son'* is illustrated in the schema below: a witch set in which two elements (father and son, for example) are endowed with a magic force; the latter invests at least two sets of bewitched. The profit from this investment goes to the witch *set*, and not to the sole witch since the latter is always solidary with his set.[13]

[12] I often heard this said. For example, a bewitched complained to me of the duplicity of her witch, who was so uneducated that she asked her to write her letters. After an unwitcher had at last revealed her witch *'in the great mirror'* – in a basin filled with water on which there suddenly appeared the image of this woman who got her naïve victim to render her services – the bewitched was astounded to see the illiterate woman warming herself on a bench in the sun reading *'a red book'*.

[13] The schemata here are taken up again and developed, pp. 199ff.

Schema (a)
Like father, like son

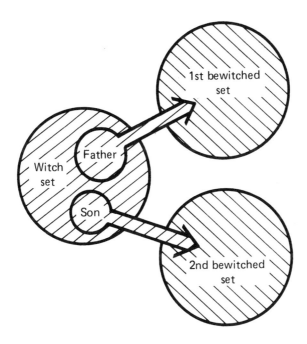

(*b*) Still according to the bewitched, it can happen that the child is totally uninterested in his parents' witchcraft; he can declare, for example, that he wishes no harm to anyone. But – and the bewitched always specifically emphasize this – whatever a person's subjective feelings, he is nonetheless '*caught*' in the definition of the set to which he belongs. As uninterested in spells as the child (or anyone else carrying the family name) may be, as unenvious of other people's riches or unwilling to obtain them magically, the witchcraft of his set is not uninterested in him. The genealogical tie constitutes a privileged contract which he cannot break, for one neither chooses one's parents nor the definition of the set to which one belongs: witch or bewitched. Even if the son has no subjective complicity with his father – the bewitched give many examples of such cases – he carries the witchcraft with him, since he belongs to the same set or family. Whether he wants to know about it or not, the son benefits from his father's plunderings, even if he himself does not exercise any magic power – in fact he has none, not having read the '*books*' – and the power of the witchcraft runs through him to reach his father's targets. While the bewitched consider him to be totally subjectively innocent, they are at the same time careful to protect themselves from him: the looks, words and touch of a witch's son are thought to be dangerous, for the innocent are used by the guilty as unwitting conductors of the family witchcraft. The bewitched say that these conductors '*pay for their father*' when the unwitcher, not '*strong*' enough to overpower the main source of his client's misfortunes, nevertheless manages to hit an element of the witch set. The subjectively innocent son is indeed more vulnerable than his father, since he has no magic force in his own name, and is only protected by that of the set to which he belongs. In Chapters 9 and 10 there are two examples of an unwitting conductor, involving first the child, then the sister of a presumed witch.

(*c*) In the third and most dramatic case, two possible fates are foreseen for the son who attempts to destroy his family's witchcraft books.[14]

On the one hand, the rebel is bewitched by his witch parent, which is equivalent to saying that he is partially excluded from the latter's set and is considered a non-relative; note that the witch set does not lose anything through this exclusion, since it pumps the vital force out of its bewitched relative.

On the other hand, the rebel is used nonetheless as a conductor of the set to which he continues partially to belong, or which intersects with his own set.

---

[14] These remarks are only valid for the child who wishes to destroy the books while his parents are still alive or in full possession of their '*force*'; the bewitched claim that a witch's child can destroy the books without incurring vengeance if he does so immediately after the witch's death, before an inheritor, who would already have read them and would consequently be endowed with magic force, arrives to take possession of them.

Schema (b)
Unwitting conductor

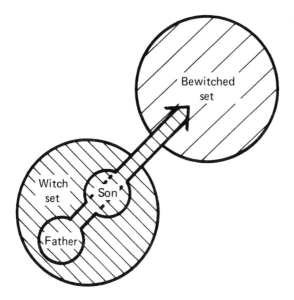

Schema (c)
Rebellious conductor

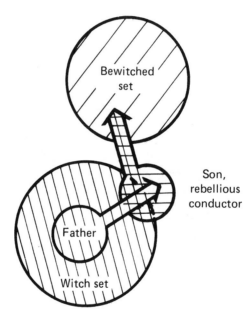

The weaponless rebel's attempts to revolt are doomed to failure, since not having read the 'books', he possesses no magic force. His vital force is then quite insufficient to overcome his family's magic force, and one can hardly imagine him turning to an unwitcher for magic force and defence, since a witch's child is always at least partially included in a witch set: in this respect, he remains, in spite of himself, a conductor of his family's witch-craft. Even more than a simple conductor, the position of rebellious conduc-tor brings out the alienation of an individual in relation to his kin, i.e. to the set which includes him and seals his fate with its sign: if he comes out of it, as Pierre Coquin attempted to do, it is only to die.

2. When I heard about the inescapable death of Pierre Coquin, I was thus 'caught' in the discourse of the bewitched. So convinced was I of its reality that I did not even wonder whether there was any other way of 'reading' this drama. It had been enough that my subjective landmarks should have dissolved on one occasion in which the possibility of my own death had become a fact. It was as if, for a few hours, I had accepted as the only possible truth the affirmations of the bewitched, according to which, in spells, one can never expect any sort of statement from witches, since they never admit being one, they pretend they do not believe in it all, and they treat those who accuse them as backward people who would be better off applying the rules of the experimental method more rigorously. Or again, they claim that the accusation is the result of a miscarriage of justice: witches exist, but for one reason or another, the divination ritual which caused *them* to be accused of witchcraft was wrongly carried out. For his part, the accused person considers himself totally innocent of the repeated misfortunes against which the bewitched is struggling. About the destiny of his children he has nothing to say, since he is not himself a witch.

The bewitched interpret these words as a sign of the witch's basic hypocrisy. However, the latter's protests must be recorded, and I would like to note here the respect in which, to the best of my knowledge, their claim to innocence is always well-founded.

The bewitched party accuses them of possessing magic books and of using them to come and lay charms in their victims' homes by pronouncing special incantations. I think these accusations are imaginary for the follow-ing reasons.

(a) Of course there are books on magic which one can inherit or buy cheaply: The *Grand Albert* for example, has recently been re-issued in paperback.[15] But whenever the bewitched give a precise description of the book, it is full of inaccuracies. For example, they maintain that all these

[15] Note, however, that only an ethnographer would be eccentric enough to buy a recent edition of witchcraft books which, in local talk, are necessarily (1) 'ancient', (2) circulated without involving any kind of monetary transaction (one obtains them by inheritance, borrowing, copying them by hand, etc.).

books are marked on the bottom of each page with the inscription: '*Turn the page if you dare, or if you understand.*' The formula in fact varies according to the speakers – who also insist they have never seen such books – for example: '*Turn the page, if you dare*' or '*if you can*' or '*if you wish*' and so on . . .

Jean Babin in particular told me: '*If I had wanted to, I could have had some*' books on magic. Indeed, a small unwitcher '*for good*' who '*was weakening*' had asked Jean to become his partner, in order to pass on his stock of secrets. He offered to show him the books, each page of which – according to the unwitcher – had the reference: '*Turn the page, if you are capable.*' Jean refused, as should any bewitched who intends to go on calling himself so. We shall see later that this episode was also intended to convince me that under no circumstances could Jean be called a witch.[16] It is also striking to see the insistence with which those around him define him as '*not capable*' of anything: of consummating his marriage, defying his witch, looking at him straight in the eyes, or of being master of himself. For an unwitcher to have proposed to associate himself with him, Jean must all the same have given the impression that he had 'strong blood'. But he says it was a misunderstanding: how could he, who is '*not capable*', undertake to read a book with the inscription: '*Turn the page, if you are capable*'? So Jean obstinately refused to have the least access to magic force, even '*for good*'. '*I said to him: I don't want to see those books.*' So when he talks to me about these books, it is from hearsay.

I personally have never seen a book on witchcraft with any such inscription, either in the Bocage or in the Bibliothèque Nationale.[17] What is most likely is that unwitchers – who claim that they alone can read such books without becoming witches – are the source of all this 'information' given by the bewitched. Convinced that any book seen in the house of a possible witch is a book on magic, the bewitched always take advantage of the smallest clue to support their interpretation.

So, when I asked Louis Babin how one recognizes a witch, he talked of some '*odd people*' into whose house he had gone unexpectedly one day: their

---

[16] Cf. pp. 180ff.

[17] There I consulted the following editions of the magic spell books most often mentioned in the Bocage:

(*a*) the 1703 editions of the *Grand* and *Petit Albert* (*Les admirables secrets d'Albert le Grand*); 1772 (*Secrets merveilleux de la magie naturelle et cabalistique du Petit Albert*); 1815 (*Nouvelles découvertes des secrets les plus curieux tirés des secrets d'Albert le Grand*); 1850 (*Admirables secrets du Grand Albert*); 1865 (*Le Grand Albert et ses merveilleux secrets; Le secret des secrets de Nature*); 1866 (*La grande et véritable science cabalistique ou la sorcellerie dévoilée*, a volume comprising, apart from two *Alberts, Le Dragon Rouge*): 1895 (*Les secrets admirables du Grand Albert*); and 1920 (*Les admirables secrets de la magie naturelle du Grand Albert et du Petit Albert*).

(*b*) For *Le Dragon Noir*, the 1896 edition (*Le Dragon Noir ou les forces infernales soumises à l'homme*, Paris, Chamuel, 122 pp.), the first page of which has the following warning: '*Do not read this book either at night from 1 to 3 and 7 to 9, or at midnight*'.

(*c*) For *Le Dragon Rouge*, the 1521 edition (*Le véritable Dragon Rouge, ou l'art de commander les esprits célestes et infernaux, suivi de la Poule Noire*), 1522, 1823.

son was reading '*a bad book*'. Louis Babin deduced that the book was bad from the '*oddness*' of the boy's parents, i.e. he suspected them of being witches. The mother then told her son: '*pick up your book*' and when the child had left the room, '*she stared at us*,' says Louis, and adds this enigmatic statement '*everyone makes money as best he can*'. For him there is no doubt that this sentence refers to the existence of the '*book*', and he repeats it several times to let its meaning sink in, then adds: '[witches] *makes a lot* [of money] *in one go, they make a lot in one go, and they make three or four times more butter than they should*' [than the state of their cows would lead one to expect].

(*b*) Witches are supposed to practice special bewitching rituals: tearing out tufts of hair from the cow which is to be dried up and pronouncing incantations over it, burying a charmed toad in front of a house or a stable, hammering charmed steel nails into walls and so on . . . No one has ever seen a witch in action: a bewitched person may have seen his neighbour with cows' hairs in his hand, but who can tell which cow they belonged to and whether there had been any incantations? Who can tell, moreover, whether it was to bewitch someone else or to unwitch himself? A bewitched may have found a toad buried under the doorstep of his house, but he only knows it was charmed by deduction; if, for example, when he has burned the toad, his symptoms disappear. When the bewitched evoke the catastrophic effects of their witch's looks, words or touch, their conviction is in the end based on the notion that the witch is a witch because he possesses '*books*' and that in them there are precise recipes for bewitchment rituals. It seems to me that even if an alleged witch had good reasons to feel guilty of the '*jealousy*' attributed to him or the '*force*' of his words, looks, and touch, and if he also had good reasons to feel threatened by the unwitcher's '*force*' opposing him, he is at least innocent of performing any bewitchment rituals.

The reader will remember that like everything else I have recounted in this book, these statements are based on my personal experience, a necessarily limited one. I nevertheless got the impression that there are no witches actually performing the bewitchment rituals attributed to them, or that they are extremely rare.[18]

Let us now attempt to formulate a few hypotheses about the possible cause of Pierre Coquin's death.

1. His father and father-in-law are held to be witches, but, even if one were to admit that they are '*jealous*', '*bad*', '*strong*' or terrifying in the eyes of the Babins, it is hardly likely that they laid any charms on the territory of their supposed victims.

[18] I was only able to collect three cases in which a bewitching ritual was almost certainly performed: curiously, in each case, it was a matter of an eccentric unwitcher at the beginning of his career, who was giving himself publicity – '*I'm going to bewitch you*', etc. – in order to terrify the people around him. The third was so convincing that his victim killed him with a gun.

2. Pierre Coquin occupies a key position in Josephine's account because his marriage links two different sets of alleged witches in a single story: that of his father, at La Gravelle, and that of his father-in-law, Ribault, at Torcé. This tie reinforces the impression that the force of witches is unlimited, especially as in the present case it is said to operate against the wish of the person who constitutes the link.

3. In the local newspaper, his death was described as an ordinary traffic accident caused by a young drunkard. In the general opinion of the village (excepting the Monniers) it is seen as the sad end of a misfit who had been going downhill for a long time. In the opinion of the bewitched, his failures are seen as the result of rebelling against his parents' witchcraft; and his death as the blatant illustration of their power.

4. According to the Babins – who, I repeat, are my only source for this story – père Coquin had always hated his son Pierre. He was constantly beating him; later on, he did not allow him to take up the profession of his choice, and openly preferred his eldest brother. These statements seem perfectly plausible, if not true, for such situations are not rare in the Bocage. One can thus suppose – for no one will ever know the end of the story – that this young misfit died one summer's day on the road to La Gravelle, the victim, anyway, of a family discourse which had written him off since childhood.

9

TAKING OVER

Each time Jean Babin recounts his misfortunes, he gives them a precise date: '*They began when I got married*', he repeats again and again. What this means is that he only began to take his bewitchment seriously from the moment when his own body was affected, and not just the running of the farm.

More discerning, Josephine refers to another event which took place at about the same time as her marriage, an event of much greater import: for the chain of misfortunes to begin, she tells him: '*you had to take over*' the farm left vacant by the death of Babin's father. Most witchcraft stories – all one needs is to remember those I mentioned in Chapter 6 – orignate at the particularly dangerous moment in which, in the space of a few months, a son buries his father, takes over the tenancy in his own name, gets into debt for a quarter of a century with the credit banks and takes a wife to help him in his tasks. Babin's father died in 1962. Jean inherited the tenancy at All Saints in 1963. According to his statements, his troubles began two months later, in January 1964. When he got married in April of the same year, eighteen months had gone by since his refusal to marry '*La Rolande*', and the death of his father and six months since he had inherited his property. When Josephine came to live on the new farm, the animals had been prey to strange accidents for three months.[1]

I. Inexplicable misfortunes

At this point in the Babins' account of their misfortunes, they never link a mishap to the presence of their witch: they are more eager to relate the first appearance of the '*abnormal*' on their farm, at a time when their case had not yet been diagnosed by any unwitcher. They are content, therefore, simply to enumerate a long series of misfortunes on the simple basis that these misfortunes resisted any attempts to explain them rationally. In other words, they are asking me to take over the annunciation made to them six years before by the healer of Laval.[2]

---

[1] Appendix 5 contains a chronology of the events related by the Babins.

[2] Cf. p. 180. This diagnosis was confirmed in November 1969 by the new priest of Torcé who said to the Babins: '*Someone is playing tricks on you.*'

So, Jean's first cow aborted for unknown reasons: *'I'd bought it with confidence, from a friend. How do you explain that?'* The bewitched always question anyone like this to whom they are telling their story, but it would be a mistake to understand this question as requiring an answer: if Jean had not been certain that, like himself, I classified these events as a series of inexplicable occurrences, he would never have told them to me: *'My friend never had any of his cows abort whereas with mine it happens all the time.'* Since abortion-provoking brucellosis is an epidemic disease, Jean's first cow could not have had it because it came from a perfectly healthy batch. Something else caused it to abort, but what? *'The vet couldn't understand it.'* [As might be expected, positivist knowledge is baffled by spells.] Since then, several cows have aborted in a similarly incomprehensible way: *'why have some cows not once aborted in six years* [for in the case of an epidemic disease, all the cows should have aborted sooner or later] *and why have other, vaccinated cows* [against brucellosis] *aborted five or six times? The vet himself vaccinated them, and he can't explain it.'* As soon as an animal aborts, they send for the vet: *'You again'*, he says discouraged, *'I can't understand it.'*[3]

In the same year in which Jean *'took over'*, several calves died for unknown reasons, as well as fifteen rabbits, *'does'*, i.e. particularly valuable animals.

Other events occurred, which indicated the presence of a witch, but in a covert way: *'And when the black cow had the milk fever'*, said Josephine to her husband, *'we heard a door* [of a car] *banging, but there was no one around.'* Another symptom of bewitchment, this time absolutely indubitable and which lasted months: *'At night, you could hear someone walking in the attic.'* Who is *'you'*? The Babins, but others as well: *'a man who worked by the day* [he lived in their house but was paid as a day-labourer] *and who slept under the attic said it was impossible to sleep there'*. Everyone heard the noises, *'even mother, who didn't believe in it.'*[4] *'As long as we were up, nothing happened, but as soon as we went to bed and turned off the light'* the strange din would begin and Jean would say to his

---

[3] At least, that is what Jean Babin said. The vet, whom I went to see, considers that the breeding situation at La Croix is perfectly clear: Jean's cows have always been affected by brucellosis. The only solution – and Jean refuses to carry it out – is to slaughter all the cows, disinfect the cowsheds and bring in new, carefully chosen animals. Jean shrinks from the expense – he is already heavily in debt over the purchase of the cows – because he refuses to take the diagnosis of brucellosis seriously on the ground that all the cows have not aborted, which, according to the vet, meant nothing special. Similarly Jean's argument that it cannot be brucellosis since the abortions had decreased in the previous three years, is apparently untenable: as long as the source of infection has not been eradicated, any animal can fall ill again at any moment. In my opinion, one would still have to explain why, ten years after Jean settled, his breeding-stock maintained itself in spite of the source of infection in his cowshed, and why the abortions indeed almost totally ceased in the last eight years, i.e. since the intervention of the unwitchers.

[4] Although Babin's mother *'doesn't believe'*, hearing of her son's sexual fiasco a month after his marriage, she took his photograph to a healer in Laval. She seemed to believe in spells and in this healer's diagnosis, but not that Ribault was her son's witch. *'Mother'*, says Jean, *'has no confidence in that. When I talk to her about it, she says: You shouldn't talk about it, the neighbour isn't*

wife: '*That's it, there he is, one of them is snoring.*' I decide to ask an ethno-grapher's question: '*one what?*' The couple look at each other, searching for an answer. After a long silence, Jean says: '*I was much too frightened to go up.*' One would have to be capable of facing the snorer to define its nature. But who would ever take such a risk, since the statements of people who were not even '*caught*' in spells – Babin's mother, the day-labourer – confirmed that it was not an auditory hallucination?

Even Josephine, who was not troubled by any physical symptoms, and who always used her protective devices with such presence of mind, could hear this thing breathe, snore and walk up and down the attic. '*Some of them even danced*', she says, convinced that she had heard more than one. The day-labourer wondered: '*It was as if someone was walking up the stairs.*' As soon as the labourer was in bed, he did not dare get up again until dawn, he lay there in bed, riveted with fear: he could hear this thing prowling endlessly between his masters' room and his own. Jean tries to describe the phenomenon precisely, miming someone with a heavy, rolling gait. '*As soon as we were in bed, it walked like this. One night they made such a row in the attic, it sounded like a tremendous clanking* [or iron scraps being dragged across the floor] *but there was nothing up there: the attic had just been cleared*' (the Babins had emptied it so as to eliminate any possible noise at night).

Josephine claimed that these kinds of mysterious incidents occur in all witchcraft stories. She remembered, for example, that on the farm where she was employed as a young girl, '*the rabbits ate each others ears*', which led to an extraordinary sight in the rabbit-hutch: '*earless rabbits*'. The vet could not do anything about it, but the '*woman from Izé*' soon put an end to the aberration. Once the rabbits were cured, however, the ducks were afflicted by an unknown ailment: suddenly, they would '*spread their wings and die*'. Narrating the event, the couple mimed these dying ducks with their heads falling to one side, as if they were drunk: '*Luckily, I spotted it in time*', says Josephine who is never short of magic remedies. '*I put salt in their beaks* [they came back to life, but] *ten more minutes, and it would have been too late.*'

II. The other witch

When Jean Babin took over his father's farm, it displeased another witch, related to his mother, who also began to '*work*' on him. Despite the precept which says that witches '*communicate*' and '*join forces*', the neighbour and Jean's uncle seemed to have operated independently; moreover they were opposed by two different types of unwitchers: the neighbour by unwitchers '*for evil*', although the Babins carefully avoided telling me about them for

---

capable of such a thing.' Later on (p. 186) we shall see that she had excellent reasons to believe that Jean's troubles did not begin with his marriage, and that they have a long prehistory: if it is to be taken into account, then the neighbours alone should not be incriminated.

some time; and the uncle by an unwitcher *'for good'*, the new priest of Torcé, whose methods and effectiveness are described in detail to me.[5] The Babins' account at that moment thus seems to consist of a demonstration in two parts of the fact that they really are bewitched.

(*a*) Ever since Jean *'took over'* his father's farm, *'things are abnormal'*.

(*b*) Some symptoms have already been relieved by an unwitcher *'for good'*: had they been caused by normal factors, they would have resisted any magic treatment.

What the Babins had already told me about the omnipotence of Ribault contained an appeal to my own magic *'force'*. Having completed their demonstration, they were to spell out this appeal. Let us therefore return to this minor witch whom the priest of Torcé quite easily mastered.

The Babins did not on that day give me any satisfactory explanation as to why their uncle Chicot – (for he has the same name as the Régnier's witch) – should want to bewitch them, except that Jean's settling on the farm seems to have brutally deprived the uncle of a few material advantages. Before the marriage, the young man's aunt – a sister of Babin's mother – sometimes came to work at La Croix as a paid day-worker; on such occasions, she would take home various farm products – milk, eggs, apples, flowers, and so on. She counted on her sister's generosity, then mistress of the farm, to improve her everyday life and to give herself status with the nuns of the Saint-Michel de Craon clinic, where she worked, by bringing them armfuls of flowers.

To simplify things, I have indicated the relations of kinship and alliance between the people concerned in figure 5.

Several months after my first meeting with the Babins, Josephine told me the prehistory of their misfortunes and I then learned that the Chicots were closely involved in it. But at this point in the story, the Babins describe the relatives bewitching them in a language comparable to that used to speak of their neighbour, providing me with evidence that the Chicots *'play tricks'* on them and that they themselves consider them to be witches. The worst seem to be *'the aunt's man'*, because, as we shall see, his death was particularly striking and his presence always produced sensational effects. The aunt would probably never have been considered a witch if she had not been married to this man – if her marriage had not included her in that set: they simply say that her presence causes damage, but they never describe her as

---

[5] Remember that the Babins constantly contrast the new priest of Torcé, who arrived in 1968, and who believed in spells and unwitched them, with the old priest they unsuccessfully consulted in 1965 and who made fun of them. I met the new priest when I already knew he had unwitched the Babins, but he refused to talk about spells, claiming very seriously *'I don't believe in those things.'* His reaction hardly surprised me, for I knew that the chaplain of the psychiatric hospital, who heard about his practices from the secrets Louis Babin had told the psychologist had gone and told the bishop...

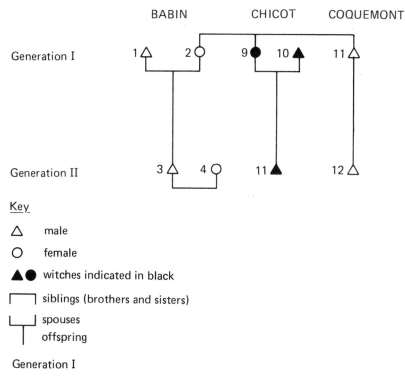

Key

△   male

○   female

▲●   witches indicated in black

⌐   siblings (brothers and sisters)

⌐   spouses
     offspring

Generation I

I, 1: Jean Babin's father, deceased.
I, 2: Jean Babin's mother, née Coquemont.
I, 9: Aunt Chicot, wife of . . .
I, 10: *The aunt's man'*, Chicot, Jean's witch.
I, 11: Uncle Coquemont, innocent witness of his brother-in-law's
       witchcraft.

Generation II

II, 3 and 4: Jean and Joséphine Babin.
II, 11: Cousin Clément Chicot, unwitting conductor of his
         father's witchcraft.
II, 12: Cousin Coquemont, innocent witness of his uncle's
         witchcraft.

Figure 5   Relationships between witches and bewitched

'*bad*', or as endowed with omnipotent attributes. As for their cousin, they tend to think of him as an innocent conductor of his parents' witchcraft.

(*a*) '*When the aunt came to work for the day*', says Jean, '*she would draw a lot of milk*' [milking Babin's cows. Their production was therefore normal before the young man '*took over*'] *and now, each time the aunt or her son come, the cow dries up*' as soon as they have turned to go home.

(*b*) '*It'll be a year in November*,' says Josephine, for whom keeping a strict count of their mishaps is an essential part of the struggle against spells, '*the black cow was about to have her calf. One of the calf's feet was out* [so, a difficult birth]. *I said: that calf is going to die, I put salt on its back* [the cow's] *and it gives birth*.' When a magic protection enables one to accomplish a difficult birth, it means that the obstacle was not a natural one; indeed, the '*aunt's man*' (uncle Chicot) had come to La Croix not long before.

(*c*) Similarly, once, after the Chicots had visited them, they found fifty '*dazed*' geese [they mimed the scene of their ailing animals to help convince me.] '*They were turning around in the farmyard. The vet didn't know what was wrong with them. We put salt in their beaks* [a particularly difficult operation], *we had a few masses said, and they got better*.' So they were ill because of a spell, otherwise the salt and masses would have had no effect. In any case, the oddness of the symptoms proves it was a spell, or to speak in the deliberately vague terms of the bewitched that '*something's abnormal*'.

(*d*) One day, says Jean, '*uncle came to pick up eating apples. Next day, I found three butterings, one of which didn't touch the ground: it didn't have any roots* [therefore butterings are not ordinary plants], *they were placed on the edge of pattes-de-chats* [ground ivy].' '*They were thick*, [he shows me his finger-joint], *one could see the cream running through them*.' This rootless plant is to them such absolute evidence of the omnipotence of '*the aunt's man*' that they were not afraid to mention the episode in the psychiatric hospital.[6] Since Jean finds cream in a '*buttering*', there must be less milk in one of the cow's udders: '*meanwhile the cow dried up*'. I tried to get a precise description of the drying-up process, but there is nothing to describe because it is always the same: '*at one meal, the cow has plenty*' [of milk, before the appearance of the '*buttering*']. '*After that, it has less. At the next meal, it has very little. After eight days, it's dried up*.' '*The aunt's man*' specialized in sending them '*butterings*': '*in '68, we got more than a hundred*'.

They did not invent these '*butterings*', for others saw them: for example their neighbours '*friends, people who help each other with work*' and who are the more reliable in that they do not believe in spells. When Josephine showed them the strange sight of these '*butterings*' sitting there on top of the flowers like a detached part of the cow's body, and when they saw the cream running under the transparent skin of this unknown plant without roots, they stared with their mouths open '*completely flabbergasted*'. That witchcraft

[6] Cf. p. 100.

is concerned is proved by the fact that the sight of *'butterings'* automatically causes astonishment, which would not be the case with ordinary non-magically invested fungus.[7] Similarly, Louis Babin would say that *'my mother's brother'* [uncle Coquemont, cited here as an impartial witness] *likes the farm. He comes here one Sunday with his boy'*, sees a *'buttering'* and rushes to meet the people coming out of church to tell Jean about the strange event which took place while the farm was unguarded. For witches also take advantage of moments when they know that the *'masters'* of the farm are away at a mass, a wedding or a funeral, to set charms or cause *'butterings'*. *'I have seen some good ones in your garden'*, he says to Jean. *'He too'*, concludes Louis *'was completely flabbergasted'*, stupefied by this evidence of witchcraft.

(*e*) They then consulted the priest of Torcé – it was in 1965 – who agreed to come and bless the place. But his benediction had no effect, for he did not believe in spells: *'he said they were old wives' tales'*, Jean said sadly. *'We said to him: wait until you yourself are caught, then we'll see what you say'*. When the *'woman from Izé'* (the Babins are careful not to name her yet) told them how to get rid of their *'butterings'*, Josephine was in constant need of holy water. *'Does she drink her holy water?'* asked the priest ironically in front of a group of the faithful. He was accusing her of getting drunk on it, and it is understandable that the joke was not appreciated by a drunkard's wife: *'Can you imagine?'* she says, *'a priest saying that!'* If priests themselves turn misfortunes and encounters with the supernatural into jokes, if they have become such *'unbelievers'*, what is the world coming to?[8]

I then ask the Babins what, in their opinion, these *'tricks'* consist in and how the witch operates these transfers of *'force'* or wealth. The couple look at each other, searching for an answer, make confused gestures and Josephine finally declares that nobody can know, but that *'the priest,* [the new one, who

---

[7] Lovecraft often describes the feeling of uncanniness produced by the sight of an apparently totally familiar object in which just one detail escapes our usual perception: it is a stone, but it shrinks; it is sculptured, but the geometry of its lines has never been seen before; it is coloured, but in an undefinable shade which is not part of the spectrum, etc. . . The hero then remembers that he read about this in cursed books, which he thought had been written by madmen (e.g. *'The Necronomicon'* of the mad Arab Abdul Alhazred). The rest of the narrative shows they were telling the exact truth. Each time a bewitched person is thus confronted by this uncanniness, witchcraft narratives, previously considered the product of a mad imagination, take on for him the character of truth. Although of course I tried to do it, it is quite useless to submit to positivist criticism the situations in which this feeling of uncanniness emerges.

[8] It is hardly likely that priests were ever over-enthusiastic about peasant witchcraft. But there was a time, which any middle-aged, church-going Bocage inhabitant remembers, when all the saints were mediators between God and believers and this was seen as a normal way of practising one's faith; it was permitted to make requests about oneself to the supernatural agencies; when the priest believed in saints and in the Devil, and peasants could allow themselves to believe in witches without being labelled mentally deranged but only superstitious; when the bishops did not check priest-unwitchers and encouraged the distribution of medals, holy water and blessed salt; when the profound distress of the bewitched was responded to by religion and not psychotherapeutics.

'believes'] says that he [the witch] *probably enters the garden, and when he says: your garden is beautiful, then the spell is cast'*. This answer immediately suggests three points: (1) the bewitched cannot know how the witch operates because an accusation of witchcraft is always a *post facto* deduction, relating strange or catastrophic events to the supposed behaviour of someone acting secretly. Furthermore, once one *'suspects'*, i.e. once one has named the witch, the bewitched's basic rule is to stay away from his witch. The best way to protect oneself from his looks is not to look at him. Consequently, only the unwitcher, whose job it is to confront the witch, can say anything about it. (2) The bewitched learn most of what they know about witchcraft from their therapist; the annunciator gives them the rudiments of an initiation which he himself has learnt from his unwitcher: most witch stories also come from the same source and are part of what the unwitcher teaches his patients. (3) In the present case the priest's explanation implies that the witch's nature is sufficiently evidenced by the open expression of a wish or by the explicit recognition that something belonging to the bewitched seems to the witch a desirable thing.

(*f*) *'Last year'*, says Josephine, *'at the Assembly*, he* [uncle Chicot] *shook hands with you: next day, there was a buttering in the garden.'* She's once again asking me to bear witness to her husband's imprudence, since he did not think of protecting himself either from his uncle or from his neighbour, and, convinced that she can count on me as an ally, she begins to upbraid him: *'Why did you go and shake his hand? You know perfectly well it would cause a misfortune!'* He, as sheepish as ever, mumbles that as soon as the *'other'* looks at him he forgets to protect himself; well, and that's just when he shouldn't, remarks his implacable wife. Even if he could, he explains to me, it wouldn't have helped: *'the aunt's man was so strong that some people were paralysed because of him'*.

(*g*) An essential proof that the Babins are bewitched, and by their uncle, is that the steps taken by the priest ended both the strange phenomena and the visits from their relatives.

The priest blessed and sprinkled with holy water the house, stables, animals and people; he distributed *'a handful of medals of the miraculous Good Virgin and of Saint Benedict'*, the saint said to be effective against witches.[9] A few were put in the cowsheds and in the poultry-yard, some were worn by each person, and holy water was habitually used at the least sign of anything *'abnormal'*: *'I always have a flask of it, always'*, says Josephine who had no intention of being caught off her guard. Masses were said for ten

---

* Assembly: assemblée: the name given to the parish saint's feast day, and a local festival.

[9] Three Benedictine monks one day discussed in my presence the credit which should be attached to the medals of St Benedict and the exorcising prayer accompanying them. The first, mature in age, found the practice 'right'; the youngest said it was 'superstitious'. The third, an old man who had been a missionary in the Far East chided the younger man, who blushed scarlet: 'What! the text was signed by the bishop of Le Mans and you find it superstitious?'

francs *'so that things would get better'*, including one to St Sebastian, the patron saint of farmers. Lastly, Jean's nervous fits were counteracted with salt: according to the intensity of the fit, either he had just to carry it in his pocket or he had also to touch it. Thus, *'the other day'*, says Josephine, *'Jean got nervous twice*, but he thought of touching the salt, and *'it didn't last'*. Salt was regularly put *'in the bottom of the milking-machine'* so that the milk would be sufficiently rich in fats, and it was also placed *'on the back of a cow giving birth'*, so as to avoid any accidents. Note that the bewitched and his animals are treated in the same way because they are included in the same set and threatened as a whole by the witch.

'*From the day the priest came*, says Jean, *uncle never came back, nor aunt. She can't pick flowers to give the nuns anymore, something is stopping her.'* Even *'aunt's son, Clément, doesn't come any more. Before, he would come all the time, and each time something went wrong the next day.'* Ever since the priest put medals at the entrance of the pathway to La Croix, Clément Chicot *'passes by, but cannot enter: he is prevented by a force* [that of the blessed medals]. *He was never able to come back.'* He is a nice boy too, the Babins like him, but like all unwilling conductors, he is dangerous. Now he is the first to be hit by the magic *'force'* of the priest's protection. The Babins remark on the fact that his life is a series of misfortunes: *'he is probably paying for the others'*.

Thanks to the steps taken by the priest, in the last few months *'things have been quiet'*. The cows rarely abort, milk and eggs are produced in normal quantities; the terrifying noises in the attic have ceased. (Only Jean is as impotent as on his wedding night, for the priest, like so many others, said to him: *'I can't do anything against that.'* But Ribault is responsible for that symptom.)

(*h*) Lastly, the uncle's unusual death is a positive sign that he was indeed a witch: *'He died in an odd way'*, after a prediction had been made, says Jean. The scene took place in the café of Torcé, on the busy market-day. Among the customers were uncle Chicot and his two accomplices, witches like him, and his wife's lovers: *'they took care of her'* at least he presumes they did, for a witch automatically has a huge sexual appetite. In comes a *'stranger'*, a man from somewhere else whom no one had ever seen before, who was never to be seen again, and who seems to have existed only to utter the predictions. Josephine looks at me and remarks: *'Perhaps it was someone like you, who came to study spells.'* This is followed by a long questioning silence on the part of the couple, but I am too astonished to know what to say, for it is clear that this stranger, who is perhaps *'studying'* spells is nothing less than an avenger who arrives at the exact moment to put things to rights through his overpowering words. Jean clears his throat and continues his narrative. The stranger goes up to the café owner and says to her, pointing at the three men: *'there are some odd people here, I don't like them at all.'* For a stranger to identify three witches in a crowd where he is not supposed to know anyone at all, for him to dare to upbraid the villagers in the village café where conflicts are usually neutralized, and for him to permit himself to base his judgement on his personal displeasure, can only mean that he really feels very sure of being in the right, or in any case of his *'force'*. Especially as he begins to utter predictions about these *'odd people'* whom *'he doesn't like'*.

'The one who lives at the top of the hill will be dead within a week.' This was uncle Chicot, who indeed lived *'on top of the hill'* and who died within the predicted time, without failing to observe the rule which holds that his *'force'* would become visible: *'When the aunt's man was near dying, his eyes were bulging out of his head, the evil was working on him'*, he was displaying the signs of his omnipotence.[10]

'The one who lives on the outskirts of the village will destroy himself.' (To 'destroy oneself' is the usual expression for suicide.) When a few months later the man killed himself, not without experiencing some final pleasures – (he was *'replacing'* the deceased Chicot at his wife's side) – he did so in a way which caught the imagination: instead of hanging himself from an apple tree or an attic beam, or drowning himself in the big pond of Torcé, the usual forms of suicide, he shot himself with the aid of an ingenious mechanism which enabled him to die in bed, wrapped in his blankets.

'As for the third who lives at the crossroads, it's difficult to kill him off', said the stranger finally. This *'third one'* says Jean, is an old man. *'The Good Lord doesn't want him, and neither does the Devil.'* Like the Babins' neighbour, he is resistant to all catastrophes: *'last year, he was about to die, but now he's walking about again as if nothing had happened'*.

This episode raised many questions, but I did not dare risk any because the Babins were manifestly asking me to fill the position vacated by the stranger. The fact that they found it unnecessary to make any comment was sign enough that they believed the predictions had caused the events announced. In such perilous circumstances, even when one comes from a civilization of speech, one thinks twice before taking any steps. Especially as Josephine, summing up her husband's misfortunes, had asked me: *'if you could do something, return evil for evil'*.

It is important to give the context in which this request was uttered. Reeling off the sequence of inexplicable misfortunes, Jean had come back to the symptoms immediately following his marriage: *'My nerves would jump around of themselves in my arms and the whole of my body'* he says to me. To illustrate this symptom, he mimes a sudden nervous twitching which jumped in his hand when he placed it, for example, on his biceps. He had been terrified by the fact that he could no longer control his constantly agitated *'nerves'*. He had gone to ask for help at the private psychiatric clinic of Dr Naveau, with whom he was vaguely acquainted because he had once

[10] An additional proof, if one were needed: *'When the aunt's husband died,'* says Josephine, *'everyone laughed'*. Cf. pp. 162–7: – 'A meaningful laugh'.

visited an aunt there. He had not been afraid to talk of his impotence, but the doctor had given him the familiar disappointing answer.

Josephine had then spoken in her turn, reciting once again the list of their misfortunes; but this time, because it was about Jean's body and his impotence, she had suddenly lost her usual self-control, her confident tone (*'I'm never ill. . .'*) and had shown by her tears how she too, was affected by the spell: *'if it had been just the animals,* she lamented *'we would have been unlucky.* [*'unlucky',* remember, is the diagnosis the bewitched himself makes before the annunciator] *and would have endured the illnesses* [of the animals]. *But that he should be ill, that we cannot have intercourse!'* What is unbearable and a sign of witchcraft, is the transition from the animal series to the human one, and the constitution of a single surface exposed to the witch's blows. Turning to me, she concluded: *'if you could do something, return evil for evil . . .'* Of course, since the priest's coming, things had been *'quiet'*; the Babins had an impressive paraphernalia with which to combat the animals' ailments and Jean's nervous fits, but his sexual impotence, that vital symptom so closely related to the *'taking over'* of his father's farm had still not been lifted.

10

TO RETURN EVIL FOR EVIL

Now that the crucial words had been let out and the Babins' demand formulated unequivocally, their talk proceeded by flashback: in witchcraft, any episode one mentions necessarily refers to something which happened before, since the spell was always there.

The reference-point in the Babins' talk is their appeal to the *'woman from Izé'*, who died the previous year but who lives for them in so many signs they see in me. Before her, however, there was the *'woman from Alençon'*. She too was called Marie; she advised Jean about his marriage, and engraved on his memory the pessimistic prediction which was to take effect at the time when they came upon me; there was the priest-doctor who cured Jean of the ailment which had prevented him from getting married, there were six unavailing unwitchers, some of whose words were remembered; and lastly, there were the spells which in the past had been cast on Josephine's parents – also on the occasion of a wedding, that of her elder brother. These spells had been promptly lifted by the *'woman from Izé'*, except for a warning from the witches as to the sexual identity of the man their daughter would marry.

Once we had finished unravelling these skeins, however, I failed to notice that what was missing was their point of origin; and when I reached it twenty months later, I was not sure that it could not itself be traced back to an even earlier origin, whose effects over the bewitched would be still active today.

Talking about the prehistory of these spells, and having myself been closely implicated in their workings, I must emphasize that in spite of its richness and ramifications, this account is probably only a fragment of a story which will never be completely known. All the same, I do not think that I am going against the precept that the ethnographer should report only well-documented cases. Indeed, I wish to seize the occasion to point out its limitations in the case of witchcraft, where any story necessarily runs on into an indefinite recession of origins. What is more, the account is only addressed to someone who, at a give moment, is in a position to put an end to it. If he cannot do this, which is what happened to me, and later to the unwitcher whom I had introduced to the Babins, he has to resign himself to the fact that just as there was a before to the account, so there will always be an after, although it will never be the same person who is invited to hear it: soon a new listener will be chosen, who, like his predecessor will become co-author of the account and in whose presence the pauses will be different because he will be asked to operate in another way.

Renée Turpin's narrative reported in Chapter 6 showed how a witchcraft story can be considered to have come to an end, although this is of course never quite true – *'the less one talks about it, the less one is caught'* – since the solution for the bewitched starts a different crisis and story for the supposed witch. The long narrative in this third part on the other hand shows the way in which speech is organized for as long as the spell has not been lifted and the main symptom not reduced. If the Babins finally managed to find the efficient unwitcher they seemed to be so obstinately looking for, I do not doubt that the narrative of their misfortunes would change radically: several episodes would be considered relevant from the point of view of the effects of the unwitching. The fact that the Babins' story is much more complex than the others does not mean that I think it is exceptionally representative of the universe of discourse on witchcraft: like the Turpins' story, it illustrates one of its particular modalities, and analysing it requires me to give even the minutest details of what I was told and asked.

I. Madame Marie from Alençon

When the Babins asked me to *'return evil for evil'*, I was so astounded by their request that I answered with a question: 'But haven't you been to see someone? [an unwitcher]'.

'Yes, we asked the woman from Izé to come. As soon as she entered the farm, she said: it's too difficult, he [Jean] *is caught too tight. There's more than one* [witch]. *It's too tangled up. The woman was shaken, she trembled like this'* [they mime the unwitcher shaken by the witches' force like a poplar-tree in a storm].

Jean stopped talking for a moment, then continued:

'Well, before that we called on a woman from Alençon, Madame Marie, she was called...'

This 'before' was in 1965, a few months after the wedding. Jean had met Madame Marie six years earlier: as a young man, he was covered with ulcerated eczema, he had it *'all over my body'*, it came over him *'especially at the changing of the seasons'*. *'Someone'* had given him Madame Marie's address, and he had gone to see her at Alençon to ask her to cure him. She had looked after him with devotion for a whole month – *'Jean loved Madame Marie like a mother.'* – She gave him *'salt baths on his stomach and back.'* She had not been able to cure him, but what she said clearly indicated that she related this symptom to Jean's chances of marrying.

In the following year, in 1966, the priest of Torcé – the first, the one *'who didn't believe'* in spells – invited a priest to preach the lenten sermons in his parish. This man – *'who had been a doctor before becoming a priest'* – was surprised that Jean, a healthy man and a good farmer, was still a bachelor at twenty-nine: *'Why aren't you married?'*

Babin's mother replied that he suffered from eczema, and no medicine had been able to heal it. *'Come back and see me'* said the missionary. And he began to treat him with prayers and a pinch of yeast every morning before breakfast. A month later Jean was cured. The priest *'didn't want any money'*, but Jean managed to make him take a small gift of five francs.

Note that the priest established an unequivocal relationship between the disappearance of this symptom and Jean's chances of getting married. It seems to me that there are two reasons why he was more effective than *'the woman from Alençon'*: on the one hand, Jean always preferred to confide in priests rather than in women; on the other, the priest limited himself to curing the physical symptom, and was careful not to interpret it in any magic context.

According to Louis Babin, the *'woman from Alençon'* had predicted to Jean that *'you'll fail every time you count on succeeding'*. That is why she had made him a solemn recommendation: *'Jean, if you take over, if you marry, I want you to come and see me before nine months have gone by.'* Louis commented on the warning in these words: *'It's because she knew the spell would start again.'* So, six years before Ribault cast a spell on Jean's sexual potency, someone had already bewitched him, and the symptom – ulcerated eczema – had something to do with getting married. But Jean never talks to me about this because he *'doesn't much believe'*, in spells, according to Louis.[1]

Jean waited to be completely overwhelmed by misfortune before consulting Madame Marie. *'He went to see the woman who said: Jean, I told you so!'*

One night she came to La Croix. Like Marie from Izé later, she was shaken by spasms when she crossed the farm threshold: *'She said there were several spells, in this direction and that they had caught tight, that they had a history to them'*, said Louis. In this way, he was giving me a hint, though a cautious one, that Jean's misfortunes had not begun with his marriage and that the spell had a prehistory; but I was not yet able to understand this at the time, although I did write his words down in my notebook.[2]

Jean claims he hesitated to ask this woman to be his unwitcher because

---

[1] It will perhaps be remembered – cf. p. 99 – that in the psychiatric hospital in 1969, Louis and Josephine had said that Jean had been ill for ten years, i.e. since 1959: were they talking of his alcoholism, for which he was in hospital, or the psycho-somatic effects of a spell?

[2] Throughout my stay in the Bocage, I wrote a diary of the events I was involved in, being well aware that it would only be thanks to this kind of a record that I would one day be able to make scientific what I experienced as an adventure. Whatever happened, I shared my time between conversations and writing these notes; I soon made it a rule to write less about my moods than about the native discourse including silences, slips of the tongue, repetitions, hesitations, and so on. . .

she seemed '*odd*': first, she looked 'fast', with too much make-up '*all that plaster on her face*'; moreover, she was '*protestant, divorced, it was too much*'; and lastly, says Josephine: '*she ate like a horse: she would sit there at table, like a queen in all her finery as if we owed everything to her*'. Of course, this is all being told to me when I am being asked to become their unwitcher, to show how much my own attitude of reserve is appreciated: according to the Babins, I am exactly the opposite of that town-dwelling unwitcher, since I don't eat much, I'm quiet, I '*look sad*', wear no make-up, and am incapable of taking money or even a fowl. Note all the same that Madame Marie had not in the least seemed '*odd*' to Jean when he asked her to cure his eczema, and his present description of her is simply a way of justifying his refusal to take her on as unwitcher; perhaps because he was afraid that her greed and provocative outfit meant she was an eccentric unwitcher. Louis reports the interview like this: '*She had taken a fairly large amount, thirty or forty thousand* [old francs = c. £30–40 at current rates]. *She would have to come back several times, she said: there are spells in all directions. They hesitated, then they felt disgusted*' and did not call her in again. '*The fact is she was asking for a lot of money and she wanted them both to wear a diamond. Oh, Fine would not have minded, but Jean found her too expensive.*'[3] She seems to have been impressed by the size of Jean's herd, and had not realized that he was '*not quite the master*' of his cattle, since he had acquired it on borrowed money. '*She was asking for too much money*', says Fine, '*two or three hundred thousand*' [old francs]. This is indeed expensive.[4] But after all, the Babins told me they had been paying that much each year for the last six years to the vet. The unwitcher tried to convince Josephine: '*If Jean would listen to me*', she said, '*it might come back* [his sexual potency] *because he still has healthy organs.*' But Jean refused, and as she left the Babins she made a pessimistic prediction, the effects of which were to weigh continually on their lives. '*If you don't do anything*', she said, '*you'll only remain married for six years.*' Note that this diagnosis gave them the chance of calling in other unwitchers, and they did not fail to use it, even if the results were relatively unsuccessful.

Even though, at least in principle, Jean '*doesn't much believe*', he then entered into a state of desperate drunkenness. Whereas '*before, he only drank by novenas*' he began to get systematically drunk, abandoning the farm for days and leaving Josephine in charge of the entire herd. However much holy salt she put in her husband's pockets, '*to prevent those harming him from making the spell worse*', he nonetheless sent his mother away from the farm, so making one of Ribault's predictions come true: '*When the mother is gone, the farm will be sad*'. Even today, he cannot explain why he did it: every time he

---

[3] Using a diamond as a magic protection is the mark of an unwitcher who is a stranger to the district, probably a Parisian.

[4] As for the payment of the unwitcher, I found there were two rules: either he asks for a lot of money, or he is extremely cheap. In both cases, it seems to me that the price asked is unlike with ordinary economic exchanges: either unwitching is almost free, or it is exorbitant.

thinks about his decision, he is seized by an uncanny feeling. The period immediately following this fiasco with the *'woman from Alençon'* was marked by an accumulation of misfortunes of crisis proportions: loss of animals, drying up of cows, *'butterings'*, car accidents, breakdowns of farm machinery, and of course the persistence of his sexual impotence.

When in December 1969, Jean was admitted to the psychiatric hospital, this was also triggered by a tremendous bout of drunkenness. He told me that despite the *'woman from Izé's'* reassurances as to the duration of his marriage, he kept thinking that she had just died, having finally *'met her master, who did her in'*, that is, a witch who had worsted her in single combat. Consequently, the prediction of the *'woman from Alençon'* was once again pressing, if it had ever been less so: in a few weeks the six fatal years would be up, which is why Jean suffered from insomnia and drunkenness.

One can also understand why the Babins so readily took me for an unwitcher when they met me: they were at a critical point with regard to the prediction of the *'woman from Alençon'* and they knew that Jean's continuing impotence endangered his marriage with Josephine. That is why they at once talked to me about this symptom, speaking of their sexual misfortune with deep disturbance. Josephine spoke about the annunciation of this still unconsummated marriage in the same terms as an unwitcher would use: *'it's deliberate. They* [the witches] *don't want us to stay together, that's what it is.'* Several unwitchers had lifted various spells and even killed a witch, but since Jean was still impotent, they were afraid their marriage would not last after the month of April 1970, which explains the particular urgency of their appeal to me.

II. Madame Marie from Izé

Since the negotiation with Madame Marie from Alençon had failed, the Babins consulted several unwitchers: *'Jean was like a madman'*, said his wife. *'Every time we were told about one, he went to see him.'* And yet he had been seriously put off by a visit to a healer who, hearing him speak of his sexual misfortune, had engaged in dirty talk and mocked at his impotence: but he was more of a bonesetter than an unwitcher. After seeing the *'woman from Alençon'* and although he *'doesn't much believe'*, in spells, Jean saw five successive unwitchers:

(a) First, the *'little lady from Torcé'*. We already know she only deals in small spells and is an unwitcher *'for good'*. But she could do nothing for him, because he was *'so tightly caught'*. So the diagnosis of the *'woman from Alençon'* – *'there are spells* [in your home] *in every direction'* – was confirmed.[5]

---

[5] The *petite mère* from Torcé had nonetheless succeeded in unwitching Louis Babin. *'But'* he said, *'our spell was weak, easy to get rid of.'* it consisted of a *'buttering'* placed in his fields, which caused his cows to dry up. The culprit was a small neighbouring farmer whose brother worked as a farm-hand for Louis Babin. This neighbour and his wife, *'are people who only think of doing harm*

(*b*) Next, four unwitchers *'for evil'*, three men and one woman. They too were useless although from what I know about two of the four, they have a great reputation for *'force'* and courage. The woman assured Josephine that Jean was *'dead caught'* and that his misfortunes would hold out *'until your husband destroys himself'* [commits suicide]. This diagnosis seemed to me to have some truth to it, since Jean was often tempted to end his misfortunes by shooting himself or hanging himself in the attic. (It was only much later that I began to understand that he thought about it especially when the unwitching had some chance of being effective. That is why I did not insist subsequently that he commit himself further with Madame Flora.) At that point also, the Babins called on the priest of Torcé – the one who *'didn't believe'* – and he blessed the farm, the animals and the people, though it did no good.

1. An embedded spell

When Fine was a young girl, she worked every day at the Brodins of La Bouronnière at Chammes, which is where she first met Madame Marie from Izé.[6] She tells me this story in a state of great excitement, for it is the most impressive one she knows:

'There was a father who wanted his daughter to die. It's his son-in-law, Gustave's his name, who called the woman from Izé. Things were getting out of hand: the father had an eye on his daughter's farm.' [The two farms were next to each other, and that of the bewitched girl was always vulnerable to the witch's murderous look.] *'It had caught so tight that the spell was fixed into the wall of La Bouronnière. The woman from Izé said: If you hadn't called me, the spell would have been fixed even further in.'*

'What do you mean, fixed in?'

'The daughter, or rather a caricature of her, was engraved in the farm wall.' [In the wall of the living room, the mortar round the stones forms a pattern which looks like a face and is interpreted as the caricature or portrait of Angèle Brodin. This representation of herself gives her an uncanny feeling and she feels mortally threatened every time she sees it: at any rate, from the moment when the woman from Izé spotted the 'engraving' and assured them that that was where the danger came from.] *'The woman from Izé was not sure she would bring it off: it's very difficult, she said, because it's fixed in.'*

---

and stealing'; the *'mère* [the witch] *used to do well, in the old days'* [she slept with everyone]; his main characteristic is greed: for instance, he wanted to take his brother's earnings: *'he wanted to draw everything from him, wanted to attract him so as to draw his money* [note that a witch always *'draws'* money, milk, force, or the other's desire]. Babin realized his neighbour was a witch when he heard about his inability to sleep *'he would get up for two or three hours every night, he was always away. That's when we said to ourselves: "it's him, the filth"* '. For if he went out at night, it was to *'travel'* and place *'butterings'* on his victim's land. Of course the brother of the witch, the farm-hand, was treated as an involuntary conductor of witchcraft: *'It made them stronger'* that their brother lived on the victim's farm; which is why *'we never talked to him'* (to the farm-hand).

[6] When a farmer names himself, he always follows his name with that of the land he cultivates. Thus Jean signed the letters he sent me: Babin of La Croix.

'What was wrong with Angèle?'

'*She had phlebitis, she had only a few days to live.*' Fine moved into the Brodin house to look after her day and night.

'How did they know it was a spell?'

Josephine then talks about the long-standing conflicts between père Poisson and his daughter: he was a '*stupid man*', a brute who drank and terrorized his family '*every time he drank his novenas*'. He always blamed Angèle because she had been '*difficult to bring up*': at birth, she had been between life and death for several weeks, and he never forgave her. Later on, when she suffered from appendicitis, he was irritated with her, but while she was being operated on '*he had a mass said for her all the same*'. Apart from Angèle, he had two sons: '*he thought little of the eldest; the youngest drank, and so was well-thought-of: at the age of eight he could drink nine glasses of cider, like a man*'. This younger son in fact died of alcoholism at the age of thirty-six.

'And the mother?'

'*Oh, the mother was sly, she didn't say anything. It's because the father was really a stupid man, she was afraid of him.*'

Père Poisson's hatred for his daughter did not come out at her wedding, but at the birth of her first child: '*The child came after nine months fifteen days. The father said: he came early*' [You were already pregnant on your wedding day]. '*After that*', says Josephine '*there were losses, many losses*', and then more children.

The neighbours looked on in silence, until one of them decided to act as annunciator. He came over to tell Gustave Brodin: '*there's a reason for it: someone wishes you ill*'. As is to be expected, the initiant was taken by surprise: '*At that time, he wasn't thinking about that sort of thing*' [spells]. But soon after, some strange events took place and confirmed the annunciator's diagnosis:

'*One day while the women were churning* [Angèle and her mother-in-law] *they heard: "Anyone in?"*' [visitors announce their presence in this way before crossing the threshold of a farm]. '*They came out, but no one was there. The next time something happened, Gustave was there: "Anyone in?" and no one there. Another time, the women heard someone walking in the dairy. They went to see who it was: once again, no one. Then, the hens kept clucking and every time Angèle went* [to collect the eggs announced by the hens' clucking] *there were no eggs.*'

These audible though invisible visitors, and the hens clucking for no reason at all are signs of witchcraft. Suspicion seems to have fallen on père Poisson because this time it was impossible to place it outside the family circle: Poisson was both the father of the bewitched girl and her objective persecutor – two reasons for an unwitcher to look elsewhere for a witch – but he was also a persecutor against whom the bewitched could do nothing. Since the birth of Angèle's first child, he had refused to talk to her; and when Gustave was out at work in the fields, père Poisson would often come to the next field, perched on his tractor, and hurl insults at him. One day, he made a statement which explicitly declared him to be a witch:

'The Good Lord has money enough to pay his people', he said to Gustave.

To me this sentence was mysterious, but Josephine said its meaning was obvious: Poisson was openly admitting that his daughter's *'losses'* were good for his own stock, and he was saying that divine authorities blessed his gains. Jean capped his wife's comment: *'Poisson was punished by the Good Lord: he lost a sow the next day.'* Since God answered his blasphemy by inflicting a loss on him, it showed that Poisson was profiting at his daughter's expense.

The series of misfortunes witnessed by Josephine herself began with the birth of a little girl after a difficult pregnancy.

'The mother [Angèle] *had to stay in bed from the third to the ninth month* [of pregnancy]: *her backbone was crooked. It was during Holy Week. On Tuesday, a cow aborts: both calves are dead. We go and fetch Madame Marie.'*

She comes, looks at the animals and the buildings, and finally discovers *'the caricature of Angèle on a wall. When it's fixed in the wall, she says, it's more difficult to get rid of.'*

'On Friday', continues Josephine, *'Angèle has phlebitis. She says to me: put the sows out. Just as I'm about to enter* [the pigstye], *in the evening, I find a sow lying stiff, near the electric wire. It's dying. We put salt in its mouth. The boss* [Gustave] *goes off to find Madame Marie at Izé.*[7] *If he hadn't gone, she would have come herself: she had the feeling something was wrong.'* The extraordinary insight of the *'woman from Izé'* is often talked about: she comes without being called because she knows the witch is at work: unlike the doctor who is never there when he is needed, the unwitcher is there before the call and always turns up at the critical moment.

When the unwitcher arrived at La Bouronnière, Angèle was critically ill – *'she was going to die'* as well as her child: *'She had diarrhoea, and was also going to die.'* Madame Marie decided that their ills had a distant cause: *'the père* [Poisson] *had touched something in the stable which had then been touched by Angèle'* – and a more immediate cause: to avoid being mocked at by the doctor whom they were expecting, Angèle had taken away her and her child's protective pouches. No longer protected against the terrible looks of a witch who was so close, they had been touched to the death. According to the unwitcher, Josephine herself, who often looked at the countryside through the attic window, had almost been caught.

'If you hadn't been carrying something [the protective pouch] *he* [the witch] *would have made you fall out of the window.'* But we know how cautious Josephine is where spells are concerned. On her walk around the farm, the unwitcher had then found several small stacks of straw, as if in preparation for a fire: *'the woman from Izé said: the fire won't be long in coming'* [luckily, I am here without having been summoned and I've come to unmask any natural and supernatural tricks prepared by the witch]. She had a saucepan of salt

[7] *'When the boss'*, says Josephine, *'went to fetch Madame Marie, it stopped him on his way'* [the force of his witch, who was trying to prevent him from reaching his liberator]. *'Every time he arrived, she gave him a good drop before he left: it makes you stronger.'*

heated and '*now he knew about it* [the witch]. *Could he feel it!*' He was suffering a thousand deaths, but Josephine did not tell me how she could check this. As far as I could understand, she knew it simply because the unwitcher showed, by her words and behaviour, that she was engaged in mortal combat with the witch. So she said one day, staggering:

'*He's coming* [the witch]. *No, he's not coming. She was in the middle of the yard: she was so hot! She wanted him to give in, she wanted to make him surrender.*'

The Babins have two indirect proofs that she succeeded in doing so.

(*a*) After these visits from the unwitcher, père Poisson met his daughter and son-in-law one day: ('*Funny, how come they met?*' ask the couple, since Poisson and the Brodins should never have spoken a word to each other.) The father then said to his daughter:

'*And mind, don't hurt us worse than we hurt you*'. As always, this sentence is transmitted to me as it stands, without any additional comment to give me some idea of the context in which it was spoken: after all, the Poissons and the Brodins were caught in a fierce family struggle, and mentioning it would have been enough to give meaning to this statement. But for my interlocutors as for the Brodins, it is a sign of père Poisson's witchcraft and his fear of unwitching: '*Angèle and Gustave didn't know what to answer, because Madame Marie had said that he who had done it was going to feel it.*' Since Poisson admitted having hurt his daughter badly and was asking her to deal out the harm returned in proportion to the harm done, this meant there was witchcraft involved. Note also that the Babins seems to consider that the witch declared himself through this very statement, which implies that before they had been able to see the effects of the ritual carried out by the '*woman from Izé*', all the bewitched could do was to '*suspect him*' and others as well: from then on, they were sure the name of père Poisson was the right one, and any other suspects could be forgotten.

(*b*) After the unwitcher had finished her work, the '*photo* [of Angèle] *remained fixed into the wall*', but its '*force*' was definitely neutralized, and all the symptoms progressively disappeared.[8]

2. Josephine bewitched

On that Good Friday when the '*woman from Izé*' saved Angèle Brodin and her child just as '*they were about to die*', Josephine Letort had been told by her parents to ask the unwitcher to come to their house, for they too were suffering from inexplicable troubles because of a witch. '*Once she was*

[8] Since Angèle and her baby were so ill, I ventured a question:
'How did the woman from Izé treat her?'
'*She saved her with herbs and grey salt. Grey salt has a stronger effect, she said, because it has been less washed*' [the unwitcher herself is dirty so as to be stronger]. Note in passing that my question itself implied that I knew in advance that unwitching cannot cure by itself, which is why I got an answer. In all the canonical narratives like the one I recounted in Ch. 6, one never alludes to the role of healer which unwitchers often adopt: the effectiveness is entirely attributed to the unwitching ritual.

done' [with her cure at the Brodins] says Josephine, *'I said to Madame Marie: things aren't too good at my father's; my parents are out of luck.'*

It was past midnight, but the unwitcher agreed to go with Josephine. *'As soon as she set her foot on the steps, she said: You've been done'* [there's a spell on your farm]. *It's always like that'* explains Marthe Babin later, when she sees that I don't know much about rural witchcraft, *'as soon as they go in, they can feel whether there are forces. Sometimes, they can hardly go forward.'*

According to Josephine, the spells at her parents' *'had been there for a long time'.* They had *'lost eleven animals within twenty months. The mares only gave birth when they were insured. If not, one was lost each time. When we had insured them all it fell on the horned animals.'* The existence of a spell is proved by the fact that misfortune tends to displace itself in this way from one species to another. In addition, the milk was getting progressively worse, to the point of being practically unsellable; the women could no longer *'churn'* the butter. *'My father managed it: he had strong blood: But his butter tasted bad . . .'* it looked like butter, but *'it was not good to eat'.*[9] A further proof that the Letorts were bewitched: *'two of the animals refused to eat. We put* [holy] *salt in their mouths and it stopped'*, they immediately recovered their appetite.

'What was wrong with those cows?'. My question is aimed at getting Josephine to repeat the vet's diagnosis, but, of course, the Letorts would not disturb him for so small a thing, and the explanation of this passing anorexia is for them irrefutably and experimentally founded.

'The spell prevented them from eating. And then we'd lost a lot before, from foot-and-mouth disease. [Finally, on another occasion and with another lot of cows] *they* [the witches] *took advantage of the fact that we'd gone to a wedding – at that time weddings lasted for two days – to go into the cowshed: and we lost three cows like that.'*

So this was a spell, for two reasons: first, because a little holy salt was enough to cure the ailing animals; second, because their mishaps were part of the series of animal diseases which, as we shall see later, appeared on the occasion of a bewitchment and always came back every time the Letorts had to go away from the farm for a social engagement.[10]

[9] 'How did your father know he had strong blood?', I asked. *'Well, he weighed 180'* [pounds, he was a tough man], says one of his daughters. The other adds: *'Well, because it worked when he churned'* [it was effective].

[10] According to Josephine, *'every time there was a burial in the area'*, her parents' cows produced thin milk. Attending funerals is one of the most important social obligations; it occupies farmers for a whole afternoon several times a year. To weddings must be added solemn communions and burials – they take up an entire Sunday – as well as attending mass followed by card games in the village café, where one sees all one's acquaintances after a week of relative isolation – and family celebrations: wedding anniversaries, births, etc. On all these occasions, actually quite numerous and sometimes unforeseeable, the farm is deserted, and the animals, which are never locked up, are said to be vulnerable to witches. Note, here, that stealing is practically unheard of in this region: which is why the farmers can, in theory, quite calmly desert their farms.

Lastly, Josephine had '*backaches*'. When she talks about this symptom, she clearly distinguished between two kinds of pain:

(*a*) Since childhood, she has had '*crooked vertebrae*', a normal phenomenon for which she sees a bonesetter. The pain appears every time she overdoes some muscular effort (carrying buckets or wheat-bales, making a clumsy gesture when she is loaded down like a beast of burden and so on) and it lasts until the bonesetter has manipulated her back.

(*b*) Passing pains, which appear for no mechanical reason and disappear just as mysteriously.

So, on several occasions she set off to the doctor's (the term never excludes bonesetters or unwitchers), but when she arrived in the waiting room, the pain disappeared, only to come back as soon as she was back at her parents' farm. Since these pains came and went in precise circumstances she makes the obvious experimental conclusion: the witch, aiming at the set constituted by the Letort family, was managing to strike the most sensitive link. The original cause was an unsuccessful marriage alliance: '*The neighbour wanted to marry my brother to his daughter.*' But, as often happens, the young man ignored his neighbour's daughter and married another: '*Remember*', says Josephine to her husband, '*the foot-and-mouth disease started on the day of the wedding.*' Before, '*my brother thought they* [spells] *only concerned the parents. Once he was caught, I said: "There you are, now you believe in it."*' She adds for my benefit, on a triumphant note: '*Now my brother believes in it: once one is caught . . .*'

'But why did it fall on her? [the spell]', I asked Josephine's sister one day.

'*Fine hadn't joined the wake for père Filoche when he died: that's why it all fell on her*', answered Marthe.

Josephine had simply told me: '*he couldn't do anything against mother*', who was being '*touched*' by a well-known healer for breast cancer, '*nor against father*'. [I don't know why, perhaps because he had '*strong blood*'.] '*So it all fell on me.*'

So, when Josephine asked Madame Marie to her parents' farm on the night of Good Friday, the symptoms of bewitchment were these:

(*a*) Her father's beasts either died or produced poor milk; no butter could be made.

(*b*) Her brothers' beasts suffered from foot-and-mouth disease, which would have seemed perfectly normal if it had not started precisely on his wedding day.

(*c*) Josephine suffered from inexplicable backaches. (Curiously her mother's cancer was not attributed to witchcraft, perhaps because it started before her brother's wedding.)

'Did Madame Marie say who was guilty?'

'*Certainly not!*' said Josephine fearfully. '*As soon as she arrived, she said: "I never say who it is because it leads to hatred."*' Josephine was silent for a moment, then said: '*But I know who it is: one day, I'm walking with the three calves on the road; suddenly they begin to run around in all directions, I just can't catch them. I turn around, and I see mère Filoche standing in the yard, looking at me. She takes two steps and looks at me. I don't lower my eyes* [unlike my weak husband]. *She takes two more steps, and looks at me. I go into the farm, and before clenching the door, I look again: she's still there, coming forward and looking at me.'* This silent clash with the neighbour seems all the more meaningful to Josephine since mère Filoche possesses the typical attributes of witches: she seems immune from death – '*The Good Lord doesn't want her, and neither does the devil*' – and her look conveys omnipotence – '*She had eyes, such eyes ... well, glassy eyes!*'

The '*woman from Izé*' only came three times, and was paid twenty-five francs and some '*fowl for her children*', and everything went back to normal. She heated up her salt pan and '*the other felt it*'; she gave out medals, kitchen salt, small pouches containing plants and bent steel nails '*to give strength*' to '*those who were caught tight*'. The others were given small bags containing ordinary nails. Lastly, she looked after Josephine's back like this: '*I had to dip a cloth in hot vinegar and salt and put it on my back for nine evenings running*', at the same time as taking three grains of grey salt every morning before breakfast.

The second time she came, Madame Marie '*came into the buildings, touched a cow and said: look at those rosary beads!* [a symptom of anaemia] *If I hadn't come, it would have died within a week.*' The third time, she came without being called: père Letort had lost and found his protective pouch, but '*luckily he hadn't worn it again, The filthy bastards had found it and rigged it.*'

'How did you know?'

'*The woman from Izé saw it. It's mad, you know, she could see in the sky, all the way from Izé, she could see the pouch was rigged. She came to tell us. If not, father could have died in* [the following] *days.* [The rigged pouch] *was thrown into the fire; the woman made a new one.*'[11]

It can be seen that the '*woman from Izé*' is just the opposite of those eccentric unwitchers I described in Chapter 4: unlike them, she is continually and utterly committed to this clash with the supernatural, it is her only passion, as can be seen by her life as well as her death. As soon as she agrees to unwitch some unhappy person, the fate of her patient becomes her sole preoccupation: apprehending the dangers which threaten him, coming to warn him of them, and immediately engaging in a ruthless struggle was part of her everyday lot. Her courage and willpower are clear: she is repeatedly shaken by spasms, has sleepless nights – '*she never slept; at night, she was worked on, while others ... honestly this job is hell; they're constantly being worked on*' – she sets off on dangerous expeditions over roads ridden with supernatural obstacles – '*after it had caught tight, the road to the farm was blocked by a shape. She would say to the driver: drive straight at it, if not we've had it!*'

One begins to understand the deep attachment of the bewitched to their

---

[11] Marthe Babin was also given a small pouch, although it contained an ordinary nail, because she was not '*caught tight*'. She no longer carries it, '*I put it aside. Actually, I wouldn't know where to look for it if something was abnormal.*' But it is not lost.

unwitcher: one can say everything to someone who is totally committed; one *must* say everything to someone who takes such risks, not only in the hope of being saved, but because the unwitcher is above all a volunteer for a suicide mission, who agrees straightaway to risk his own life to save the patient having to do so himself. If there is little doubt that the unwitcher gets a deep satisfaction from this situation – which, in my view, is his real reward, the monetary fee only serving to give this satisfaction in an acceptable symbolic form – it is still a fact that being a volunteer for death requires immense courage and strength. This is why, when certain people are considered to possess magic *'force'* and an annunciator promises to initiate them, it is hardly surprising that most of them refuse to commit themselves any further, and shrink from the idea of spending the rest of their lives engaged in ruthless combat.

For instance, one of Josephine's relatives: *'We have an aunt who has strong blood. If she wanted to, she could lift spells.'*

'How does she know?'

'Once, at a wedding, she met père Coquin.[12] *She was the dressmaker, she'd made the bride's dress, that's why she'd been invited. Père Coquin* [who was sitting opposite her at the banquet] *was forced* [because of the strength of the aunt's 'blood'] *to look at her, he couldn't help it. But as soon as she looked at him, he lowered his eyes over his plate.'* She herself could not understand what was going on, since she did not know he was the Monniers' witch and she had never imagined she could be stronger than a witch. She said to the person next to her: *'that old man is completely batty!'* Intrigued, she questioned her healer who told her that, having come out victorious in a battle of looks with a witch, *'she could avert spells'*. But she vehemently refused: *'That kind of work is hell, you have to fight all the time.'*

A second book will be almost entirely devoted to showing how the efficacy of a cure is essentially based on the patterning of a certain form of speech which is necessarily forgotten as soon as it has had its effect. The bewitched only remember the series of misfortunes as established by the interpretation, and, in a vivid manner, the moment when the ritual began. This is why I know almost nothing about the words exchanged between the Letorts and the *'woman from Izé'*. They could not remember them at all, and all Josephine could tell me was that they talked a lot at the beginning – they had to *'tell it all'* so that the facts could be interpreted and the guilty party identified – and a lot at the end: the particular story of the Letorts had to be integrated in a set of witchcraft stories witnessed and part-composed by the unwitcher.

I was also not told what words were exchanged between the Letorts and their witches, the Filoches. Everything leads me to think that it is less a matter of words (since one must above all not say anything once the witch

[12] Cf. pp. 116–23.

has been identified) than of a message, in a very general sense. Between one day and the next, everything in the Letorts' behaviour accused the Filoches, beginning with that sudden silence which cannot be explained by preceding conflicts – since the Letorts had continued seeing their neighbours until the arrival of the '*woman from Izé*' – and this frenzy on the part of the bewitched to '*clench*' doors and windows, animals and people, cars and agricultural machinery, in a region where people usually leave their key in an empty bakehouse when they go away so that it can easily be found by possible visitors.

One can also count as a message those silent battles of looks, refusals to shake hands, moments when questions or greetings by the witches are answered by the bewitched by simply repeating their words; and the systematic refusal to continue any relationship. Lastly, remember that the presence of an unwitcher cannot escape the notice of the accused: Josephine said that the first time, Madame Marie was worried because her arrival had been given away by the dogs barking; more generally, I have often noticed how closely the goings and doings of other people are watched, and how attentively noises are listened to. No stranger can enter a farm, even at night, without all the peasants in the neighbourhood noting the hour, the number of the car and attempting to find out the exact reasons for the visit.

Even when someone thus accused of witchcraft is totally innocent – which seems to me to be the case nearly every time – he is bound to be worried at the idea of being accused in front of an unwitcher as powerful as the '*woman from Izé*', whose legendary feats and determination he must have heard about. When, after her visit that night, he saw from the behaviour of the bewitched that they thought he was responsible for their misfortunes, it would not surprise me if this silent accusation, which is in fact the equivalent of a long speech, sent him into a panic. This seems to have been the case with the Filoches, whose farm soon collapsed, so that they were obliged '*to sell out*' their belongings after a few months. Mère Filoche who, according to the bewitched, so liked to '*draw butter*' from others, i.e. to cause their cows to give poor milk and to prevent the farmers from churning, died, appropriately, while making butter.[13] Her children were incapable of keeping on any farm, and were always '*forced*' to '*sell out*' every time they settled on one.

In the Letort home, on the other hand, everything went back to normal. Josephine was immediately cured of her backaches; her brother was from then on '*lucky*' in cattle-rearing.[14] Their parents died, but it was considered to be a natural death, since it happened after the witch's defeat. The only

[13] '*She died suddenly while making butter: she met her master*', said Josephine who recalls that during the period when her mother could no longer churn, the woman from Izé had said '*the bitch passed by the end of the path*'. Since mère Filoche died while churning, '*the bitch*' must have been her.

[14] '*From the day the woman from Izé came, we didn't lose a thing. My brother even has good luck now.*' For a long time he corresponded with Madame Marie, asking her advice '*every time something abnormal happened: he'd been caught tight, had to be careful*'.

remaining dark spot was a warning from young Gabriel Filoche who said to his neighbour, three weeks before Josephine's wedding (at the time of Jean Babin's accident, to which he imputes his sexual impotence) '*make sure you don't marry a nanny-billy*', i.e. according to the terms of the person concerned, a being who would be '*neither a nanny-nor a billy-goat, neither a man nor a woman, a man who can't make love*'. But I was only to hear about this much later, at the time when I took her to my unwitcher.

3. A meaningful laugh

So when the Babins talk about the '*woman from Izé*', it is to boast of her victories: she lifted both the spell weighing on the Brodins – although it was '*really hard because it was fixed in*' – and the spell cast on the Letorts. She won her third victory over père Coquin on behalf of Josephine's brother-in-law, Monnier, the deputy mayor at La Gravelle. As usual, the story of this exploit is introduced by a preliminary account, which I shall run through since it will help the reader to follow the windings of the story and also because its point was to prove to me the futility of trying to get rid of one's witch by any kind of direct or violent clash with him.[15]

For once, it was Jean who spoke: Jean, who, according to his wife and brother '*didn't much believe*' in spells, and who usually left any conversational initiative to his wife. He spoke in order to describe a situation in which an innocent person became the conductor of a spell simply because she was related to a witch: she was married to one. Angot, the man bewitched – a '*good neighbour*' of the Babins, they helped each other in various ways – had married the sister of Foubert, his witch. It is likely that this accusation of witchcraft is the result of a belated interpretation, at least subsequent to the marriage: otherwise, the entire situation would be incomprehensible since an inhabitant of the Bocage would never wittingly expose himself to the evil contact of a witch by choosing to marry the relative of one, for the charms of love are totally out of proportion to the guaranteed danger from a witch set. And yet I was unable to discover the prehistory of this story, which was told to me to illustrate the notion of innocent conduction.[16]

'*Every time Foubert* [the witch, the brother-in-law] *went round to the Angots*', says Jean Babin, '*the cows dried up.*' The expression '*to go round*' [*faire le tour*] needs a comment here, since it is often used in the Bocage with different meanings:

[15] It will be remembered that in Ch. 6, I described a victory by the '*woman from Izé*', when her ritual took effect on the predicted day and drove the presumed witch to the psychiatric hospital and to a rapid death. Her victory was so exemplary that the bewitched felt unable to take it in and shut themselves off behind what I called the barrier of the unspeakable. From the preceding pages, it will have ben understood that unlike the Régniers, the Letorts considered their witches' death and their children's ruin as a sign that justice had at last been done, since Josephine could talk quite calmly of the consequences of the intervention of that merciless '*unwitcher for evil*'.

[16] Cf. Ch. 8 Death at the crossroads and '*Ex post facto*', pp. 117–36 and Ch. 9, p. 142.

(*a*) Generally, without any connotation of witchcraft, it simply means '*to go round and see someone*' whom one knows well, to call on him.

(*b*) At a pilgrimage, and especially one for a saint who is a protector of animals, '*to go round*' is to follow the procession around all the parishes which believe in the saint's effectiveness.

(*c*) In the case of witchcraft, '*to go round*' or '*to do the rounds*' [*faire la tournée*] can mean: either the witch circles round the land and buildings of his victim, laying charms in strategic places (at least this is how the bewitched says he imagines the witch's actions); or the unwitcher or the bewitched go round in the same way, but to place magic protections: blessed salt, medals of Saint Benedict, and the rest.[17]

This is an example of the basic ambiguity of the discourse of witchcraft.

(*a*) The context always determines whether the expression '*to go round*' is used in its general sense – to visit someone – or in one of its three particular senses, each one referring to a way of encircling: religious, magic-aggressive, or magic-defensive. I use the terms circle or encircling on purpose, to bring out the relation – carefully hidden in local talk – between magic healing practices which are not supposed to have anything to do with spells, and witchcraft practices.[18]

(*b*) When witchcraft is involved, it is also the context, but more particularly the relationship between the speaker and whoever is said to '*go round*' which determines the meaning to be given to the phrase.

So, when Jean Babin uses it to speak of the witch, he is emphasizing the vulnerability of the bewitched (which relates to his own vulnerability) since Angot could never know in advance whether Foubert was meaning to pay him an ordinary visit, as would be usual for a brother-in-law, or whether he was taking advantage of the situation to encircle his victim's goods with the help of his evil force, i.e. to '*clench*' them, lock them, and bewitch them.

To find out, he had to wait and see whether Foubert's visit had any effects: none, if he came as a relative; disastrous, if he came as a witch. Until that moment, the significance of the visit could not be ascertained,

---

[17] On the eve of 1 May and 24 June, said Louis Babin – when witches '*travel most. . . because they work for the whole year*' – '*you must throw salt*', i.e. '*go around*' the farm throwing salt in strategic places: '*you must put salt on the fences*', he said, '*you must put salt around the buildings; the farm must be encircled. At each fence, each opening, you must make a sign of the cross with the salt*', i.e. throw it in two perpendicular lines, as if one were making a sign of the cross. '*All the time I say prayers, Aves*' because the Virgin Mary is said to be '*strong*' against '*evil ones*'. According to Babin, unwitchers never miss an opportunity to tell their patients to '*do the rounds*'. At the risk of disappointing folklorists, I should like to point out that the two dates given me by Louis Babin are not the only ones thought to be particularly favourable to the actions of witches.

[18] One evening, I had a long conversation with a locally highly-regarded encircler. Unwilling to tell me his secrets, especially in front of his wife who apparently hoped to take advantage of this situation in order to learn them, he preferred to get me to tell him stories about spells, and asked me each time for details of the unwitcher's ritual. A remark made by his wife made him absolutely furious: she had dared to say that with an unwitcher, '*it came to the same*' as with an encircler and that '*it's probably the same thing*'.

especially since no one has ever seen a witch laying charms. Remember that a witch always operates either hypocritically or secretly, and in any case, if that is what one is afraid of, it is better not to watch him so as to avoid being exposed to his terrible look.[19]

However hard I questioned the Babins about the relationship between the Angots, there was not the least trace of any marital conflict: '*Oh no, there was never any question of that!*' was their reply. Madame Angot was absolutely innocent of any witchcraft, as well as of any natural evil. She was an agreeable and hospitable woman, whom her neighbours liked to meet. Her husband would never have dreamed of casting in her teeth the fate which condemned her to be the conductor of her brother's witchcraft. (Note, in passing, that a woman who gets married does not cease to belong to her set or to her original line; just as '*taking over*' does not systematically cancel a man's debt to his line; in either case it is a question of interpretation.) Père Angot averted this fatality as much as he possibly could, for example by not allowing his wife to go near the cows, forcing himself to milk them morning and evening, which is no light task. One wonders too how they decided about this, since the job of milking is usually carried out either by the farmer's wife alone, or by the couple together. But I was unable to get any information about this.

Jean wanted simply to insist on his unfortunate neighbour's vulnerability: however many protections he accumulated, his cows always dried up whenever Foubert '*came round*'. If an unwitcher did intervene – though no one mentioned it – he was totally ineffectual. In fact, not knowing where to turn, the bewitched man had a direct clash with his brother-in-law: '*Angot*', said Babin, '*punched him in the face; now they no longer talk to each other, but it's not finished*', the cows still dry up. Like Angot, the Babins presume that the witch will be obliged to hide himself more skilfully, to operate under the cover of night, '*going round*' the fields and cowsheds of his victims when they are asleep.

Like all the bewitched who have not yet exhausted the possibility of resorting to magic – for example, they ask me to '*return evil for evil*' to their witch – the Babins emphasize their view that any attempt to break the encircling (the locking, the clenching) of the witch by physical force is imprudent and absurd.

(*a*) It does show that one is not afraid of confronting one's witch; but this

---

[19] '*When one doesn't know* [that one is bewitched] *one never sees them*', says Louis Babin. But when one does know – or rather when '*one suspects someone*' – one still doesn't see them. '*They come at night, they wait till you're asleep*'. – But why not be on the look-out? – '*Better not, it would be frightening, I can feel his evil* [the witch's]. *You must leave him alone, not attack him, you mustn't make things worse*' because at that moment no one could resist his omnipotence. Cf. p. 69 the episode where the witch, '*all electrified*' destroys his victim by simply being present. Even when one has identified the culprit, said Louis, '*it's no use grumbling. You must act as if nothing had happened, avoid them. The healer deals with them, either by pushing them back or by completely turning them*'.

makes physical contact unavoidable, and the witch is bound to use his evil touch.

(*b*) Since a witch never considers himself beaten until a magic force superior to his own has been mobilized against him, being beaten up by his victim will only make him the more eager to use his magic tricks to avenge himself for the blows received.[20]

For the Babins, the way in which the '*woman from Izé*' taught Monnier how to overthrow père Coquin is much more interesting. On meeting his witch (at the municipal council of La Gravelle, for example), the bewitched, well provided with protective devices and convinced that the unwitcher was battling on her side, had to get a firm hold of the tail of the witch's jacket. (This implies that the bewitched had to make sure he did not directly touch his witch's body.) The result surpassed Monnier's expectations, for he suddenly saw his witch lose countenance: '*Coquin didn't know where to put himself, he lowered his eyes, he was all agitated*' by this outburst of force by the bewitched party. The public was involved on this occasion, for I was told that everyone laughed at Coquin's confusion and that it was the first sign that his magic force was at last overcome: '*he didn't know where to put himself*', and having thus lost face in a public confrontation, he stopped playing his '*tricks*' on Monnier.

It is important to understand the difference the Babins thus established between a private hand-to-hand fight, like Angot's unsuccessful effort, and a public confrontation in which the bewitched, supported by his unwitcher's magic, just grabs the witch's clothes. In the second case, the public's laughter is equivalent to an interpretation: since the audience is laughing at Coquin, the witch has been beaten by the bewitched.

However, it is hardly likely that those who laughed at the municipal council had any shared notion of the witch's downfall, for two closely related reasons.

(*a*) So far as I know, there is no such thing in the Bocage as a common agreement about who is a '*village witch*', since witchcraft is always a matter of a dual relationship between two families only. If Coquin is said to be a witch, it can only be by the Monnier family. Any other bewitched from La Gravelle, complaining about his witch, will not name Coquin, but Truffaut, Beinvenue or Barrillon.

(*b*) The main reason preventing the common agreement that so and so is a witch is that a bewitched never talks about spells for fear of ridicule, except to his close relatives, his annunciator, and his unwitcher. '*One doesn't talk about that*' – not even to one's friends or '*good*' neighbours, I was told many times: '*they would only laugh at us*', the bewitched often say.

The bewitched, who is so afraid of being laughed at for talking about

---

[20] It would be pointless to use verbal violence here: '*Shouting doesn't change anything. You have to keep quiet*' and not show the witch you've discovered who he is or that you '*suspect him*', or his hatred would only be more intense.

spells nevertheless uses this laughter as an argument to prove that so and so is a witch. For example, I asked the Babins if others besides themselves in Torcé considered their neighbour Ribault to be a witch: '*one never talks about that*', says Jean. '*But each time he falls ill, everyone laughs*', for, according to my interlocutor, it is good to know that '*someone stronger than him is making him pay*'. Similarly, the bewitched often recall the laughter which shook the procession at their witch's funeral as evidence that his true character had long been known to public opinion, and that the Babins were certainly not the only ones to suffer from his supernatural evil or to rejoice in the fact that he had at last '*met his master*'.

So it does not enter the minds of the bewitched that the town council of La Gravelle could laugh at père Coquin's confusion simply because the incident struck them as funny, or possibly out of pleasure at seeing a disagreeable man being put in his place. When the Babins use as an argument that '*they're terrified of Coquin down there*', at La Gravelle, they are playing on the perpetual ambiguity of the discourse on witchcraft. This ambiguity allows them to suggest the supernatural origin of bad moral traits: if all the villagers agree to call Coquin a '*filthy bastard*', a '*bad man*' or '*terrifying*', this permits them to call him a witch. This is perhaps why the term '*witch*' is almost never used; his victims merely point at him in terms of bad character. This demonstrates their perpetual need to find a symbolic guarantee in public opinion of the well-foundedness of their accusation: the proof that the '*terrifying*' Coquin derived his power from supernatural sources is that everyone laughed with relief when it was finally destroyed.

In conclusion, I should like to emphasize one essential feature of the discourse on witchcraft, which we shall return to later. The characterization as a witch, as such, cannot in any circumstances be made in public; one can laugh and call him a '*filthy bastard*', but one never explicitly states that he is a witch. The name of the unwitcher, on the contrary, can be mentioned and repeated by all and sundry: despite the precautions he uses in taking on patients, in a way it is just as if he were running a flourishing business. Of course, the unwitcher operates under the cover of night, as the witch is said to do, but this is only so as to counter the surprise-attack of the '*evil one*' by a surprise-defence.[21] Everyone in the village can say that so and so is an unwitcher, even though they may say so ironically or disdainfully; no one but his victim can ever think that so and so is a witch. Correlatively, whereas the unwitcher always acknowledges himself to be such, the supposed witch always denies having committed the evil deeds he is accused of.

---

[21] '*Just when he* [the witch] *is least expecting it, he* [the unwitcher] *catches him*', said Louis Babin. The unwitcher comes at night, out of caution. '*He comes at night so he won't be seen* [by the witch]. *He* [the unwitcher] *doesn't want it to be known* [his visit to the bewitched farm] *because the others* [the witches] *want him to die.*' In support of this claim, Louis Babin told me the story of an unwitcher from Jublains who let herself be surprised by the witches she was fighting: '*She was paralysed in one arm by the others. But she fought, and it came back*' [the use of her arm].

This basic difference between the two positions of aggressor and magic avenger acquires its full significance when we inquire whether and how the unwitcher provides a symbolic guarantee that the real misfortunes of the bewitched are provoked by an imaginary witch.

4. The copula

When the Babins met me, their time had run out for the prediction made by the 'woman from Alençon' namely: 'if you don't do anything, you'll only stay married for six years'. Although the unfortunate couple had consulted several doctors and unwitchers, they felt that nothing had really been done to cure Jean's impotence, since all the therapists had been ineffectual. In particular, the 'woman from Izé', who had won victory after victory in every fight that Josephine had witnessed, at once ruled out the problem: 'it's too difficult' she had said, 'he [Jean]'s too caught. There's more than one [witch]. Things are too mixed up.' So she refused to engage in an unwitching ritual, but gave her clients some powerful protections.

Remember that in my first interview with the Babins, I had totally misjudged their reasons for talking to me so freely. I naïvely imagined that I had at last met some good 'informants', i.e. people who took me for an ethnographer. They talked continuously: I listened and took rapid notes, sometimes stopping to ask an ethnographer's question. My stupidity reached its height when we came to the most powerful of these protections.

It was a parcel which had been given to them by Madame Marie, with the solemn recommendation: 'Always keep it, otherwise you'll no longer be together'. Until the death of the 'woman from Izé' four months before, her recommendation had effectively cancelled out the prediction of the 'woman from Alençon': even if the Babins had not met any efficacious unwitchers, so long as they kept this parcel they would be sure to stay married despite the husband's impotence. So it seems appropriate to define this parcel as a 'copula', since it was supposed to take the place of their sexual relations.

I had already seen medals of St Benedict, little bags containing various things, scapularies and Sacred Hearts of Jesus, but no one had ever spoken to me of 'parcels'. Without stopping to think, I asked them to show it to me, for my curiosity had at once been aroused. But on seeing them hesitate, I immediately withdrew my request, awkwardly excusing myself. After all, 'secrets' did not really interest me. Josephine, however, suddenly got up and went to fetch the copula from the cupboard, where she had carefully placed it among the pile of sheets which were part of her trousseau. Jean explained to me that he was only afraid that opening the parcel would 'harm the woman from Izé' (who, having just died, seemed to be out of danger, so to speak). Josephine put the parcel on the table and said she was sure I was 'for good' and certainly didn't intend 'to harm the woman from Izé'. One can hardly say more explicitly that one unwitcher replaces another, but this was just what I did not want to hear.

Josephine had put the parcel, well tied up by the unwitcher, in a tin that had held cattle-cure: she had been afraid that in time it would deteriorate. The Babins had never thought of opening it till then, and they discovered its contents with me. I untied the strings and wrapping-paper and discovered seven plants, of which they could only name four – pimpernel, fern, laurel and box. They were wrapped around two metallic objects: a bit of harvester blade: *'It's made of steel, very strong, I always have some on me'* commented Josephine – and a horseshoe nail: *'the nails have to be heated over a fire; she heats them, then bends with her teeth; she bends the little pointed bit'*, to avert the witch's force and prevent him from perforating the body of the bewitched.[22] *'Look, it's not bent'*, said the astonished Jean, who from that moment on seemed totally perplexed. What, indeed was one supposed to think of this paradox: *'the woman from Izé'* had refused to unwitch him on the pretext that he was too *'caught'*, but she had put a straight nail in the parcel, usually used with those who are only caught by a *'small spell'*; and he also knew that the protective bags she made him wear next his skin contained a bent nail as well as holy salt and plants, the absolute proof that in the eyes of the unwitcher, he was *'caught tight'*.

When I finished examining the parcel's contents, Josephine packed it up quickly, without taking any particular precautions or even tying it up again: all the contents were pushed randomly into the tin box which she put back in the cupboard.

This episode was a turning-point in my relationship with the Babins: not knowing then that in witchcraft no words are guileless, I thought I had just asked a routine question; but they had never conceived of being mere informants, because nothing is more foreign to witchcraft than a relationship based on information. The very fact that I had dared do such a thing as open the magic copula confirmed their feeling that I was the intrepid unwitcher they were waiting for. The unreflecting words I had uttered were thought part of my *'force'*, which had arrived at the right moment to replace the disappearing one of the deceased Marie from Izé. From then on, they only mentioned her when they wanted to identify me with her, that is, they were asking me to replace her and, if possible, to attempt what she had not dared: *'to return evil for evil'* and cure Jean of his impotence.

III. If you feel capable. . .

I mentioned above the misunderstanding between me and the Babins, a misunderstanding due to the fact that for one thing I was faced for the first time with a situation of this kind, and for another that I felt incapable of fulfilling their demand. Determined to stick to my conviction that I was an

---

[22] The metaphor is my own: I have called the *body* of the bewitched the set constituted by himself, his family and his belongings – a set that the bewitched represent as a single surface or a bag always in danger of being perforated by the witch.

ethnographer, I expounded my views on what I then knew of the Babins'
story at the department seminar at the University of Nanterre. I had hardly
opened my mouth, when I was interrupted by an Africanist, who asked me
the relevant question: 'How much do you pay your informants?'

'They want to pay me.[23]

Even then, I had not understood all the implications of this simple,
though crucial fact: the ethnographer usually has to pay his informants
because he knows he is asking for something which is of no use to the native;
if, therefore, I was offered payment in the Bocage, it was because the
situation was reversed: the fact that I was asking the questions, like all
ethnographers, meant something only to me; the bewitched, for their part,
could only understand this request for information in terms of their own
request for which they must pay me; that is, that I was talking about
witchcraft from the position of the unwitcher. Rereading these notes today,
I am still astonished at my inability or unwillingness to hear what was in
fact being expressed quite unequivocally.

I had arranged to see the Babins again a few days later. I read through
my notes and thought about it during the eighty kilometer drive which
separated us. It was only when I stopped my car in their yard that the logic
of the situation struck me: this time, they were going to ask me to unwitch
them; in some sense they had *told me everything*' and my refusal to be paid, at
our previous meeting, was equivalent to a refusal to accept the position they
had given me. Aware of their confusion, I decided without really knowing
what this implied, to follow them wherever they would lead me.

Jean left his tractor and took me into the farm where Josephine was
washing the dishes. While we were drinking coffee, Jean complained about
feeling constantly sleepy, of headaches, and how his *'strength'* was failing.
He showed me the drugs Dr Davoine had given him – tonics – as if I would
know why they were no use. Stupidly, I advised him to arrange an
appointment with the doctor, as had in fact been agreed between him and
Jean a few weeks earlier; he had asked me to do it for him, on the ground
that he was afraid the doctor would refuse and that his secretary *'had a kilo of
plaster on her face'* (like Madame Marie from Alençon). As I thought it better

---

[23] My reply aroused the indignation of one colleague, who expressed it in conversations in the
corridor once I had left: well, if she is getting paid by the natives, she cannot be considered
an ethnographer and it is truly scandalous that the Centre National de la Recherche
Scientifique is supporting her adventure, etc. More generally, my enterprise produced three
kinds of comment: (1) what she's doing is not science; (2) the woman is mad, psychotic or in
any case seriously neurotic; (3) other, more humane colleagues, simply waited for me to
suffer such spectacular setbacks in the field that I would come back to Paris and take refuge
in the warm atmosphere of the scientific community, having understood the impossibility
for an ethnographer of any subjectivizing approach. If I went on doing fieldwork in the same
way, it was because I did not see how I could do it otherwise. But for a long while I felt
intimidated by my colleagues' objections, which is why it took me so long to begin writing
this book.

to let him run his relationship with Dr Davoine on his own, I did no more than jot down the telephone number of the hospital. The conversation dragged on for a good half-hour: they were waiting for me to start talking. Since I did not do so, Josephine boldly spoke out: *'So what d'you think? Can you cure him?'* I answered that I had myself been cured by *words* and I tried to explain, using the terms of witchcraft, what a cure by words consisted of. All Josephine could gather was that I had myself been bewitched and had pulled through: *'The others wanted to get you!'* Thinking about my aversion to being paid – for at that time I still could not accept it – I declared that my own cure had left me with an unpaid debt, since my therapist had said: *'You'll cure someone as I cured you.'* They, of course, did not take it like that: they were obviously fascinated by the fact that I had managed to escape the clutches of a witch, thinking it absolutely normal that I was indebted to my therapist for my cure; but so far as they were concerned, they *must* pay me.

At the end of our conversation, Jean, foreseeing my unwillingness to receive any money, said to his wife: *'Fine, go and get the fowl'*, and she brought me an enormous cock, plucked and dressed.[24] I accepted it, and said there should be nothing more for the time being, on the spurious ground that it was *'not good'* for Jean's therapy. I knew that in doing this I shocked them in their convictions, but I could not yet bring myself to accept payment. Today I can say of this modesty that in one sense it was altogether well-founded: I proposed to operate with words, that is, with some sort of psychotherapy – about which I did not even know very much at the time – because I did not consider myself as belonging to any magic tradition. Things were to be altogether different a few months later when, having become the assistant of my unwitcher, I could associate myself with her teachings and practices, and bring in patients who wished to be unwitched: their presents in money or in goods no longer bothered me, even when they imagined they were giving them to an unwitcher.

To return to the beginning of the conversation. According to Josephine, Madame Marie of Izé's death was to be taken as a defeat, which is why the Babins then turned to me. *'The woman from Izé'*, she says, *'found someone stronger than herself, who did her in* [who killed her magically]. *They* [unwitchers] *always die like that.* [Of course, everyone knows that] *Madame Marie had*

---

[24] Giving a cock to one's unwitcher is of course quite a step for someone who is asking the unwitcher to lift his sexual impotence. My way of recoiling at the Babins' request – in spite of my explicit intention of agreeing to it – can be seen in this story. That evening I came back home and showed the cock to my young son, saying: 'A bewitched man gave me a hen.' He instantly noticed my slip of the tongue and laughed. Next day, when we ate what I cautiously called the *'fowl'* he reminded me once again that it was a cock. This time I had a better excuse, or a more devious one, since Jean Babin himself had called it a *'fowl'*. But the fact that he himself may have been caught in the effects of the witch's words to his wife – who had predicted she might marry a *'nanny-billy, neither a nanny-goat nor a billy-goat, neither a man nor a woman'* – was certainly no reason why I should share this confusion about the sex of the animal Jean had given me.

cancer, but she must have found someone stronger. . .' The medical aspect of the illness which carried off the unwitcher is not unrecognized; but in the interpretation, it is only considered to be a secondary cause. Since spells are involved, the first cause of any death, even a natural one, must be found in a witch's will, a necessarily *'stronger'* will than that of the deceased.

'And didn't you go and see Madame Auguste?' I asked, trying to find some solution suitable for the Babins, and one which would also avoid my getting further involved.

'*Ah'* says Jean admiringly *'a powerful woman, she is! Tall and strong, she would not be afraid of a farmer!'* She is thus a woman vigorous enough to fight a man, if it came to that, and her exceptional strength is interpreted as a sign that she automatically qualifies as a possessor of magic force.[25] This is perhaps why Madame Marie chose her as an assistant and *'passed the spell on to her before dying'.* Madame Auguste, the former driver, assistant and confidante of the *'woman from Izé'* is now an unwitcher in her own right and has the good taste to be surprised: *'it's funny'*, she often says, *'but it* [the magic force] *works on me as much as it did on her* [Madame Marie]. *I didn't expect it.'* In the eyes of her patients Madame Auguste's surprise at this anonymous force now living inside her and which *'works on'* her, proves that she is not an impostor. Josephine in fact thinks her an effective magician now that one of her brothers-in-law *'who was caught tight'* is being unwitched by her.

But the Babins did not call her in, though they cannot tell me exactly why. I can, however, make some assumptions as to the reasons for this refusal.

(*a*) Before being bewitched, Jean was an exceptionally vigorous man: '*At the corn-chandler's'*, says his brother Louis, *'he would carry hundred-kilo sacks, and he was never tired. Now he wouldn't even be able to carry one.'* Similarly, during the harvesting season, when the village boys have competitions to show who is strongest, Jean had the reputation of being a clear winner. But when three weeks before his wedding, Ribault cast a spell over him, his vigour, strength of character, and sexual potency suddenly vanished. Since then, he persistently defines himself as a fundamentally weak person.

When his progress from unwitcher to unwitcher is examined, it becomes clear that he is unable to ask a strong woman to cure his weakness: the only one he ever trusted, Madame Marie, looked particularly fragile. This was not the case with Marie of Alençon, who could not cure him of his eczema and whom he refused to take on later as an unwitcher, or with Madame Auguste.[26] It would seem that Jean Babin's difficulties, either in getting

[25] The physical appearance of an unwitcher is always interpreted as the visible sign of his magic force: (*a*) either, as in the case of Madame Marie, her apparent frailness contrasts with her actual magic force, so that the absence of physical force is then a sign of the presence of magic force; (*b*) or the unwitcher's sturdiness and build reinforce the patient's belief in his magic force.

[26] Remember, even before the appearance of his sexual impotence – Jean's main symptom, which he asked me to lift – the ulcerated eczema which led him to Madame Marie and made it impossible for him to get married.

married or in consummating his marriage, cannot be overcome by a woman unwitcher who also had these characteristics: physical strength/strength of character/magic force. For reasons which have to do with his own mental organization, at least one of these attributes had to be severed from the others.

(*b*) The '*woman from Izé*', the only unwitcher he had dared ask outright to unwitch him, had refused to do so, and had only guaranteed that his marriage would survive as long as he kept the copula. She had thus tried to isolate his sexual impotence from the other symptoms – loss of livestock, accidents, and so on. But she had been frustrated by events: true, the Babins were still together, although they had not been able to consummate their marriage, but they could not remain indefinitely passive before the crisis, the mounting up of other symptoms. This drove the Babins to consult the priest from Torcé, the one who '*believed*'. But in so doing they were changing unwitchers and might wonder whether the copula still had any effect.

(*c*) The priest of Torcé was eaily able to overcome the Babins' secondary witches, the Chicots – with the help, admittedly, of the stranger who made those fatal predictions in the café at Torcé – but he finally declared himself powerless in the face of Jean's impotence. But in some sense, the priest succeeded where the '*woman from Izé*' had failed: by lifting all the symptoms except the sexual impotence, he kept this last relatively isolated, and the Babins seemed to have been content for a few months with the guarantee offered by the copula.[27]

(*d*) Unfortunately, Madame Marie died in 1969. The Babins never explicitly related her death to the events which followed, but I may note that Jean once again felt dominated by the awe-inspiring gaze of Ribault, his main witch, and the cause, according to him, of his sexual impotence. Instead of going to consult the powerful Madame Auguste, who intimidated him, or any other unwitcher, Jean threw himself into the bout of drunkenness which led him to the psychiatric hospital.

In other words, the Babins met me at the very moment when they should have called for Madame Auguste, and they immediately identified me with her structural opposite, represented in their minds, by the late Madame Marie. Like her, according to Josephine, I am '*small, thin, and we can see that what we said is working on you. That means the others* [Babin's witches, but also those of my other interlocutors, who, as Josephine was clearly conveying,

---

[27] In my opinion, remember, the missionary who came to preach for Lent at Torcé had succeeded in·curing the eczema which prevented Jean from getting married by depending on these factors: (*a*) he was himself a man, a man marked with the sign of sexual abstinence, and therefore in a position to make statements that it was the Divine Will that a healthy farmer ought to get married; (*b*) he had interpreted and treated Jean's symptom outside any witchcraft context, using magic-religious means. His refusal to take any payment for the cure made it quite clear that he considered himself to be an operator of the Divine Will and not someone exerting any kind of personal stake in the matter.

could in no way be informants] *that means the others are now working on you.*' She already knew I was hearing other accounts of witchcraft, and could hardly imagine that they produced no effect on me; I admitted that I dreamt of it at night and sometimes suffered from insomnia. Fine looked at her husband and declared sententiously: '*That's it, she's struggling like Madame Marie! These small women, they look delicate, but they're tough!*'

The Babins then asked me about my life and circumstances. Like Madame Marie, I had two children; like her, I was not fond of money; like her, I was courageous, '*always on the roads alone*', a characteristic which weighed with Jean since he no longer drove unless it was absolutely necessary from fear of accidents caused by Ribault's gaze; lastly, the Babins noted that, just like Madame Marie, I had '*trembling hands*', a reliable sign that my interlocutors' witches were '*working on me*'.

Josephine could even prove that I was the person they said I was: after our previous conversation, Jean had met his witch as he was on his way to shop in Torcé. For the first time in months, Ribault had avoided his victim's eyes, an important event immediately credited to my '*force*'. '*The other didn't feel strong enough to play tricks*', said Jean. Josephine then repeated her request: '*if you feel capable of stopping the other from playing tricks on him. . . of recovering your force, Jean*' she said, looking at each of us in turn. She immediately warned me that Ribault would not hesitate to attack me '*as soon as he feels capable of taking his* [Babin's] *force again*', a borrowed force, which, passing from me to her husband, had victoriously demonstrated itself against the witch.

We were interrupted by the arrival of the vet, who had come to examine a sick animal. As soon as he knocked at the door, Josephine quickly took me to a store-room: I had decisively passed over to the side of magic knowledge, which, as it is outlawed, must never confront positivist knowledge. Taking advantage of the fact that her husband was temporarily detained at the stable, Fine turned to me with great vigour: '*If you would only cure him!*' she begged. This time, she was asking me to understand that Jean was so '*weak*' that he was not even capable of wanting to be cured, and that I had to want it for him (or against his will). '*You know*', she reminded me, '*my brother-in-law wanted to see the doctor. . .*' to persuade him to operate on Jean's '*kidneys*' without his knowledge. But I knew that no cure, either by magic or by words, could be attempted without the formal commitment of the person concerned, and I replied that only he could ask me to cure him. As he entered the store-room to fetch us, he overheard my words. Fine looked at him critically, and ostentatiously left: '*well I'd best be getting back to my work, I'll leave you*'.

Once he was alone with me, Jean looked as though he had literally been struck dumb. I tried to tell him how I conceived this unwitching by words, and he faintly approved the principle: '*I don't mind. . . I'm willing to start, but there's the doctor's treatments. . .*' That he should talk about medical knowledge in this way only a few minutes after his wife had treated me as a magician seemed to me to demonstrate his resistance: Jean himself did not want to embark on any kind of cure; all in all, the doctor's tonics seemed less disturbing, although probably quite ineffective because all he had to do was to swallow them passively. The psychiatrist had merely asked him a few technical questions about his sexual life; as usual, Josephine had answered in her husband's place: *'it's over before he's ready'* she had explained, meaning by this that Jean suffered from premature ejaculation. The doctor had responded to this statement by writing a prescription.

For my part, I do not think I was driven by any wish to perform miracles, either through words or through some kind of unwitching ritual. I had accepted the idea of facing the Babins' request because it was put to me in such an urgent and desperate way that it would have been inhumane to back out. When, however, it became obvious that Jean had absolutely no desire to commit himself personally, I thought it right to put off my proposal to undertake a cure; I told him to call me back, if he wished, once he had finished with Dr Davoine; and I left without making a new appointment. At that point he offered me the *'fowl'*, a word which for several days kept reminding me both of Jean's mysterious attitude to his troubles and my own concerning the role I meant to play in this story.

In January and February 1970 I met them again a few times, as well as Louis and Marthe Babin, to fill in a few details of their story. My presence and questions seemed justified by my status as a town unwitcher: *'Of course'*, said Jean, *'they don't play the same tricks on you in town. So, if you want to understand the tricks that are being played on me. . .'* The awkwardness of the situation was nevertheless obvious to us all, since Jean Babin did not seem in the least anxious to undertake any cure at all, either by words, as I had suggested, or by the magic methods current in the Bocage. That I had been able to *'take on myself'* his story seems to have momentarily comforted him, as can be inferred from the episode of the meeting with his witch and from the peace which settled over his farm during those few weeks. Having both decided I was an unwitcher and contrasted me with the image of the *'woman from Alençon'*, he was to a certain extent lessening the urge to *'do something'* to save his marriage; having been given the chance to call me in spared him from having to consult the great Madame Auguste. But at the same time, since he asked no more of me than that I should serve as formal guarantee, we no longer had any reason to go into his story: speaking immediately calls for a commitment on the part of both unwitcher and patient. So, when he ended a conversation with the sentence: *'we'll write to you if anything abnormal happens'*, I had already decided I would not need to come back to La Croix.

NOT MUCH BELIEVING

Sixteen months later, in June 1971, I went back to see the Babins, guessing that they still had not met the magician 'capable' of 'pulling them through'. My progression through witchcraft had taken a distinct turn ever since an old bewitched man, père Séquard, had acted as my annunciator and had brought me to his unwitcher, Madame Flora. They both thought that the mere fact that I listened to the stories of the bewitched endangered me: my interlocutors' witches could not fail, at some point or other, to turn against me. In one sense their interpretation was quite relevant: the discourse of the bewitched affected me deeply, and I was continuously torn between the fascination which made me go on listening and the fear which sometimes paralysed me for weeks.

When, after a period of fear and uncertainty, I began an unwitching cure with Madame Flora, I immediately felt relieved. My previous progression from bewitched to bewitched she instantly interpreted as simply suicidal: I had let myself get '*caught*' in the discourse of witchcraft without providing myself with any symbolic guarantees. (Positivist ideology, which had so effectively protected my colleagues against this possibility, could be of no use to me since it cautiously avoided considering the real power of the discourse of witchcraft except by using the effects of suggestion as an explanation.) That this discourse could cause an effect of panic seemed absolutely obvious to Madame Flora, who not only proposed to unwitch me but also to help me in my work. Of course, she carefully avoided communicating her '*secrets*' to me, just as I never asked her to; but, as the months went by, she invited me more and more often to her consultations, in which I was given a far from negligible role. She was also favourable to the idea of my publishing a book, probably because she imagined she would find her competitors' secrets in it as well as the kinds of stories she relished.

The fact that she could thus stand surety for my state as one bewitched, my position as assistant unwitcher, and my undertaking to write about spells at last enabled me to present myself in the Bocage in a way that enabled me to recognize myself. The brilliant way in which she managed her cures – including my own – provoked my admiration, so that I thought it natural to speak of her to the Babins: this time, I would not be proposing a hypothetical cure through words, since I now had a base in a magic tradition; also, for my own convenience, I could propose the name of an unwitcher they did not know and whose passionate interest in her work showed she was '*stronger*' than I.

I should say here that my decision to see the Babins again to propose the services of Madame Flora was based on a certainty that they keenly wished to be unwitched and that it was simply due to circumstance that this had not yet been achieved. Jean had only met two unwitchers whose frail appearance – at least in his eyes – suited him. The '*woman from Izé*' had backed out on the ground that Jean was '*caught too tight*', and I had not been able to understand from his account what had justified such a view: he was of course seriously bewitched, but he seemed less threatened than other patients of Madame Marie's, the Brodins of La Bouronnière, for example. On the other hand, now that I had met several unwitchers and often taken part in Madame Flora's work, I understood better the way in which I had disappointed the Babins: (1) even when an unwitching cure takes place through words only – as was the case with Madame Flora – this is never explicitly said. (2) In any case these words are pronounced in highly ritualized situations. (3) Although it is essential for the bewitched to put forward his request for a cure and his desire for the death of his witch, the unwitcher '*takes it all on himself*', including what his patient does not say, and expresses it in his stead with a degree of violence I should certainly have been incapable of.

It seemed to me that by not following up my proposition to unwitch him by words, Jean Babin had shown elementary wisdom. But my self-criticism still left me with the impression that he really was seeking the magician who would pull him through. When I went to talk to him of Madame Flora, I had no idea he was going to refuse, or the way in which Josephine would decide to undertake the cure I was proposing. I then learnt that, for reasons to do with the prehistory of the spell on his sexual potency, Jean was in an inescapable situation with regard to witchcraft. His wife summed it up in this way: '*The trouble with him is that he doesn't much believe*' ... in spells. This chapter is an attempt to understand how she was able to say that and how he was able to live with it – or die from it.

I. If she can work from a photo...

I found the Babins at La Croix, seated at table with their neighbours, who had come to help them bring in the hay. They greeted me very warmly, but an approaching storm meant they had to finish their work quickly, so as not to lose the harvest. They suggested I come back the next day.[1]

---

[1] This time I did not take notes – in fact I never took notes during a conversation, except on my first visit to the Babins. When I saw them again in 1971, I sometimes worked with a

When I arrived, Jean was out, which displeased Josephine: '*He knew, he knew you were coming!*' I paid no attention to this, thinking he was kept longer than expected by one of those unforeseeable events which occur every day in a farmer's life. Josephine immediately took up the conversation where we had left off sixteen months before:

'*I'm all right*' she began '*but for the boss* [Jean], *things haven't changed: my husband and I still haven't had intercourse.*'

'What about the animals, is everything all right?'

'*Yes, things are all right . . . well, we've lost four calves since the beginning of the year!*' These losses were not very great, given the size of their herd, and apparently she thought they were natural, since she described these failed calvings in great detail. Yet she unexpectedly concluded: '*it's normal in a way, but still . . .*'

Since the Chicots, their secondary witches, had been defeated, I asked her about her principal witch:

'What about your neighbour? [Ribault].' I learnt that they had at last found an efficient way to protect themselves from him.

'*Well, we don't see him. My husband sent him packing last June or July* [1970], *I can't say what hour* [at which moment exactly Jean sent him packing]. *He* [Ribault] *came to say hello* [to Jean, who had the courage this time to refuse the neighbour's outstretched hand and to declare firmly:] – *I'll shake hands with you when your hands are clean, but not before.* [Notice the ambiguity of this statement, which can be explained either by a previous conflict between the two farmers, or an accusation of witchcraft]'. '*I wasn't there,*' said Josephine '*but still, I know that Jean sent him packing. And now he* [Ribault] *leaves him alone.*' As support for her husband's declaration of war against their witch, Josephine had faced him in a silent staring-match. Since then, Ribault had not talked to the Babins, had avoided their eyes and no longer offered to shake hands. Because of this, the cattle were doing well – except for a few possibly questionable calvings, and the Babins could be said to be prospering, if it were not for the fact that their marriage still had not been consummated.

I announced the purpose of my visit: 'I came to see you because I've met a . . . Since I last saw you, I've met many people who lift spells . . .'

'*Have you, have you now?*' said Josephine, her eyes suddenly sparkling.

'In particular I've met a woman in the Manche département, at Taron, a fortune-teller who knows about spells.'

'*Really?*'

'I have been going to see her for more than a year now. It's because I myself got caught, in the end . . . You know, getting involved in these things:

tape-recorder intended, in principle, as a safeguard against my own forgetfulness. But later on we will see how illusory this safeguard was, since I was incapable, for example, of writing out part of this recorded conversation, precisely the part I did not want to hear. The presence of the tape-recorder nonetheless explains the extra animation of the dialogue.

I kept falling ill and having car accidents. And one day, a farmer told me: *"But you can't go on like that! Listening to all those stories ..."'*

'*Ah yes*', Josephine filled in, '*someone* [a witch] *set upon you.*'

'He [père Séquard] lost seventy fat pigs. [He was therefore well placed to be my annunciator].'

'*Ah yes!*' Josephine said, warmly.

'So he went to see her to ask her to pull me through. He said to me: '*I'll get you an appointment because the mère* [Flora] *is secretive; you have to go with someone she knows, otherwise she won't see you, she'll say: "I don't do it."* [I don't unwitch].'

'*Well, well.*'

'The woman from Taron uncaught me in three or four months. [This was Madame Flora's conviction, although she did not explain to me why I was still needing to be unwitched, at the rate of one séance a month].'

'*Really!*' exclaimed Josephine, visibly impressed.

'At the same time she took a liking to me, she is interested in what I'm doing and she lets me help her sometimes ...'

'*In other words, you work with her!*'

'A couple of weeks ago, I thought of you, and I said to her: "Look, I met a couple last year, who were unable to consummate their marriage." She said to me: *"did they suffer losses too?"* – "Yes" – "*Well*", she said to me, "*I know what that is, I can do it.*" [In such cases, I know how to unwitch]. "She gave me five or six examples such as yours where she succeeded. Since I have been going to her, I have never met anyone who was unable to consummate their marriage, but I have seen her 'pulling through' people who suffered losses, illnesses ..."'

'*Yes, yes ...*'

'I only recently thought of mentioning you to her. Since I had no news, I thought that ... perhaps ...'

'*No, no*' said Josephine who understood I was alluding to the doctor's prescription for tonics. '*Absolutely not! I'll never go back to that doctor. Never!*'

To tell the truth, I was not in the least surprised by Josephine's decision, or by her outburst of anger. In 1970, a few days after my first encounter with the Babins, Dr Davoine had asked me about them; he wanted to know how long those silent peasants had agreed to talk to me. My answer – 'three hours' – had at first flabbergasted him. After a short silence he said to me: 'I know why: it's because you didn't stop them.' Astonished in my turn, I had asked for what reason I should have stopped them: 'In the cause of reality', he answered. This otherwise extremely sensitive doctor (but it seems that no one escapes from the psychiatric dictum, which has it that any false idea can produce delirium) had then taken advantage of the Babins' next visit to oppose their convictions.

'*He said one has to be mentally ill to believe in spells*', Josephine then told me indignantly. (Remember that her complaint was justified in that the Babins would never have talked about witchcraft in the hospital if they had not specifically been asked to do so.) '*We went together, Jean and I. At one point, he told me to go next door, and he came to talk to me* [in a case of 'collective delirium', it is good practice to separate inductor from induced]. *He said his brother* [Louis Babin, Jean's brother and Josephine's ally, and, in the eyes of the psychiatrist, the co-inductor of this collective delirium]. *He said his brother ought to mind his own business* [i.e. he ought to stop urging the doctor to have Jean operated on without his knowing] *and that one had to be mentally retarded or mentally deranged to believe in spells. Ah, I can tell you I wasn't pleased!*' '*Me neither*', said Jean, '*he told me to drop those fairy tales*'.[2] After that, whenever I met the doctor, I avoided mentioning the Babins and only talked about my work in vague terms. But to come back to my conversation with Josephine, in June 1971:

'*I'll never go back to that doctor!*' she exclaimed. '*Because he says to me, all that* [spells], *in the old days people were so backward he says. But now, we mustn't believe in all that.*' She vividly remembers the humiliation he inflicted on her: '*he treats us like real idiots. So, he said to me, Madame Favret is going to cure you, is she?*' Convinced of his own superior knowledge, he kept making fun of her convictions: '*We doctors, he said, are much stronger, science is the strongest!*' She was not impressed in any way, but could not forgive him for his arrogance: '*Ah, did he talk! It didn't do any good, though, because I'm certainly not going back to see him! He had no call to say that I'm totally backward! Well, really, he's trying to put us on . . . you can't imagine! I said it must be a spell. But you're not going to believe in that, he said to me! There was an accident* [the beam which fell on Jean three weeks before the wedding] *but it has nothing to do with it! Peasants are so retarded, he says . . . In the old days, it was all right* [to use spells as an explanation of a biological misfortune], *in the old days, it was all right, but nowadays, you mustn't believe in all that! And your brother-in-law* [Louis Babin], *whose business is he minding, he says to me? You've got to get all that* [spells] *out of your head, it's not true, they cannot exist. We . . . science is so modern that it's able to deal with any illness!*[3] *Well if that's not something* [to make such arrogant speeches], *if that's not something: with all the losses* [we've had] *and all that! I'd like to see your brother-in-law, he said to me, there are a few things I want to say to him! I think that if Louis had come, he would have punched him on the nose!*' she ended laughing.

She only told me the real reason for her deep resentment against the doctor in front of her husband a little while later. Dr Davoine had tried to convince her that the responsibility for Jean's impotence was not due to spells but to Josephine herself: '*He said I was to blame, because he said Jean is normal. He said it was my fault. That's not very subtle, I can tell you. That's not very subtle!*' she sobbed.

'Why did he say you were to blame?'

---

[2] On the psychiatric notion of 'collective delirium' cf. Appendix 4, 'The yardstick of truth', pp. 250–66.

[3] Through Josephine's way of reporting the speech of Dr Davoine, one cannot fail to hear Dr Wahl's remarks on 'archaic delirium': cf. Appendix 4, 'The yardstick of truth'.

'*He said if things were like that* [if Jean is impotent] *it was my fault because . . . I don't know, I wasn't loving enough!*'

'What does he know?' I was astonished, for if anything, it seemed to me that the opposite was true: from what I knew of the Babins' sexual life, Jean was continuously terrified at the idea that his wife would try and awaken his desire, and every night he carefully waited for her to be asleep before getting into the bed. Jean, who spoke so little, seized the occasion to give a sign of his presence:

'*Well, he's not in the bed! That's what I told him. I told him!*' he repeated banging his fist on the table.

But to get back to the conversation which took place between me and Josephine while we were waiting for Jean to arrive. Since an appeal to the medical world was now impossible, I asked about unwitchers:

'Otherwise, have you been to see anyone? [an unwitcher].'

'*Ah well, I mean, we never went to see Madame Auguste, because my husband doesn't have any confidence in all that, since . . .*'

The notes I took in 1971 from a tape recording of this conversation contain the following astonishing passage, quite typical of the deafness that so often descended on me in the course of my work: '*This is followed by an inaudible story, about an unwitcher — not Madame Auguste, but someone else — who accused Jean Babin of being one of his neighbour's witches. "Some people were in trouble* [bewitched], *here, in our quartier and they said my husband had done it."*'

Of course, Josephine's remarks were ambiguous, as always where witchcraft is concerned: thus, she said '*in trouble*' for bewitched, '*done it*' for cast a spell, and so on. But by June 1971, I had a perfect understanding of this kind of allusion and I myself used these terms without difficulty: note, for example, that I had spoken of going to see '*someone*' rather than explicitly saying an unwitcher. On the other hand, it seems incredible to me today that this particular passage should have been inaudible, since, later on in the recording I could hear the drone of the Babins' washing machine, but could still understand their words. At the most, Josephine had been talking to me hastily, because she wanted to tell me everything before Jean's arrival, but I was used to that too. The most likely assumption then is that I did not want to hear her account of a crucial episode – about which I did not ask a single question – because taking it into account would have meant revising my version of the Babins' story: if their troubles originally came from this accusation of witchcraft, what could they expect from an unwitcher and what exactly had they wanted of me the year before? Had they talked about this accusation to the '*woman from Alençon*', or only of his eczema, and then of a spell? Had the '*woman from Izé*' backed out because they told her, or because she sensed they were not telling her everything? Why had they not mentioned a word of it to me? Would they be willing to talk about it to Madame Flora?

My confusion can be partly explained by the fact that Josephine had not in the least situated this crucial episode in the time-scale of her story, so that for one minute I thought the accusation had been made by the great Madame Auguste. Jean had always thought of her as formidable, and I must admit that I shared his opinion. In January–February 1970, I had been eager to meet her so as to hear about the life-story of her initiator, Madame Marie, whom the Babins had described in such striking terms, and in the hope that I would be able to follow her nocturnal wanderings. The Babins had considered my wish quite normal: knowing her would help me to understand the subtleties of rural witches and to become more efficient in unwitching Jean. Moreover, their brother-in-law, then a client of Madame Auguste, had already asked to meet me and he could easily act as intermediary. Once he was stopped by ice on the roads as he was going to Izé to talk to her about me. Then the Babins never spoke to me of her again.[4] I lived impatiently through those days of waiting – at last I was reaching my goal – but at the same time I was terrified: this fierce woman who had a man's name and who could lift up a farmer at arm's length gave me nightmares. My plan of getting her to talk about Madame Marie also caused me some misgivings: after all, the Babins had definitely identified me with her, but she was dead and everyone thought that a witch had *'done her in'*. I was not in the least impressed by the alleged force of witches, but I had already tested, on certain dramatic occasions, the tremendous force of the language of witchcraft. It was obvious to me that I could not both admit being *'caught'* and not run any risks. By June 1971, anyway, I had several times experienced my inability always to avoid the consequences of my involvement in this discourse.

Hence my stupid question to Josephine, as a result of which she stopped telling me about the initial accusation against Jean, and began to complain about the uselessness of the unwitchers they had so far consulted:

'Was it Madame Auguste who said that? [that Jean was the neighbour's witch].'

'*Oh no, no, no, no! He* [Jean] *went there a long time ago* [to see Madame Auguste] . . . *Well, at that time, it wasn't Madame Auguste, but Madame Marie, and she said: You know several of them* [witches] *are on him. I can't do anything. He's been to see four or five* [unwitchers] *and nothing doing. He went to see the woman from Alençon who was supposed to cure him and she didn't! So I don't know what to say to him* [Jean]. *He says: "How come? She cures others and it doesn't do a thing for me. It* [unwitching] *succeeds with others, but with me, nothing." So, what do you expect? he's losing confidence!*'

So if Jean *'didn't much believe'*, in spells, it was because he had several times got to the limits of an unwitcher's competence. (1) One of them had wrongly accused him of bewitching his neighbours. (To avoid any confu-

---

[4] In June 1971, Josephine told me that Madame Auguste had actually refused to meet me because she was afraid of being denounced to the police. '*She said to my brother-in-law: well, I was caught* [once before], *I don't want to see anyone, because suddenly, huh, you're under arrest.*'

sion, I would like to add that this neighbour has not yet appeared in my account.) (2) So far, no unwitcher had been able to lift the spells which he was subject to.

From the point of view of a bewitched, I thought that Jean's scepticism was not equally well-founded in both cases, and that he himself must realize this. He could hardly be surprised at his therapists' failures if he had given them the same version of the facts that he had given me (a version in which he carefully omitted any reference to the fact that someone else thought he was a witch, even and especially if the accusation was unjust) and if he had presented himself as an ordinary bewitched (in so far as such people exist), or if he had not *'told everything'* to his successive unwitchers. I hope it is clear by now that if I have taken so much trouble to describe this story in its minutest details, it is because it brings out a typical situation, in which the bewitched identifies himself as such after being accused of witchcraft. If one thinks that for any bewitched person there is an innocent witch whose survival depends on his capacity to face such an accusation, the Babins' erratic course illustrates some of the difficulties of this situation: they cannot, it seems, ask for the help of an unwitcher except by breaking an essential rule of the cure, which is to *'tell everything'* to one's therapist.

Josephine thought that if her husband got no better *'perhaps it's because he has powerful blood: it works on him, oh yes, it works on him!'*. In this way, it seems to me, she was expressing the dramatic ambiguity in which her husband had been struggling for so long: Jean was big, red-faced and well-built; but at the same time, he felt fundamentally *'weak'*. His *'blood'* had seemed *'strong'* enough for a healer to propose to initiate him into his secrets; but Jean sharply refused to have access to the *'force'*, even if it were *'for good'*. Some neighbour had called Jean a witch, but he himself claimed to be bewitched, obstinately repeating over and over again that he was not what everyone took him to be: despite the way he was talked about and all that his strong constitution might suggest, he said he was *'not master'* of himself, and he behaved irresponsibly like a drunkard or a bewitched person. Nonetheless, whatever he said or did, his *'powerful blood'* – like an anonymous force, like an *'it'* from who knows where – *'his powerful blood works on him'*, and regularly frustrated the *'force'* of the unwitchers.

When Jean finally turned up, Josephine had already questioned me at length on the way in which Madame Flora worked. She had a keen desire to go and consult her, but she was afraid of her husband's resistance: *'It's just that he doesn't believe much, he doesn't have any confidence in all that sort of thing'* she kept repeating. As for me, disconcerted as I was by what I had just learnt – and almost certain that Jean's long hesitation had been caused by his fear of me or of unwitching – I would have preferred to put this conversation off and take some time to think. So I talked with him about meaningless things, dragging out as long as possible this moment of 'phatic' exchange, as Malinowski would say. Seeing, however, that Josephine was bursting with

impatience, I preferred to speak about Madame Flora myself, so I regret-
fully came to the heart of the matter. Fine, who thought I was not going fast
enough and not emphasizing the essential points – those which could
convince her husband – kept interrupting me. She triumphantly insisted on
the episode of my own bewitchment:

'*And she* [Madame Flora] *told you that one* [a witch] *had fallen on you!*'

Jean was startled and asked me exactly when this diagnosis had been
given. My answer, totally in accord with the historical truth – 'last year, at
Easter' – narrowed his eyes, which had been shiftier than ever, and, as
usual, hidden by smoked glasses. If this were true, I was confirmed in the
position he had previously attributed to me, of '*taking it all on myself*', for it
was at that time that the '*woman from Alençon's*' prediction was supposed to
have come true: '*If you don't do anything, you will stay married only six years.*' The
fact was that after meeting me in 1970, not only had they remained married
but he had found enough courage to protect himself in any form of contact
with Ribault.

I gave a detailed explanation of Madame Flora's methods, price, and the
frequency of the séances. Jean, in an extremely excited tone of voice,
interrupted me and asked: '*What about a photo, can she read from a photo?*'

I answered I had never seen her work in that way and that I thought it
unlikely: I knew how keen Madame Flora was for her clients to commit
themselves body and soul to their cure. Jean was immensely disappointed.
He then began to give me a series of plausible arguments which were to lead
to his refusal:[5]

'*Taron's not that near!*' he mumbled.

'No, it's not near, but some people come a hundred kilometers,' I tried to
argue.

'*I'm not denying that*', answered Jean, annoyed. '*After all I did go as far as
Alençon and it didn't change a thing* [it didn't get me cured]. *To Taron, every three
days!*'

'*No, no* [exclaimed Josephine] *three times in nine days to begin with, then once a
month, until you're cured!*'

'*That's enough!*' interrupted Jean, banging on the table.

'You're fed up with all that sort of thing?' I asked, relieved that he had
dared to refuse so quickly. But he felt obliged to give me other reasons.

'*Well in the first place, you have to spend the day there* [which was of course
untrue]. *If she wants my photo* [without my having to go there], *she can try, I'm
willing.*'

Josephine suggested going on a Sunday, to see. Jean became quite angry.

---

[5] One can compare the arguments Jean Babin put forward with those of Louise Régnier, when
I suggested we make an appointment for her to discuss their story with her husband and me.
Later on, it will be seen that if it had not been for his wife's insistence, Jean Babin, like Louise
Régnier, would have barricaded himself within what I have called the domain of the
unspeakable. Cf. Ch. 6, pp. 77–91.

'*Yes, but it comes to the same thing, on Sundays!* [You know I am making hay every day of the week, in this foul weather, and that soon it'll be the harvest season]. *I will not go to Taron, and that's that! You can go if you like but I'm not going.*' He then asked me another question.

'*Can you ask her if she can do it from a photo?*'

'Of course, but I don't think she does . . .'

'*Can she work from a photo?*' he repeated, without heeding my reply. I then remembered having seen her look at a photo in a particularly tricky situation, where the father of the bewitched was the only objective persecutor and a furious one at that; she had not been able to avert the accusation away from the family circle, as she usually did.

'What I do know is that if the witch is a member of the family, she asks for a photo. But, it's the one who's got something [the bewitched] who must go to the consultation. My reply was accurate, but particularly unfortunate: for it could be taken to mean that in the eyes of my seer only a witch, i.e. someone who was hiding his true identity could appear on a photograph which, in some sense, spoke up for him. Jean then remembered the unjust accusation which had been made against him:

'*Yes, but sometimes people can think someone is something he isn't*', he said. His scepticism overrode all our arguments: '*As for me, I won't go. If she wants my photo* [that's all right, since one cannot ask a photo to "*tell all*". If not] *I won't go and get my face smashed in again!*' [in a car accident, as has so often happened]. '*I would rather go back to the hospital with the lunatics*', he remarked laughing, '*and do nothing all day long* [carefully protected by the hospital's high walls and my status as a passive patient] *I'm fed up with going to every Tom, Dick and Harry!*' [all those unwitchers, who are so good at lifting other people's spells but unable to deal with mine], he shouted. '*Let her go once if she wants to* [Josephine, who believes] *but for me, I don't give a damn!*'

'*You're afraid to go by car*', his wife pointed out in a soothing voice. '*Well, the lady* [Madame Favret] *can come and fetch us* . . . [she is not afraid of driving].

'*I'm fed up with the whole thing!*' Jean screamed. '*You can go if you want, I'm not going!*' For he could only respond to his wife's unanswerable arguments with an outburst of violence or a reminder that he had weak nerves: '*It's going to take me the whole afternoon*' he grumbled.

'*It's his nerves*', explained Fine. '*It's his nerves that are working on him*', because he was worried by the idea of unwitchment. Seeing his sensitivity thus acknowledged immediately calmed Jean: he spoke to me at length about entirely trivial matters in a warm and friendly tone, then proceeded to leave us, saying that I could make an appointment with Madame Flora for his wife. As for himself, he would only appear in the form of his wedding picture.

II. The bewitched as witch

I shall not go into Josephine Babin's unwitchment here, as I propose to describe it at length in a second volume. I will only say that for all the time it took, like the others it had no effect on the central problem: the Babins were still not able to consummate their marriage. But I would just like to mention one thing about it. Josephine never said a word to Madame Flora about the unjust accusation which had formerly been made against her husband, but she often talked about it to me after the day I had been to see her, in June 1971.

If she was able to do this, I think it was because in her eyes I had definitely lost my position as unwitcher: even though my relationship with Madame Flora implied that I would one day become a magician, she would never again consider me as being in charge of her destiny. She did begin to pay me, giving me several presents of meat or money, but, in theory, this was to pay my petrol expenses. We were then both Madame Flora's clients, and as she was present at my consultations, she was able to estimate my weakness. So we soon formed a friendship, a complicity between two women, and during the journey from Torcé to Taron and back, two hours each way, we would talk about our lives and comment on our respective consultations.

She spoke for the second time about this accusation of witchcraft during a conversation about her husband's drunkenness: Jean had been the favourite child of his father – himself a confirmed drunkard – who had taken him on his drinking bouts in the cafés of the region while he was still a child; but Josephine considered that her husband had only really become a drunk at the age of 28, after a neighbour, Nouet of La Grimetière, had accused him of being his witch.

This account, which she repeated on several occasions without ever changing a word of it, is quite short: according to Josephine, the Nouets had already lost a lot of animals when, in 1959, the *'mistress'* of the farm fell ill. An unwitcher was consulted, and showed them how to identify their witch: *'The first person to ask you for help is doing it'* [bewitching you]. Note that, as always, when the accused speaks of his accuser's unwitcher, the method used is necessarily rudimentary, if not stupid. The next day, Jean's motorbike broke down at the beginning of the path to La Grimetière, and he wanted to borrow a tool. The Nouets first refused to answer him, then to his astonishment, they began to accuse him vehemently: *'So it's you, you filth! So it's you who's doing it to us!'* Jean unsuccessfully tried to explain matters, then went home, totally bewildered. *'That's why'*, concluded Josephine, *'ever since, he doesn't much believe.'*

From that day on, Jean claimed he did not believe in spells and still less in the competence of unwitchers. Note, however, that he then began to get drunk systematically with his father, and that everyone at the Babins' – except his mother, whom I shall talk about in a moment – interpreted his drunkenness as the effect of a spell because it was so totally unexpected and wild in the opinion of all those who knew Jean. His wife told me explicitly that in her opinion the Nouets had asked their unwitcher to '*work on*' Jean in this way – turning him into a drunk – and she did not doubt that he had succeeded.

Mère Babin, remember, did not believe in spells any more than her son did. One could now wonder whether she was not trying to clear him of the accusation: for if there are no spells, Jean could hardly be a witch. But remember, too, that sometimes she did seem to believe in them – like anyone else – for example, when she said that Ribault could not be Jean's witch because he was '*not capable*', which implied that she thought others were. It would seem to me that by thus stating: 'Jean's witch is not Ribault but someone else' she was perhaps referring to that initial episode of accusation which, unlike the other members of her family, she could not disassociate, in her interpretation, from her son's later misfortunes. (Once again I can only make assumptions, since the earlier violence of Jean's relationship with his mother naturally prevented me from asking her opinion on the subject.)

The way in which the Babins' case is paradigmatic is now clearer: it illustrates the typical situation where a bewitched person, '*caught*' in the repetition of biological misfortunes following an accusation of witchcraft, is faced with the impossibility of talking about it to any unwitcher. This impossibility seems to be part of the discourse of witchcraft itself: for I have never heard a bewitched person complain to an unwitcher of having been accused of being a witch; indeed, none of the many stories I was told contain this situation which, however, cannot be a rare one, since every time someone considers himself bewitched, he has to name a witch: so there are as many witches as there are bewitched. The problem, then, is to know how this large number of accused people deal with this imputation, since they at least know they are innocent of possessing '*books*' and using them to lay charms.

In my experience, three choices are open to the alleged witches.

1. Either the accusation hits them head on: of course they know it is materially untrue, but they are so convinced of the unwitcher's magic power that they behave as if they were condemned to death. Some, like mère Chicot, who was accused by the Régniers, die rapidly of an inexplicable illness; others, like Tripier, Manceau's witch or Filoche, the Letorts' witch, go bankrupt and leave the district.

I was of course unable to question them: for survivors still have a chance so long as they are prudently silent about the past. Even if I omit the fact that I only heard about them through their accusers (and I cannot say this is not important), it is difficult to see what they could have said, or to whom. For they could hardly claim both that the accusation was unjust and that the unwitcher's ritual had done them so much harm.

2. On the other hand, an alleged witch can reply to an accusation with irony and sarcasm: I am not guilty of being your witch, they say in effect, for the simple reason that spells have no objective existence and one must either be backward or mad to believe in them; whoever convinced you that I was your witch is a mere charlatan himself, and so on. If, as sometimes happens, they can really maintain this attitude, the unwitcher is foiled: however much he pierces ox hearts, or throws salt in red-hot pans, '*the other*' does not '*feel it*'.

I met a few people like this, but I was often struck by the fact that the conversation would always come to a dead end at the slightest crack in their scepticism, which appeared as a defence system. (I must say that they were able seriously to maintain this position during the first months of my stay in the Bocage, when my inability to handle the language of witchcraft implied that I myself was a sceptic. Later on, they always got bogged down in such blatant contradictions that they were afraid I would think them witches myself.) One, for example, began to say, laughing, that these accusations, like spells in general, were '*rot for the backward*'; but he then boasted that because of his '*strong blood*' he had foiled the unwitcher. Another, less bold, neither laughed nor boasted, but pointed out as proof of his innocence that the ritual had not had the least effect on him, whereas his alleged victims were still beset by misfortunes. This could of course mean that spells are a pure figment of the imagination, but it could also mean that my interlocutor had more '*force*' than the unwitcher who had to fight him. An accusation of witchcraft goes so deep that they could not see how to escape from it in the eyes of someone who, like me, was in everyday contact with magicians and bewitched people. For all they could prove was that the slur had not caused them to tumble into a sequence of biological misfortunes.

3. Others, like Jean Babin, declare that they do not believe in it, but their behaviour is in continued conflict with their words: once they are accused, they are caught in the process of repetition. They are then engaged, sometimes for many years, in having to constantly reinterpret their story, until they can present it as that of an ordinary bewitched: they must suppress all allusion to the accusation in the past and find an unwitcher who will be convinced and who will authenticate this revised version of their story.

When I met the Babins, they were just starting on the last-but-one stage of this revision. The account they gave me contained many allusions to the past accusation – which I was of course incapable of understanding before Josephine told me the full story, but it probably had not escaped the notice of the preceding unwitchers, particularly the '*woman from Izé*'.

First, it is relevant that the appearance of the '*woman from Alençon*' in the Babins' life was closely related to this initial accusation, since the ulcerated eczema, which prevented Jean from marrying before the age of thirty-three, began as early as 1959 shortly after Nouet had called Jean a witch. The Babins do not say how Jean presented himself to Marie from Alençon: as a patient simply suffering from eczema who wanted a healer to suppress his symptom, or as an ordinary bewitched person requiring an unwitcher. What is certain is that the '*woman from Alençon*' was unable to cure the eczema, which she treated with traditional methods, and that she gave some hint of a spell, since she advised the patient to come back and see her if he got married or if he '*took over*'. '*She knew*', said Josephine, '*the spell would come back*'. (This is probably why the missionary who came to preach for Lent in Torcé was able to heal Jean: he was only concerned with the symptom, eczema, from the point of view that he had been a doctor and that God wanted healthy farmers to get married; and he never referred to spells.)

It is also significant that Josephine – so long as she was not talking to an unwitcher – said that Nouet's unwitcher cast a spell on her husband (which gave him eczema and made him take to drink) and that Jean's witches were called Ribault and Chicot. How the first got eliminated from the interpretation in favour of the others is what we must now try to understand.

Since Jean presented himself as an ordinary bewitched whose misfortunes had begun at the time of his wedding, any unwitcher was bound to ask him this question: since you are suffering because you cannot consummate your marriage, whom are you offending through your choice of wife? Ribault then became an obvious witch, since he had tried so hard to impose his servant on Babin and had been openly offended by the young man's refusal.

The naming of Chicot, on the other hand, was the result of a far more complex process. Remember that in 1970, the Babins told me they had identified him as a witch because of the resentment he felt when his nephew established himself. With Jean also presenting himself as bewitched after he '*took over*', the unwitcher's question would then have been: whom are you offending by establishing yourself? Chicot could then be identified as the witch, without the Babins having to mention the events of 1959. Although the injury done to '*the aunt's man*' was slight – he could no longer get flowers and produce from the farm – the unwitcher would have been convinced of his guilt by the wave of '*butterings*' after each visit from one of the Chicots. It occurred to me in 1971, though, that if the Babins were so keen to point to Chicot as their witch, it was because of the close link he had had in the past with La Grimetière: he had been the farmer just before Nouet settled there. Babin probably never said this to an unwitcher since he could not say that he had been the target of an accusation, but he certainly had it in mind, as can be seen from these statements by Josephine:

'*Could be it was him* [Chicot]', she said, '*who did it* [who bewitched the Nouets, because he was jealous of seeing them establish themselves on a farm he had had to leave], *and it fell on Jean.*' [What thus '*fell*' on her husband was both an accusation of witchcraft and the spell which his accuser's unwitcher necessarily cast on him.]

The use of the expression '*could be*' calls for some comment: (1) It cannot be understood as a form of uncertainty, since, in further conversations, Josephine took it for granted that Chicot had been guilty from 1959 onward; she also said, in similar terms, that she '*suspected it was Ribault*' after it had already been well established that he was responsible for her husband's impotence. (2) This expression has more the stamp of a personal view, never submitted to an unwitcher's interpretation. Otherwise Josephine would not have hesitated to shield herself behind an unwitcher's authority, by saying, for example: 'The woman from Izé said that . . .'

Although they were not able to obtain the authority of an unwitcher's word on this matter, the Babins' reasoning seems to me to have been as follows: since the Nouets' witch is not Jean – Jean knows perfectly well that he has no '*books*' and that he has never set any charms on anyone's property – it can only be '*the aunt's man*', Chicot, since he had obvious reasons to resent his successors at La Grimetière.

I shall now attempt to formulate the series of shifts in the Babins' story through which the name of the Nouets' witch was gradually obliterated and exchanged for that of Chicot. To do this, I shall use diagrams like those I used in Chapter 6 to display the stages in a witchcraft crisis from the point of view of the bewitched; the diagrams are based on a provisional distinction between magic force – exclusively held by unwitchers and witches – and the vital force belonging to any individual, whoever he is.[6]

1. According to the Babins (it is, of course, their point of view which is given here) in 1959, Uncle Chicot bewitches his successor at La Grimetière, Nouet. Nouet is thus bereft of magic force, weak (–), and continually losing his vital force: his animals die, his wife falls ill; or, to express the situation in the same terms as those I used in Chapter 8, his *set* is affected by various misfortunes, due to a super-powerful witch, (+), Uncle Chicot.

Bewitched (1) ——————————→ Witch (1)
(–)   (+)
Nouet   Chicot

2. Nouet, for his part, does not know who is '*drawing*' his vital strength away. So he consults an unwitcher, who provides him with a method of identifying his witch. Unfortunately, the magician is incompetent and his method results in Nouet naming Jean instead of Chicot. But Chicot is still a witch, although only the Babins are in a position to say so, several years later and because of the course of events.

---

[6] Cf. pp. 70–1.

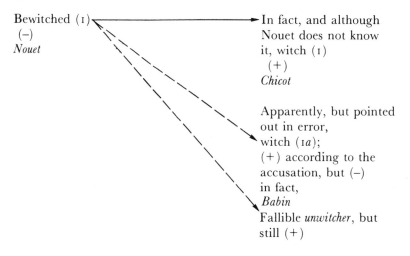

Bewitched (1) ————————————————————→ In fact, and although
(–)   Nouet does not know
Nouet   it, witch (1)
                                            (+)
                                            Chicot

                                            Apparently, but pointed
                                            out in error,
                                            witch (1*a*);
                                            (+) according to the
                                            accusation, but (–)
                                            in fact,
                                            Babin
                                            Fallible *unwitcher*, but
                                            still (+)

According to Babin, he should not be credited with magic force, or a (+) plus sign, when he is totally without it (in spite of his robust appearance) but should be given a (–) sign.

3. The unwitcher then engages in a magic fight with the alleged witch. Jean, being naturally weak, is easily overcome. But contrary to the unwitcher's expectations, the situation is not reversed from witch to bewitched since the victim is an innocent man and the real culprit, Chicot, retains his magic force intact. (Babin cannot have lost any in the process since he did not have any at the start.) On the other hand, the unwitcher's ritual causes another kind of reversal: an ordinary individual – not in any way involved either in spells or magic force – becomes bewitched. For the unwitcher's ritual, (although he is a hopeless seer he is still an effective unwitcher) causes Babin's vital force to be '*drawn*'. And as a result Babin becomes an alcoholic and covered with eczema. The story does not say whether Nouet, the initially weak man, recuperates his vital force after the operation; what we do know is that Babin loses his.

Bewitched (2) ————•————————————→ Witch (2)
(–)   (+)
Babin   the incompetent but
                                      effective unwitcher

4. So the initial witch, Chicot, has not lost his magic force and, like all witches, must use it all the time.[7] Babin is then his uncle's obvious victim:

---

[7] It is one of the system's essential presuppositions. I shall return to this later: the witch is obliged to use his magic force unceasingly – it is said that he '*must play a trick a day*', otherwise his force will turn against him and destroy him. If it can be said that the witch possesses his victims, it is no less true that he himself is possessed by his '*force*'.

Chicot had already managed to affect him in 1959 through an incompetent seer. When Jean '*took over*' his father's farm in 1963, the witch, on the pretext that his nephew's establishing himself would deprive him of some material advantages, bewitches him – this time directly:

Bewitched (1)—————————————► Recidivist witch (1)
(–)   (+)
Babin   Chicot

5. Babin can only call in an unwitcher so long as he keeps quiet about the past and dates the beginning of his career as a bewitched from the time he '*took over*'. But because he is closely questioned each time either this initial accusation comes into the open or Babin falls silent, and the professional unwitchers – at least the '*woman from Izé*' – back out. It is striking that the Babins are only able to get rid of Chicot through benevolent unwitchers: first a priest, then a passing stranger. The first gives them magic protections, while the second kills the witch with a prediction.

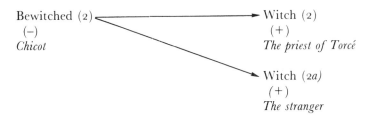

Bewitched (2)◄——————————► Witch (2)
(–)   (+)
Chicot   *The priest of Torcé*

                                            Witch (2a)
                                            (+)
                                            The stranger

I think there are two reasons why the Babins talked to me about the Chicots, although they no longer needed anyone's help to fight them. (1) In 1970, they were still totally fascinated by the recent death of '*the aunt's man*'; (2) by talking to me about it, they were hinting at the position they wanted me to occupy, namely that of an occasional unwitcher, like the stranger – '*perhaps he was someone like you, who had come to study spells*' – who accomplished his mission as avenger and left Torcé for ever. This was later proved by the fact that Josephine never said a word about the Chicots to Madame Flora – a professional unwitcher. She presented herself as a victim of Ribault only. And so the last connection linking the events of 1959 with those of 1963 – disappeared.

The Babins now knew how to tell their story as that of ordinary bewitched: in the version Josephine gave Madame Flora, her misfortunes had begun three weeks before the wedding; Jean had been hit on the head by a falling beam and had become impotent because of Ribault; at the same time, Filoche's son had warned her not to marry a '*nanny-billy*'.

But Jean was not cured of his impotence because he was never able to go in person to see Madame Flora. The unwitcher's failure was caused, I think, by the basic limitations of any magic cure and probably of any cure whatsoever; for no one can cure a person for whom preserving his central symptom is a question of life or death. For I think that Babin's sexual impotence was for him the only way he could hold his ground as an autonomous person in face of the family coalition, which had decided on his fate in his stead.

'*It was always understood that Jean would have La Croix*', said Josephine; after he had settled there, his elder brother – who plays an important role in the whole story – married him to the twin sister of his own wife, on the grounds that Jean was 33 years old and that he needed a wife to help him look after his farm. Actually, all this would have been quite sensible, were it not that Jean had no desire to be a farmer, or to marry his sister-in-law.[8] By not consummating this marriage – one thing no one could decide on or do instead of him – Jean, in my opinion, was attempting to frustrate the fate to which he had been committed against his will. The fact that he had never even tried to have sexual intercourse except at the beginning of his marriage and after the visit from the 'woman from Izé', and that he threatened to kill himself every time his wife asked him to co-operate in Madame Flora's cure, was evidence enough that he was trying to preserve the symptom, whether for the vital reasons I have given or for others which he could give, if he agreed to talk.

In conclusion, I would like to make a purely logical remark: it is very likely that most of those who are accused of witchcraft manage, at some point or other, to transform their story into that of an ordinary bewitched. If one reflects that (1) the accused are innocent and (2) it is extremely difficult to escape the discourse of witchcraft – the sceptics only manage to preserve their conviction so long as they are spared the series of biological misfortunes – one is led to assume that a significant proportion of those who have been bewitched is made up of former alleged witches. However, this initial episode belongs to a foreclosed past which no one – apart from the accuser – will ever know about. Not even, it goes without saying, an ethnographer.

If the utterance '*you are my witch*' is to be transformed into '*I am bewitched by So and So*', one must once and for all shut off the episode of the initial accusation from that of the final bewitchment. For this, at least three conditions must be fulfilled.

(*a*) The person accused by the bewitched must in no way be related to the person who first accused the bewitched.

(*b*) The bewitched must bear the responsibility of infringing the requirement to '*tell everything*' to his unwitcher. (In my experience, every

---

[8] Jean, who was intelligent and gifted at school, would have liked to continue until the *Certificat d'études primaires* and become a nurse, but his family was against this. And although he seems to have had a feeling of respect and affection for his wife, he never seems to have physically desired her, so far as one can ever know these things.

bewitched is confronted some day or other by this unavoidable step. For the only way to avoid becoming totally alienated by the unwitcher's will is to summon up the courage to hide some parts of one's life from interpretation.)

(c) Without talking about it to anyone else, the bewitched has to get by, making use of the system's fundamental contradiction: some unwitcher once perpetrated a miscarriage of justice to my own detriment; but some other unwitcher will be telling the truth when he accuses someone or other of being my witch. In other words: though it is true that I can be bewitched (caught in a repetition of misfortunes) by someone else, it is not true that anyone can put me in the same position as that someone else.

This accusation cannot be verbalized and the discourse of witchcraft can only be effective so long as each individual gets along by himself in silence: without this, naming a witch would not have any point, since it would become clear that 'the witch' only intervenes as a logical prop, in a system enabling the repetition of biological misfortunes to be understood and dealt with, often successfully. But, in my opinion, it does not follow that this discourse is less true or more illusory than any other. Rather, like any discourse, it meets both the conditions for and the limitation of its efficiency by obscuring a specific part of reality.

MID-WAY SPECULATIONS

Having gone a certain distance along these sometimes tangled paths, the time has come to develop some concepts which can be used as a basis for further development. It would not have been appropriate to offer general statements about witchcraft in the Bocage without having first shown how unwitchers effect their cures, and before attempting to define those elements of the bewitched's misfortunes which are solved, and at what price. It would also be premature to take a definite stand on the epistemological questions raised by my approach, since it cannot yet be seen just where it leads.

I can, however, clear the way for a theoretical statement by putting forward in this final chapter a reconstruction of the set of concepts which, in my opinion, underlines the system of witchcraft in the Bocage, or at any rate the position of the bewitched.

Those who like tales of witchcraft will be disappointed by the dryness of this outline. They would do better not to read it. The themes of the fight to the death, of breaking in and of loss are central to this part as they were in the narratives. But here they are expressed in a supposedly less involved tone, that of logic.

At two points in the course of this book, I have attempted to represent the progress of a witchcraft crisis from the victim's point of view.[1] For that purpose, I made a provisional distinction between the magic force wielded by witches and unwitchers only, and the vital force which everyone possesses. A witchcraft crisis has these elements: a witch sets out to attract, by magic means, the vital force of some ordinary individual, that is an individual totally without magic means with which to defend his vital force. When a bewitched is invested in this way, all he can do is call on a magic avenger: the unwitcher. This person must be capable of opposing the aggressor with an even more intense magic power, so obliging him to return to his client the stolen amount of vital force. If not, the bewitched will progressively lose his vital force and inevitably sink in ruin or death.

[1] Cf. pp. 70–1 and 188–92.

Remember, on the other hand, that the defeat of a witch is marked, for him as for everyone else, by a partial loss of his vital force, or even its total loss, the equivalent of death.

Defining two categories of force enabled me to suggest that what is exchanged in a witchcraft crisis is vital force, whereas what promotes the exchange is magic force.

By calling the force of a witch or an unwitcher 'magic', I am conforming to a widely-used convention in the social sciences: ethnographers and folklorists use this notion to characterize a force allegedly different from those operating in nature or in physics, i.e. empirically identifiable and measurable forces. But it must be granted that this is only a negative definition, relating the native to his 'otherness', and so sparing the ethnographer from having to question the nature and the workings of the 'magic' power. In effect, the ethnographer is asserting that the Zande say that such a force exists; it's only the Zande who say this, and you and I can agree that the notion is basically absurd.

The aim of my book on the other hand, is to take magic force seriously, and not to be content to describe it as a logical error, or someone else's belief. So, if I have used the expression so far, it was only provisionally and to indicate something which needed elucidation. Like everyone else, I gave it a negative definition. It takes into account the peculiar characteristics of Bocage ways of thinking: to say that there are beings who possess a magic force is to attribute to them the capacity to increase their potential of vital force without having to work, steal, or use any of the normal legal and economic means. But this tells us virtually nothing more than we knew. Moreover, I think it is time for me to ask why the inhabitants of the Bocage do not feel any need to distinguish between two types of power and use just one term – 'force' – to mean both what causes the exchange and what is exchanged in a witchcraft crisis. It should be possible to draw up a description of their conceptual system that would do justice to their lexical choices.

I have attempted to do this in the following pages. In a way, this is a speculative exercise: we shall see native notions being progressively replaced by others which I thought more susceptible to logical manipulation. In reading this outline, think of the episodes in the narratives which first prompted me to work out these notions.

I could not indefinitely postpone venturing this attempt to reconstruct the conceptual scheme underlying the representation the bewitched use to describe what they are caught in. Actually I have no disregard for speculation, so long as it is frankly seen as that. My attempted reconstruction is certainly not the only one possible, but it is the best I could manage, or at any rate the one which represents the present state of my thinking.[2]

[2] My successive attempts at writing this chapter were greatly helped by several conversations I had with François Flahaut (whose theoretical imagination and critical rigour have provided me over the last two years with a continuous source of mental stimulation), Radmilla

I. Concepts and presuppositions

1. A bewitched and his domain

A witch's target is the head of an economic unit (whether agricultural or not) and also the head of a family. It is always he who is said to be bewitched, even though he may not be suffering at all, while his wife or his rabbits are clearly suffering as a result of the witch's violence. The witch who is following a policy of escalation measures his misdeeds according to two criteria:

– the distance between the target element and the head of the economic unit or of the family: each attack hits the bewitched more or less directly;

– the resistance of each element to magic aggression: it is more difficult to lay charms when everything is 'clenched' and a whole assortment of counter-charms has been preventively set up.

This escalation-policy presupposes that the witchcraft offensive is of fairly long duration, as in a war of attrition. Only the long series of blows enables the bewitched to go on considering himself such.

Whatever the elements attacked, they are never attacked in themselves but because of their relationship with the head of the unit or of the family: they are *his* crops, *his* cows, *his* rabbits, *his* poultry, *his* children, *his* wife, etc. Let us call these elements the bewitched's *possessions*, and their set (in which the bewitched himself is included), his *domain*.

Even when the target possession is a human being (wife or children), the attack is aimed at the sole possessor. The latter is affected by what happens to any elements of his domain: his being is inseparable from the set. Ultimately, the witch's target is the body of the bewitched. But from the start of the offensive, the bewitched defines himself completely differently from what Descartes, for example, would mean by 'subject': a *cogito* ideally distinct from all the attributes of the *ego*. The 'I' of the bewitched is the set made up of himself and his possessions, i.e. the set which is socially bound to his name. In such a set, one cannot distinguish between body and belongings because the belongings are one with the person whose name they carry. This is why I have called this set either the *domain* or the *body* of the bewitched.

2. The bio-economical potential of the bewitched

The bewitched and/or each of his possessions is subjected to a weakening of his '*force*', i.e. his capacity to:

– survive (illness and death of animals and people)

Zygouris, Dominique Iogna-Prat, Anne Levallois, Jean-Max Gaudillière, Françoise Davoine, Patrick and Dominique Guyomard, Elise and Claude Poyart, Albert and Isaac Turkieh, Michel Crozon and Marc Keller. Naming them here in no way implies that I consider that they agree with my views, for which I assume full responsibility.

reproduce (sterility of animals and people)

produce (exhaustion of work-energy, deterioration in the means of production, drying up of cows, sterility of the soil, and unavoidable unproductive expenses).

These three dimensions are not distinguished in local parlance. The spell is said to be *'tighter'* or *'stronger'* if it affects the capacity to survive rather than the two other types, and less *'tight'* if it only affects productive capacity. In any case, the bewitched considers that ultimately it is his capacity to survive which is at stake: that is why there is no need to distinguish these three dimensions.

I earlier used the expression *vital force* when referring to this capacity to survive, reproduce or produce, although the inhabitants of the Bocage call it simply *force*. But whatever it is called, it can be defined as a capital or a bio-economic potential belonging to each possessor of a domain.

3. The system's two presuppositions

This representation is bound to be abstract. However, until this point the reader could easily flesh it out by recalling some of the words that were spoken to me. I must now break away from the actual discourse of the bewitched and state two presuppositions without which the whole system (or discourse) would be unintelligible.

1. There is no vacant vital space, there are no new frontiers to push back, and no virgin lands to occupy: vital space is entirely registered, or stamped with the name of an owner.

2. In any of the situations considered, one must distinguish between the dynamic point of view (*'force'*) and the topological one (the field of investment in which this force operates).

topological: every head of a family has a domain marked in his name; its area must fully express how he stands with regard to others.

dynamic: this domain is invested with the force of its possessor.

In order to represent the various situations involved in a war of witchcraft, I have drawn up several diagrams which should be read on both sides of the page simultaneously and in reverse.

The obverse or recto corresponds to the topological approach, i.e. to the dimension of what is visible: for a given situation, one can see the objectively locatable variations of the domain (of the body, etc...) of each protagonist.

The reverse or verso corresponds to the dynamic approach, or to the dimension of what is invisible, showing which conditions are presupposed by the bewitched so that these visible variations become meaningful.

4. Sufficiency or excess of force in relation to space

From the topological point of view, there is a vital space completely occupied by domains each carrying the name of their possessor.

(a) *The case of the ordinary individual* (cf. Schema 1.) One cannot talk of magic as long as the force (the bio-economic potential) of an individual is totally invested in the area marked with his name: whether he is working, exchanging, producing or reproducing, all these activities belong to the range of normal symbolic mediations, in other words they are strictly contained, for any individual, within the limits of his name. One can also say that, in this case, the force, the name and the area of the domain coincide exactly.

Exchanges set up between owners maintain this force (this bio-economical potential) at a constant level: there is no danger of its running down, so long as the domain is sufficiently enclosed to resist ordinary aggressions, i.e. so long as the system of names is enough to regulate social relations.

(b) *The case of possessors of magic force* (cf. Schema 2) Their force is such that it exceeds the area marked in their name, or overflows it.

There are beings such as witches who are able to increase the bio-economic potential of their domain without using ordinary symbolic mediations – i.e. without having their activity confined within the system of names: this is what the bewitched say. Listening to them, however, it is impossible to locate the witch's force as such: no bewitched has ever seen a witch laying a charm, since witches act under the cover of night or of invisibility. No bewitched has ever read a book on witchcraft, the alleged source of a witch's power, since reading one would turn him into a witch, rather than the victim he claims to be.

This is why the bewitched are content to infer *ex post facto* and by relying on interpretation the existence of this force which no one knows of directly: is my force diminished after a witch has been here? Does it remain constant when he is far away? And so on.

Even the outward or objective signs of this force – for example, bulging, '*blurry*' or '*glassy*' eyes – are the product of an *ex post facto* interpretation: a bewitched concludes, on the ground that his vital force decreases after the visit of a witch, that the latter's eyes are a sign of omnipotence. (The most contradictory things have been read in my ethnographer's eyes, ranging from fear to force according to the position I was given.)

The unwitcher's strength also cannot be directly located: unlike the witch who has never been seen laying a charm, the clients of an unwitcher see him performing rituals. But these rituals act at a distance (for the witch is not there in person, there is only an object representing him) and metaphorically $\left(\dfrac{\text{an ox heart}}{\text{a witch}}\text{ is pierced}\right)$. Is this a pantomime or a struggle? Is there any force involved, or is this just an idea? One can only answer these questions afterwards, by seeing what happens to the protagonists in the crisis, and by inferring, from these visible effects, the presence or absence of this invisible surplus force which I called 'magic' for reasons of convenience.

SCHEMA 1
The domain of an ordinary individual

Visible
domain

It may be seen from the verso that all the force belonging to an individual possessing a certain domain is exclusively invested within the limits of the area marked with his name; the owner's force exactly covers the limits of his name.

Invisible force

Force exclusively invested in the limits of the domain

SCHEMA 2
The domain of the witch

Visible
domain

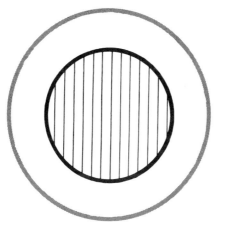

It may be seen from the verso that there is a surplus of force which cannot be invested in the domain marked with the name of its owner, and that it overflows its area.

Invisible
force

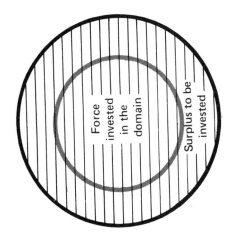

– Does the witch (as well as the unwitcher) behave as if he were acted on by an outside force dominating him? Is a loss in his force observable?

– Does the bewitched behave as if he were protected by a screen? Does he get back his force?

According to the bewitched, a witch's force is of an unknown magnitude, but in any case it is immeasurably superior to their own: as soon as a witch appears, he presses on the boundaries of their 'enclosure' with an intensity which those boundaries were never meant to withstand; so a breach is opened, through which the bewitched's force will begin to leak away.

Similarly when the bewitched mention the force of a witch, it is in order to say that before they were victims of it they did not believe in it; their positivist mentality was reluctant to acknowledge the existence of a non-material force in a fellow human being; or else it is in order to lament that they did not know anything, which is why the witch was able to 'catch' them so easily. This supernatural force is said to be greater or less in different witches. One can however only assess this force by opposing to it the beneficial forces – though of equally unknown magnitude – of various unwitchers: who will overpower whom? Who is stronger than whom?

In local discourse the witch is a fundamentally 'jealous' being; in my own terms, I would say he is jealous because his domain is never big enough for him to use up the whole of his power. Since all social space is registered, or appropriated, the witch is then obliged to invest domains marked with the names of other individuals, and to mark plots with his own name, i.e. to draw them into his own domain.

What is 'magic' in the witch is thus this basic overflow, this surplus of force relative to his name (or territory): a witch is a being who never has enough vital space in which to invest his force. One can also say that a force is 'magical' in that it cannot be contained within the system of names. This is enough to make the force produce its effects without using ordinary symbolic mediations.

The inhabitants of the Bocage usually say that the witch 'has' force; but they also say that he is 'forced to play a trick a day'. If the witch 'has' force, it is no less clear that the force 'has' the witch, that it possesses him and obliges him to work constantly, like a slave: indeed he has force but he will never stop being owned by it. It would therefore be more correct to say that this necessarily unbounded surplus force operates through the body/the name/the domain of the witch. (This is also true of the unwitcher, who always complains of this force which works on him and alienates him; anyone who might possibly become an initiate he invites to rid him of this force once and for all by taking it all on himself.)

One can infer from this that the witch represents a *lack of vital space* due to his surplus of force. This lack is of course not an empirical reality: for, like everyone else, the witch has his domain, whose area could be increased by the usual legal and economic means. Rather, this lack is an ontological ?

property: whatever the quantity of space available to the witch, he is always in need of more to invest his surplus force. The domain he does have at any point in his life is nothing compared to what he needs, and what he knows is to be found in other hands. This is why I have attributed a minus sign to the witch's domain (or body).

In the following diagrams the signs $(+)$ and $(-)$ therefore indicate the adequacy or inadequacy of a domain, given the force to be invested. Signs on the reverse side do not refer to a visible, objectively locatable datum, but to a presupposition of the bewitched (cf. Schema 3).

The representations of both domains (that of the witch and that of the ordinary person) are strictly complementary: the lack in one exists only with respect to the other's sufficiency and conversely.

Let us specify that the witch's force is only aimed at harnessing the force of the bewitched, at enlarging his domain to the detriment of those of others, without having to submit to ordinary symbolic mediations (work, exchange, theft, etc.).

Others, in this case, can only be ordinary individuals, and not witches or unwitchers. On the one hand, witches never attack each other; they are accomplices, they 'communicate', they 'join forces': this is an absolute rule. On the other hand, when the witch defends himself against the unwitcher's attack, it is because the latter chose to interpose his force between that of the aggressor and that of the victim, so preventing the witch from tapping it. Apart from this situation, the witch is not interested in the fact that the unwitcher also has a surplus of force.

Note that in these fights between 'magicians', none of the protagonists have the time, in theory, to begin a war of attrition over their possessions as a whole. It all takes place through a single duel or through a limited number of moves in which the other's death is the objective, that is, the cancellation of his bio-economic potential. Of course they do not kill every time, but one gives the other a foretaste of death. This amounts to saying that duels between 'magicians' aimed at cancelling the opponent's bio-economical potential, do not involve one particular kind of force – the one I had named 'magic'. This is so true that a bewitched discovers that his witch's 'magic' force has been cancelled by looking at the visible signs of transformation in the bio-economic potential of each magician: have witch and unwitcher survived the clash, i.e. have their domains grown or diminished? Do their bodies show signs of the struggle?

Any impairment in magic force, whether it is that of the witch or that of the unwitcher is thus conveyed by a single effect: the transformation of the domain where this force is invested. All the rest is mere inference.

Suppose, then, that there is only one force; it may circulate between two poles, a positive and a negative one: the witch, who lacks space in which to invest it, sets out to capture the domain of someone who has enough space, the ordinary individual. The inhabitants of the Bocage say that the witch

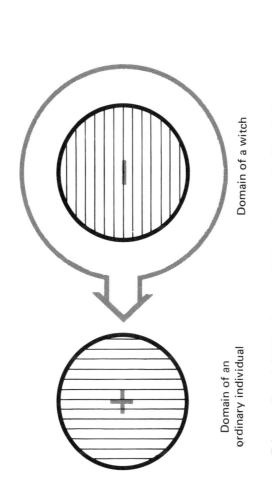

Visible domains

SCHEMA 3
Normal situation:
the domain of an ordinary individual, and that of a witch

Domain of a witch

Domain of an
ordinary individual

Take an ordinary individual; he invests all the force he has at hand into his domain (verso), which is enclosed so as to resist ordinary aggressions. If this domain increases or diminishes, this is wholly due to biological or socio-economic constraints; in other words, the owner's force never exceeds the area defined by his name, or – this space is adequate (+).

Invisible
forces

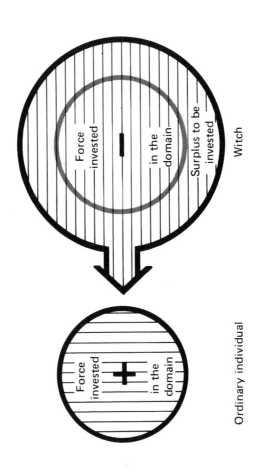

Witch

Ordinary individual

It is however assumed that there is a witch somewhere, who lacks vital space (−) in which to
invest his surplus force, and who is eager to conquer other people's domains.

'*draws the force*' of his victim; at the same time, he '*draws*' segments of his victim's domain (the witch grows richer, his health prospers, his cows are more and more productive; while the bewitched grows poorer, wastes away, and so on. . .)

In such a system, life is thought of as a full sack that may empty, or as an enclosed field that may open; death is thought of as the end result of suction by a vacuum, is the active principle which alone causes the force to circulate. In a peasant said to be stupid, to have invented such a system implies some philosophical talent.

II. Attack by witchcraft and its warding-off

Schemata 4 and 5 show what a witchcraft attack is and what its effects on each protagonist are.

The witch's 'magic' force – i.e. the capacity with which his negative force can attract the positive force of his victims – is all the greater when:

⊘he witch has not been identified: so long as he is not included in the system of names, he can operate freely because '*no one suspects him*'.

⊖o 'magic' force (i.e. marked with a minus sign) has interposed itself in the path of his own and obstructed it: the witch's force flows freely from himself to his victim.

This force belonging to the witch oscillates between extreme powerfulness (as for instance in the case of a witch who has '*never met his master*') and extreme weakness (when a witch has been overpowered by an unwitcher stronger than himself). The state of weakness can be compared to that of the bewitched: the witch is in danger of losing his entire bio-economic potential, i.e. he is threatened by ruin or death so long as the unwitcher exerts his force on him.

There is therefore a surplus of force which circulates and tries to occupy the possessions of others. Ontologically a witch is a being whose energy has no specific domain (since it always overflows it), which is why his set is marked by the sign (−). The (+) space available to him at any point in his life is a borrowed one: if the witch's domain exists, it is because its possessor is always trying to make up for this basic lack by removing finite amounts of (+) territory from the domain of others. So one must never forget that his set, his body or his domain always include some elements marked (+) (See diagram 6).

At this point in the crisis, the unwitcher comes on the scene. He will make it possible to name the witch and will set out to fight him. Like any other individual, the unwitcher has a domain marked in his name, and one liable to vary according to biological and legal or economic circumstances. But the bewitched define his ontological status by two features.

①Unlike the witch and like the ordinary individual, the unwitcher is not '*jealous*', he is not greedily seeking to lay his hands on other people's possessions. What he has is always enough, and if he wants to get richer, for instance, he does so through the ordinary symbolic mediations (work, purchase, and so on). In principle, he always has a job (farmer, gelder, hairdresser, etc.) and a social standing independent of his function as an unwitcher, which he performs over and above all the rest. Since the vital space he has is sufficient, one can therefore attach a positive sign to his domain.

②. And yet he is, like the witch, endowed with a surplus force which produces effects without using the ordinary symbolic mediations, and he must invest this force in domains marked in another person's name.

He has made an ethical choice in that instead of occupying the domains of ordinary individuals, he occupies those of domain-stealers, i.e. witches. But because his own domain is enough for him, bringing his force into play does not increase his possessions. In other words, the unwitcher is such that:

⊖ he has enough with his own domain. It can therefore be given a positive sign.

⊖But he considers he lacks the segments of his patients' domains which were stolen by the witch, so one can also mark his domain with a negative sign.

This point of view takes it for granted that the unwitcher *joins forces* with his patients, which is why I have represented the pair constituted by the bewitched and his magician as a whole; one can also say that the bewitched is threatened because he has no surplus force of his own. But as soon as he calls in an unwitcher, the latter's surplus force will be joined to his.

The unwitcher thus possesses a domain with two signs, positive and negative. (Note that the unwitcher's *set* is thus marked by two signs, and not, as in the witch's case, the set marked by one sign and its elements by the other.) The unwitcher who thus has both plus and minus can act as a *logical transformer*: the witch has plugged his negativeness into the bewitched's positiveness; by opposing his own $(-)$ to the $(-)$ of the witch, the unwitcher switches off the lethal circuit. Because he himself does not lack vital space, because his set is marked by a $(+)$ sign, his $(-)$ can only be used against someone who also has a $(-)$ sign.

For it is said in the Bocage that an unwitcher never attacks ordinary individuals, or the bewitched, or other unwitchers, or even witches so long as they are not harming his patients. (This, at least, is the official theory of the bewitched; in fact, any unwitching implies, on the part of the patient, a certain degree of unease as to the use an unwitcher might make of his negativeness, or force, in relation to himself, at some critical point or other in the cure: and what if the transformation operation failed? Remember, also, that sometimes an unwitcher calls his competitor a witch, without seeing that by thus monopolizing the function of logical transformation, by attributing it only to himself and considering himself as the only saviour, he is destroying the faith of the bewitched in the institution he represents.)

SCHEMA 4
A witchcraft attack

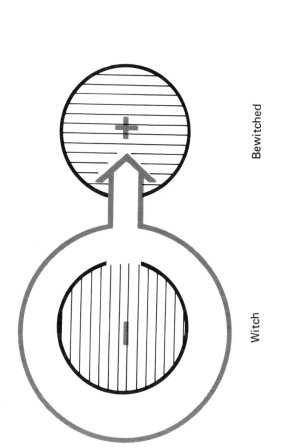

Visible
domains

Witch   Bewitched

A witchcraft attack involves nothing less than the 'tapping' of the witch's negativeness (or greed) into the positiveness (or threatened sufficiency) of an ordinary individual. The domain of the bewitched (recto) is then invested by the witch;

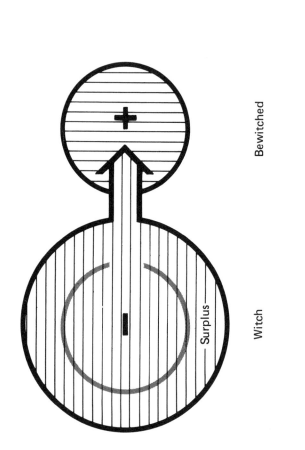

Invisible forces

Witch   Bewitched

Surplus

one may likewise say that the surplus force of the witch is 'invested' in his victim's domain and *'draws'* it (verso). The witch enters the 'body' of his victim and sucks his vitality like a vampire.

Visible
domains

SCHEMA 5
The effects of the attack

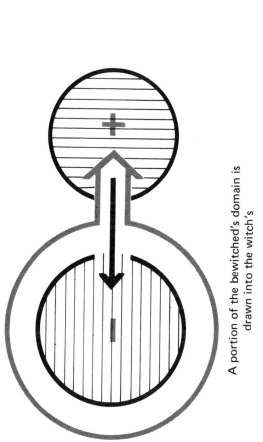

**A portion of the bewitched's domain is
drawn into the witch's**

For the bewitched, the visible effect of this attack (recto) is a decrease in his domain. He might say, for example, that he has had '*losses*' of stock, that his cows don't keep their calves when they are '*carrying*', that his child '*has no strength left for anything*', etc. Note here that only a repetition in the attacks or '*losses*' of all sorts justifies a bewitched in speaking of himself as such. Correlatively, the witch's domain is increased by the portion he has taken from his victim.

Invisible
forces

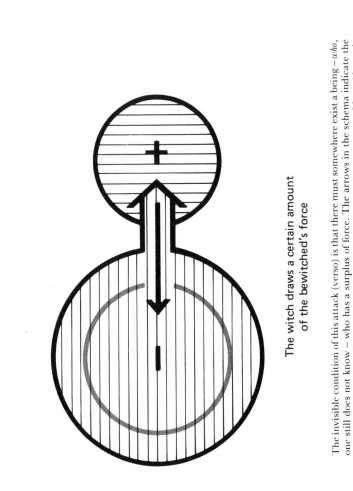

**The witch draws a certain amount
of the bewitched's force**

The invisible condition of this attack (verso) is that there must somewhere exist a being – *who*, one still does not know – who has a surplus of force. The arrows in the schema indicate the circulation of portions of domain (topological viewpoint, recto), or amounts of force (dynamic viewpoint, verso). The quantity (of force, of territory) taken from the bewitched then supplies the witch with some positiveness.

SCHEMA 6
The witch set

Visible
domain

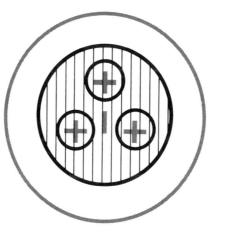

The set, basically lacking in territory, is marked by the sign (−); whereas some elements,
taken from others, are marked by the sign (+).

Invisible
forces

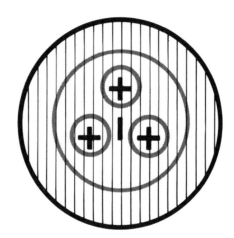

The proof that the unwitcher is disinterested, not jealous, and so on. . . . lies in the fact that he demands no possessions for himself after he has overcome the witch: he obliges the latter to give back the possessions stolen from his victims and makes him lose an extra amount to punish him for his bad intentions, but this share gets lost in the wilderness without anyone profiting from it (I shall return to this point).

In a witchcraft crisis, the unwitcher's only role is to isolate the witch from the bewitched, i.e. to prevent the witch's negativeness from bursting into his victim's 'enclosure'.

For this interposition to succeed, the superiority of the unwitcher's negativeness over the witch's must be ascertained. (Of course the operation sometimes fails: if the unwitcher is not killed on the spot – but this is a purely theoretical case – he withdraws, saying he *is not strong enough*, in which case the witch stops attacking him.) (See Schemata 7 and 8.)

The first consequence of a successful unwitching is that the bewitched gets back his initial domain, while the witch sees his own decrease and the unwitcher's remains constant. (In fact, the unwitcher is shaken by the impact of his clash with the witch, and he experiences a momentary loss which is not represented in the schema because it only lasts an instant. What is important is that the unwitcher comes out victorious.)

Note that the witch loses two segments of his domain: the first represents what he had taken from the bewitched, the second the punishment inflicted by the unwitcher for all his unfulfilled intentions. This segment is of no benefit to anyone: it leaves the circuit. Let us take a few examples: ① The witch dried up two of his victim's cows but he intended to dry up three. After the unwitcher's intervention, three of his cows are dried up, while the two cows belonging to the bewitched become productive again. ② The witch caused the impoverishment of his victim, but he intended to ruin him. After the unwitcher's intervention, the bewitched recovers his former position, and the witch is ruined. ③ The witch caused his victim to fall ill, but he intended to cause him to die. After the unwitcher's intervention, the bewitched is once more in good health, while the witch either dies or is seriously ill.

When the witch is obliged to sell off some of his possessions cheap as the result of the unwitching, the event is obviously profitable to someone. But it is interpreted in terms of ordinary legal-economic exchanges: the buyer does not know he is dealing with a witch. It is in this sense that I said that this segment taken from the witch is of no benefit to anyone and leaves the circuit.

If it were taken by the unwitcher, he could no longer claim a (+) sign, for he would then lack possessions for himself and, like a witch, he would benefit from investing his surplus force in the domain of others. But according to the principle stated above, no two witches can ever attack each other. The following (Schema 9) thus illustrates the difference between an unwitcher and a witch.

The second consequence of the unwitcher's victory over the witch is that, unable to plug into the possessions of the bewitched and manifestly improverished by his defeat (for he possesses fewer (+) elements in his set than before the aggression), the witch must urgently attack some other victim elsewhere to get back his fill of possessions. For the time being, he is doubly in deficit.

He must therefore set up as fast as possible a new battleground with some ordinary individual who has no negativeness to oppose to him. If his victim calls in an unwitcher, the situation I have just described begins all over again. Remember what I said above about the result of these struggles: it is often the unwitcher who is overcome, which is why it makes sense for the witch to attack other victims even if he himself was defeated in a previous fight, for he can hope that his new victim will know nothing of his defeat – these things are kept so secret – and that he will be opposed by a weaker unwitcher.

In the case of both the witch and the unwitcher, there is therefore a surplus of force not invested in the domain of each. The witch's surplus has to be invested in the domains of ordinary individuals: he has, apparently, to 'play a trick a day'. The surplus force available to the unwitcher, on the other hand, seems to maintain itself as it is. Now we must try to understand which symbolic landmarks enable the unwitcher to wield this non-invested surplus force.

SCHEMA 7
The successful intervention of an insulator

Visible
domains

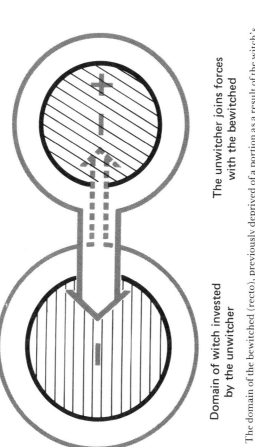

**Domain of witch invested
by the unwitcher**

**The unwitcher joins forces
with the bewitched**

The domain of the bewitched (recto), previously deprived of a portion as a result of the witch's attack, and that of the unwitcher join forces; and the domain of the witch, enlarged by the portion he took from the bewitched, is now invested by the unwitcher.

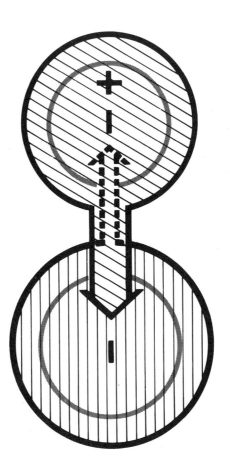

Invisible force

The witch's force is invested by the unwitcher's

The domain of the unwitcher, with both signs: (+) and (−); the broken lines represent the witch's surplus force, still 'tapped' into the domain of the bewitched; the solid line represents the unwitcher's surplus force, which invests the witch's.

Note that the situation of Schema 7 is exactly that of Schema 4, except that it is reversed: the robber is being robbed.

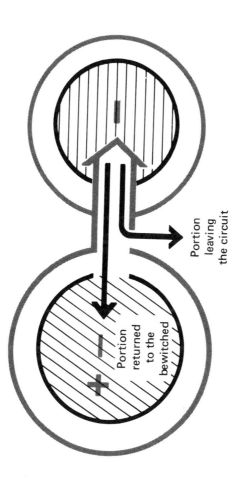

SCHEMA 8
The effect of unwitching

Visible
domains

Portion
leaving
the circuit

Portion
returned
to the
bewitched

The unwitcher takes two portions from the domain of the witch

Invisible
forces

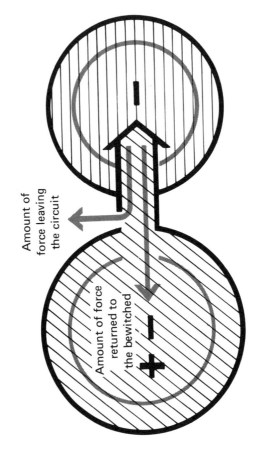

Amount of
force leaving
the circuit

Amount of force
returned to
the bewitched

The witch force is diminished by two portions

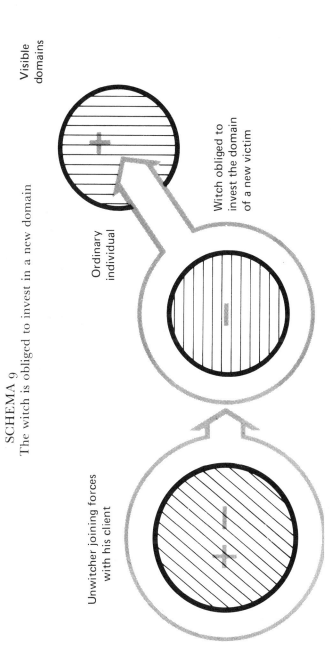

SCHEMA 9
The witch is obliged to invest in a new domain

Visible domains

Ordinary individual

Witch obliged to invest the domain of a new victim

Unwitcher joining forces with his client

Invisible forces

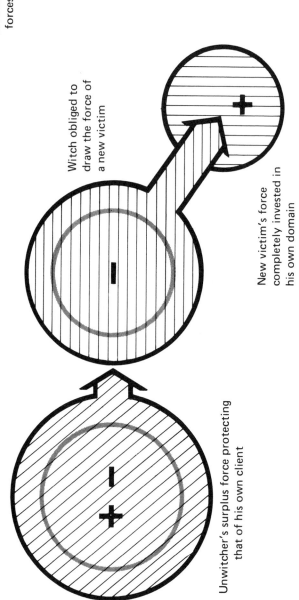

Witch obliged to draw the force of a new victim

New victim's force completely invested in his own domain

Unwitcher's surplus force protecting that of his own client

APPENDICES

(translated in collaboration with Alan Duff)

APPENDIX I

THE EXPLORER OF DARKNESS

The following text was published in *Critique* (April 1972, no. 299) under the heading 'Witches and peasants'. It concerns a television film entitled 'Witches in the Berry', shown as part of the programme *Objectifs*, the magazine of 'Information première' [news programme] prepared by Pierre Dumayet and Jean Cazenave; it was reported by Patrick Pesnot and Jean-François Ribadeau, and televised on 6 August 1971.

The film starts with a series of eerie pictures: sneering devils, owls nailed to doors, bats . . . Disquieting sounds, screams are repeatedly heard. The dictionary of peasant fear and credulity must be displayed from the start. These peasant features are in advance placed far from the viewers by the setting of an archaic landscape: secret groves, ancient houses, horses reflected in ponds, scattered manure. Signs of modern life are carefully erased from the picture: no Formica or plastic in the Berry. Nothing but primitiveness and the howling wind of fear.

When the peasants come into the picture, their place is already set: they are of a different type from the film-makers and viewers. Witchcraft is *still* believed in, but elsewhere, in the Bas-Berry. In this respect, the film is part of the ethnographic tradition, which objectifies other people and confines them elsewhere. Let us simply praise the team of 'Information première' for having admitted – which no ethnographer ever would – their incapacity to make obstinately silent peasants talk.

That, then, is the gist of the programme: a reporter – i.e. a hero of positivist discourse – goes and asks bewitched peasants and their unbe-witchers if they believe in witchcraft, for the benefit of a viewer assumed to be incredulous. The peasants are not in the least taken in, and answer with silences or innuendoes: can one talk of witchcraft to someone who refuses to acknowledge that he or she too is *somewhere* implied in the belief? From then on, the interview proceeds as a long misunderstanding: either the peasant states that he does not believe in *that*, and he is caught blatantly lying by the reporter who points him out to the viewer as an erring child: both credulous and a liar. Or else the peasant admits he *does* believe in *that* a bit, and he begins a conversation which is soon repressed by a nervous laugh or a lasting silence. When the local squire speaks, the content of the exchange is no different (I was bewitched, etc.) but the delivery is: the tone is amused, as that of an adult who hears himself talk like a child. The reason is that the reporter, the squire, and ourselves are part of the élite. That is, if it were not for the content of the discourse which *does* refer us back to the childish part of us all.

The eerie iconography which punctuates the interviews makes up for the peasants' silence. If they won't talk, pictures will: those of Dürer, for instance, since we must have some culture somewhere. Yet the peasants' faces, in their silence or uneasiness, are eloquent enough: this film would have been authentic if its director had had the courage to meet the challenge of those held-back words, immediately withheld when given, always taken back. In one of the sequences, for instance, a farmer's wife asks the reporter to come back to see her because she has something to tell. She meets him again and does not say a word. The reporter does not understand that everything there is to say has been said and questions her, quite absurdly.

APPENDIX 2

IGNORANCE AS A PROFESSION

To avoid a boring, purely academic debate, I shall simply put forward two statements which underlie my argument, without attempting to justify them.

1. Although I read the theoreticians' reflections with great care, I cannot understand how they could hope to develop folklore as a scientific field distinct from ethnography: neither their method, nor their object – whether it is called 'habits and customs', 'popular traditions', 'the study of popular mentality in a civilized nation', and so on – is significantly different from what we know under the general heading of 'ethnography'.

2. It is not enough to aim at being scientific to become so. The fact that Van Gennep, to take the most outstanding example, should have dedicated his entire life working towards this goal – and in heroic circumstances: he was deprived of the support of scientific institutions in which so many 'semi-scholars'[1] pontificated – makes one admire such a degree of obstinacy. But when one takes a closer look at his work, one fails to be convinced. I am not forgetting 'passage rites', a clever scientific finding; but its scope is limited.[2]

I shall first take the indications given in the *Manuel de folklore français contemporain*, a handbook explaining how to collect and interpret facts related to the magic-religious field, and I shall show that whatever Van Gennep's general claims at objectivity, he cannot meet them in this particular case since he is trapped in the same ideological situation as his predecessors.[3] We shall see, however, that he came closer than anyone else to understanding what it is to believe. I shall also use his descriptions of regional folklores to show that his questions, categories of classification and ideas on research priorities made it unlikely that he could grasp what is at stake in a witchcraft crisis.

[1] Apart from his scientific work, Van Gennep wrote a delightful pamphlet against the scholarly life: *Les Demi-Savants* (1911).

[2] *Les rites de passage, étude systématique des cérémonies de la porte et du seuil, de l'hospitalité et de l'adoption, de la grossesse et de l'accouchement, de la naissance, de l'enfance, de la puberté, de l'initiation, de l'ordination, du couronnement, des finançailles et du mariage, des funérailles et des saisons, etc.* (1909).

[3] *Manuel de folklore français contemporain* (1938–1958).

According to Van Gennep (*Manuel*, I, p. 73), the field of 'beliefs and feelings', to which witchcraft eminently belongs, is the 'most delicate part of folklore': no doubt because the 'facts' consituting it are made up of words only and one cannot cling to reassuring material objects. When one can only talk – and no longer, for example, collect or make maps – the two interlocutors are caught in the bilingual trap. For, according to Van Gennep, peasants speak a primitive language and think with a pre-logical mentality; whereas the folklorists speak a civilized language. 'Popular mentality does not evolve on the same level as scientific mentality because it uses mostly analogic and participationistic reasoning, which lie at the basis of symbols, beliefs and rites, as has been shown by Lucien Lévy-Brühl' (*Manuel*, I, p. 15). When the people involved in a folkloristic investigation talk to each other and do nothing beyond that, two factors impede communication. On the one hand, common people are simple-minded, 'it is all the more difficult to obtain precise information as the people we are studying are themselves simple-minded' (*Manuel*, I, p. 73). On the other hand, the scholar is encumbered by his learning: 'but here we must be very cautious because we, the "civilized" find it very difficult to think in a participationistic or associationistic manner, to put ourselves in the other's place, to eliminate what we know, to become ignorant again, at least in some domains' (*Manuel*, I, p. 100). Note that the inverted commas around the word *civilized* are only there to attenuate the brutality of the implicit judgement contained in the statement: while we are civilized, the others, the peasants, the common people, are savages or primitives; what is more, they are ignorant and if they think at all, it is in a pre-logical manner.

In 1880, Paul Sébillot, author of the monumental *Folklore de la France* (to whom the convenient theories of Lévy-Brühl were not available), quite openly expressed the prejudices of the scholarly élite concerning the peasantry: 'In general, one can say that the French peasant belongs to an inferior stratum of civilization, at least in some respects; inferior, that is, to the inhabitants of towns who have at least acquired something of a literary veneer. If one acknowledges that these are men of the nineteenth century, many peasants can then be said to be two or three centuries behind; sometimes, even, their culture is from the Middle Ages.'[4] He simply advised folklorists to play a double game in order to extract the precious folkloric matter from the peasants: 'Collecting folk-literature is not so easy as one imagines', he wrote in his *Questionnaire*;[5] 'in order to succeed, one needs tact, patience, and a certain degree of know-how. For should you fail to be gladly accepted by those you question or should you let them suspect you think [the truth, i.e.] that their beliefs and legends are ridiculous, then you will

---

[4] Paul Sébillot (1887). The anachronism of peasants is a favourite cliché of the scholarly élite: they are quite convinced that they possess the right sense of history. On this matter, cf. pp. 3–5 and Ch. 4.
[5] Paul Sébillot (1880).

obtain nothing – they will start making up stories or saying things which are quite different from what actually happens.'[6]

What, from Sébillot to Van Gennep, has been left uncriticized, is the definition of French ethnography as *folklore* (the science of the 'common people') and the stereotype of infantile and ignorant common folk.[7] Lévy-Brühl's theories gave support to the notion that the common people do not think but imagine, feel and participate: only the scholar can be said to really think. Thus: when interpreting, said Van Gennep, one must be sure to stay 'in a specifically folkloric atmosphere', i.e. popular or non-scientific. The scholar in him seemed to find it quite difficult to define this atmosphere, 'more imagined and felt than thought out and constructed' (*Manuel*, 1, p. 105).

To help us understand how ignorant people think, Van Gennep introduced the notion of the 'world as if': 'all humans', he said, 'except where true science in concerned, are in the same mental and emotional state as children listening to fairy-tales or looking at a puppet show; they behave *as if* they really believed in the reality of the characters, in the plausibility of the metamorphoses, although they know that in everyday life there are no fairies or Punches who hit policemen without taking any risks' (my italics).

If I may put Van Gennep's statements in my own words:[8] *I know*, says the child, that Punch can't hit the policeman without taking any risks, *but still*, if this were possible, what a great revenge against authority; or again: I *know* that fairies don't exist, *but still*, if only one of them could transform me, etc.

Van Gennep is perfectly right to emphasize the fact that only scientific statements leave no room for the *but still* – i.e. for the fulfilment of an impossible desire – since the *I know* takes up all the room. But he became inextricably confused by counter-balancing the scholar with the illiterate. We have only to recall, for example, the text cited above in which he wrote how difficult it was for 'civilized people' to think in a pre-logical manner, 'to eliminate what they know, to become ignorant again'. For the child is aware that fairies are mythical beings: perhaps it is because he knows this that he takes pleasure in being told tales in which humans can be physically transformed or authority ridiculed without peril to himself.

The very notion of a 'world as if' that Van Gennep proposed as the key to popular mentality is completely hampered by this misunderstanding. Within the space of a few lines (ibid., pp. 105–6), it takes on three different

[6] Another version, taken from 'Instructions et Questionnaires' (op. cit.): if you have been 'nice to the peasants, not arrogant, as they say, there comes a moment when they no longer feel embarrassed, and you can then obtain valuable information without seeming to do so. But you have to watch yourself: whatever you hear, you must not protest at its absurdity, or smile at its naïvety: in other words, you must appear to agree with them, to laugh at their vulgar humour, and be interested in their legends (which is not difficult, since many of them have a certain charm) and accept their beliefs and superstitions without further discussion.'
[7] On this point, cf. Michel de Certeau, Dominique Julia, Jacques Revel (1970).
[8] Cf. pp. 51–2.

meanings: the 'logic and the feelings of the common people' are defined as those for whom the metaphysical or mythical world is:

(*a*) as if it were understood: 'It is best, here to refer to Vaihinger's philosophical theory of the world as if (*die Welt als ob*), which almost corresponds to the mathematical formula: let us consider the problem solved. Astrology, divination in all its forms, occultism, magic medicine, mythology and folk-literature are all based on the principle that if such and such a thing is *known* the rest follows and is also *known*.'

(*b*) as if it were real: 'one presumes that things took place, or take place in such and such a way, and one acts correspondingly; whereas scientific method does not allow such extrapolations [. . .] This conception of the world as if, of "make believe", of "behaving as if it *really* happened" has the advantage, for the folklorist, of etc.'

(*c*) as if one believed it: 'folklore as a whole is immersed in the World *as if*. Most humans, when they are methodically and precisely questioned, are not absolutely *convinced* of the existence of a Judging God, or of the intervention of Providence in our lives [. . .] or of the material reality of miracles. But they behave as if they *believed it*' [again, my italics].

It seems to me that Van Gennep would have been spared many difficulties if he had stated that the metaphysical world is simply seen as if it were *still possible*. He would then have taken advantage of his analogy between popular mentality and mathematical reasoning, which consists of drawing conclusions from a hypothesis whose truth value is temporarily left unquestioned; from his considerations about children who know, *but still*; and from the extension of pre-logical mentality – i.e. the stating of the *but still* – to anyone who is not at the point of the *I know*, involved in scientific discourse.

Instead of which he completely opposed the primitive to the civilized, the uneducated to the scholarly, the child to the adult – and considered all these oppositions as equivalent – as if these positions were once and for all taken up by each person: a child lies sleeping in each of us, he said in substance, but in the folklorists' parlance, it is the adult who speaks. Or, to say things differently, Van Gennep considered logical mentality (the *I know*) and pre-logical mentality (the *but still*) as characteristic of two distinct categories of humans and not as two set positions of opinion liable to be occupied at different moments by any speaker, be he primitive or not.[9] For

---

[9] Sometimes he does give precise indications of the contrary, but he does not use them to advantage. Thus: 'In folklore above all, he says, one must carefully avoid establishing scales of value or placing personal involvement before logic. In fact, one habitually thinks in two different ways, and one continues to do so at various times or in certain circumstances. Both ways of reasoning and drawing conclusions, both modes of *action* are constitutive elements of the human race' (*Manuel*, 1, p. 97). Van Gennep does not seem aware that these two frames of mind are mutually incompatible: (1) that pre-logical mentality is not related to any particular social category and (2) that it relates to what is 'popular' (e.g. in 'popular mentality does not evolve in the same way as scientific mentality'), while logical mentality relates to the

this reason, Van Gennep could not solve the mystery of their interrelationship, and advised the scholar who wished to have access to folklorist materials to play the simpleton, or the child; for this is what catching 'the specific folkloric atmosphere' comes to. Thus one will hardly be suprised that it could be understood as an invitation to condescension: 'if the folklorist internalizes this view [of the world as if]', says Nicole Belmont in all seriousness, 'he will place himself on the level of popular logic and sentiment.'[10] At least the nineteenth-century folklorist who studied peasants had the excuse that they were their servants, farmers or flocks.

It may be remembered that, in the *Manuel* (IV, p. 557), Van Gennep introduced the topic 'magic and witchcraft' as follows: 'If one were to stick to the facts, one could almost put the whole of French folklore under this heading, since so-called popular acts and concepts differ precisely from so-called scientific ones by a mistaken application of the law of causality. The scope of this logical mistake has varied throughout the ages', etc. This reduction of witchcraft to a logical mistake goes very much against a principle put forward by the same author: one should absolutely avoid interpreting folkloric facts in the terms of scientific logic (e.g. *Manuel*, I, p. 106). It was to avoid just this reduction that the notion of the 'world as if' was so painstakingly developed.

When reading the chapters of Van Gennep's regional monograph devoted to witchcraft, it is rather offputting to see that his informants are almost always schoolteachers. For there are reasons to suspect – even and especially when they are of peasant origin – that they have a score to settle with the irrational. Actually, the *Manuel* (I, pp. 69–70) contains this peculiar indication: 'priests, schoolteachers, directors and professors of teacher-training schools can be excellent witnesses ... especially with regard to the *secret* domain of folk medicine and witchcraft'. Since these domains are secret and hence normally forbidden to an outsider such as the folklorist, Van Gennep proposed to sidestep the difficulty: the folklorist should send a questionnaire to the schoolteacher – who is assumed to be well-integrated in local life – and he should question his pupils and their families, and send his report to the folklorist. This survey by mail meets, in a few rare cases, with 'half-witted refusals' from informants who write back to the folklorist: 'Do you take us for savages? We are civilized people.'[11] It is striking that Van Gennep, who saw the uselessness of this procedure where witchcraft was concerned – in his *Le Folklore du Dauphiné*, he admits that when the survey is successful it is 'by luck' – should nevertheless have continued to give his questionnaires to the schoolteachers of all the

---

'civilized' (we, the civilized, etc.'). Note too that Lévy-Brühl's theories are like fairy-tales: both are too good to be true or to be repudiated. Although Lévy-Brühl often insisted that one had to admit this, the folklorists cannot make up their minds to give it up once and for all: 'I know it's not true', Van Gennep seems to be saying, 'but still, it's quite useful'.

[10] Nicole Belmont (1974), p. 114.   [11] Van Gennep (1932–3).

provinces where he chose to work and should have recommended its use to his colleagues.[12]

I think that Van Gennep carried on with such absurd methods because, on the one hand, he was convinced that the state school was the people's school; hence there could not have been any distance between the school-teacher and the milieu in which he worked. On the other hand, like all folklorists, he was obsessed with a feeling of urgency: like many others in the previous hundred years, he often repeated that what was left of popular traditions must be collected before it entirely vanished.[13]

This is why Van Gennep undertook extensive surveys of regional folk-lores, thus checking out, commune by commune, the existence and form of 'folklore facts' that had already been identified by his predecessors.[14] The shortcomings of extensive surveys are well-known.

(a) The breadth of a survey is always achieved at the expense of significant detail, which is particularly detrimental when, as in the case of witchcraft, complex symbolic systems are at stake. What, for instance, is the point of in-forming us that 'at Méribel-les-Echelles, cows that gave no milk were be-witched; milk would immediately coagulate on coming out of the udder; it was impossible to have cream and butter; or, conversely, it was impossible to make cheese. The same milk, once taken out of the bewitched house, would react normally in neighbours' or others' houses. At Vaujany, witches were people with an uncanny look who predicted the future and helped one find lost objects. One had to do what they wanted, to be very submissive, or else they would cast evil spells on the house, etc.?'[15] So many communes, so many informants, so many fragments of a symbolic system, presented in disconnected form.

(b) The exhaustiveness of this investigation is contingent upon the qual-ity of the informants and on the greater or lesser ease with which a given phenomenon can be put into words: it is hard to imagine how school-teachers could break the walls of secrecy that protect witchcraft, either in the commune in which they live, where it would create an eventful scandal, or in the other communes of a region. On the other hand, if it is obvious that the investigation will not be exhaustive, why undertake it and come up with

---

[12] Trusting Van Gennep's advice, I questioned a few schoolmasters and teachers in the Bocage including a retired head of 'l'Ecole normale'. I have never come across such paltry infor-mants: most of them knew some witchcraft stories, usually concerning eccentric unwitchers whom they had read about in the press, or had heard about from local gossip drawn from the press. Some, very few, remembered having heard stories during their peasant childhood, but their narratives were governed by an overwhelming desire to blot out this pre-logical past.

[13] And yet nothing can be further from a scientific approach than this eager haste, which usually gives priority to quantity rather than to the relevance of the data collected.

[14] *En Savoie*, vol. I: *Du berceau à la tombe*, Chambéry, Dardel, 1916; *Le Folklore du Dauphiné*, 1932–3 (op. cit.); *Le Folklore de la Bourgogne (Côte-d'Or) avec une discussion théorique sur le prétendu culte des sources*, Cap, Louis Jean, 1934; *Le Folklore de la Flandre et du Hainaut français (département du Nord)*, Paris, G. P. Maisonneuve, 1935, 2 vols; *Le Folklore des Hautes-Alpes*, Paris, G. P. Maisonneuve, 1946, 1948, 2 vols; *Le Folklore de l'Auvergne et du Velay*, Paris, G. P. Maison-neuve, 1942.   [15] *Le Folklore du Dauphiné*, op. cit. p. 474.

statements such as 'at X, ritual A is practised'; 'at Y, ritual B has fallen out of use', 'at Z, C is still believed to be effective'?

(c) As what has been said may have shown, mere 'folklore facts' boil down to names without bodies, to entries in a file. That each one should be in its place in a classification does not necessarily mean that this classification actually refers to the empirical system to which it is meant to give order. With regard to witchcraft in particular, Van Gennep does nothing more than to put the findings of his predecessors in order, without ever questioning their relationship to the empirical system studied. Even when he knows the region well – as is especially the case for the Dauphiné – he uses the same questionnaires which yield the same results: a monotonous list of witchcraft agents, objects, rituals, anecdotes. That these anecdotes are characteristic of one and only one type of exchange; that in no way could they be called *legends*; that objects and rituals are less interesting than the agents of witchcraft; that no separate question can be asked about these agents, since what is at work in witchcraft is their reciprocal relationship and nothing else: these principles entirely escape Van Gennep whose only worry is to check out, commune after commune, whether such agents, such objects, such rituals or such anecdotes are still extant.

Here, for instance, are the questions about witchcraft he asks his informants in Savoy:[16]

'To whom are diseases (human and animal) attributed? Witches. Men or women with the evil eye. Bad encounters.

– Use of certain animals in healing and in witchcraft (dormouse, bear, viper, toad, mole, grasshopper, crayfish eye, pigeon, etc.).

– How are people or animals "dried up"?

– Who can obstruct a fire; dam up flooding (formulae, prayers)?

– How are storms, lightning stopped or warded off (bells, saints, formulae to be recited)? How are spells cancelled?

– What are the means to give or interrupt the act of love; make oneself loved; have children?'

The reader will have observed that the unwitcher is absent from this questionnaire where formulae and rituals are stressed. There is no concern expressed about who utters or performs them. Van Gennep is interested in what can most easily be made objective: beliefs ('to whom are diseases attributed?') or practices. But by thus isolating them from the context of an exchange of views and a situation which invites opinion, he cancels their meaning once and for all and in fact reduces them to mere *logical mistakes*.[17]

---

[16] *Manuel*, III, pp. 32–8: 'Questionnaires sur les moeurs et coutumes de Savoie, Barrer ce qui ne se fait pas. [. . .] Questionnaire n° 3' (on disease). Van Gennep liked to use these Savoyard questionnaires: he would say they 'worked well' – so well, in fact, that he simply adapted them for other regions.

[17] These reflections, which I have centred on the works of Van Gennep, apply to folklorist writings as a whole, except for the work of Marcelle Bonteiller. I shall talk about this in the forthcoming volume.

APPENDIX 3

ROBERT BRAULT, 'PROPHET' OF ARON

As I wished to avoid overloading this work with too much additional detail, I chose to reserve for the appendix the material available to me on the 'magus' from Aron (Mayenne).

When I was carrying out my fieldwork, Brault was living in clandestine seclusion on the farm of one of his disciples. It was rumoured that he was being sought by the police, even though the law had not succeeded in charging him with any crime whatever. At the beginning of my stay, the doctor in charge of the psychiatric hospital, wishing to assist me in my research, mentioned my work to the Public Prosecutor; the Prosecutor, it appears, thoughtfully suggested having the 'prophet' arrested so that I might submit him to questioning at a psychiatric examination (which, by the way, I was not qualified to conduct). This may have been no more than a polite offer by men who were eager to be of service, and I cannot say for sure that the 'magus' would actually have been arrested if I had in fact accepted their proposal. This conversation, however, put an end to my dealings with the authorities. Two months later, I was beyond the pale: the farmers had taken to hiding me away whenever the priest, the doctor or the veterinary surgeon happened to call in while they were talking to me about witchcraft.

As I knew that Brault had been cornered, I avoided working in his area, and even refrained from following up leads which might have given me the opportunity of meeting him. The figure of Brault (and his followers) afforded a fascinating subject of study, but it seemed clear to me that, whatever my intentions might be, I would have the police and the law at my heels, and that I could not avoid being partly responsible for his arrest.

The 'magus', anyway, would have had reason enough for mistrusting me since he had already suffered as the result of a previous study carried out by a psychology student from the region in preparation for her thesis on 'the portrait of a sorcerer'.[1] This student had prematurely divulged her dis-

[1] Which is tantamount to saying the portrait of 'The Invisible Man', since the bewitcher is an imaginary being, who only has an imaginary reality. One wonders what were the musings of Professor Lagache, who assigned this research topic to her.

coveries and at the same time, it appears, expounded her enlightened *a priori* judgements to members of the local Rotary Club (or it may have been to their rival, the Lions Club). She subsequently began receiving threats against her life.

Although I never feared physical aggression while carrying out my investigations, I knew there was one rule of the game by which I had to abide. In this particular case, the rule was that I should make no attempt to meet the 'prophet' nor to get his closest followers to speak to me, until the inevitable misunderstanding he had of my intentions had been removed, i.e. at the very least, he should feel confident that I would in no way involve him in any legal risk, as he was in a most precarious situation; but also that I would not use the information I had gathered to denounce him publicly or to expose him to ridicule. By the time he died, in 1971, I still had not succeeded in getting to the heart of the matter.

The notes which now follow are based, therefore, on press cuttings. This means they should be treated with caution. Nevertheless, they do offer partial insight into the development of a breakaway cult in a region where religious innovation would seem to be the last thing expected. (During my work, I had very close relations with another religious group, based on the conviction that 'the End of the World was at hand'. The members of this group were all farm-workers, and they too had been bewitched. But I could not speak of them today without identifying them completely to those among whom they live; and these people would not be slow to exploit my disclosures for stirring up a scandal comparable to the one described in Part II, Chapter 4. Hence I prefer not to discuss this group in the book.)

Robert Brault (1915–71) began his working life in Nantes as a metal-worker. After the death of his father, who had been a taxi-driver, then a miller at Aron, Brault returned to the land to replace him. The flour-mill, it seems, swiftly went bankrupt, and Brault worked for some time as a level-crossing guard. His wife died in strange circumstances in 1948, killed by a bullet shot from a revolver by a friend; the police inquiry, however, established that the death was accidental.

Brault then became an animal healer and spell-breaker, making use of large quantities of consecrated salt and a team of informants who reported to him on how things were going in the local cattle-sheds. When he turned to curing women of sterility, it is claimed he also rounded up a team of sturdy young men to serve as 'stallions'. He seems to have belonged to the category of eccentric unwitchers; at all events, I never heard anything said of him that might allow a different description.

In 1962, following a religious crisis during which he taught himself about the various religious traditions, he claimed that twelve years before, i.e. shortly after his wife's death, he had received a secret commandment from

God, and he now undertook to preach to the bewitched who came to find out about the doctrine he had devised.

This doctrine, which Brault explicitly stated was not a new religion but a purified or reformed Catholicism, was based on four main tenets.

(a) The time of the great misfortunes is nigh; only those who have faith in Brault will be saved. With this message of doom as his basis, he uttered a series of prophecies, generally expressed in rather vague form: 'in a short time hence the disbelievers will be sorely deceived'; 'great happenings are soon to occur' (Le Courrier de la Mayenne, 26 December 1964). These prophecies always refer to a future that is close and catastrophic, although the form it is to take is not specified. On occasions, however, when pressed by a journalist or goaded on by the urgent need to win the full trust of his followers, he did risk more detailed statements: 'It is no longer a matter of days but of hours' (Mayenne-Républicain, 21 February 1965); 'Christ will return to Earth this year'; 'in 1964, you will see the Son of Man' (Le Courrier, 23 January 1965); 'before the end of the year there will be a great earthquake; only those who believe in me will be spared' (Le Courrier, 22 January 1965); [in 1964], 'we shall be covered by thick shadow from Wednesday of Holy Week until Easter Sunday' (Le Courrier, 23 January 1965). (When it was pointed out to Brault's disciples that not one of these predictions had been fulfilled, they replied, as followers of doom movements generally do; 'They have been fulfilled elsewhere and for others; soon it will happen to us.' cf. Le Courrier, 23 January 1965.)

(b) The Devil is the cause of evil and sickness; but through personal purification ('when the soul is pure it cannot be sick') and through the power with which the prophet has been endowed to fight the forces of the Devil, the doctor's attentions can be rendered unnecessary.[2]

(c) The Catholic priests cannot absolve sins, for they themselves are sinners (idle, cowardly, ignorant, and lascivious); it is better to do one's own penance, to fast (Brault claimed to have fasted fifty days on end), to abstain from meat and animal fats, and to mortify the body.

(d) Contrary to the pronouncement of the Catholic Church, marriage is not indissoluble since it is a human institution.

Brault's precepts for the conduct of life are simple in the extreme: 'Follow the Bible, above all the Gospels; whiten the soul; say no to the way of wickedness; direct your path towards perfection' (Le Monde, 21–2 February 1965). But his followers seem to have been primarily fascinated by the contempt shown by the 'magus' towards work and material goods, includ-

---

[2] Le Monde, 21–2 February 1965. The Courrier de la Mayenne devoted an article ('A sect member dies', 17 April 1965) to the fact that a disciple of Brault's had died without being offered medical aid, implying that this could constitute a reason for laying criminal charges against him. When the 'prophet' died in 1971 in the same conditions, the farmer in whose home he had sought refuge was charged with failing to offer assistance to a dangerously ill person, and was imprisoned at Laval.

ing inherited property; they were also attracted by the commitment to devote their lives to aiding those in distress, starting with the 'frères' of the sect. In a district where the supreme good was conceived solely in terms of increasing the inheritance and where disregard for all non-relatives was looked upon as a cardinal virtue, these precepts were bound to attract local dissidents who might otherwise have become militant *avant-garde* Christians.

Thus Brault rapidly attached some hundred followers to his cause, many of them young farm-labourers or prominent churchgoers. 'Healthy souls, only yesterday, often the backbone of the community', *Le Courrier* of 2 January 1965 notes with concern, 'and today, utterly under the sway of this enchantment, speaking as though they had completely lost their reason'. On 23 January, the same paper states that: 'The letters we receive show that at present the superstition in Mayenne is by no means in a state of semi-lethargy and that it is gaining a hold even on the young. The sect that has emerged in Aron and is based on belief in magic spells has given an unexpected and dangerous lease of life to this superstition, so powerful that it has reached the point of totally disrupting the life and customs of certain farming families. By playing upon the ingenuousness of some of the young farm-workers, it has now led to the financial ruin of several farmsteads, the heads of which, transformed into missionaries and apostles, have now taken to roving round the countryside with their entire families in search of suffering and misery to relieve, totally disregarding the fact that the first among the unfortunate in need of aid are their very own children, and that the first distress in need of relief is likewise their own.' Finally, the parish priest of Aron observed the anxiety felt by priests in his district 'on occasionally finding parishioners, whom they had hitherto considered among the most devoted, turning aside from the straight and narrow', i.e. choosing the teachings of Brault in preference to their own (*Le Courrier*, 2 January).

On entering the sect, the disciples were given new designations: some became known as the 'Parfaits', others as the 'Apôtres', and most of them as the 'Frères' (*Le Courrier*, 23 January). This represented a radical innovation with regard to the traditional nomenclature of the Bocage, where a person's individual status, his position as a son or father, and his land-ownership status would be conveyed, for instance, as: 'Pierre du Plessis' (the son), or 'père Vaujois des Gaudinières'. (While Brault was described as *'Prophète'*, *'Réformateur'*, *'Evnoyé spécial du Très-Haut'*, etc.)

The disciples were distinguished from the rest of the population by their physical appearance: they went barefoot, in sandals, wearing their hair long (which in 1964 was no slight provocation), with a necklace or beard, to 'overcome pride' and to indicate that they were not concerned by what others thought of them (*Le Monde*, 21–2 February 1965). Furthermore, they observed frequent fasts and had adopted a strictly vegetarian diet, which was a sure way of alienating them even further from the local people, for whom meat in abundance represented not only wellbeing or good living but also the main precondition for a healthy mind.[3] A reader, writing to the *Courrier* of 23 January, says: 'Their diet for Lent consisted of: 4 biscuits, *bouillon* [soup], and fruit – nothing else all day. They never ate meat or butter.' As a result of this diet, says the editor (6 March), 'their health was seriously undermined', and he notes, on 9 October, 'the physical and moral decline caused by Brault's insalubrious doctrine'.

Like all other sects, this group replaced the traditional ties of solidarity (between relatives, neighbours, etc.) with new attachments: members were to keep company only with the 'frères' or with those who came to beg their assistance, most often the bewitched who were in distress; likewise, traditional occupations (cultivating the land to increase the heritage, performing one's duties as a parishioner together with the other inhabitants of the district) were replaced by new activities: healing, unwitching, and generally being of assistance, in addition to participating in the religious life of the sect rather than that of the parish. For Brault celebrated mass and evensong, preached and administered the holy sacraments in a building he had had restored, which was close to his mill and served as a chapel.[4] 'These farmers, who are no longer farmers except in name', says the *Courrier* of 9 July 1966, 'are primarily interested in the ceremonies that are held all week long at the Mill of Aron: the "baptism" or "confirmation" of a child of the sect, and other ceremonies and rites. During this time, the animals manage as best they can';[5] 'the followers of this sect are required to be present twice a week at the "mass" celebrated by B(rault). [. . .] "what mass?" a reader asks indignantly, and adds that some children "no longer go to Catechism, or even to school, because they are caught up at prayer-meetings that often last late into the night." ' 'Fasting is observed and mourning worn on all sorts of occasions', observes the editor of the *Courrier*.[6]

[3] This explains why, in the small town where I was staying, how in spite of all my learning, I could be 'bound' by spells: as I ate little meat, it followed that my nerves were particularly frail (*'she doesn't eat meat, she'll have thin blood'*, etc.). For the same reason, certain people thought I had been initiated by the 'magus' from Aron.

[4] 'Everybody was gathered together in a room consecrated as a chapel, furnished with a long table, two benches and stools. Hanging in state above a cupboard was a colour print of a pietà. On a blackboard was a commentary on Christ's words about brotherly love' (*Le Monde*, 21–2 February 1965). 'It was a clean, low-ceilinged room. On the walls, several holy pictures and a blackboard bearing a painstakingly copied-out passage from the Gospels; the furnishings were completed by a rough wood table, stools and a censer' (*Paris-Jour*, 16 February 1965).

[5] The *Courrier de la Mayenne* did not hesitate to label them as 'deserters from their farms' (21 August 1966) – which is quite an insult in a region where the great public occasions revolve around the celebration of memories of heroism in the two World Wars.

[6] The *Courrier de la Mayenne* of 2 and 23 January 1965. When the 'prophet' died in 1971, I overheard the following exchange between two villagers discussing the famous 'vespers': *'There was a bigger congregation at the prophet's vespers than there was at the priest's'*, admitted the one.

The ideological and emotional binding-force for the sect was Brault's word, which he claimed to be directly inspired by God and by Christ. The 'prophet', like his disciples, healed and unwitched, but on important days for the sect his main activity was to speak, preaching to his disciples with widespread arms, in the chapel or on the roads (falling silent at the approach of a curious onlooker), and advising them on the conduct of their lives in numerous personal discussions. The substance of his teaching was so secret that certain disciples preferred to pay a five-hundred-franc fine [some £50 at current rates] than to reveal details of his instruction to the magistrate.[7]

In spite of the rustic simplicity of his theology and, it seems to me, because he adopted a stance so firmly opposed to local values, Brault held considerable sway over his followers and was so influential that he could with calm and confidence defy their families, local opinion, the Church and the law. An indication of this influence is given by a child who, when being questioned on Catholic dogma, told the priest, without a hint of brashness, 'I know far more about it than you' (*Le Courrier*, 23 January 1965).

The 'prophet's' predictions caused sufficiently powerful reverberations among the people for the clergy to become alarmed: between 1964 and 1965 it was possible to hear priests from the region of Aron personally refuting Brault's arguments and referring to doctrinal works for support. The parish priest of Aron (who told me he believed Brault to be a person genuinely concerned with religious matters) published an interesting cautionary note in his parish bulletin: while recognizing the possible curative powers of the healers, he denied their right to instruct people's consciences as to the conduct of their lives, '*for this is a right that belongs only to God*', that is to say, to his delegate the priest. The line of his argument was as follows: just as Christ proved that he was God, so too every prophet must prove his mission. 'When Christ came to preach his Gospel, he took the Jews by surprise. Some were scandalized, but Christ proved that he was God by carrying out his prophecies in person and by performing the many miracles recounted in the Gospels – curing the sick, raising the dead, and being resurrected. (Generally, the local priests play down the importance of the miracles performed by Christ in order not to be required to draw conclusions from the miracles the local healers claim to have accomplished. But here, in referring to the raising of the dead and to Christ's resurrection, the parish priest from Aron was fully confident that no healer could make equal

'*The priest's vespers? There hasn't been one for a good long time*', sighed the other. Michel Legris in *Le Monde* (quoted above) fully grasped this connection between the proliferation of breakaway religious cults in western France and the weakening of the Church's image since the Vatican Council.

[7] As an exceptional measure against the disciples, this magistrate felt obliged to revive a certain article 109 of the Penal Code – which had since fallen into abeyance – enabling him to impose a heavy fine upon them if they persisted in their silence.

claims, although – as we shall see later – Brault seems to have done so.) Can anyone, without proving his mission or without being in some way specially delegated (by having been ordained to the priesthood, for instance), provide religious instruction? (It should be noted that the key issue for the parish-priest from Aron is the church's monopoly over religious instruction, an issue which is identical to the one raised at the time of the first heresies.) Can one teach freely in religion or, further, make an amalgam of all the religions which have become familiar from literature? I do not think so.' (The 'prophet's' doctrine was indeed a compound of various religious traditions; but one might also recall that Catholicism was not formulated in a single day or in any one place.)

'Such thinking already existed at the time of Saint Paul, who wrote in his second epistle to Timothy, 4. 3–4: "For the time will come when they will not endure sound doctrine; but after their own lusts shall they hear to themselves teachers, having itching ears; And they shall turn away their ears from the truth, and shall be turned into fables." ' [In quoting this text, the priest was killing two birds with one stone: (1) he was basing his argument on a passsage from the Holy Scriptures, the truth of which Brault himself would have recognized, in order to brand the 'prophet's' teaching as a 'falsehood' and his disciples as scatter-brained people, governed by their passions; (2) he was challenging Brault's claim to have introduced any religious innovation whatever, since his coming had been eternally predicted in the holy texts.]

'This thinking continues to exist today, a fact not difficult to prove. One need only give ear to the witness of Christians worthy of religious belief, to the testimony of priests responsible before God and before their bishop for spreading the Gospel in their parish', and so on (What is being implied here is that Brault's words do not carry the slightest weight since he is not responsible to any hierarchy.) Hence the priest's final admonition: 'Whatever may be the real or presumed holiness of the person who acts of his own accord in the domain of religion, such initiatives, it seems to me, constitute a flagrant abuse; and I hope it is not too late, to say to those who have chosen the wrong path: reflect, pray, consider, and return to the fold so that there may be one flock alone, and one Shepherd.'[8] But it is hardly likely that these deviants, the followers of the 'Prophet', would have been tempted by the prospect of rejoining the 'flock'.

A short while afterwards, the *Courrier de la Mayenne*, a conservative Catholic paper which nonetheless regarded itself as a 'weekly news-sheet', launched a 'detoxification campaign' against this modern poison, the 'new religion' preached by the miller from Aron. The *Courrier* devoted a long series of articles to him, which had a two-fold effect: (*a*) they helped form a movement in public opinion hostile to the 'prophet', culminating in the

---

[8] Quoted in the *Courrier de la Mayenne* of 2 January 1965.

demonstrations of February 1965; (*b*) they served as documentary material for the press as a whole once the scandal broke. (The *Courrier* openly acknowledged having played this role when, after the first incidents, it carried the following statement on 20 February: 'Once facts of sufficient gravity had been brought to its attention, the *Courrier de la Mayenne* was the only paper to pursue an unrelenting campaign of detoxification in every one of its issues from 17 December (1964) onwards. One must give credit where credit is due; if the media in Paris (Radio Station *Europe 1*, *France-Soir*, *Paris-Jour* and so on) have now been alerted and if we are about to see this tragi-comedy brought to an end, then your paper is doing its job!').

It is worth giving a moment's reflection to this type of literature in order to observe the press in action when it is concerned both with demonstrating a belief to be heterodox and contrary to the concept of an 'enlightened faith'[9] and with demolishing its tenets (which are potentially subversive of the established religious order): for instance, by reducing this faith to mere sado-masochistic scheming between gullible fools and charlatans.

It will be seen at once that the editors of the *Courrier* seem to have had no shortage of derogatory expressions to describe the 'prophet's' doctrine: most often, this teaching is referred to as an 'evil',[10] but other terms are also employed, such as 'the weird and mysterious rites' of the 'obscure religion known to us', or again, 'this heinous doctrine based on fatalism' (which, as we shall see, is a sound reason for reproof), 'this dangerous prattling', 'this brainwashing', 'this bunkum'. Brault is designated as 'the false one' or 'the famous prophet', 'this lugubrious individual' motivated exclusively by his own acquisitiveness, whose teachings lead to catastrophic effects. Which may also be put down as: the 'disastrous results of this so-called doctrine', or the 'dangerous consequences of certain superstitious beliefs'.[11]

The essence of the *Courrier's* argument is contained in the following passage dated 20 February 1965, significantly headed: 'What the healthy-minded public does not understand.' I shall take the liberty of commenting on the passage within the quotation: 'It is indeed difficult to understand how, in this third quarter of the twentieth century [a reminder

---

[9] A frequently-recurring theme in post-Concilium sermons in parishes in the Bocage.

[10] The *Courrier de la Mayenne* of 2 and 9 January, 20 February, 6 March and 2 October 1965.

[11] The *Courrier de la Mayenne* of 26 December 1964, 9 January, 13 and 20 February, 6 March, 2 and 9 October 1965. *Ouest-France* likewise defined Brault as an 'unscrupulous fellow' (11 February 1965), reigning as a 'grand potentate' over a 'sect of visionaries' (23–4 October) – the visionaries here being contrasted to members of the Enlightenment as an extreme in relation to the norm; the editor also speaks of 'the deplorable duping of Aron' (22 February) or 'the venture inaugurated by reprehensible individuals and taken up by weak, gullible people' (11 February). The liberal weekly, *Mayenne-Républicain*, offers in turn a restrained and cautious account of the affair in its edition of 21 February: this paper, like all the others, makes use of contemptuous terms ('charlatanism', 'credulity', 'abuse of influence and trust', 'frauds', the 'deplorable nature of certain facts', etc.), without ever stating clearly to whom these terms are being applied, or else putting them down to unverifiable reports.

that the subject of witchcraft and prophecy is scandalously anachronistic] a man with a questionable past [the editor is alluding here to the strange circumstances in which Mme Brault met her death] could practise his methods of stupefaction on people from the most respectable families [for some of Brault's disciples belonged to the better-off farming families, and not to those of drunkards and riff-raff, although it was popularly held that only people from such primitive backgrounds could believe in spells], a stupefaction that has led to the suffering of many children, to whom no meat is given [the theme of the child martyrs] because it is forbidden by M. Brault [the theme of the 'prophet's absolute sway over his disciples]. It is likewise hard to comprehend how hitherto sensible people may be so stupefied as to commit the worst of errors and perform acts of incomprehensible stupidity, dragging them into bankruptcy and ruin [the all-important theme of the squandering of the inheritance]. [...] If these men are mad [for one would have to be mad to believe in this teaching], they should be locked away, with their 'Pope' at the head; if they are subverters [for one would have to be perverse to make others believe], they should be arrested' [the theme of resorting to the Law].

Now let us see how some of these themes were expanded in the *Courrier*.

(a) The 'prophet's' absolute sway over his disciples

One of the early articles went no further than to speak of 'this vague something, a sort of hold or threat hanging over them' (26 December 1964); but Brault's influence rapidly became equated with 'designs for psychological and moral seduction' (2 January 1965), and later with 'the most dangerous form of bewitchment': 'Those who have been bewitched by Brault are completely done for', writes the relative of a follower of the sect. 'They will never work again; to start with, they are reduced to a lamentable physical state, annihilated, and from then on are more helpless than children for looking after themselves. [...] This is straight bewitchment [...] the most dangerous form of bewitchment' (6 March). The notion that the disciples were thus deprived of their free-will had been aired, as it happens, a few weeks previously (2 January) by the editor of the *Courrier*: 'With their freedom crushed, their acts and actions are now absolutely dependent on the "ideas" of B[rault] their great leader'![12] Then, once the scandal had erupted and legal investigation was under way, certain interesting leads were suggested for the law to pursue, including hypnosis and drug-taking: there was a farmer, so it was said, 'who had narrowly escaped being bewitched by Brault – which was the only real danger – and who

---

[12] On 9 July 1965, the editor of the *Courrier* was again to say of Brault: 'nothing is done without his orders', not even the sowing. While *Ouest-France*, making heavy weather of the metaphor, speaks of 'the leader of the sect at Aron [...] extending his tentacles like an octopus, [...] to assert a formidable influence over his victims', etc. (12 February).

related how Brault had always tried to get him to look into his eyes while he was talking ... in order to bewitch him properly. Many people swore that Brault's followers drank special concoctions, which disturbed their minds and explained their state of exaltation' (17 April); 'certain people wondered if a blood specimen, taken at the right moment, might not one day reveal that the bewitchment of some of the followers was being prolonged through the taking of drugs' (15 May).

(b) The disciples' fatalism

On 2 January 1965, the editor of the *Courrier* carried an account of a 'true conversation' between a farmer, who was a follower of the 'prophet', and his creditor:

'*Who will give you the money you keep hoping to have tomorrow?*' asked the creditor.

'*God.*'

'*But if you are always looking after other people* [an allusion to the disciples' solidarity and to their pledge to help the bewitched] *and not after your lands, who will do your work?*'

'*God will provide* [...]. *We are not on this earth to earn money.*'

The disciple then went on to justify his attitude saying it was anyway pointless to consider repaying his debts since an earthquake would occur before the end of the year. The editor concluded:

'No need to work, then! – that's clear. What do these poor creatures make of sayings such as: "God helps those who help themselves" and "Charity begins at home"?'

Writing in the same vein, the editor of the *Courrier* reminded the disciples, in his edition of 30 January, 'that even though the birds of the air may give no thought to the morrow, they do at least take the trouble to gather their own food'; and he referred again to that popular saying – here elevated to a moral precept of absolute validity – 'Charity begins at home.' So whether the prophecy was true or false, the only response was a catch-phrase.

(c) The children, martyrs of their parents' convictions

On this issue, at any rate, the editors of the *Courrier* felt sure of gaining unanimous disapproval of the sect: in a stock-breeding region, such as the Bocage, vegetarianism is inevitably an outrage against normal existence. When the parents believe, the children suffer the consequences: 'But when one thinks of all those innocent creatures, eating nothing but margarine and being deprived of meat, milk and butter on account of him [Brault], the heart bleeds!' (30 January 1965); 'and their poor children, deprived sometimes of even the necessary minimum – cases could be quoted – suffer the consequences of these profligacies' (2 January); for several months, the paper never failed to mention 'deprivation of food, for which the weakest pay the cost' (20 February), the 'poorly-nourished children', the 'bad treatment which the children suffer as a result of their diet' (21 August) – all of which, remember, is quite simply the outcome of following a vegetarian diet.[13]

(d) The breakdown of traditional bonds of solidarity, and particularly of family attachments and neighbourly relations

On the one hand, the followers are separated by their faith from their families: 'One mother was *turned out of doors* by her daughter, who was a follower of the sect. A grown-up son, who had come to visit his parents, whose superstition he did not share, was likewise turned out of the house, after which the parents washed down their doorstep with disinfectant' (23 January 1965). What the editor does not mention is that the mother and the son were probably disinclined to allow members of their families, followers of the 'prophet', to interfere with the family inheritance, and that the discussion which followed must have been more like the violent disputes over inheritance common among families of the Bocage than calm discussions between persons of differing views. On the other hand, accusations of witchcraft and of adherence to the precepts of the 'magus' stir up discord in groups bonded by natural social ties: 'The families affected', explains the editor on 2 January, 'are often divided. They become morally self-isolating and driven to mistrust all others, sometimes even their neighbours. [...] The neighbours, in turn, soon become bothered and disturbed by the mysterious demeanour, the prolonged absences, and the far from reassuring appearance of a former companion who has let his hair, beard and moustache grow, and who now walks around barefoot and in sandals, holding forth incoherently. The man is hardly recognizable!' (This last remark should be stressed: rallying to the banner of the 'prophet' means becoming unrecognizable to one's own people.)

(e) Squandering the inheritance

'This fatalism which backs down under any pressure' (29 January 1966) necessarily results in the disintegration of one's inheritance. There seems to be little doubt that some of Brault's disciples were swiftly led to ruin

---

[13] *Ouest-France* states on 11 February 1965 that: 'The "adherents"' children, deprived as they are of requisite nourishment, are often in a wretched physical state'; on 15 February, the same paper offers its sympathetic support to the relatives of a group of disciples who had come to take away by force 'these lost creatures and their three children, weakened by lack of food, since meat and butter were forbidden to them'. In the same vein, *France-Soir* (16 February) also reports that: 'It is common to see families eating nothing all day but red cabbage and grated carrots, as the teacher explained to me. As a result, the children could end up suffering from rickets.'

through putting his principles into practice: most farms in the Bocage are normally in dire financial straits, and it is only by incurring constant debts that the farmer is able to meet his running expenses.[14] The *Courrier*, therefore, proudly proclaims that 'the publicity given [by them] to the desertion of homes and farmsteads [...] had the splendid effect of attracting the attention of suppliers, guarantors, bodies offering credit facilities, and landlords – who then reacted' (21 August 1965). At all events, these small landholdings, which subsidized mainly from rearing milch-cows, beef-cattle and pigs for slaughter, would have been unable to survive without regular work: milking twice-daily at fixed hours, cleaning the pigstys, feeding the cattle, and so on. The crops required less regular attention, but the work still needed to be done on time. The *Courrier* also gave a gloomy picture of the economic effects of this 'new religion': 'That is how ruin and misery come beating at the doors of the followers of B[rault], and the animals and the lands are left to abandon in several of the many farms in the forty or so communes affected, so they say, by this evil [...]; farms are no longer in business, debts accumulate' (2 January). It is all very well for the followers to maintain solidarity towards one another, but they swiftly become incapable of re-stocking the flocks and herds seized by the creditors.[15] Furthermore, despite their determination to sever all links with their families, the disciples cannot escape the deep concern of parents and relations (who had often stood as guarantors for loans they contracted before joining the sect) at the prospect of their children's impending bankruptcy: there are social links which cannot be broken simply by the declaration of adherence to a religious principle.

This is the context in which the demonstrations against the sect must be understood, as a reaction by the families to the schism (the term used by

[14] Cf. for instance, Armand Frémond, *L'Élevage en Normandie*, Caen, Association des Publications de la F.L.S.H. de Caen, 2 vols, 1967. (In particular, vol. 1, part 2: 'Le Bocage normand: une tradition d'incertitude'). René Musset, *Le Bas-Maine*, Paris, Colin, 1917, is still essential reading.

[15] The Mottais affair (or Mottier, in some versions) typifies the tension ruling at that time in the Bocage; on 27 September 1965, this farmer, a disciple of Brault's, had his forty head of cattle seized and sold to repay his creditors. The '*frères*' of the sect succeeded in buying back only six or seven cows, two horses, and several calves (*Le Courrier de la Mayenne*, 30 October). But this event gave rise to demonstrations: two thousand people came to attend the seizure; some days later, a posse that was trying to collect evidence of Brault's action, came to the mill to photograph the animals that had been bought back and were being kept there in transit. The interlopers were greeted with gunfire, and the photographer chose to make himself scarce. The person who appears to have contracted him for the job, and who had been organizing demonstrations against the 'prophet' for several months, was summoned to appear before the court in Laval. In his defence, he revealed that, as the relative of an 'Apostle', he had endured the break up of his family, his nephews' troubles, and so on. He was sentenced to pay a five-hundred-franc fine. (Cf. *Le Courrier de la Mayenne* of 2 and 9 October 1965, and 29 January 1966.)

Ouest-France, 15 February 1965) of those of their members bent on following the 'prophet'. 'Some families' – as the same paper notes on 11 February – 'deeply distressed by the involvement of the most naïve of their kin and by the sad consequences of their joining the sect (bankruptcy, deterioration of mental and physical health, etc.), have become justifiably upset by this sorry state of affairs. And since this situation has lasted far too long, and they still have no hope of seeing it finally brought to an end, they have decided to move into action.' The *Courrier*, in turn, systematically reported all the signs of this dissent, beginning with the most obvious ones: 'The local inhabitants, and above all those families with members belonging to the sect, have become exasperated at seeing all their former neighbours, parents and friends attending "mass" on Sunday morning, and later "evensong", with their bushy hair and beards often unkempt, in B[rault's] farmyard. They are ashamed of what happens there, of what is said, of seeing their fellows behaving like mental deficients . . . letting their business go to rack and ruin, refusing to give meat to their children, "salting" man and beast alike, etc.' (13 February; salt is used against witches).

'The purification cleansing campaign' (as the same issue of the *Courrier* called it) which the families now launched against their children who had been led astray, initially took the form of a spearhead attack on the visible signs of adherence to the sect: on 5 and 7 February, demonstrators seized followers as they were coming out from a religious ceremony and cropped those who were 'completely bewitched' (*Le Courrier*, ibid.) and who refused to go to the barber.[16]

But this intervention soon took on a more violent turn, which led to a call for the police: on 14 February, close on five hundred people gathered to surround Brault and his disciples as they came out of 'evensong'. They pulled down the fences, erected barricades, overturned cars, hurled stones and insults at the sectarians, and wounded the 'prophet' in the face with a

---

[16] We note the pleasure that the *Courrier de la Mayenne* takes in describing how the disciples had their heads shaved: the demonstrators 'returned to the town carrying locks of hair and beards in plastic bags like trophies'. One disciple, 'who had arrived late for the ceremony [*'vespers'*] was seized by a group of demonstrators who hacked away at his beard – a handsome ginger one – with scissors which tore away at the "scrub" rather than cutting it. Will this second, somewhat painful operation be a lesson to him?' (13 February 1965).
    'A thousand people set upon the (bearded) followers of the bewitcher at the Mill at Aron (Mayenne), to shave them . . . They wanted to shear them of their magic power', proclaims *France-Soir*, abiding by the great tradition of the national press (cf. Part II, Ch. 4, '*Someone must be credulous*'). The followers were described as homosexuals to be held up to ridicule, and the shaving ceremony as a scene of rural lampoon: 'Woe to bearded people in the Mayenne. For several days, the enemies of a new religious sect, founded by a miller-prophet, have been systematically attacking the bearded and long-haired followers who come to pray at the Mill at Aron with scissors and razors. Looking like the Beatles when they arrive, they leave shorn as smooth as eggs. Yesterday, a large-scale punitive expedition took place at the time for evensong. Close on a thousand people surrounded the prophet and his effeminate flock [etc.]'

stone. Brault, utterly serene, received representatives of the national press who had travelled down for the occasion, and impressed them with his dignity and composure. In answer to a reporter from *Paris-Jour*, who had asked what his feelings were about the hatred being shown him, Brault replied in Christ's words: 'Whoever you may be, your words do no more than brush past my ears' (16 February). When Michel Legris of *Le Monde* asked him if he were not afraid of losing his life by being shot, the 'prophet's' only remark was: [in that case] 'my earthly mission would be ended there' (21–2 February). At any rate, he refused to lay charges as he was determined to remain faithful to the principles of non-violence (*Ouest-France*, 15 February).

The following Sunday, 21 February, the demonstrators returned, but the 'prophet' was missing. Only his daughter, Sylvie, and the police were there (*Ouest-France*, 22 February). On 28 February there was a heavy frost, and there were no more than three hundred demonstrators. They began by trying to smoke Brault out, then they broke their way into the chapel, which was rumoured to be a venue for orgies. But they were to be disappointed, for all they came across were biblical inscriptions and a library, 'the foul food of the followers' (*Le Courrier*, 6 March; the metaphor should be noted: these thin-blooded vegetarians, who eat no meat, are poisoned by assimilating these 'foul' works). Brault had disappeared, seemingly at the advice of the authorities (*Ouest-France*, 6 September 1974).

The *Courrier de la Mayenne*, catalyst to the resurgence of public opinion against the 'prophet', paid lip-service only in condemning the violence that attended each demonstration. Thus, on 9 October 1965, it writes: 'These reactions are, clearly, to be deplored, for nothing can be settled by violence. Do not forget, however, that people are regularly driven to such acts through their irritation at finding that, in spite of the personal rifts that have arisen, which are engendered even within families, occasionally embracing feelings of hatred, in spite of the material ruin and the physical and moral degeneration caused by Brault's doctrine, he and his followers continue to perform their activities in freedom. How much simpler it is to arrest an exasperated counter-demonstrator [the implication being that the real demonstrators, the true *provocateurs*, are the members of the sect, and that those who have come to attack them are no more than 'counter-demonstrators'] than to put an end to this brainwashing!' And, on 6 March, *Le Courrier* warns that: 'Violence against the followers would serve only to make martyrs of them and to rouse the pity of those whose mindless sensibilities have already led them to the brink of the traps set to ensnare them by this pathetic fellow.'[17]

---

[17] Cf. also the *Courrier de la Mayenne* of 13 and 20 February. *Ouest-France* considers these demonstrations as 'a movement of popular discontent' (11 February), a 'popular reaction' (15 February), and even a 'a mass popular reaction' (23–4 October). Regular readers of the paper could not help being surprised at finding these militant terms being used for once without inverted commas and in a favourable sense.

Following the first demonstrations, the authorities opened up a file on the sect; in spite of their drastic methods, however – a raid on the chapel on 9 May, with a five-hundred-franc fine for the followers present who refused to talk – they were unable to extract any declaration that might have been used against the 'prophet' and his followers. All that was produced was a hefty file full of '*it-is-said-that*' statements, i.e. ones for which the speaker was not prepared to accept any responsibility.[18]

It appears that the 'prophet' must then have sought refuge for several months outside the region of the Bocage – his followers continuing to hold their meetings at the mill, with Brault's daughter presiding – since he later returned to live clandestinely among his followers until his death. The local press did not fail to greet this event with its customary irony. From *Ouest-France* of 23 June 1971: 'The Mayenne police made a raid on Haute-Courie, a farm at Châtillon-sur-Colmont. In one of the rooms of the farmhouse, they made a macabre discovery: the corpse of Robert Brault, who had died fifteen days previously, was laid out on his death-bed. His followers, respecting Brault's own prophecy, were awaiting his resurrection! After seeking refuge in this farm more than a month ago, the man who believed he was Christ died of cancer of the throat without having received any treatment whatever.'[19] One senses in this passage a conservative opinion swelling with satisfaction at establishing that the basic, scandalous challenge to its own faith (the resurrection of a man who claimed to be God) was at last relegated to a past that was done and finished, i.e. mythical and of no further effect.

Bibliographical note

The *Courrier de la Mayenne* opened the hostilities against Brault with two leading articles: 'Miller, healer, prophet – where are he and his followers heading?' (26 December 1964), and 'Magic and sorcery: incredible claims' (2 January 1965), followed by four 'Readers' Letters providing information on the 'magus' from various vexed people (most often from parents of his followers disturbed at the risks this new doctrine imposed on the families' inherited wealth), on 9, 16, 23 and 30 January. Subsequently, the paper was

---

[18] Cf. The *Courrier de la Mayenne* of 15 May, *Mayenne-Républicain* of 21 February, *Ouest-France* of 12 February, which speak of 'the legal action for which we all long' and blame the sobriety of the 'prophet's' disciples: 'Through their obstinate silence, these people – for the most part victims of schemes seemingly linked with bewitchment, – slow down and delay the desired outcome with the result that all the good folk who pity these too easily-influenced followers proceeding under the yoke of the "new religion" become understandably impatient.' Cf. also *Ouest-France* of 13–14 February and 23–4 October, and *Le Monde* of 21–2 February 1965.

[19] *Ouest-France*, 6 September 1974: 'Retro ... Satanas'. Cf. also *Ouest-France*, 24 and 25 June 1971, and the *Courrier de la Mayenne*, 26 June 1971, which, with fine optimism, buries with Brault the 'last of the Mayenne bewitchers'.

to mention the 'magus' in connection with various local scandals during
1965: 13 February – 'Aron: display of public wrath'; 20 February – 'The
"Prophet" from Aron's *grande première*: when will this tragi-comedy end?';
same date – 'Brault demystified: five hundred farmers who no longer fear
his spells surround the Moulin-Normand'; 6 March – 'The ways of the
"Prophet": a tragic experience'; 27 March – 'Incidents at Aron'; 17 April –
'Death of a follower'; 15 May – 'At the mill of Aron'; 21 August – 'What's
become of Brault?'; 2 October – 'At Chailland, court orders sale of the
property of a farmer belonging to the Aron sect'; 9 October – 'Acts of
violence at Aron'; 16 October – 'Aron, a correction'; 30 October – 'Brault
summoned before the police-court'; and, finally, 9 July 1966, a last article
on a disillusioned note – 'The sect of Aron continues to wreak havoc' – until
the debate was closed at the death of the 'magus', 26 June 1971: 'Witchcraft
in mourning: the body of the "Prophet" of Aron discovered at a follower's
house.'

In the local press, the following headlines also appear: 'Time to end the
scandal that has lasted far too long: a movement of popular disapproval
emerging around Aron', *Ouest-France*, Mayenne edition, 11 February 1965;
'Countless and disturbing side-effects of the Aron affair: court penalties
imposed on un-cooperative witnesses', id. 12 February; 'A visit to the Aron
"Prophet", where things are bubbling and long hair is in', id. 13–14
February; '"Prophet" of the Moulin-Normand jeered and heckled by
several hundred, and hit in the face by a stone', id. 15 February; 'The Aron
affair', in *Mayenne-Républicain*, 21 February; 'Twilight of the murky tale of
Aron: the "Prophet" vanishes, his followers scatter', in *Ouest-France*, 22
February; 'Accused of illegal medical practice, the Aron "Prophet" fails to
appear in court', id. 23–4 October. And at his death: 'After several years'
disappearance, Robert Brault, the Aron "Prophet", found dead at a follower's house in Châtillon-sur-Colmont', in *Ouest-France*, Mayenne edition,
24 June 1971; 'The "Prophet" had been dead for 13 days', id. 25 June;
Jacques Hardouin, 'Retro ... Satanas', ibid. 6 September 1974.

In the national press, cf. *Paris-Jour*, 15 February 1965, 'The witches are
among us', and 16 February, Ph. Javron, 'Police had to protect "Prophet"
from "anti-magus" demonstrators'; *France-Soir*, 16 February, Ph. Leroux,
'A thousand farmers attack the (bearded) followers of the bewitcher and
shave them at the mill of Aron (Mayenne)'; *L'Humanité*, 19 February, Cl.
Picanti, 'It's the Devil's fault if meat is cursed and fat is damned, the
bewitcher of Mayenne told me'; *Le Monde*, 21–2 February, Michel Legris,
'A "Prophet" in Mayenne: the farmers of Maine fall a prey to mysticism'.

APPENDIX 4

THE YARDSTICK OF TRUTH

The psychiatrist *'says to me you have to be mentally deranged to believe in spells. Because, he says, in the old days people were so backward! But now one mustn't believe in that. We doctors, he says, we're stronger, medicine's stronger. We ... science is so modern that it's able to deal with any illness ...'*

Joséphine Babin

I have shown several times that there was never any scientific thinking on witchcraft, merely a learned ideology which took advantage of witchcraft to confine an imaginary peasant to his position of credulous being. Nor is psychiatric thinking in any way exceptional as regards this attitude. If, however, I have chosen to refer here to psychiatric thought, it is not because I wish to prove the same point yet again, but because two important features emerge in the rationale of this discipline:

1. Since psychiatry has sprung up from the solid basis of medical science, it may presume to dispense entirely with the necessity of scientific proof, which doubtless explains why, in writings that reflect this way of thinking, one will come across a vast number of unfounded assertions, for which the only scientific backing is the academic status of the person by whom they are proposed.[1]

2. Psychiatric theory, as soon as it touches upon witchcraft, may appear

---

[1] The more ideological a psychiatric text is, the more immediately it establishes an unbridgeable gap between on the one hand the medical profession and the learning from which it draws its authority, ('I should like to recall the interpretations put forward by experts such as X and Y', 'at this point we might mention the excellent works of Professor X, our colleagues Y and Z, and many others', 'like Professor X, we too consider that...', 'my old colleague Y rightly concludes that...', 'we psychiatrists', etc.) and, on the other hand, the humble mass of patients ('these degenerates', 'the feeble-minded', 'the backward', 'a primitive subject', 'he was a semi-idiot with numerous stigmata of degeneracy' [which, of course, it would be pointless to enumerate, since we are addressing readers who know the meaning of imbecility and degeneracy], 'this mentally and socially retarded person', 'in spite of their vaunted religious enlightenment, these backward people will never understand that...', 'a good, honest priest confided to me that...', 'his wife, a fine housekeeper', 'a hot-headed virago with an impetuous temper', etc.)

singularly deficient to researchers trained in other disciplines. Neverthe-less, it enjoys considerable importance since it is applied in the establish-ment of legal decisions: the psychiatrist is frequently called in to assess the state of mind of one of the bewitched, and this he does with the aid of the erudite references offered by his discipline. I shall give examples of precisely how the official classification of a 'sick-person's' behaviour – a classification authorized by the application of theory and reproduced in an expert medico-legal report or in a hospital record – can have profound after-effects on the life of the person concerned.

Writings on witchcraft constitute a purely minor branch of French psychiatric literature: until 1970, when the school of Limoges began its publications, the only writers to take an interest in witchcraft were those too apathetic to grapple with the central problems of their discipline, or else mental health workers, all equally attached to the established practice of the Enlightenment.[2]

All are agreed in thinking that a patient who talks about witchcraft is simply delirious, that is – mad. For description of oneself as a bewitched person is the same as confirmation of one's subordination to will of another – the witch – with whom contact produces devastating effects on the person and property of the victim. Which amounts to speaking of psychotic ten-dencies.

Judging by the fact of the real delirium of some of the bewitched, the psychiatrist comes to the sweeping conclusion that belief in spells is also a form of delirium. One can better understand the reasons for this amalgama-tion by appreciating that psychiatric literature defines delirium as pertain-ing solely to the dimension of being in error. Thus, for instance, one finds the following definition in the latest edition of the *Manuel Alphabétique de Psychiatrie*, under the entry 'Delirium': 'Whenever there occurs an error in perception or a deviation in judgement, the mind may produce false ideas. The false idea becomes a delirious idea when it militates against reality or is contradicted by the evidence. Delirium consists of a delirious idea which is maintained and followed through. It is then the disreal or de-realistic (see the definition of this entry) thought that is basically characteristic of delirium at the intellectual level.' Under the entry 'Dis-real, De-realistic (thought)', one finds the following: 'Mental construct in blatant disagree-ment with reality' – the illustrations offered being schizophrenia, dreams, daydreams, and states of high excitement.[3] The notion of delirium, then,

[2] In the notes that follow the more important psychiatric writings relating to witchcraft are cited. Anyone who takes the trouble of consulting these works will realize that my choice of quotations is in no way contentious, and that if psychiatric thought on witchcraft appears to be a caricature of a scientific approach it is through no doing of mine.

[3] Antoine Porot, *Manuel alphabétique de psychiatrie clinique et thérapeutique*, 4th edition, revised and reissued, Paris, 1969, P.U.F. (1st edition 1952). It is beyond question here that it would be of interest to establish a relation between psychotic statements and the utterances of the bewitched; readers interested in the question of psychosis will have sensed, in reading this

presupposes the existence of a reality which has features upon which general agreement can be reached. Indeed, this reality seems to be so unquestionable that it must be recognized from the evidence available. The medical psychiatrist is therefore implicitly defined as one whose profession confers upon him the right to apply the yardstick of measurement for the degree of veracity, reality, demonstrability or rightness (all these terms being equivalent) of the ideas and outlooks of his contemporaries. A delirious person is someone who stoutly maintains a position the doctor pronounced to be false.

1. Archaic delirium and pre-logical mentality

In the nineteenth century, what is today known as the delirium of witchcraft figured in the clinical picture as a nosographic entity introduced by Esquirol and described as demonomania or demonopathy.[4] Today, this is considered to be an outdated classification, but it is by no means immaterial for our argument to note that it involves exactly the same view of delirium as an error of judgement – and of the peasantry as a bastion of credulity – as we find in the modern notion of witchcraft delirium.[5] Esquirol's conclusions here are significant: [... Demonomania, which includes the statements of the bewitched] 'has, as a remote cause, the ignorance, prejudice, weakness and pusillanimity of the human mind [...]. It is provoked by anxiety, fear, and dread [...]. The delirium, the actions, and the resolution of the demoniacs [amongst whom are included the bewitched] spring from the principles of false ideas on religion and from extreme moral depravity [...]. This disease has become rarer ever since religious instruction, improved education and more widespread schooling have led to all classes of society being more equally informed.'[6] 'For a considerable time now,' he says elsewhere, 'demonomania has attacked only a few weak and credulous minds [...]. Certain inaccurately observed phenomena reinforce the belief of these simple, timid and credulous people, and witchcraft still retains some obscure and despised vestiges of its former power.' As for Logre, he does not

book, that the issue is constantly present in my writing, although generally in an implicit sense. The reflections given on the psychiatric interpretation of witchcraft are simply intended to help gauge the extent of the dead-end into which one is led by the initial postulate which says that an error of judgement lies at the source of all deliriums – a blind alley which so many authorities offer as the only way forward.

[4] Esquirol, De la démonomanie, Paris 1911; Des maladies mentales, vol. 1, pp. 482ff., Paris, Baillière, 1838.

[5] Le Dictionnaire alphabetique de psychiatrie (op. cit., article on 'Démonomanie (archaïque), démonopathie') says the following: 'These archaic groupings [of deliriums classified together under the term of demonomania] only have a bare historical interest, and even their denominations are no longer used to describe the diabolical interference which still generates delirium and the superstitious explanations given by many primitive people.'

[6] Esquirol, Des maladies mentales, p. 516.

hesitate to state that: 'In almost all cases, the persons affected were country simpletons, illiterate – or scarcely literate – farmhands and most of them Bretons.' To declare that one is being manipulated by devils or witches is patently less creditable, because it is less modern, than to claim that one is directed by sonic waves or electronic circuits: in the latter case, it must be mentioned, the authors never speak of credulity or ignorance, only of delirium.

The foundation of modern research into witchcraft delirium was an article by Dr Wahl, in 1923, which first introduced into psychiatric litera-ture the term 'archaic delirium', an expression that subsequently became the regular reference whenever the question of witchcraft entered into the case-study of a patient.[7] If, generally speaking, delirium is produced by a false idea, archaic delirium is generated by an anachronistic false idea: 'What we refer to as archaic delirium is a state that was once extremely common but has now tended to become increasingly rare, even to the point of extinction,' The archaic madman (i.e. one who utters opinions that are today repudiated by the medical authorities) is described as a degenerate, alcoholic individual, who draws the stuff of his delirium from the fund of delirium-producing associations common to the environment in which he lives: i.e. from what the ethnographer would describe as his traditional culture.[8]

The description given by Wahl of these backward environments – in spite of the pompous formulation, '*circumfusa* of madness' – reflects just those everyday points I have already mentioned in referring to non-professional thinking on witchcraft.[9] To quote Wahl: [In these archaic regions], 'the continuous development of civilization seems to have been brought to a complete standstill ever since an era that is difficult to determine but is at all events extremely remote'. 'One may well imagine that in such surroundings [where the houses are "hovels" and "shacks", where everything is "timeworn", "scattered higgledy-piggledy", "grimy" or "insalubrious"], leftovers of the Middle Ages, you might say, modern ideas will not have penetrated.' 'The deeply-rooted hatred of anything new (misoneism) in these rural environments'[10] means that for the inhabitants the 'modern world does not exist': 'What are modern science, modern culture, modern life doing for them!' These 'minds, which are inferior or not yet normally

---

[7] Dr Wahl, 'Les délires archaïques', in *Annales médico-psychologiques*, March 1923.

[8] When Wahl published his study, the theory of madness as a degeneracy of the individual had nevertheless already been under criticism for ten years. The reference to alcoholism is compulsory for anyone seeking to identify an organic cause of madness.

[9] Cf. pp. 3–5 and Ch. 4.

[10] In psychiatric terminology, 'misoneism' is defined as 'hostility towards whatever is new. Mental tendency frequently encountered in elderly persons closely attached to the past and who are often resistant to mental and moral progress' (Antoine Porot, op. cit.). The use of psychiatric terminology to describe social groups is a distinctive ideological trade mark which will often come up again.

developed, are incapable of understanding the modern scientific explanation of physical, chemical, biological or social phenomena': 'In the backward rural areas which are under discussion [...] people still hold the old ideas on witchcraft, evil spells, magic, the Devil, God or the Virgin.' 'Intellectual life assumes a chiefly religious and mystical character'; this is why 'if madness becomes manifest', it will take on 'the mystic forms of delirium, which are the most frequent aspects of archaic delirium'. Naturally, Wahl refrains from disparaging the 'true transcendental mystics', those 'high intellects', those 'grand figures of humanity': he only comes down hard upon this rustic's mysticism 'which springs from utter mediocrity and is of the lowest moral value', the mysticism of the 'mentally deficient', which is always 'pathological, insofar as it is a translation of thoughts of an inferior type of person produced by an abnormal brain'.

This facility for 'unrestrained belief' already belongs to pathology: all those who give evidence of this tendency are persons 'predisposed', who verge on the limits of madness (they are said to be 'subnormal'). On the other hand, those who could be explicitly described as mad are people who claim to be founding a religion ('theomegalomaniacs'), attaining sainthood, prophesying, being possessed by the Devil or being bewitched – the latter category is referred to as 'madness through belief in spells and sorcerers'. One must therefore be mad to believe in spells or to lay claims to innovation in religious matters, for these are anachronistic preoccupations. Anachronistic – please note – in relation to the concerns of the doctor, who holds the yardstick by which historical time or meaning is measured.

It is noticeable that these much-belaboured stock attitudes towards the anachronism of the peasantry are far from harmless: if, in addition, these attitudes can find a haven where they can bloom in peace – behind the high walls of a pseudo-medical science, for instance – they will be sufficient to legitimize the diagnosis of madness and the order for confinement. To believe in spells, you have to be backward, so they say in the Bocage; and to be backward, you have to be mad, say the psychiatrists, taking the statement one step further.

In 1934, Doctors Lévy-Valensi and Delay presented a case of archaic delirium which they discussed in terms of the highly convenient notion of pre-logical mentality.[11] With the introduction of this concept borrowed from ethnography – a concept nevertheless so problematic that its originator expressly disowned it – the missing features of the notion of

---

[11] Lévy-Valensi and Delay, 'Délire archaïque: astrologie, envoûtement ... magnétisme', in *Annales médico-psychologiques*, July 1934. Cf. also, J. Lévy-Valensi, 'Mentalité primitive et psychopathologie', in *Annales médico-psychologiques*, May 1934. The author is here setting up Lévy-Brühl's theories on primitive mentality against those of the psychiatric theoreticians for whom psychosis is a regression or degeneracy, i.e. a return to one of man's primitive states. He concludes that an analogy does exist between the two mentalities – primitive and psychotic – but that they are not identical: the one is reminiscent of the other.

archaic delirium could now be added: those suffering from delirium, and especially those who spoke of witchcraft or enchantment, were not merely anachronistic beings, but creatures with a mentality radically different from our own, to which, it so happened, the works of Lévy-Brühl provided access.

The work of Lévy-Valensi and Delay consisted simply in compounding an amalgam composed of the description of a clinical case and the two expressions, archaic delirium and pre-logical mentality. The case concerns a woman who was said to have been bewitched by Hindu hypnotist to whom she had given a photograph of herself: the authors refer to her delirium as 'archaic' because her case-history is reminiscent of others in the remote past of Europe.[12] 'This delirium', they conclude, 'is of such a nature that, taken as a whole, it may justifiably be called archaic. Belief in spirits; revelatory dreams; resurrection of the dead; hallucinations; logolatry – we have here all the features of primitive mentality. [This woman] displays all the incarnations of superstitions throughout the ages, from astrology through medieval bewitchment to mesmeric hypnotism. [...] The same imperviousness to sensory experience, the same blind, absolute belief in the one devouring mystical experience, and as with primitive peoples a special logic – Lévy-Brühl's pre-logic – governs by the law of participation.'

One suspects that the notion of pre-logical mentality, which was introduced to account for the ideas of the bewitched (or for their 'delirium'), did not persist because of the intellectual rigour with which it was formulated but simply because of its ideological convenience. This, no doubt, is why it withstood criticism for so long. Right up until the time of the studies by the school at Limoges in 1970, writers would regularly refer to pre-logical mentality, feeling thereby that this notion served to explain the peasants' thought processes from which they meant to keep well clear, in common with all the learned élite.

Thus in 1964, Jean Morel, wrote in Chapter III of his thesis on *Witchcraft and its psychiatric effects in the department of Orne*[13] ('An explanation of the causes of this belief'): 'As we have seen, then, a considerable proportion of the rural population in the Orne still believes in witchcraft. [...] Are the explanations they offer for the major events in their lives all that different from those given by certain primitive peoples? ... The author then quotes Lévy-Brühl and his description of the magically-influenced behaviour of the Papus of Kawai: 'Are our peasants of the Orne département so far

---

[12] The case-study of this delirium contains a sweeping judgement. 'She was a mental defective who had always been credulous, suggestible, and superstitious.' Only the first of these qualifying adjectives has a place in psychiatric terminology, but it is obviously brought in here simply to bolster the layman's terms with one of pathological connotation.

[13] Thesis for a medical doctorate, Medical Faculty of Paris University. Cf. also G. Jacquel and J. Morel, 'Sorcellerie et troubles mentaux: étude faite dans le département de l'Orne', in *L'Encéphale*, January–February 1965. This article is a condensed version of the hub of Morel's thesis.

removed, then, in their behaviour from the primitive peoples? ... Among
the peasantry, whose intelligence is often low, whose way of life ancestral,
whose mentality primitive, superstitious ideas acquire a most intense
power of attraction, etc.'[14]

2. Witchcraft as a collective delirium

In the late nineteenth century, classical French writers developed the
notion of *folie à deux* (shared madness) or passed from one to another. From
Legrand du Saulle (1872) and Lasègue and Falrest (1877) to de Clérambault, whose publications on this subject appeared from 1902 to 1924, these
writers asked themselves why certain forms of delirium, far from causing a
breakdown in communication between the afflicted person and those
around him, are in fact perfectly understood and even shared. What forms
of delirium can thus be readily communicated or transferred, what is the
category to which delirious people belong who are able to get others to share
their convictions, and to what category do these others belong, and, finally,
what are the characteristic features of the systems of communication set up
by these forms of delirium? These questions were discussed with a most
unusual freshness and open-mindedness, which cannot fail to strike the
reader who uncovers these writings after half a century.[15]

The inventors of this notion of transferred madness drew a sharp distinction between the person who transmitted the delirium (the '*inductor*' of
Lasègne and Falret) and the receiver (the '*induced*'): only the former should
be regarded as mentally ill, the latter is merely the passive receiver of a
delirium passed on by someone else. The treatment suggested for these
forms of multiple delirium consisted simply in isolating the transmitter

[14] Note that for Morel, belief in spells must be distinguished, at least in principle, from
witchcraft delirium. But as will be seen later, he makes hardly any practical use of this
distinction. In connection with the use of the concept of primitive mentality as a means of
describing those who believe in magic, mention should also be made of Mme Michelin-
Germain's thesis (*A propos de quelques cas de délires démonopathiques dans le Morbihan*, Faculté de
Médecine de Paris, 1964), and particularly Dr H. Aubin (*L'homme et la magie*, Paris, 1952,
Desclée de Brouwer, Bibliothèque neuropsychiatrique de langue française). Judging by the
frequency with which he is quoted, the author appears to be highly thought of in psychiatric
circles, but the nuances of his colonial doctor's liberalism may escape those who have not
been brought up to the brutalities of the seraglio. His argument seems to boil down to stating
that primitive mentality and that of French rural dwellers or countryfolk display a point-
by-point resemblance: thinking of the one makes one think of the other and yet, says the
author, it is not quite the same thing; but he is not too sure why.

[15] Cf. Legrand de Saulle, *Du délire des persécutions*, Paris, Plon, 1871, pp. 218–78; Ch. Lasègue
and J. J. Falret, 'La folie à deux ou folie communiquée', in *Annales médico-psychologiques*,
November 1877; E. Régis, *La folie à deux ou folie simultanée*, Paris, 1880; M. Baillarger,
Recherches sur les maladies mentales, Paris, Masson, 1890; Marandon de Montyel, 'Des conditions de la contagion mentale morbide' in *Annales médico-psychologiques*, March–April and
May–June 1894; G. de Clérambault, *Oeuvre psychiatrique*, vol. I: '*Délires collectifs et associations
d'aliénés*, Paris, P.U.F., 1942.

from the receivers, i.e. breaking down the system of communication established by the delirious person.

The relatively frequent setbacks encountered in this therapy gave rise to the suspicion that the receivers might not be as passive as they appeared to be and that they were using the communication circuit to convey their own delirious messages. Strictly speaking, then, no originator or transmitter of multiple delirium could be distinctly separated from the receivers. All those involved in collective delirium from now on seemed to be more or less caught up in a general psychosis, and discussion centred on the mechanism which generated it.[16]

The intellectual precision that had characterized the discussions on transferred madness was later to offer scientific corroboration for a purely ideological interpretation of witchcraft as a multiple delirium or collective psychosis: since delirium results from an error of judgement, any false statement, i.e. one which is not substantiated by medical knowledge, can be described as a delirium; and any false statement supported by a particular social group – e.g. witchcraft, by the peasants – becomes a collective psychosis.

This interpretative twist was soon to be made by Professor Heuyer and his students:[17] 'The notion of psychosis', he reminds us, 'involves a state of mental pathology. It is a mental disturbance, a delirium; that is, a false idea in which the sufferer or the group firmly believes ... For we psychiatrists, the criterion of an individual psychosis is the same as that of a collective psychosis. It is necessarily social. [...] It consists in the inability, occasioned by the emotional, instinctive, or temperamental elements of the [collective] psychosis, to become integrated into the rational organization of a society. This inability [...] represents the pathological nature of a collective psychosis. It is more than just "ebullient behaviour"; it is unsociable and insufferable collective behaviour.' And, clearly, in determining this outlook, it is the psychiatrist who holds the yardstick of rationality by which the sociable and the tolerable are measured.

Psychiatric history will perhaps comment upon the extent of the impact made by Heuyer's work. The assumption which springs to the layman's

---

[16] The title of Clérambault's last publication on this subject is 'The question of collective deliriums is closely linked to that of the generating mechanisms of psychoses'. The long holidays are over: for several years we have been enjoying ourselves dismantling systems of communication; now we shall have to get back to dealing with the sickness itself.

[17] Cf. C. Heuyer, Dupouy, Montassut, Ajurriaguerra, 'Un cas de délire à cinq', in *Annales médico-psychologiques*, February 1935; Heuyer, 'Contact avec les guérisseurs' in *La vie médicale*, special issue, Christmas 1954; Heuyer, 'Les psychoses collectives' in *Revue du Practicien*, 21 May 1955; Heuyer, 'Les psychoses collectives: rôle de l'instigateur et des circonstances', in *Congrès des médecins aliénistes et neurologistes de France*, Nice, 1955; M. Letailleur, J. Demay and J. Morin, 'Délire collectif de sorcellerie', in *Congrès des médecins aliénistes et neurologistes de France*, Nice, 1955.

mind is that his writings present the prejudices of the greatest number in extreme form – albeit backed by the authority of a Professor. Doubtless this accounts for why his declarations have been so rarely contested. I have only encountered one criticism, and most politely worded that: '. . . nevertheless, semantic confusion over the term "delirium" or "psychosis" is encountered even among authoritative writers such as Professor Heuyer in a recent article, etc.'[18]

Heuyer supports his argument with the research work of his predecessors on *folie à deux* – 'we are here on firm ground, which has already been explored by Baillarger, Régis, and de Clérambault' – and with the fact that in 1935 he came up with a case of *folie à cinq* (quintuple madness): for five is greater than two; five is already a social group.[19] This case involved a Parisian family said to have been bewitched by a priest aided by several assistants. Without wishing to quibble with the eminent Professor over the question of knowing how many delirious people are required for a psychosis to be described as collective, I should nevertheless like to point out that in the case he presents there are not five but four delirious people. The fifth, a young farm-girl who had come from a region where people had experience in spells, did no more than interpret in witchcraft terms whatever the family of her Parisian lover expressed in delirious terms.[20] But since it is singularly misleading to say that one can be the victim of a witch, Heuyer treats this farm-girl in the same way as the other delirious people, merely expressing astonishment that her 'delirious convictions should have persisted in spite of her isolation': had she been the receiver of a transferred madness, the isolation ought to have induced her to correct her delirium. This isolation therapy does indeed seem to have been helpful to her four partners, if one may judge by the victorious report published by their energetic doctor: 'It was sufficient to keep our patients under observation for several days at the Special Infirmary and then to have them confined to bring them back sharply and somewhat roughly to reality and thus allay their short-lived persuasions.'

The outcome of Heuyer's interest in this operation by which *folie à deux* is transformed into collective psychosis was that psychiatry began to examine

---

[18] J. Alliez, M. Dongier, R. Pujol, 'Quelques observations sur les délires à deux', in *Congrès des médecins aliénistes et neurologistes de France*, Nice, 1955.

[19] Heuyer, Dupouy, Montassut, Ajurriaguerra, op. cit.

[20] 'She was a simple country-girl, lost in Paris, where she worked as a general household help. Child-like and easily influenced, she came from a family that believed in bewitchment. We met her elder sister, who was still living in the country and who shared the same belief. [. . .] For a long time, she had been believing in the practices of witchcraft: "Where I come from," she said, etc.' The symptoms offered by the authors as justification for their diagnosis of delirium are extremely lightweight: the girl had nightmares; she attributed an illness from which her son was suffering to the fact that a fairground entertainer, assistant to the chief sorcerer, had studied a photograph of the child; she heard a voice that told her, ' "You can go there, but there won't be a place for you".'

social pathology, which thereafter entered the therapeutic domain on the same terms as individual pathology: 'Psychiatry', he says, 'is rich in knowledge already acquired (concerning, for instance, *délire à deux*). Reinforced by new information (on delirium affecting more than two people), and its domain extends to the observation, examination and treatment of collective psychoses. These psychoses are as old as the hills; they are still frequent today, and dangerous for the mental health of the community.'

One will not be surprised, therefore, that everything Heuyer considers counterfeit is lumped together under the diagnosis of collective psychosis; nor dismayed that the instigators of delirium – referred to as the 'ringleaders' by the doctor, who seems to draw his terminological inspiration from the police interview room – should be denounced and opposed: 'faith-healers, hypnotists, mesmerizers, occultists, mediums, diviners, astrologers, to whom we can add the psychoanalytical psychotherapists working without medical supervision, all of them attracting the sick and the unfortunate by their declarations, unchecked and unproven, and running small chapels which are nothing but centres of collective psychoses'.[21] Finally, among the day-to-day functions of psychiatry is the control of information conveyed by the *media*: since a collective psychosis results from the conjunction of a false idea, fear, and a public, it is appropriate that a Scientific Committee for Radio Transmissions has been set up in which Mental Health workers are actively engaged. 'It is only by accident that information which is tendentious, or dangerous for the mental stability of listeners, ever succeeds in slipping round the barrier that has been erected', explained the committee's watchdog.

In 1955, three research workers made reference to the writings of Heuyer in presenting a case of 'collective delirium resulting from witchcraft' at the congress of specialists in mental illnesses and neurologists at Nice, where the notion of multiple delirium had been placed on the agenda.[22] When reading their observations, particularly if one has any experience of witchcraft in the Bocage, one cannot fail to be struck by the ease with which the authors pronounce their diagnosis of delirium: as far as we can judge by what the doctors tell us of this case, none of the central figures was delirious, but each was in his own way under the effects of spells. An examination of

---

[21] Another version of the same old song in 'Contact avec les guérisseurs', op. cit.: 'The faith-healers [etc. the list of charlatans is the same in both versions], all alike – knowing nothing of the disorders they claim to be able to cure, incapable of recognizing them, ignorant of the symptoms, causes, or development of an illness, shameless and conceited – they exploit or try to exploit the sick, whom they lure on with unchecked and unproved assurances.' Why should this be so surprising, since 'the faith-healer is by definition a person with no scientific knowledge of medicine who claims to be able to cure, as a matter of routine, illnesses about which he knows nothing'. By definition.

[22] Letailleur, Demay, Morin, 'Délire collectif de sorcellerie', op. cit.

the data offers an opportunity of contrasting the thought processes and the terminology of psychiatry with those of witchcraft.

The case concerns a 47-year-old craftsman from Normandy who attempted to break the grip of the spell in which he and his family had been held for six years by firing three revolver shots at one of the witches. Following this attack, he was charged with attempted murder, examined by a specialist in mental disorders, and confined to the psychiatric hospital of Evreux with a diagnosis of persecution delirium resulting from witchcraft.

The drama arose over the sale of a piece of property: an unsuccessful rival buyer appears to have threatened this man, after the conclusion of the sale, by saying that he would show him 'what the *Grand Albert* [a *grimoire* frequently invoked in Normandy] was'. Six months later, the man's wife began to suffer from various disorders: headaches, disturbances of vision, associated with the impression of having needles thrust into her head; for a long time she lay prostrate, complaining of pain, and unable to eat. 'The doctors who were consulted found no objective indications to explain these symptoms, and their treatment remained ineffectual', so the family called in the unwitchers. One of them asked: 'Does anyone have a grudge against you?' The craftsman then recalled his rival's threat, and saw in it an explanation for the afflictions being suffered by his wife and by the other members of the family.

As it turned out, the man's daughter had also been attacked by headaches and was bed-ridden for three months after her mother's disorders had begun. (But she was pregnant, and recovered on the night of her wedding, to be able to open the dancing in high spirits.) Some months later, the husband too began to feel pains: burning sensations, pressure, suffocation, constriction of the throat. Last of all, the two small boys were affected, though less violently, with intermittent headaches and minor ailments; like everyone else in the family, they heard the furniture shifting around at night, and could confirm the next morning that it had been displaced.

Seeking protection, the family turned to various unwitchers and diviners. They turned to the police, too, but they refused to help. They then tried to offer the house and a sum of money to their sorcerers, in an attempt to avoid the death of the two women from bewitchment. The son-in-law, who had taken up the case for his wife's family, and who was not afraid of witchcraft, went round to deal with the witches. But he ended up paying a fine for assault and battery and failed to bring the symptoms to an end. The persecuted family, now practically ruined and deeply depressed, left the area and moved into the Aisne district. After several months' respite, however, the troubles began again. The husband now began writing threatening letters to his witches,[23] but seeing that this move was unsuccessful, he went back to his old home, determined to kill one of them. After

---

[23] There were three witches: the rival buyer mentioned above, his wife and her uncle.

seriously wounding one of the men, he considered himself henceforth unwitched. His wife hanged herself shortly after his imprisonment.

The only element that seems to me untypical in this story is the witch's threat: '*You'll find out what the* Grand Albert *is*.' I have never heard tell of a witch silly enough to unmask himself so openly, though this does not of course exclude the possibility of occasionally coming across such naïvety. In all other respects, this is a typical instance of an abortive unwitchment: the symptoms are comparable to those encountered in all dealings with witchcraft;[24] there is nothing, however, that would enable us to discern the reason for the unwitchers' inability to perform their task. On the other hand, it is readily understandable that the victims should have had recourse first to the law and subsequently to direct confrontation as the only possible way of settling the crisis.

For the authors of this paper, there could nevertheless be no doubt about the pathological state of the craftsman and his family: the accused was described as 'a fine Norman with an unblemished record, clear-headed and alert, well-balanced, with a good memory, and of average intellect, who manifested with absolute and unshakeable conviction a fully systematized persecution delirium that had been developing over a period of six years'. Had he not described himself as being bewitched, the doctors would have regarded him, then, as being completely sound of mind, since he gave evidence of no other clinical symptoms. The mere fact that he and his family believed that a threat of bewitchment could actually be put into effect was sufficient reason for the doctors to pronounce a diagnosis of delirium, all the more so since the persons involved admitted that they had never ascertained whether their witch did in fact possess the incriminating book. (It should be mentioned that a bewitched person will never take the risk of going to his witch to carry out a search – not even in order to convince a psychiatrist – for the simple reason that once his persecutor has been named, he must avoid all physical contact with him.) And lastly, because the 'delirious person' was able to recount his story in all its complexity, his delirium was described as being 'perfectly systematized'. Members of his family were likewise regarded as 'delirious persons', and so were his friends and those of the villagers who accused the same witch and his wife of having cast evil and harmful spells upon them. None of the central figures in this affair, not even the witch herself, was excluded from the block diagnosis of archaic or collective delirium: 'In fact,' declared the doctors, confident that it was they who held the yardstick of judgement, 'the woman is mentally ill; our colleague who attended her during the fit which was brought on by the attacks in which her uncle had been victim, informed us that she had long been manifesting a delirium of influence which was also related to witchcraft involving incantatory rites. Her strangeness, her weird behaviour

[24] With the exception of the girl's symptoms, which seem to be open to a different explanation.

[which had led to her being pronounced a witch by the villagers and by her neighbours, the craftsman's family], and her eccentric actions, were all attributed to a state of possession and to diabolical powers [let it be added that the doctor had probably never heard anyone, not even the witch herself, speak of possession or of diabolism: these are terms he must have borrowed from psychiatric works, which classify the deliriums of witchcraft with demonopathic deliriums], although she too was striving to free herself from evil spells.' Let us accept that this witch did claim to be bewitched herself – how long for, and by whom, is not known – and that, since nothing so closely resembles an unwitching ritual as a ritual of bewitchment, her neighbours should have accused her of being the cause of all their misfortunes. The doctor freely interpreted her behaviour as being that of a misfit or an 'eccentric' (relative to the rational aims which every healthy-minded being is supposed to pursue?) and that she manifested a 'delirium of influence'; the 'incantatory rites' here acquire a pathological connotation, as does the understandable crisis – described as a fit – which led her to seeing the doctor after the attacks in which her uncle had been the victim. Whatever she may have said, medical parlance turned her into one of the 'mentally ill'.

Similarly, the behaviour of the craftsman and his family was described in psychiatric terminology, and thus became irrevocably defined as pathological: 'What it amounted to in the end was a question of interests developing into a collective persecution delirium induced by means of witchcraft. The delirium spread from the couple C. to the rest of the family, to the man who was to become the son-in-law, and then to family friends and to a group of people in the village who had come out in sympathy with the persecuted. Each person reacted in his or her own way: the mother, through depression ending in suicide, the father through manifestations of hypochondria, cenestopathia, and paranoia, the daughter – a girl of low intelligence – through various symptoms of hysteria, the son-in-law – of fairly limited mental capacity – through permanent subexcitation and an emotional state which drove him to violence, and the children through minor reactions. All shared the same delirious convictions, equally unshakeable eight years after the beginning of this affair, and nearly two years after the drama they had unleashed.' The authors are fully confident that here they are confronted with a collective psychosis of the type defined by Heuyer: the convergence of a false idea, fear, and a public. They conclude by noting the need to battle against 'outdated prejudices' and rural anachronism, considering this to be the 'best prophylactic for collective psychoses'.

This case-study might seem merely comical if it only reflected an exceptional practice of the odd psychiatrist.[25] However, we only have to consult

[25] Even though this comic aspect may not strike those who quote this work. Cf., for instance, Alain Péron, *Sorcellerie et psychopathologie, à propos d'une étude ethnographique et psychiatrique pratiquée dans le département de la Haute-Vienne*, Medical thesis, University of Bordeaux, 1970, part VI, p. 26.

specialist medico-legal case-studies and hospital reports to realize that belief in spells is commonly held to be associated with pathology, delirium, or collective psychosis. Here are two more examples, drawn from Jean Morel's thesis on *Witchcraft and its psychiatric effects in the Orne district*.[26]

Case no. 1. Involves a roadworker aged 48 who stabbed his witch. Expert opinion was: 'Basically, the only mental anomaly observed in D. [the roadworker] – but it is a consequential one – lies in our knowledge of his positive conviction that B., through magic power, by means of witchcraft, had transformed him into an absolute robot...' The accused related his story – a real classic – and the expert concluded: 'This account of D.'s is genuinely characteristic of a delirious state. D., a peaceful and generally well-esteemed man, became directly transformed into a criminal under the influence of a persecution delirium based on witchcraft, and restricted to one sole concern: the persecutions to which he and his wife had been subjected by B., who had cast a spell on them, and the domination under which they lived. [...] Belief in witches is still widespread in our area. Court records contain sworn evidence given by several people who shared all D.'s delirious convictions. [...] What was involved, in this case, was a non-hallucinatory persecution delirium, a variety of paranoia, founded on interpretations and illusions. D., in spite of his composure and his speech, which was normal on all subjects other than that of his troubles with B., was none the less a mentally deranged man, a delirious person, who under the influence of his delirium became an assassin.'

The roadworker was declared not responsible for his crime and was confined for 2 years to the psychiatric hospital at Alençon, in spite of which he 'retained all his belief in the magical ploys of bewitchment'. He demanded that a second specialist opinion be given on his case, and obtained his release; he died, however, in a traffic accident after just a few weeks of freedom.

Case no. 6. A farmer had shot a witch and killed him. 'The case-file', said the expert, 'contained excellent information concerning H., who was considered a gentle person and a good worker. He was not a drinker, but was convinced that he was the victim of spells that had been "cast" on him by his neighbour, L... The highly detailed account given to me by H. of his misfortunes – which according to him were proof of the schemes of witchcraft of which he believed himself to be the victim – leave us in no doubt as to the pathological state of his mental faculties. The man involved is undoubtedly suffering from a persecution delirium.' His wife, who was considered to be the instigator of the delirium, 'fully shares her husband's delirious convictions. The accused woman, like her husband, manifests a persecution delirium centred on witchcraft... This is a form fairly often observed in *délire à deux*. She is a delirious paranoiac, with underlying

---

[26] Op. cit. Of the eight case-studies offered by Morel, only one – the fifth – seems to justify the diagnosis of *délire à deux*.

elements of alcoholism and persecution, who affords numerous interpretations of a witchcraft theme.' After two years' confinement, the couple were released, completely ruined.

3. Witchcraft as a counter to delirium

In 1955, Alliez, Dongier and Pujol raised an isolated protest against the equation, so generally accepted in psychiatric circles, between belief in spells and multiple delirium.[27] In 1970, the researchers of the Limoges school undertook to re-examine this question from a far wider viewpoint, which led them to recognize that witchcraft did have some use.[28]

In their studies, they referred to the work of Lévi-Strauss on the therapeutic function of the bewitcher and to American works on transcultural psychiatry. These references did at least have the advantage of recognizing some autonomy in the symbolic field – which was no longer identified with that of rationality – as well as a certain right to be different for the peasantry, no longer thought of as a stronghold of anachronism.

To be quite frank, three of their sociological postulates strike me as being ill-founded: (1) that the peasantry constitutes a fundamentally different society or social group; (2) that this society or rural culture is 'in a state of equilibrium'; (3) that witchcraft is a normal belief and that it is uniformly recognized by this rural society. In their haste to postulate a different state of normality, which they wished to see established, they underrated – or so it seems to me – the deep-rooted ambiguity of country dwellers in their attitude towards witchcraft. For if rural society were not incorporated into (or alienated from) the national culture, if it constituted an autonomous society, inherently balanced and fully operative in its 'being different', one would have had no need for the work of Professor Léger to know this: the press would daily recount the efforts of Jacobin power to overcome this dissidence.

Nonetheless, these references brought home to Péron, Professor Léger's pupil, the need to range beyond the confines of the hospital to assess the importance of witchcraft in local society. In adopting this approach, he made a decisive break with medical practice: Morel, for instance, considered himself sufficiently well-informed on the sociological aspect of witchcraft after studying the statistics[29] and consulting hospital patients,

---

[27] Op. cit.

[28] Alain Péron, *Sorcellerie et psychopathologie*, op. cit. J. M. Léger, R. Léger and A. Péron, 'Aspects actuels de la sorcellerie en Limousin, ses relations avec la médecine, son importance en psychopathologie', in *Revue de médecine de Limoges*, 1971, 2, no. 3. J. M. Léger, A. Péron, J. N. Vallat, 'Aspects actuels de la sorcellerie dans ses rapports avec la psychiatrie (peut-on parler de délire de sorcellerie?)', in *Annales médico-psychologiques*, 1971, 2, no. 4; 'Forum: le médecin, le malade et le sorcier', in *Concours médical*, 29 January 1971.

[29] A proper reckoning of 'witchcraft deliriums' would in fact require the patients' willingness to communicate their secrets and equal willingness on the doctor's part to listen to them; this is why I am surprised at the praise Péron gives Morel for his statistics.

and in some cases their families; but as he was unable to free himself from the idea that every hospital patient must be 'sick', he concluded that, if the family shared the patient's convictions, it meant that one was dealing with a family delirium. By contrast, Péron undertook an ethnographical study which brought him into touch with outlooks and ways of thinking on witchcraft that were quite different from those he encountered at the hospital.

The results of these studies can, I think, be summarized as follows.

1. It is pointless to speak of 'collective delirium caused by witchcraft' when a patient is merely using the language of the social group to which he belongs. In substance, the beliefs expressed by Péron's patients in no way differ from those collected during his ethnographic survey; the interview he conducted with the families of bewitched persons who had been hospitalized – after performing an act with medico-legal implications (e.g. assault) – enabled him to conclude that 'the beliefs were not necessarily expressed in a more delirious manner by the hospital patients'. The peasants are separated from the medical profession by the distance between one set of standards and another, but not by the space between reason and delirium: 'Either we can no longer speak of delirium, or else the entire group (of rural dwellers) is composed of delirious people.' Clearly, the ideas of witchcraft are 'false ideas that run counter to reality and contradict all the evidence' – which is the definition given by Porot of delirium. But can one say that delirium is present so long as the subject is perfectly adapted to his family and social group, or should one simply say that his symbolic system of reference is different from the doctor's? (The reader will have sensed that Péron has introduced a decisive shift in the criterion of delirium: it is no longer truth or error that is in question, but the possibility of communicating.)

2. When an unwitching cure succeeds, the psychiatrist hears nothing about it: it produces no delirium, but it does re-establish a circuit of communication. Only the failures of witchcraft end up in the hospitals.

(a) The patients suffering from functional disorders who are sent to the psychiatrist by the local doctor after no objective cause for their symptoms has been found. Although convinced that they have been bewitched, these patients generally make no mention of this either to the psychiatrist or to their local doctor.

(b) Patients suffering from thymic disorders: a state of depression accompanied by signs of anxiety, asthenia, gloom, and suicidal behaviour. Or, conversely, a state of exasperation accompanied by irritability.

(c) Patients suffering from psycho-sensory disturbances (visual or aural hallucinations), cenesthetic disorders, and the sensation of being acted upon by an external influence. None of these disorders, however, can be classed as a delirium (Péron speaks of illusions, hysterical pseudo-hallucinations, exacerbation of the patient's suggestibility, etc.).

The origin of the disorders in these three categories of patients is still largely unknown to the doctors, since the bewitched do not admit to their bewitched condition.

(*d*) Patients who have reached the hospital via the medico-legal route, following acts of aggression (punch-ups, murder or attempted murder of the witch) or via the local authorities (town council, police), whose patience is exhausted by people taking the law into their own hands to rid themselves of their witch. In this event, the patient cannot avoid speaking of his bewitchment to the doctor. But, instead of concentrating on trying to find out whether or not these patients are delirious (and such cases are exceptional), the doctors should be trying to work out what process has brought them to this pass.

3. Among the bewitched entering hospital there are some who definitely are delirious, but it is not witchcraft that make them so: 'witchcraft delirium occurs only when witchcraft has ceased to play its role', i.e. that of re-establishing the communicative links threatened by the disorders of the bewitched.

The psychiatrist, as such, is no more deaf than anyone else, once he has agreed to release his hold on the yardstick of truth.

Appendix 5

CHRONOLOGICAL LANDMARKS IN THE BABINS' STORY

1. The pre-history of spells (1928–60)

1928
- Birth of Louis Babin at La Croix en Torcé;
- of Marthe and Josephine Letort at Chammes.

1931
- Birth of Jean Babin at La Croix en Torcé;
- Goes to school as far as the *Certificat d'études primaires;*
- Jean is his father's favourite son;
- Father takes Jean drinking with him in the cafés while he is still very young, and encourages him to share his drunkenness,
- Father considers Jean his successor to the farm.

1952
- Jean does his military service in Alençon as a medical orderly.

1955
- Louis Babin, 27, marries his childhood friend, Marthe Letort;
- The couple move into La Roë because Babin's father is still active on the farm at Torcé;
- Louis will say later that Jean was then sexually normal.

1958
- Louis is bewitched by a neighbour. He finds '*cheeses*', until 1968, but the '*petite mère of Torcé*' always 'pulls him through'.

1959
- Jean, 28, is accused of being a witch by his neighbour, Nouet of la Grimetière.
- He denies it, says he does not believe in spells ('*since then*' says Josephine '*he doesn't much believe*'),
- but a short while after, he becomes decidedly alcoholic,

– and suffers from a purulent eczema.

– He goes to consult a healer in Alençon, Madame Marie, who looks after him devotedly for a month, giving him salt baths. The treatment fails to cure him. But she makes a recommendation: *'If you take over, come back and see me before nine months have gone by.'* Through this, she already seems to think that Jean is bewitched, but he *'doesn't much believe'*.

– (In 1969, his wife and his brother will say in the psychiatric hospital that Jean has been ill for ten years: because of alcoholism, for which he was hospitalized, or the psycho-somatic effects of this accusation of witchcraft?)

1960

– A priest on a mission to Torcé wants Jean to get married and succeeds in curing him of his eczema with prayers and yeast.

2. *Spells (1961–3)*

1961

– While Babin's father is ill, Ribault, his neighbour, tries to get Jean to marry his servant and mistress.

– When Jean refuses, he makes the following prediction: *'In a few years time, the farm will be sad'*. It takes just three years for the prediction to come true.

1962

– Death of Babin's father.

– Aunt Chicot, who used to live in the farm next to La Grimetière, comes to La Croix to work for the day, until Jean's marriage.

All Saints 1963

– Jean *'takes over'* his deceased father's farm and lives there with his mother.

3. *The misfortunes begin (1964)*

1964

– From January on, epizootic abortions, loss of animals (calves, 15 doe rabbits).

– In March, three weeks before his wedding, Jean is hit on the head by a falling beam, is knocked out, and afterwards considers that the spell cast by Ribault materialized through this incident:

– Jean, who was physically very strong, becomes weak;

– He was sexually potent (he was said to have had a mistress in the village), he becomes impotent;

– Lastly, he suffers with his kidneys.

– At the same time, his fiancée, Josephine Letort, hears a prediction uttered by their neighbour's son, Gabriel Filoche from Chammes, that she will marry a *'nanny-billy'*, i.e. according to her, someone who is *'neither a nanny-goat nor a billy-goat, neither a man nor a woman, someone who can't make love'*.

– In April, Jean Babin, 33, marries Josephine Letort, 36, the twin sister of his sister-in-law Marthe.

– It is a marriage of convenience between a bachelor and a spinster.

– Jean is unable to consummate his marriage, he seems to be suffering from premature ejaculation: *'It was done before it was ready'*, says Josephine.

– Jean consults Dr Naveau, a psychiatrist in Placé, who treated his mother and aunts. He complains of his nerves and his sexual impotence.

– The doctor is unable to cure him and sends him away with these soothing words: *'It'll come back.'*

– Seeing the doctor's failure, Babin's mother goes to consult a healer in Laval, who acts as annunciator and declares: *'Someone's played a trick on him.'*

– In January 1970, Jean considers that his marriage provoked the anger of two witches:

(*a*) Ribault, whose servant-mistress he refused to marry;

(*b*) Chicot, the *'aunt's man'*; Jean's marriage deprived him of certain material advantages.

Jean's sexual impotence is due to the first witch alone; all the other misfortunes affecting the animals and humans are caused by either witch. In the psychiatric hospital, Jean will say he has been bewitched for six years, i.e. since 1964.

4. Attempted unwitchings (1964–9)

1964–5

– Jean consults a healer in Laval, but the latter apparently makes fun of his impotence.

– Jean then remembers (1965?) Madame Marie d'Alençon's recommendation made in 1959. He has her come to La Croix, but changes his mind because of the unwitcher's high price and shady looks. Although she confirms the diagnosis made by the unwitcher of Laval (*'There are spells in all directions'*, she claims), he refuses to let her operate. She then predicts: *'If you don't do anything, you'll only stay married for six years'*, i.e. until 1970.

– Jean takes up drinking again,

– and chases his mother out, by which he fulfils a prediction made by Ribault: *'when the mother has gone, the farm will be sad'*.

– The misfortunes continue: loss of animals, drying up of cows, *'butterings'*,

car accidents, breakdowns in the farm machinery and, of course, Jean's sexual impotence.
- The Babins then consult several unwitchers who confirm the initial diagnosis but are unable to lift the spells:
  (a) first, the *petite mère from Torcé* reputed *'for good'*,
  (b) then, four unwitchers 'for evil', three men and one woman.
  The latter assures Josephine that Jean is *'caught to the death'* and that the misfortunes will continue *'until your husband kills himself'*. Actually, Jean is sometimes tempted to hang himself in the attic or shoot himself.
- He calls for the priest of Torcé who blesses the farm, the animals and the people but who doesn't believe in spells and makes fun of Josephine's superstitious practices: *'Does she drink her holy water?'*, he asks, in front of his parishioners. Because he doesn't believe, his benedictions have no effect.
- The Babins then fetch Madame Marie, the unwitcher of Izé who helped Josephine's family in the past: this unwitcher *'for evil'* declares, as she crosses the threshold of La Croix: *'Its too difficult. He* [Jean] *is too caught. There's more than one. It's too muddled up here.'* She thus withdraws but gives the Babins magic protections and a fetish which I have called the *copula*: *'Always keep it'*, she advises them, *'if not, you'll not stay together.'*
- The misfortunes continue:
  In 1968, a hundred *'butterings'* provoked by *'the aunt's man'*.
- That year, a new priest *'who believes in it'* arrives at Torcé in September.
- In November, he comes to La Croix to place protections, succeeds in overcoming Chicot (helped, it must be said, by the stranger's fatal prediction) but declares himself incapable of curing Jean's impotence: *'I'm not strong enough for that'*, he admits.
- In 1969, death of Madame Marie of Izé who *'met her master'*. She is replaced by Madame Auguste, of whom the Babins are afraid.
- In May of the same year, two cows dry up because of Ribault;
- The Babins have masses said, but it has no noticeable effect.
- Jean cannot withstand Ribault's look; he begins to drink again and provokes brawls in the local cafés.
- On 25 November, Jean has a nervous fit (to name but the dated misfortunes).
- On 18 December, Jean is admitted to the psychiatric hospital for a drying-out cure following a brawl. It is more or less imposed by his doctor. Jean, on his part, claims he entered the hospital only *'because of the nerves'*; he asks Dr Davoine for a treatment against impotence and is given tonics. His brother Louis Babin makes an unsuccessful attempt to persuade the psychologist and Dr Davoine to operate Jean on his *'kidneys'* without him knowing it. Jean leaves the hospital disintoxicated but still impotent.

5. Interventions of the ethnographer (1970–3)

1970

– In January and February, I have several conversations with the two Babin couples: Jean and Josephine at Torcé and Louis and Marthe at La Roë.

– During our very first conversation, Josephine asks me whether I can 'return evil for evil' to her witches. Too engrossed in taking notes, I don't answer. At the end of our conversation, I refuse to be paid.

– During our second conversation, Josephine asks me whether I can cure Jean of his sexual impotence. Unwitching through words – what I propose – seems utterly derisory to them. Jean avoids the issue by saying he prefers to finish Dr Davoine's treatment before beginning with me. I shall see them again later when I try to meet Madame Auguste, unsuccessfully. As Jean takes his leave at the end of our last conversation, he says: 'we'll write to you if anything's abnormal'.

1971

– Having become the assistant of an unwitcher, Madame Flora, I suggest to the Babins they be unwitched by her.

– Since I last saw them, they have given up on medical treatments: Dr Davoine, displeased by the fact that I have such a special relationship with them, lectured them several times in the name of reason and modernity. What is more, he accused Josephine of being the cause of Jean's impotence. They feel they have been definitely humiliated by the outright contempt of his words.

– Josephine accepts to meet Madame Flora through me, while Jean refuses to go there but prefers to delegate his wife and a photograph of himself. This is the beginning of a long unwitching cure which I shall follow to its (unsuccessful) end in 1973.

References

Balandier, G. (1957) *L'Afrique ambiguë*, Eng. tr. H. Weaver, *Ambiguous Africa: Cultures in Collision*, London, 1966.

Beattie, J. (1964) *Other Cultures*, London.

Belmont, N. (1974) *Van Gennep, le créateur de l'ethnographie française*, Paris. Eng. tr. D. Coltman, *Arnold Van Gennep, the Creator of French Ethnography*, Chicago, 1978.

Benveniste, E. (1966) *Problèmes de linguistique générale*, Paris. Eng. tr. M. E. Meek, *Problems in General Linguistics*, Coral Gables, Fla., 1971.

(1970) 'L'appareil formel de l'énonciation', *Langages* 17.

de Certeau, M., Julia, D., Revel, J. (1970) 'La beauté du mort: le concept de culture populaire', *Politique aujourd'hui*, December.

Chatelet, F., Derrida, J., Foucault, M., Serres, M. (1976) *Politiques de la philosophie*, Paris.

Clausewitz, K. von (1968) *On War*, edited with an introduction by A. Rapport, tr. J. S. Graham, Harmondsworth.

De Martino, E. (1966) *La terre du remords*, Paris. Fr. tr. by C. Poncet of *La terra di rimorsa*, Milan, 1961.

Evans-Pritchard, E. E. (1937) *Witchcraft, Oracles and Magic among the Azande*, Oxford.

(1973) 'Some Reminiscences and Reflections on Fieldwork', *Journal of the Anthropological Society of Oxford* (4) 1.

Favret, J. (1969) 'Le Crime ne paie plus', *Critique* 271.

(1971) 'Le Malheur biologique et sa répétition', *Annales E.S.C.*, 3–4.

Foucault, M. (1961) *Histoire de la folie à l'âge classique*, Paris. Eng. tr. R. Howard, *Madness and Civilization: a History of Insanity in the Age of Reason*, London, 1967.

Jakobson, R. (1960), 'Closing Statement: Linguistics and Poetics', In T. A. Sebeok (ed.) *Style in Language*, New York: French translation (1963) in *Essais de linguistique générale*, Paris.

Leach, E. (1967) 'Virgin Birth. The Henry Myers Lecture 1966', *Proceedings of the Royal Anthropological Institute*. Reprinted in *Genesis as Myth*, London, 1969.

Legendre, P. (1974) *L'Amour du censeur, essai sur l'ordre dogmatique*, Paris.

Leiris, M. (1934) *L'Afrique fantôme*, Paris.

(1948) *La Langue secrète des Dogons de Sanga* (Travaux et mémoires de l'institut d'ethnologie, vol. 50), Paris.

Lévi-Strauss, C. (1955) *Tristes Tropiques*, Paris. Eng. tr. J. and D. Weightman, *Tristes Tropiques*, Harmondsworth, 1976.

Lovecraft, H. P. (1955) *Dans l'Abime du temps*, Paris. Fr. tr. of 'The Shadow out of Time', first published in *Astounding Stories*, June 1936, reprinted in *The Lurking*

Fear, New York, 1947, London, 1964, etc., and *The Shadow out of Time*, London, 1968.

Malinowski, B. (1923) 'The Problem of Meaning in Primitive Languages', in C. K. Ogden and I. A. Richards, *The Meaning of Meaning*, London.

Mannoni, O. (1969) *Clefs pour l'Imaginaire*, Paris.

Monod, J. (1972) *Une riche cannibale*, Paris.

Morel, J. (1964) *La Sorcellerie et ses incidences psychiatriques dans le département de l'Orne*. Thesis for doctorat de médicine, Faculté de médecine, Paris.

Nadel, S. F. (1951) *The Foundations of Social Anthropology*, London.

Porot, A. (1969) 'Echolalia' in *Manuel alphabétique de psychiatrie clinique et thérapeutique*, 4th ed., Paris.

Rendu, M.-A. (1965) 'Incroyable, cette campagne est envôutée', *Constellation*, March.

Royal Anthropological Institute (1971) *Notes and Queries on Anthropology*, London.

Sébillot, P. (1880) 'Essai de questionnaire pour aider à recueillir les traditions, les coutumes et les légendes', *Revue de Linguistique* 8.

(1887). 'Instructions et questionnaires: sur l'art de recueillir', *Annuaire de la Société des Traditions populaires* 2.

Todorov, T. (1970) 'Problèmes de l'énonciation', *Langages* 17.

Van Gennep, A. (1909) *Les rites de passage, étude systématique des cérémonies de la porte et du seuil, de l'hospitalité, de l'adoption, de la grossesse et de l'accouchement, de la naissance, de l'enfance, de la puberté, de l'initiation, de l'ordination, du couronnement, des fiançailles et du mariage, des funérailles et des saisons, etc.* Paris. Eng. tr. M. B. Vizedom and S. T. Kimball, *The Rites of Passage*, London, 1960.

(1911) *Les Demi-Savants*, Paris. Eng. tr. with an introduction by R. Needham, London, 1967.

(1932–3) *Le Folklore du Dauphiné (Isère). Etude descriptive et comparée de psychologie populaire*. Paris.

(1938–58) *Manuel de folklore français contemporain*. Paris.